Pictured Key
Nature Series

How To Know

THE
TREES

Howard A. Miller
Marietta, Georgia

H. E. Jaques

SECOND EDITION

WM. C. BROWN COMPANY PUBLISHERS
Dubuque, Iowa

Copyright 1941, 1946 by H.E. Jaques

Copyright 1972 by
Wm. C. Brown Company Publishers

ISBN 0—697—04878—0 (Paper)
ISBN 0—697—04879—9 (Cloth)

Library of Congress Catalog Card Number 70-167733

THE PICTURED-KEY NATURE SERIES

How To Know The—

AQUATIC PLANTS, Prescott, 1969
BEETLES, Jaques, 1951
BUTTERFLIES, Ehrlich, 1961
CACTI, Dawson, 1963
EASTERN LAND SNAILS, Burch, 1962
ECONOMIC PLANTS, Jaques, 1948, 1958
FALL FLOWERS, Cuthbert, 1948
FRESHWATER ALGAE, Prescott, 1954, 1970
FRESHWATER FISHES, Eddy, 1957, 1969
GRASSES, Pohl, 1953, 1968
GRASSHOPPERS, Helfer, 1963, 1972
IMMATURE INSECTS, Chu, 1949
INSECTS, Jaques, 1947
LAND BIRDS, Jaques, 1947
LICHENS, Hale, 1969
LIVING THINGS, Jaques, 1946
MAMMALS, Booth, 1949, 1970
MARINE ISOPOD CRUSTACEANS, Schultz, 1969
MOSSES AND LIVERWORTS, Conard, 1944, 1956
PLANT FAMILIES, Jaques, 1948
POLLEN AND SPORES, Kapp, 1969
PROTOZOA, Jahn, 1949
ROCKS AND MINERALS, Helfer, 1970
SEAWEEDS, Dawson, 1956
SPIDERS, Kaston, 1953, 1972
SPRING FLOWERS, Cuthbert, 1943, 1949
TAPEWORMS, Schmidt, 1970
TREMATODES, Schell, 1970
TREES, Miller-Jaques, 1946, 1972
WATER BIRDS, Jaques-Ollivier, 1960
WEEDS, Wilkinson-Jaques, 1959, 1972
WESTERN TREES, Baerg, 1955

Printed in United States of America

INTRODUCTION

This revision covers 312 species, varieties and hybrids of native and exotic trees; 21 species have been added; 16 species appearing in previous editions have been deleted through varietal transfer, reduction to synonymy and hybrid; 10 species have been expanded to cover additional varieties now recognized.

Subject matter in this edition differs greatly from former editions. Not only is the tree described as an individual, but also as a member of a forest ecosystem. To know a tree one should not only be able to identify it as an individual but also, have knowledge of its relation with associates and behavior within the communities where it may occur. This is the theme of this revision.

As in the former editions common and scientific names were taken from "Checklist of trees of the United States" U.S.D.A. Handbook No. 41. This nomenclature was up-dated by correspondence with Elbert Little, Jr., Dendrologist, Forest Service. "Silvics of forest trees of the United States" U.S.D.A. Handbook No. 271 and the author's own field notes are the basis for discussions of trees in relation to their environment.

Forest cover types mentioned appear in "Forest cover types of North America" a publication of the Society of American Foresters.

Much of the basic information on forest pests and air pollution was taken from "Proceedings of the 5th annual forest pest control conference" 1970, Southeastern Area, Forest Service, particularly the presentation on air pollution by Francis A. Wood. Additional air pollution information was taken from papers presented at the "Symposium on trends in air pollution damage to plants" American Phytopathological Society, 1967. Avery Rich, University of New Hampshire, furnished information regarding the effects of road brine on tree growth.

The majority of information on dendrochronology came from publications of staff members of the Laboratory of Tree-Ring Research, University of Arizona, through the courtesy of Bryan Bannister who reviewed this section.

Size and location of the largest tree comes from the American Forestry Association's "Social register of big trees." This list was started a quarter of a century ago by the Association as a nation-wide hunt for largest specimens of various typical American trees. Measurements consist of circumference, to the nearest inch taken at a point 4 feet 6 inches above the ground; total height and average crown spread, to the nearest foot.

The trees that follow are from the most recent listing of 1969. We should recognize that these are senior citizens of the tree world and as such are subject to the vagaries of age. We can only hope that the yoke of years will continue to rest lightly and they will grace our lands for yet many decades.

The author wishes to acknowledge the help received from his former colleagues in the Forest Service and the Bureau of Sport Fisheries and Wildlife. It would be difficult to enumerate each but Russell K. Smith in Forest Pest Control and certainly Alfred W. Johnson in the fields of taxonomy and ecology, must be mentioned for their valuable assistance.

Mozelle A. Funderburk is the artist responsible for the line drawings which illustrate the text.

Yvonne R. Turner typed the final manuscript.

Last but not least, my appreciation to Erma Edwards Miller, a pianist who forsook the keyboard, to help organize material, shuffle range maps, read galley and page proofs; my wife.

All photographs and range maps are by the author, except as noted.

TO THE MEMORY OF
Hiram S. Doty, Scientist,
Counselor, Friend.

CONTENTS

Fig. 1. Trees frame the majestic grandeur of the Northwest (1a) become a tapestry of fall color (1b); or inviting shade on a summer afternoon (1c). Their root buttresses form a protective environment for spring flowers (1d).

HISTORICAL

Trees have been a dominant vegetative cover over much of the earth's surface for many millions of years. Throughout the greater part of geological time, climate on the earth was much more uniform than at present. Climatic zones which now exist were scarcely recognizable in early geological periods. Probably the first clear definition of climate appeared in the Pliocene era which just preceded glaciation.

Earliest tree-like plant forms were tree ferns and cycads which reached their greatest development during the mid-part of the Mesozoic era some 150 million years ago.

Earliest tree-forms resembling present-day species were gymnosperms, or conifers. These reached their greatest development during the early Mesozoic era, but unlike the tree ferns and cycads, continued to become more specialized. They are unmistakably a dominant tree-form in the present-day forest.

Flowering plants or angiosperms, which include the hardwoods, originated in the latter part of the Mesozoic era about the same time tree ferns and cycads were at their zenith. Paleobotanists estimate that the flowering plants have not as yet reached their greatest specialization and development.

During the Pleistocene era, extensive glaciation resulted in many changes in tree distribution in the Northern Hemisphere. Following recession of the ice shield, open land was first invaded by tundra-forming sedges followed later by boreal tree species. At the peak of glaciation, boreal species occurred much farther south than at present. The overall general warming trend, following recession of the ice, permitted extension and intermingling of warmer climate species such as slash, shortleaf and loblolly pines, oak and hickory into northern species, spruce, fir, beech, birch, and maple.

Some of the early Tertiary trees which are still with us today, yellow poplar, sweetgum, sassafras, walnut, and hickory, are still undergoing development. The ginkgo-tree is the sole survivor of a large order of gymnosperms which flourished in the early Mesozoic era.

Dating and ecological interpretation of the pre-historic past is possible by examination and analysis of fossil wood, tree-ring analysis, carbon 14 dating, and peat and pollen analysis. Findings from these sources constitute valid lines of evidence connecting the pre-historic past with the present.

1

THE TREE AS AN INDIVIDUAL

A tree is composed of a crown, trunk, and roots. Roots serve to anchor the tree in the soil, are storage areas for food, and take up moisture and chemicals from the soil. The trunk, often called bole, holds the tree erect and serves to transport water and other materials between the roots and crown. It may extend to the tip of the tree as in the conifers, or be lost in branches to the crown as in hardwoods. The trunk is the portion of the tree usually utilized as lumber or for other wood products such as pulp and veneer. The crown is composed of small branches, twigs, leaves, flowers, and fruit. It is the display rack for the beautiful fall colors associated with hardwoods.

Crown

Green plants are the major source of oxygen in our atmosphere. Trees are leaders in this field. It has been suggested that the deciduous forests of Eastern United States produce about 1000 times more oxygen per unit area than the average cover of the earth's surface. There are literally acres of leaf surface in a mature hardwood crown. Leaves carry on the unique process of photosynthesis which utilizes radiant energy of sunlight to synthesize energy rich carbohydrates from water and carbon dioxide. This is accomplished by the chlorophyll in the palisade cells of the leaf. (Fig. 2) These cells, with their chlorophyll, give the leaf its green color.

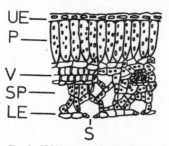

Fig. 2. SECTION OF LEAF. (UE) Upper epidermis. (P) Palisade cells. (V) Veins. (SP) Spongy parenchyma. (LE) Lower epidermis. (S) Stomata.

A transparent layer of cells, the epidermis, covers each side of the leaf and light readily passes through these to the palisade cells. The epidermis is punctured with many tiny openings called stomata through which the needed carbon dioxide may pass. In the process of food manufacture and growth, quantities of free oxygen and water are released into the air through the stomata.

All plants must carry on respiration as well as photosynthesis. In photosynthesis, action takes place only in the palisade cells of the leaf. Production of oxygen and carbohydrates from carbon dioxide and water is accomplished during daylight. Respiration,

2

on the other hand, takes place continuously in all living cells. Raw materials are oxygen and carbohydrates and the products, carbon dioxide and water. Respiration or "breathing" is not only through the stomata of the leaf, but through special pores in the bark and roots called lenticles. Coniferous leaves which are needle-like or scale-like serve the same purpose as the large leaves of broadleaf trees. Shape, size, and surface characteristics of the leaf are useful in determining tree species. These are described in the key, glossary and species descriptions.

Like other flowering plants, trees bear flowers; some are very showy such as yellow poplar and magnolia. Others are quite inconspicuous as in the conifers. They have the same parts as the typical flower. (Fig. 3) Stamens, composed of a slender filament with a pollen sac on the end called an anther, produce the pollen and are the male part of the flower. The female portion is the pistil which is composed of a flared portion, stigma, on top of a slender style and an enlarged base called the ovary where the seed is developed. Some flowers have both stamens and pistils and a tree bearing such flowers is said to be both male

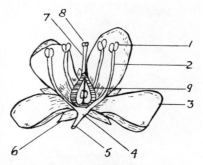

Fig. 3. PARTS OF A FLOWER. (1) Anther. (2) Filament. (3) Petal. (4) Receptacle. (5) Stem. (6) Bract. (7) Style. (8) Stigma. (9) Ovary (with 2 ovules).

and female. On some flowers only stamens or pistils appear, but not both. Trees having both staminate and pistillate flowers are said to be monoecious such as hickory, birches, and pines. If the staminate flowers are found on one tree and the pistillate on another of the same species as on maidenhair tree, the tree is said to be dioecious. They are, of course, definitely male or female.

Flowers are born singly or in several different groupings. A cluster of flowers and their arrangement is an inflorescence. When the top-most flower on a stem or rachis blooms before those below it, the inflorescence is said to be determinate. If the flowers bloom progressively from the base to the top, the inflorescence is referred to as indeterminate. A cyme is a determinate inflorescence which consists of a central rachis bearing a number of pedicelled flowers. If the pedicels are all of the same length, it is cylindrical; if of uneven length, flat-topped.

Seven flower arrangements are indeterminate. They are: Spike, a central rachis with a number of stemless flowers; Catkin or ament, a spike bearing apetalous unisexual flowers; Raceme, consists of a central rachis with a number of flowers with stems of nearly equal length when mature; Panicle, a branched raceme; Corymb, a central rachis bearing a number of branched stems, the lower ones much longer than the upper, giving the inflorescence a round-topped or flat appearance; Umbel, consists of several stemmed flowers with a common point of attachment; Head, a number of sessile flowers clustered on a common receptacle—it may be either globose or flat-topped. These characteristics are illustrated in the key, glossary, and Fig. 4.

After fertilization, the ovule develops into a seed which is a young tree with an embryonic root, stem and leaves. Some seeds germinate as soon as they come in contact with a favorable site.

Fig. 4. FLOWER TYPES. (a) Strobili of pine (Photo courtesy U. S. Forest Service) (b) Upper; staminate and pistillate catkins. Lower; Strobili of Alder (Miller Photo) (c) Strobili of birch (Miller Photo) (d) Panicle of sourwood (Miller Photo) (e) Head of buttonbush (Miller Photo) (f) Corymb of mountain laurel (Miller Photo) (g) Perfect flower of yellow poplar (Miller Photo)

Others over-winter and germinate the following spring if conditions are favorable. Still others have a hard seed coat which permits them to be dormant for a period of months or even years.

Coniferous fruits may be either dry or fleshy. Dry seeds are usually born on fleshy scales arranged around a central axis to form a cone. Others are covered by a pulpy material called an aril.

Broadleaf fruits are also either dry or fleshy. Dry fruits which split on definite lines for release of the seeds are dehiscent and are: a legume, splits along two lines; follicle, splits along a single line; and capsule, splits along several lines. Dry fruits lacking such release openings are indehiscent. They are called: achene, a small unwinged but usually plumed fruit; samara, a winged achene-like fruit; and nut, usually one seeded and covered with a bony or leathery material. Some fruits are fleshy and are called: pome, with an inner wall of tough papery material encasing numerous seeds; drupe, a one-seeded fleshy fruit and; berry, a several seeded fruit in which the seeds are embedded in a pulpy mass. These characteristics are illustrated in the key and Fig. 5.

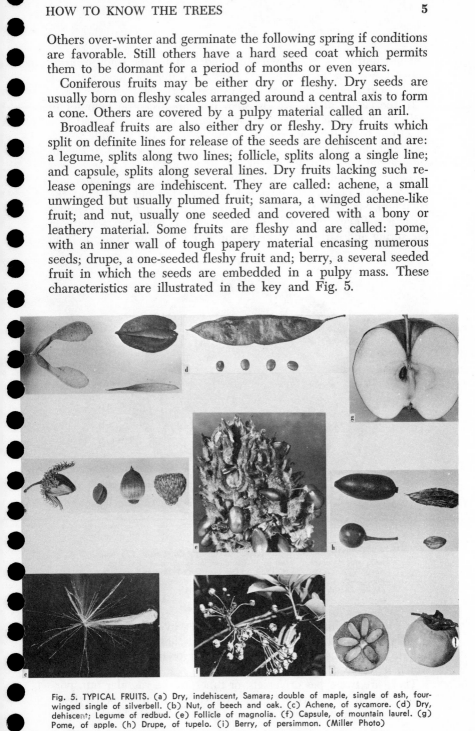

Fig. 5. TYPICAL FRUITS. (a) Dry, indehiscent, Samara; double of maple, single of ash, four-winged single of silverbell. (b) Nut, of beech and oak. (c) Achene, of sycamore. (d) Dry, dehiscent; Legume of redbud. (e) Follicle of magnolia. (f) Capsule, of mountain laurel. (g) Pome, of apple. (h) Drupe, of tupelo. (i) Berry, of persimmon. (Miller Photo)

Trunk

The trunk holds the crown erect and contains the transportation network between the leaves and roots for water and food material. Limbs and twigs are a part of this transportation system.

In the center of the woody stem is a small central cylinder of pith. (Fig. 6) It is surrounded by a region of wood enclosed in a sheath of bark. Between the bark and wood is the growing tissue, the cambium layer. Growth consists of adding new cells to the inside of the bark and outside of the wood. Each year a new layer of wood is added to the outside of the existing wood cylinder and a new layer of bark is intruded between the old bark and the cambium. Stretching the bark by an ever-enlarging wood cylinder gives it a flaky, furrowed appearance. High cambium activity in the spring and early summer slowing to more deliberate growth in

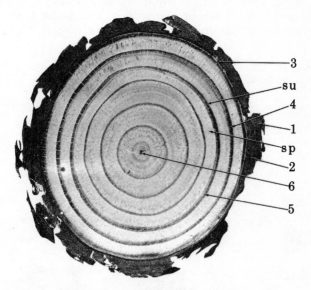

Fig. 6. CROSS SECTION OF WOODY STEM. (1) Outer bark. (2) Inner bark, area of phloem vessels. (3) Cambium, growing tissue. (4) Annual ring. (su) summer wood. (sp) spring wood. (5) Medulary ray. (6) Pith. Stem is too young for heartwood to be developed, see Fig. 8. (Miller Photo)

later summer, followed by cessation in the winter, in most climates, divides the wood into annual rings. From these it is possible not only to tell the age of a tree, but also the growing conditions under which it survived. (Fig. 8)

There are two types of vessels, or tubes, in the vascular transportation system of the tree trunk. The xylem, in the woody tissue carries water and mineral elements from the roots to the leaves and, the phloem in the inner bark carries materials manufactured in the leaves to the roots, except in the spring when growth starts and movement is upwards. When storage space gets too crowded in the leaf and roots, materials are stored in the wood, fruit, and seeds. Lateral travel between the vessels and wood storage areas is through the medulary ray which appears as a plate extending from the surface of the wood towards the center of the trunk. These rays serve to bind the rings together as well as to transport and store food. Bundle scars in the leaf scar on the twig are evidence of this transportation system between the roots and leaves.

As trees age, the older wood toward the the center of the tree becomes darker as a result of foods stored in the vascular system. This inactive area is called heartwood as compared to the lighter colored sapwood of the active distribution area. (Fig. 8) Heartwood gives colour and character to finished woods in furniture and veneer.

Roots

The root system holds the tree firmly in place, gathers water and soluble food material from the soil and stores excess food materials. Water and raw food are delivered to the leaves through the vascular system of the roots, stems, and leaves. Root systems are either branched and spread out in all directions, or depend largely on a single large tap root which descends deep into the ground. Trees with deep tap roots are likely to be more windfirm than those having a shallow branched system.

There is an important relationship between the roots of a tree and their immediate soil environment. Fungi, mostly the group we call mushrooms, form an association with the root hairs when their mycelium envelopes or sometimes enters the root hairs of the tree. This, in short, adds the "root system" of the fungus to that of the tree. This mutual arrangement benefits tree growth. (Fig. 7) Food materials manufactured by the mycelium are available to the tree. This fungus-root association is called "mycorrhiza."

a   b

Fig. 7. (a) One of the common mycorrhiza forming mushrooms, the peppery milk mushroom *Lactarius piperatus.* (b) Mycorrhiza on root hairs of loblolly pine. Mycelium has enveloped the root hairs. (Miller Photos)

General Characteristics

Trees have certain characteristics or a "personality" of their own. They are said to be tolerant if they can grow in the shade of, or in competition with, other trees. This is probably an over-simplification of a complex relationship involving such things as age, soil moisture, fertility and overall site quality. The light relationship, however, is one easily understood and apparent by observation. Trees which are intolerant, or which do not do well in shade, many times are more tolerant in the seedling and sapling stages of their lives. Others remain tolerant or intolerant as the case may be throughout their entire life. Tolerance has much to do with the ability of a tree to grow in competition with other trees in the forest ecosystem. Some intolerant species are black walnut, yellow poplar and eastern redcedar. White pine, red maple, and white ash are considered intermediate. Tolerant species are sugar maple, flowering dogwood, American beech, and rosebay rhododendron.

Species differ greatly in rate of growth. Some are fast growing, some about average and others slow growing. Rate of growth is measured in the number of rings per inch. In other words, the number of years (rings) it takes a tree to grow one inch in radius. Three to five rings or less per inch is considered rapid growth, 8 to 10 rings per inch is a good medium growth rate. More rings per inch is considered slower growth and of course the larger the number of rings, the slower the growth rate. Growth rate is important particularly in younger trees when they are in competition as seedlings and saplings. Slow growing trees in the forest community do not grow into sapling and pole sizes unless they are extremely tolerant. Fast growing species get the jump and over-top slower growing associates becoming the dominant trees of the new forest.

Rate of growth is important when considering trees to plant in newly developed lawns and parks. Fast growing species such as Lombardy poplar and Chinese elm give early shade but are short lived. They must be replaced by early planting of slower growing but longer-lived species such as the large crowned oaks, silver maple, or American elm. Loblolly pine, red maple, sycamore and yellow poplar are fast growing species while white pine, sugar maple and black tupelo are moderate growing trees. Eastern redcedar and baldcypress are slow growing species.

Rate of growth, while being inherent to particular tree species, is also affected within the species framework by site. Site is a combination of biotic, climatic, and soil conditions on the particular area upon which the tree is growing. Site quality, like fertility, influences the rate of growth of a tree. Site quality is measured by the average height growth of dominant and codominant trees growing on the area at a given age, usually 50 years. This height is called the site index of that particular area. For example, if the average height of dominant and codominant trees at the age of 50 years on an area is 100 feet, that would be a 100-foot site index. A poorer site might be 75 feet.

Longevity, often closely associated with rate of growth is another specific characteristic. Trees whose life span is less than 150 years are short-lived species. From 150 to 500 years, medium lived and those living over 500 years are long lived. Short-lived species are Virginia pine, aspens, willows and blackjack oak. Southern red oak, black cherry, slash pine and eastern redcedar are of moderate longevity while red spruce, baldcypress, white pine and Douglas-fir are long lived.

Trees have an affinity for soil moisture in varying degrees. Certain species require moist, well drained soils while others will tolerate heavier and much wetter soils. Some seem to prefer dry sites. Examples of species having an affinity for dry sites are shortleaf pine, pitch pine, scarlet oak, and chestnut oak. White pine, sugar maple, and sweet birch prefer moist soils. Baldcypress, river birch, and sycamore prefer wet soils, or those of high moisture content.

Trees have ability to fit into the dynamic vegetational changes which take place in the forest ecosystem. Pioneer or primary species are those which are capable of invading bare areas often in large numbers. They are likely to be intolerant and light seeded. They persist until displaced by the next succession. Secondary or sub-climax species are those which follow the pioneer community and are usually at least moderately tolerant. Climax species occur in a more stable community and are generally long lived and tolerant. Examples of pioneer species are redcedar, Virginia pine, sweetgum, the aspens, and gray birch. Yellow, sweet and river birches, white ash, lodgepole pine, and most of the oaks are considered subclimax species. White oak. American beech, flowering dogwood, and eastern hemlock are common to more stable long-lived communities.

These are the more common characteristics of tree species which determine their occurrence in the forest ecosystem. When trees are used in single plantings as in yards and parks, many of these characteristics are not too important except to put species on sites where they will do best.

Dendrochronology

Tree-rings and their interpretation have long intrigued scholars as a window into the past. Tree-rings tell us not only about the past activity of the tree itself, but are a reliable calendar into past events and climate. As early as 1901, A. E. Douglass, an astronomer, was inquiring into the relationship of tree-ring patterns to climatic conditions. From his early work has grown the present sophisticated study of dendrochronology.

Experience has shown that the best trees for dating purposes are located in areas where some climatic factor such as precipitation or temperature, or a combination of both, strongly influences the amount of tree growth each year. When the environment during a given year becomes limiting to growth, all of the trees in the affected area add a narrower than average annual ring. (Fig. 8) During a year when climate is especially favorable to growth, the trees will tend to add a wide ring. Over a period of years under such conditions, each tree builds up a pattern of wide and narrow annual rings. The ring pattern of any one tree is closely duplicated in the others. Such trees are said to "crossdate" with one another and the variable ring series they contain are referred to as "sensitive." Trees growing in a mesophytic climate where there are no great stresses for water, light and soil nutrients exhibit a uniform ring series and are not useful as calendars except to document the history of that particular tree or stand. Ring series in such trees are referred to as "complacent."

a   b

Fig. 8. (a) Sensitive pattern of Douglas-fir. Periods of stress result in diagnostically narrower than average rings at 1227, 1186 and 1182. Wider than average rings at 1201 and elsewhere. (Courtesy Laboratory of Tree-Ring Research, University of Arizona) (b) Complacent ring series, typical of trees growing in a mesophytic region. Loblolly pine; as a seedling and sapling free to grow, then became crowded when its crown touched those of its neighbors and slowed down. At about 30 years it reached dominance again and was free to grow and maintained good growth for the remainder of its life. (Photo courtesy U. S. Forest Service)

The best material for ring dating is found in the semiarid regions of western North America, particularly the Southwest. Ponderosa pine, Douglas-fir, pinyon pine *Pinus edulis,* bristle cone pine *Pinus aristata,* and giant sequoia *Sequoiadendron giganteum* are typical of the coniferous species which dendrochronologists usually study. The oldest and most sensitive trees are often gnarled, stunted, and isolated individuals which grow on dry, windswept, rocky ridges. Ring patterns from these trees are useful in archaeological dating, determination of climatic cycles and periods of stream course downcutting.

To establish a tree-ring chronology, samples from living trees containing sensitive ring patterns are first studied and crossdated with each other. Since the actual year in which the samples were collected is known, calendar year dates can be assigned to each ring of the crossdated sequence by starting with the outside ring and counting inward. The dated chronology will extend from the year of collection to the earliest pith ring of the oldest tree. Distinctive ring patterns in yet older specimens, long dead but still sound trees, logs from prehistoric ruins, etc., can be matched against the early part of the dated chronology to push back the calendar even further in time. In the Southwest, many thousands of overlapping archaeological tree-ring samples have been used to roll back the ages into the centuries before Christ.

Use of rings in archaelogical dating is illustrated in Fig. 8a, a section of Douglas-fir furnished through the courtesy of the Laboratory of Tree-Ring Research. It represents a section of a timber recovered from the archaeological ruin known as Five Kiva House located in Johnson Canyon in southwestern Colorado. The pith ring was put down in AD 1113, the outside ring in 1240. Following the procedure described above, diagnostically narrow rings characteristic of the southwestern Colorado tree-ring chronology can be seen at 1227, 1186, 1182 and 1166 for example. A study of this calendar indicates that the tree was cut sometime after the growing season in 1240 and placed in the structure at about that time, thus dating the ruin.

A climatologist would look at the ring pattern for a climatic "window" to drought and rainfall cycles, through the ages, and revealed by wide and narrow ring sequence. Such information could be correlated with geological changes in stream courses.

Tree-ring analysis frequently serves to further pinpoint conclusions reached from carbon 14 dating, peat, and pollen analysis and fossil woods. The Laboratory of Tree-Ring Research at the University of Arizona is the focal point in the United States for studies relating to dendrochronology.

THE TREE AS A MEMBER
OF A COMMUNITY

A forest community is a group of trees containing one or more species growing in a specific area. Trees growing in a forest community compose a complex environment of plants, animals, soils, air, and water. This vegetative cover type is called a forest ecosystem and is constantly changing both in time and space.

A forest ecosystem is developed vertically into three layers—overstory, understory, and lesser vegetation. (Fig. 9) The overstory comprises the dominating tree species of the main canopy. Understory extends from the ground to just beneath the intermediate crowns and is made up of woody shrubs, vines, and trees which will never reach the overstory. Grasses, forbs, fungi, and other plant forms occupy the ground and in this discussion are considered lesser vegetation. Although soil biota is a part of the forest ecosystem, it will not be discussed herein.

There is a characteristic vocabulary used in describing the forest community. A forest association is an assemblage of plants and animals occupying a common environment. The term forest type refers only to the overstory trees and is useful in grouping stands of similar composition.

Forest types are further divided into stands. A stand is an aggragation of trees occupying a specific area and sufficiently uniform in composition, age, or condition so as to be distinguished from other groups of trees in adjacent areas. Stands are selected on the basis of composition, age, size, and condition. For example: by composition, a pine or hardwood stand; by size, pole timber, seedling or sapling stand; by age, 1 to 20 years or 21 to 40, etc.; by condition, fully stocked or understocked.

A seedling is a tree grown from seed and encompasses the time following germination until it becomes a sapling. A sapling is a young tree less than 4 inches diameter breast high but larger than 2 inches d.b.h. Pole is a young tree over 4 inches d.b.h. but not over 8 to 12 inches. Trees larger than poles are considered either saw timber size or mature. Maturity covers a wide spread of years, especially in long-lived trees. Maturity ends when growth falls off or decay begins. Trees are measured at a point 4 1/2 feet above the ground, commonly called breast high and abbreviated d.b.h. Measurement is diameter, outside bark, in inches, unless otherwise indicated.

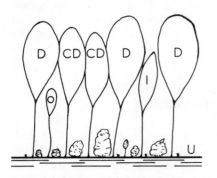

The overstory is described both by species comprising it and their vertical position. Crowns are either dominant, codominant, intermediate or overtopped. (Fig. 9) Species of trees making up the overstory are usually the basis for naming the forest type.

Forest communities are dynamic and ever-changing, without disruption they succeed each other from pioneer through secondary suc-

Fig. 9. Crown classes.

cessions to climax almost as though each prepared the way for the next.

Silviculture, or the planned manipulation of a forest community, takes advantage of forest dynamics to retain type groups having high commercial, watershed, wildlife, or recreational values, or a combination of all. Southern pine pioneer forests and subclimax mixed hardwoods having a high percentage of oak and yellow poplar are maintained by silvicultural methods. Unplanned disturbances such as wildfire, flooding, and windthrow usually adversely affect succession.

The term climax, in the discussions that follow, relates to a more or less stable community of long-lived, mostly tolerant trees which develops late in plant successions and in the absence of disturbance.

Pioneer communities are frequently composed of intolerant, light seeded tree species. A common example of a pioneer association is found in the reversion of fields, formerly cultivated, to trees. (Fig. 10) These pioneer species are often eastern redcedar, gray birch, sweetgum, or loblolly pine. None of these could be considered stable as they will soon be displaced by more

Fig. 10. Pioneer eastern redcedar and sweetgum invading abandoned farmlands. (Miller Photo)

tolerant species unless some form of disturbance occurs to the site. Secondary or subclimax associations are composed of a large number of mostly mid-tolerant species. Frequently remnants of the intolerant pioneers, as well as advance tolerants of more stable communities, are encountered.

a   b

Fig. 11. (a) Spruce and fir replacing aspen in transition from pioneer to subclimax. (Photo by Forest W. Stearns) (b) Early subclimax pine-hardwood forests are attractive to many species of wildlife, including white-tail deer. (Miller Photos)

Some of the more common forest types which are subclimax in the east are: Northern Red Oak-Basswood-White Ash, Sweetgum-Nuttall Oak-Willow Oak, White Pine-Northern Red Oak-White Ash. In the west: Western White Pine, Lodgepole Pine, and Pacific Douglas-Fir.

Examples of some of the more stable, long-lived associations considered climax are: in the eastern forests, White Spruce-Balsam Fir, Hemlock, Sugar Maple-Beech-Yellow Birch, White Oak-Red Oak-Hickory and Beech-Southern Magnolia; in the western forests, Red Fir, Interior Douglas-Fir, Interior Ponderosa Pine, and Pacific Ponderosa Pine.

Subclimax forests are more common, contain more commercial products, have a wider variation of species, occupy more important watersheds, furnish more favorable environment for wildlife and in the fall probably display more beautiful foliage than either pioneer or climax associations. (Fig. 12)

Fig. 12. A subclimax composed of such species as northern red oak, yellow poplar, yellow buckeye, white ash and black cherry, is pleasing to the eye, attractive to wildlife, a good soil builder and a source of valuable wood products. (Miller Photo)

Forest types which, because of disturbance do not appear to be either pioneer or subclimax, are referred to as transitional. These often follow heavy cutting or fire.

ENEMIES OF TREES

Enemies of trees are lightening and wild fire, windthrow, ice breakage, insects, disease, wild animals, polluted air, contaminated soil and abrupt changes in water table resulting from flooding and drainage.

Lightning and Wild Fire

Lightening is dangerous as it may destroy the tree by a strike, rending it asunder or it may ignite a crown or ground fire consuming the tree along with others in the same area. Lightening fires are more common in the western mountains than in eastern United States. Combustible material must be plentiful and dry for a lightening strike to start a fire. Accumulations of dead plant material, too abundant to decay rapidly, are potential fire hazards. There are about 8000 lightening fires in the United States each year, or about 7 percent of the total number of fires. Most lightening fires seem to occur in areas of difficult access.

Wildfire damages trees of all ages and there are about 110,000 man-caused forest fires annually. Many times the tree is not killed outright but the base of the trunk scarred, the cambium and inner bark laid open and exposed to attack by fungi and insects. This is particularly true of hardwood species. Conifers seem to be able to throw off fungi attacks from fire scars better than do hardwoods. Many conifers have a thick bark which acts as insulation against the heat of surface fires. Thin bark species are, of course, more susceptible to damage by surface fires than those with thick bark. Fire under control used in growing conifers in the southern Coastal Plains and elsewhere is used in such a manner that it is not considered an enemy.

Windthrow

Windthrow is prevalent in shallow rooted species growing in swampy and moist sites, such as larch and balsam. Shallow rooted species however, regardless of site, are subject to windthrow. Trees of poor vigor and those with root rots are good candidates for wind damage. These trees have a poor anchor and thus are readily blown down.

Ice Breakage

Ice breakage occurs sporadically where heavy sleet storms are prevalent and particularly when accompanied by high winds. Many times breakage in itself is not too damaging but the fresh wood exposed is an attraction to insects and disease.

Wild Animals

Deer, moose, and elk browse heavily on certain tree species, particularly hardwoods. Willow, yellow poplar, tupelo and maple in seedling and sapling stages are frequently killed or their height growth destroyed by browsing. Gnawing animals such as beaver, rabbits, and porcupines damage trees by exposing the cambium, performing a girdle. In cases where the tree is not completely girdled, it is laid open to attack by insects, frequently bark beetles. Control of wild animals may be accomplished either by hunting, trapping, or biological means.

Insects

Insects and disease rank along with fire in the magnitude of destruction to trees and forests. Damage caused by these pests is usually less conspicuous but nevertheless substantial. Large areas of a single species of tree is an inviting environment to insects as well as disease. These pests attack trees in all stages of their life from seed to maturity.

Foliage of trees furnishes attractive food for a host of insects. Fortunately, the majority of leaf eating insects occur in comparatively small numbers. A few species will, however, build up in large numbers causing extensive defoliation for one or more years. Loss of growth is usually the principal damage, but several years of repeated defoliation may kill some tree species. Defoliation checks the manufacture of food materials in the leaves and interfers with transportion and translocation of materials within the tree. All this is reflected in a slow-down in rate of growth and vigor which may lay the tree open to attack by bark beetles and other insects.

a   b

Fig. 13. TREE INSECTS—DEFOLIATORS. (a) Leaf skeletonizer on Alder. (b) Eastern tent caterpillar and web. (Miller Photos)

Some of the more common insect defoliators are leaf miners and skeletonizers which feed upon the succulent leaf tissues between the veins. (Fig. 13a) Others consume the entire leaf. Defoliators belong to the leaf chewing type of insect. Other leaf eaters are the spruce bud worm *Choristoneura fumiferana* which attacks the true firs and Douglas-fir. The gypsy moth *Porthetria dispar* attacks a great variety of species, but the greatest damage has been to the oaks. It is now spreading southward and expanding to other hardwoods. The eggs are often deposited on campers and trailers, thus rapidly expanding the insect's range. Canker worms *Alsophila* and *Paleacrita* often called "measuring worms" attack elms, willow, and many other deciduous trees. The larch sawfly *Pristiphora* is one of the most serious defoliators of larch in the east and west. Pine sawflys *Neodiprion* **spp.** are injurious defoliators and attack all southern yellow pines, spruces, and lodgepole pine. The forest tent caterpillar *Malacosoma disstria* prefers sugar maple, aspen, and oaks;

the eastern tent caterpillar *Malacosoma americanum*, cherry. (Fig. 13b)

Other insects attack the meristem tissue of the terminal parts of the tree, leaders and tips of branches. For the purpose of this discussion, meristem insects are arranged into three logical groups based on the part of the tree which they attack.

The first group feeds on the terminal parts, twigs, tips, shoots, and small roots. Some of the more common and injurious of these are the pine tip moths *Dioryctria spp.* and *Rhyacionia spp.* which feed on ponderosa, Virginia and white pines as well as some other species. The pales weevil *Hylobius pales*, an enemy of young pines, is usually found following logging in natural reproduction or in new plantations. Damage is to the seedlings. The white pine weevil *Pissodes strobi* attacks jack pine and eastern white pine killing the leaders and causing forked and crooked boles. The white grub *Phyllophaga spp.* feeds on small roots beneath the ground, attacking them wherever they happen to occur. They are extremely damaging in nurseries. White grubs are the larvae of the May beetle which emerges in early spring and may feed as an adult on the foliage of trees. Infrequently, they may cause defoliation injury but their greatest damage is in the larval stage to the rootlets. In addition to white grubs, there are a number of other insects which feed upon the small rootlets. One such group is the wireworms *Elateridae*, the larval stage of which are commonly found in heavy moist soils containing a considerable amount of decayed plant material.

The second group of meristem insects attack the cambium region of the trunk and branches. They live in the cambium throughout their early development and some of their adult life. They are commonly referred to as "borers." The pitchmass borer *Parharmonia pini* rarely kills the tree but causes defects and loss of vigor. The sugar maple borer *Glycobius speciosus* and two-lined chestnut borer *Agrilus bilineatus* attack chestnut, oaks, and beech. This latter species is generally distributed east of the Rocky Mountains. It frequently works in conjunction with a root rot, *Armellaria mellea*, the honey mushroom, which is a parasitic fungus on many oaks. (Fig. 15a) Twig girdlers are particularly damaging in appearance to shade trees. They attack small branches and twigs, working toward the base of the branch, encircling, girdling, and causing its death. There is usually a litter of small twigs and branches under trees infested with twig girdlers. The bronze birch borer *Agrilus anxius* is one of the more common of this group. Another group of insects attacking the cambium are bark beetles *Scolytidae*. They comprise a large family and have a characteristic manner of work which may be helpful in identification. All excavate galleries in the cambium region and deposit eggs. (Fig. 14b) Hatching larvae work outward in the succulent tissue of the cambium and inner bark forming a characteristic pattern of tunnels. Many of the bark beetles are secondary and attack only when trees are reduced in vigor. The genus *Dendroctonus* contains most of the bark beetles which are considered to be primary pests of trees. Among these is the red turpentine beetle *Dendroctonus valens,* the black turpentine beetle *D. terebrans,* the western pine beetle *D. brevicomis,* the mountain pine beetle *D. ponderosae,* the Douglas-fir beetle *D. Pseudostugae* and the southern pine beetle *D. frontalis.* These attack many of the western and southern conifers. (Fig. 14a) The engraver beetle *Ips* **spp.** is particularly damaging to southern pines. Pine beetles and the engraver beetle work in definites areas of the trunk. Engraver beetles work from the ground to the tip of the crown. Southern pine beetles from near the ground level to about half the crown length. Turpentine beetles work from ground level up to 4 or 5 feet above ground. Bark beetle infestation may be identified by pitch tubes. (Fig. 14c). They are about the size of a wad of gum and may be white, yellow or red-brown and are found on the lower trunk. Pitch tubes are the result of the tree's effort to drown the adult beetle when it enters the tree.

a   b   c

Fig. 14. BARK BEETLES. (a) Lodgepole pine killed by bark beetles. (Miller Photo) (b) Pattern of galleries made by larvae of southern pine bark beetles. (Photo courtesy U. S. Forest Service) (c) Pitch tubes of bark beetles on southern pine. (Photo courtesy U. S. Forest Service)

The last group of meristem insects are those which attack both cambium and wood. They are commonly called "cambium-wood" insects. For the most part, these insects are pests of dying trees and freshly cut logs. Those occurring in living trees, for example, are the locust borer *Megacyllene robiniae,* poplar borer *Saperda calcarata,* and carpenter worm *Prionoxystus robiniae.* They normally tunnel in solid wood. In the spring however, the larvae attack the cambium for a short time before entering the wood. Some of the more common insects in dying trees and logs are the flat-headed borers *Buprestidae* and the round-headed borers *Cerambycidae.* Damage is principally to the wood which would be used for lumber.

Another group of insects which damage trees are the sap sucking insects. They do not have developed mouth parts for chewing plant material but have a beak which can be inserted in the plant tissue enabling them to remove juices. These insects rarely kill trees directly but may reduce vigor to a point where other primary insects can kill it. They injure the tree in two ways—by sucking the sap thus robbing the tree of part of its food supply and, by indirectly disseminating plant diseases. Some of the more common sucking insects are those which are referred to as "plant bugs," the boxelder bug *Leptocoris trivittatus*, the tarnished plant bug *Lygus lineolaris*, and lace bugs *Tingidae*. The most damaging of the sucking insects are the true aphids or plant lice. Blue, Engelmann and Sitka spruces are attacked by *Adelges coolyi*. The balsam wooly aphid *Adelges piceae* is damaging Fraser fir in the east. Other more common sucking insects are oystershell scale *Lepidosophes ulmi*, cotton maple scale *Pulvinaria innumerabilis* and beech scale *Cryptococcus fagi*.

In the forest ecosystem, there is some loss from insects each year. These are endemic and are often measured only in reduced growth, deformities, and lowered commercial quality. Seldom is the tree actually killed. Epidemic conditions occur when the environmental balance is disturbed. This may be triggered by reduction of predators or stresses on host trees from drought, fire, and windthrow. These weaken the tree, thus making it easier for establishment of the insect. Breeding habitat of the insect may be suddenly expanded such as would result from new logging slash or wind breakage. When all or even a part of these conditions exist, epidemic populations may occur.

Considering shade and ornamentals any attack is serious and steps should be taken to give the infested tree protection. Attacks are usually recognizable by fading foliage, loss of vigor, and in the case of bark beetles, the appearance of pitch tubes.

Disease

Diseases attacking trees may be grouped into those which affect the leaves, heartwood, and roots. They may appear as leaf spots, dieback, decay, rots, rusts, and cankers. Probably the most common diseases are those of the heartwood, called heart rots. These are caused by a great number of different fungi which enter the trunk through fire scars and other wounds. They rarely kill the tree but do reduce its value for lumber as well as contribute to windthrow and breakage. Some of the fruiting bodies of sap rotters are edible mushrooms, such as the honey mushroom *Armillaria mellea*, (Fig. 15a), the sulfur polyphore *Polyporus sulphureus*, and the oyster mushroom *Pleurotus ostreatus*. Many of the hedgehog fungi *Hydnums* are common sapwood rotters. As a rule, only a single fungus is responsible for heart rot in any one tree. Heart rots are not like insects which may follow one another. Diseases are damaging in various degrees. White pine blister rust *Cronartium ribicola* at one time was serious enough to attract national attention. Due to aggressive control measures and cooperation, the disease was controlled in some areas. Fusiform rust *Cronartium fusiforme* (Fig. 15b) of southern pines does not become a primary cause of death, but it does contribute to breakage and reduces growth. Another disease demanding national attention was the chestnut blight *Endothia parasitica* which caused complete destruction of commercial numbers of the American chestnut. (Fig. 15c) Chestnut blight was the greatest botanical catastrophy within the memory of man. Dutch elm disease *Ceratocystic ulmi,* which is presently a serious threat to the genus Ulmus, oddly enough enters the tree through wounds and is carried by means of two bark beetles, *Scolytus multistraitus* and *Hylurgopinus rufupes.* "Elm Street" is disappearing from many cities. The disease does not go from one host to another by itself but is wholly dependent on insects for mobility. Control has become involved with some of the more damaging hydrocarbons such as DDT. These do immeasurable damage to the ecosystem as residues do not deteriorate but remain potent in the soils for many years. Soil fauna suffers and many insectivorous songbirds have been killed or rendered sterile from eating insects which carry residues of hydrocarbons in their bodies. Other pesticides which are biodegradable can be used to control the bark beetles carrying the Dutch elm disease.

Nectria *Nectria* **spp.** and strumella *Strumella coryneoides* cankers are damaging to many oaks, elm, and yellow poplar. Oak wilt *Ceratocystis fagacearum* attacks red and white oaks.

a   b   c

Fig. 15. DISEASES OF TREES. (a) *Armillaria mellea,* the fruiting body of shoestring root rot. (b) Canker of fusiform rust on southern pine. (c) Canker of chestnut blight. (Miller Photos)

The annosus root rot of pines caused by *Fomes annosus* is damaging to white pine, slash and loblolly where they occur in plantations. Little leaf disease of shortleaf pine caused by a soil fungus *Phytophthora cinnamomii* is a "disease" associated with low quality sites and poor internal soil drainage.

Control of insects and diseases is an involved and complex process. Shade trees and ornamentals should be inspected frequently and if lacking in vigor, color, or general well being, an entomologist or pathologist should be contacted. Many times this service is available through the State Forester's office.

Air Pollution

Over 3000 foreign chemicals are presently polluting our atmosphere. Some of these are or can be harmful to trees. (Fig. 16) Materials causing air pollution may be separated into primary pollutants which immediately upon emission are phytotoxic and secondary, those which must go through a chemical change often triggered by light or reaction with another chemical before they become harmful.

Both primary and secondary pollutants damage trees by killing leaf tissue, destroying photosynthesis and reducing growth, thus lowering vigor of the tree. Primary pollutants are sulfur dioxide, flourides, oxides of nitrogen, hydrogen chloride. Secondary pollutants are ozone, peroxyacetal nitrates and terpenes.

Fig 16. Air pollution by sulfur dioxide from smoldering mine dump. Hardwoods are first to go. (Miller Photo)

Sulfur dioxide is one of the more common of the primary pollutants. Combustion of coal and oil produce the greater amounts of sulfur dioxide. There are numerous instances of serious vegetative damage resulting from emissions from coal burning power plants. Other less frequent sources are production, refining, and utilization of petroleum and natural gas; manufacture and industrial utilization of sulfuric acid and sulfur; smelting and refining of ores, especially copper, lead, zinc, and nickel. Sulfur dioxide is one of the least toxic of presently known air pollutants.

Symptoms of exposure to sulfur dioxide are yellowing between the veins of the leaf, frequently with die-back from the tip in broadleaf trees. Die-back from the needle-tip is a common symptom in conifers, frequently accompanied by reddish banding of the needle. On some broadleaf species such as red maple, the dying interveinal leaf tissue becomes reddish brown. There is a marked reduction in growth rate which occurs even without these external symptoms.

Flouride compounds, another of the primary pollutants, originate principally from aluminum reduction processes, manufacture of phosphate fertilizer, steel manufacturing plants, brick, pottery and ferroenamel work, and refineries. Flourides are toxic at much lower concentrations than other air pollutants. While the annual volume of emissions does not compare with common pollutants such as sulfur dioxides, flourides represent a major problem in tree damage. Flourides, particularly hydrogen flouride, are the most toxic of presently known air pollutants.

Flouride symptoms differ from those associated with sulfur dioxide. The die-back and chlorosis of the leaf instead of being inter-veinal is evident on the margin. Fluoride compounds are mobile within the tree and move through the vascular system from the leaf to accumulate elsewhere. Because of this ability of movement and accumulation, flourides have been found toxic to animals. Browsers eating leaves and shoots of contaminated plants often develop a disease called "flourosis." There have been serious out-breaks of flourosis in cattle herds in the western states where live-stock was browsing on contaminated vegetation.

Oxides of nitrogen are a third primary pollutant. These have been discovered more recently and are serious in view of the amounts emitted. Oxides of nitrogen originate from gasoline combustion in motor vehicles, the refining of petroleum and the combustion of natural gas, fuel oil and coal. Incineration of organic wastes is also an important source of the pollutant.

Hydrogen chloride is a fourth primary pollutant. It has long been recognized as damaging to vegetation, but processes producing the compounds had been changed to the point that harmful emissions were minimal. In recent years, there has been a reappearance of, and damage attributed to, hydrogen chloride. Sources of hydrogen chloride include refineries, glass making, incineration, and scrap burning. Polyvinal chloride which is used in ever-increasing quanti-ties in the manufacture of packaging material and wire insulation is a source of hydrogen chloride. Combustion of polyvinal material is the basis for emission of hydrogen chloride and other compounds. Predictions are that hydrogen chloride will become increasingly common as an air pollutant.

Ozone, usually a secondary pollutant, has been recognized for many years. It has been only in the last 10 to 15 years, however, that its origin and activity in smog over cities has been recognized. Ozone comes from electrical storms and photochemical reactions. Some of the ozone present in our atmosphere is brought in during violent storms in the troposphere. A more common source of ozone, however, is from photochemical reactions in polluted atmosphere. Oxides of nitrogen resulting from motor vehicle combustion and a variety of industries and utilities often react in the presence of light with the oxygen in the atmosphere to form ozone. Hydrocarbons emitted by motor vehicles and some industrial processes can react to form ozone. Ozone from this origin is the major ingredient of "urban smog." Ozone is less toxic to trees than the flourides, but more so than sulfur dioxide.

Symptoms of ozone damage to plants and trees is frequently characterized by metallic flecking or stipuling on the upper leaf surfaces. Broadleaf trees such as ash, oak, and yellow poplar show the stipuling on their upper leaf surfaces. Coniferous leaves show a mottling pattern of green and brown, added to tip die-back of the needle.

Peroxyacetyl nitrate commonly called PAN is another secondary pollutant. The major source of this compound is hydrocarbon emissions from motor vehicles combining with oxides of nitrogen to form PAN. It is rated along with ozone in toxicity.

Terpenes which originate from the distillation of coniferous materials can react photochemically with oxides of nitrogen to form ozone or PAN. Terpenes present in the atmosphere in the vicinity of power plants, for example, could result in the formation of either pollutant.

Symptoms of PAN poisoning on plants is glazing or silvering on the lower surface of the leaf. There is but fragmentary evidence at this time indicating that PAN is damaging to trees. They appear to be more resistant than herbaceous plants.

Particulates commonly originate from the same sources as sulfur dioxide, oxides of nitrogen and hydrogen chloride. Damage to plant tissue is more closely related to these chemicals rather than the smothering effect of particulates.

Normally, trees do not show violent external reaction to low continuous or intermittent emission of the various air pollutants. More insidious is gradual reduction in condition and vigor thus subjecting the weakened tree to attack by insects and disease. Damage to trees from polluted air in past years has occurred largely in areas where high concentrations of industrial pollutants have been present. Today's multitude of motor vehicles, new processing plants and the incineration of organic wastes in larger volumes, will significantly increase and expand the pollution hazard. Under these conditions not only will shade and ornamental trees in urban areas suffer, but vast acreages of forests may be subject to the pollution threat.

Soil Pollution

Another enemy of the tree is soil pollution. Early indications of this are marginal leaf scorch, early autumn coloration, defoliation, and reduced shoot growth. Later symptoms are death of entire twigs and limbs with ultimate death of the whole tree. If the tree does not succumb, its vigor is so lowered that it is open to further damage from insects or disease.

There are two major sources of soil pollution. One being from septic tanks where the by-pass field is filled with caustic soaps, detergents, and other non-biodegradable chemicals foreign to the ecosystem. This is particularly true in soils of low porosity where the caustic materials are held in close contact with the root hairs of the trees. The only solution where individual septic systems have poisoned the ecosystem is municipal sewage.

Brine run-off from salt applied to roads for the purpose of melting ice and snow is another source of soil pollution. Hopefully some non-toxic ice melting chemical may be found for use on roads to assure winter driving safety. Until such time however, planning for plantings along roads and in new developments should make use of salt tolerant tree species. Some of these are black cherry, bigtooth aspen, black locust, yellow and sweet birches, red and white oaks. Salt intolerant species are sugar maple, hemlock, white pine and red pine.

Distance between the tree and the source of the brine is an important factor. On the average, trees beyond 30 feet from the roadway have a better chance of survival than those closer. This distance of course varies with the direction of the slope. Up-slope plantings may be closer than those on down slopes. Depressions where brine run-off might accumulate should be shunned as planting sites.

Where there is early indication of moderate pollution, gypsum may be applied to soil around the trees. Gypsum improves the soil structure which was broken down by the brine. The best solution at this time appears to be in selecting salt tolerant trees and planting them beyond the safety zone.

Water Manipulation

During germination and early seedling development, the root system of a tree becomes established on the basis of the moisture cycle peculiar to that site. Any abrupt changes in this cycle alters

the entire tree-site relation and has a definite impact on the tree itself. In the case of flooding, even trees normally found in swamp sites such as baldcypress and swamp tupelo cannot stand permanent inundation. (Fig. 17) Neither can trees established in a mesophytic environment tolerate drainage. When the water table is abruptly lowered below that in which the tree became established, its well being is endangered.

Fig. 17. Even trees normally found in swamp sites cannot withstand flooding. In this case baldcypress. (Miller Photo)

Man-made development such as flood control and hydroelectric impoundment change the water regimen drastically not only within the flooded area, but in the adjacent lands as well. Trees which were occupying dry slopes of the valley become subjected to a water table higher than that in which they became adjusted. On such sites, there is a gradual invasion of species better adapted to higher moisture conditions. Roots of the trees which were established on the basis of the former water table will be drowned.

Temporary flooding during the dormant season, as is practiced in green tree reservoir manipulation for waterfowl, does not adversely affect growth.

Beaver impoundments adversely affect the site in the same way as other permanent flooding.

Drainage has the same effect as flooding, but in reverse. Drainage of bottomlands abruptly drops the water table and leaves the tree's roots stranded. Bottomland tree species are very sensitive to changes in moisture and either die or lose vigor and are crowded out by species more adaptable to dryer conditions.

HOW TO USE THE KEY

Keys such as the ones that follow are built on the basis of multiple choice, a familiar type of examination. The general key contains 195 entries; the winter key, but 81. Keys require a decision from several opportunities. Let's say, for example, we have a specimen from a broadleaf tree. Turn to choice 1 and observe that the leaves are not opposite but are alternate and only one growing at each node. Turn to choice 3 and determine that the veins are palmately arranged; that is, they arise from the base of the leaf blade. Following this decision, turn to 122. Here we find that the twigs do not have stipular rings nor are the axillary buds covered. This leads us to 124 where we find that the leaves are not in 2 rows on the stem (2-ranked) and go to 135. Note that the leaves are more or less star shaped with 3 to 7 radiating lobes. We check the pith of the twig and find that it is 5-angled. This species then is sweetgum. (Fig. 219) By elimination of characters that are not found on our specimen, we have arrived at the correct genus and species. Further checking of the species description, leaves, twigs, bark, and flowers, will verify the decision.

PICTURED KEY FOR IDENTIFICATION
OF THE MORE COMMON TREES

Fig. 18.

1a. Leaves with netted veined expanded blades, Dicotyledons. Fig. 18 ....
....................THE BROADLEAFS, p. 71

Fig. 19.

1b. Leaves needle-shaped, linear, awl-shaped, or scale-like. Seeds borne in cones. Trees evergreen (except *Larix* and *Taxodium*). Fig. 19 ....
......THE CONIFERS, p. 27

1c. Leaves fan shaped, veins equal in size and diverging from base of blade; borne on thick wartlike dwarf branches ....
.....................MAIDENHAIR TREE *Ginkgo biloba* L. Fig. 20
MAIDENHAIR TREE ....*Ginkgo biloba* L.

Imported from China and Japan where it had been cultivated in Temple Gardens for centuries. It is a medium-sized tree, sparingly branched, often into a conical shaped crown. The wood is resinous. BARK: gray, irregularly fissured and loose scaly. LEAVES: fan shaped, 1 to 2 inches long and 1 1/2 to 3 inches broad, often 2-lobed, with parallel veins, leathery, bright green, turning yellow and shedding in the fall. FLOWERS: dioecious, greenish, staminate in catkins; pistillate small. FRUIT: about 3/4 inches long, egg-shaped, yellowish with ill-smelling pulp which surrounds a whitish nut. The kernel is edible and often roasted and eaten by Orientals. Ginkgo is a living fossil, related to conifers and the sole survivor

Fig. 20. Ginkgo biloba.

of its family. It is used in the United States for street and ornamental planting. It is resistant to smoke, dust, wind, and ice; free from insect injury. Male trees are preferred because of the disagreeable fruits of the female.

THE CONIFERS

2a. Leaves in definite clusters on the side of the branch. Fig 21
....3

Fig. 21.

2b. Leaves scattered singly on the stem, linear. Fig. 22 (Read 3b also) 10

Fig. 22.

2c. Leaves opposite or whorled or feather-like. Figs. 25-30 5

3a. Clusters of 2 to 5, long needle-shaped leaves. Retained for more than one year (evergreen). Fig. 212.   THE PINES 21

3b. Clusters of seven to many shorter needle-like leaves, borne on permanent wart-like dwarf branches. (Leaves of first year scattered) Leaves dropping each fall, trees bare during winter. Figs. 21b, 23, and 24. The LARCHES 4

4a. Cones 1/2 to 3/4 inch long, leaves an inch or less, native and growing in wet places. Fig. 23.

TAMARACK ....*Larix laricina* (Du Roi) K. Koch

Tamarack is a small to medium-sized tree 40 to 80 feet in height. It has a long cylindrical bole and open pyramidal crown. It is a fast growing species when young but slows down from about 40 years of age. It has a moderately long life span. BARK: thin and smooth on young boles, becoming thicker and slightly scaly, gray to reddish brown. LEAVES: needle-like and in tufts, pale green, 1/2 to 1 inch long, deciduous. FLOWERS: appearing in the spring with needles, staminate, yellowish green; pistillate, red. FRUIT: a small cone, short stalked, erect 1/2 to 3/4 inch long, remaining open on the twigs for a year or two.

Fig. 23. Larix laricina.

Tamarack occurs in cool swamps, bogs, and better drained moist lands where its best growth is attained. It cannot withstand prolonged flooding and is a characteristic tree of the northern bogs. Tamarack is extremely intolerant and can stand forest conditions only if it is the dominant tree. It is a pioneer species in acid bog sites. Although it occurs extensively in even-aged, pure stands, it does grow in association with black spruce, balsam fir, northern white-cedar, and black ash. Typical understory shrubs and lesser vegetation found under tamarack are green alder *Alnus crispa,* speckled alder, bearberry *Arctostaphylos uva-ursi,* several huckleberries and blueberries *Vaccinium* **spp**. The principal enemies of tamarack are fire, in bogs where where peat burns kill the roots, but on upland sites it is moderately resistant to fire; windthrow as a result of the shallow root system. Larch sawflies periodically become epidemic and defoliate large areas. Following defoliation, bark beetles attack the weakened trees. Tamarack is frequently attacked by heart rots and root rots. Porcupines strip the bark from the upper stem, causing deformation. White-tail deer may browse seedlings in winter deer yards. Since the species is deciduous, it furnishes little winter protection to deer as a winter yard; if there is a high percentage of spruce and balsam, deer may yard in the type.

The largest living tamarack of record is 9 feet 8 inches in circumference, 95 feet high with a crown spread of 50 feet. It is growing near Jay, Maine.

4b. Cones 3/4 to 1 1/2 inches long, leaves one inch or more, grows in dry ground, cultivated. Fig. 24.

EUROPEAN LARCH ....*Larix decidua* Mill.

European Larch is a tall pyramidal-shaped tree with drooping horizontal branches. It reaches heights of 90 to 120 feet. It is a native of northern Europe. BARK: grayish-brown, thin, and in rough loose scaly plates. LEAVES: short needles 3/4 to 1 1/2 inches long in tufts. They are deciduous. FLOWERS: developing with the needles in the spring, staminate, yellowish; pistillate, red. FRUIT: small cone, 3/4 to 1 1/2 inches long, the wings of the seed extending to the outer margin of the scale. Cones persist, opened, for several years on the twigs. European Larch is subject to the

Fig. 24. Larix decidua.

same insect and fungus enemies as Tamarack. Since it usually occurs in urban area, dangers from changes in water levels are not high. While its use as an ornamental is probably more frequent, it does make good lumber and pulpwood. The largest European Larch living of record is 6 feet 8 inches in circumference, 106 feet high with a crown spread of 30 feet. It is growing in the Buckloons Recreational Area in the Allegheny National Forest in Pennsylvania.

5a. Leaves arranged feather-like as pictured on deciduous dwarf branches. Trees bare during winter. Fig. 25.

Fig. 25. Taxodium distichum.

BALDCYPRESS ....
.... *Taxodium distichum* (**L.**) Rich. **var.** *distichum*

PONDCYPRESS ....
.... *Taxodium distichum* var. *nutans* (Ait.) Sweet

Baldcypress and pondcypress are perhaps two of the most unusual trees found in the south. They are restricted to very wet soils consisting of muck, clay, and silt where the moisture is abundant and fairly permanent. They will, however, grow under well drained conditions on high lands. More than 90 percent of natural baldcypress and pondcypress is found on flat topography less than 100 feet above sea level. On wet sides, baldcypress is a slow growing long-lived species. Virgin stands are 400 to 600 years old; individual trees up to 1200 years old have been reported in Georgia and South

a   b

Fig. 25 a-b. (a) Cypress festooned with Spanish moss *Tillandsia usneoides* is a trade mark of the low country. (b) Typical cypress "knees." (Miller Photos)

Carolina. Height growth of baldcypress averages about 1 foot per year, second growth stands grow faster. Baldcypress has a distinctive root system. The descending portion provides anchorage but many wide spreading shallow roots on wetter sites put up structures known as "knees." The function of the "knees" is not definitely known but it is believed that they improve aeration. Growth characteristics of pond and baldcypress are similar. Bark: reddish-brown, fibrous, and flaky. LEAVES: feather-like, yellow-green 1/2 to 3/4 inch long and deciduous in baldcypress. In pondcypress they are nearly flat and scale-like against the twig, 1/8 to 3/8 inch long. FLOWERS: monoecious, staminate purplish in large cluster; pistillate borne singly, terminal. FRUIT: a cone, spherical, 3/4 to 1 inch in diameter. The northern limit of the range of pondcypress is shown by the heavy line on the range map.

Baldcypress and pondcypress both occur in pure types and are considered intolerant. Where baldcypress occurs in swamps, it is considered a subclimax species. Baldcypress is commonly associated with water tupelo. Other associates are pondcypress, black willow, swamp cottonwood, red maple, overcup oak, and water hickory. On drier sites, it occurs along with sweetgum, Nuttall oak, loblolly pine, slash pine, and pond pine. Understory species are few, buttonbush, coastal leucothoe *Leucothoe axillaris,* Carolina rose *Rosa carolina,* possumhaw, poison sumac, and Virginia sweetspire *Itea virginica.* In many cypress swamps unique ferns, vines, and epiphytes are present. Due to the high moisture content of the sites in which baldcypress grows, fire is not too frequent. A brown pocket rot of the heartwood known as "peckiness" is caused by *Stereum taxodii.* Insects do not appear to be too damaging. Baldcypress is becoming rare due to several reasons—difficulty in regeneration, drainage of wet lands where it normally grows and, conversely, drowning of wet lands by flood control impoundments. Cypress lumber is in demand where long lasting qualities are desired. It is popular for interior paneling and "pecky" cypress is used extensively for this purpose. Selection of just the right amount of "peck" can result in a uniquely beautiful panel. Dry land species of wildlife are not generally attracted to cypress stands. Waterfowl, however, find it well suited for wintering grounds and where it grows with oaks it is especially high quality feeding range. Swamps are good escape cover for white-tail deer.

The largest baldcypress of record and now living is 38 feet 8 inches in circumference (above the butt swell), 122 feet high with a crown spread of 47 feet. It is growing 3 miles west of Sharon, Tennessee. The largest pondcypress living and of record is 21 feet 10 inches in circumference (above butt swell), 121 feet high with a crown spread of 90 feet. It is growing at Statesville, Georgia. Baldcypress is the State Tree of Louisiana.

5b. Not as in 5a **6**

6a. Leaves scale-like, very small and tightly overlapping, less than 1/8 inch long. Fig. 26 ....**7**

6b. Leaves awl-shaped, not closely overlapping, 1/4 to 3/4 inch long. Fruit a bluish, berry-like cone. Figs. 28 and 29 ....**9**

7a. Young leafy shoots very much flattened and fan-like, in a horizontal plane; scale-like leaves 4-ranked. Fig. 26.

NORTHERN WHITE-CEDAR .... *Thuja occidentalis* **L.**

Fig. 26. Thuja occidentalis.

Northern white-cedar is normally about 40 to 50 feet tall and has a wide pyramidal crown. The tapering bole is supported by a shallow, wide-spreading root system. It is slow growing and long lived. BARK: 1/4 to 1/3 inch thick, brownish in color and fibrous, peeling in strips. LEAVES: small and appressed, 4-ranked on flattened fan-like sprays, yellow-green. FLOWERS: monoecious, both staminate and pistillate cones very small and terminal. FRUIT: a cone, 1/3 to 1/2 inch long, erect and oblong, opening in the fall but persisting on the twig during the winter.

Northern white-cedar occurs in a cool, humid climate and grows on a variety of soils. It makes its best growth on soils of limestone origin. Although often associated with swamps, good drainage is required for best development. The species is tolerant and considered a climax species. It occurs in pure stands and associated wtih other conifers and hardwoods. Some of its associates are white spruce, balsam fir, black spruce, tamarack, hemlock, red spruce, yellow birch, red maple and paper birch. Common understory shrubs are gray dogwood *Cornus racemosa*, red-osier dogwood *Cornus stolonifera*, willows, American mountain ash, mountain maple, honeysuckle *Lonicera* **spp.**, and western thimbleberry *Rubus parviflorus*. White-cedar is susceptible to fire, windthrow, and changes in moisture conditions. It is seldom attacked by insects and disease. Deer, during winter yarding, browse heavily on young seedlings and saplings. Moose and snowshoe hare do equal or greater damage. Northern white-cedar swamps are prime deer wintering yards. White-cedar is very durable and used for poles, railroad ties, posts, box lumber, tanks, and building construction. Cedar oil is extracted for medicinal purposes. It is widely planted as an ornamental. The largest northern white-cedar living of record is 17 feet 2 inches in circumference, 111 feet high with a crown spread of 38 feet. It is growing on South Manitou Island, Michigan.

The ORIENTAL ARBORVITAE, *Thuja orientalis* L. is often planted as an ornamental. It may be distinguished from T. occidentalis by the young leafy shoots which usually stand in a vertical plane with both sides alike, cones which stand erect, and seeds which have no wings.

7b. Young shoots not conspicuously flattened 8

8a. Leaves scale-like, all nearly the same. Young shoots cylindric or but slightly flattened. Fruit a dry brownish cone. Fig. 27.

ATLANTIC WHITE-CEDAR ....
....*Chamaecyparis thyoides* (**L.**) *B.S.P.*

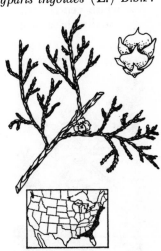

Atlantic white-cedar is characteristic of fresh-water swamps and bogs of the Atlantic and Gulf Coastal Plains. It is not a large tree, sometimes reaching heights of 90 feet. The crown is small, narrowly conical and is composed of slender branches which droop. The root system is shallow. It is slow growing with a medium life span. BARK: reddish-brown, 3/4 to 1 inch thick, scaly. LEAVES: glaucous or light green, awl-shaped in opposite pairs, a conspicuous gland on back, some with keels. FLOWERS: are small monoecious terminal cones. FRUIT: a cone, 1/4 inch in diameter, at maturity bluish-purple and glaucous, later turning brown. Atlantic white-cedar occurs in extensive pure stands. Although tolerant of shade,

Fig. 27. Chamaecyparis thoides.

young seedlings and saplings do not survive under the dense shade of older growth. Pure stands are even-aged. Where fire or cutting has taken place, the associated species are about as follows—pond pine, baldcypress, swamp tupelo, slash pine, titi, red maple, and black gum. Atlantic white-cedar is considered an intolerant subclimax species which when disturbed by cutting is replaced by swamp hardwoods. Dense even-aged stands are not conducive to development of a vigorous understory, but in openings loblolly-bay, sweet pepper bush *Clethra alnifolia* and Virginia sweetspire *Itea virginica* will often develop. In the northern portion of its range, the protection by dense even-aged cover for deer in the winter is important. Fire and windthrow are damaging to white-cedar. It has no serious insect enemies. Few fungi attack it. White-cedar is a durable wood and used for posts, small boats, exposed siding shingles and porches. It is also a popular ornamental. The largest living Atlantic white-cedar of record is 15 feet 6 inches in circumference, 87 feet high and is living near Brewton, Alabama. Atlantic white-cedar is the State Tree of New Jersey.

8b.   **Leaves of two kinds—many small and scale-like often forming a 4-angled shoot; other 1/4 to 3/8 inch long; awl-shaped and sharp pointed. Fruit a bluish-white berry-like cone. Fig. 29. EASTERN REDCEDAR.**

9a.   **Leaves awl-shaped, all the same, upper surface concave with white center stripe and narrow green margin, green below, usually three at each node. Fruit dark blue, axillary. Fig. 28.**

COMMON JUNIPER ....*Juniperus communis* L.

Common juniper, sometimes called the "pasture juniper," is a small sprawling, bushy circumpolar shrub common to many sections of eastern and northeastern United States. It may be recognized by its peculiar bushy habit of growth, its long awl-shaped leaves. It is slow growing. BARK: is shreddy, dark and resinous. LEAVES: 1/4 to 1/2 inch long, often curved, rigid, sharp tips, lustrous dark green below, white above, in whorls of 3. FLOWERS: dioecious, axillary, cone-like and small. FRUIT: blue, glaucous, berry-like and fleshy with 1 to 3 bony seeds.

Fig. 28. Juniperus communis.

Oil obtained from both the wood and the leaves is used in the manufacture of perfumes and medicines. Gin derives its characteristic taste from juniper "berries." It is used as ornamental, foundation, and corner plantings. Deer browse the new shoots. The largest living common juniper of record is 10 inches in circumference, 14 feet high and has a crown spread of 7 feet. It is growing in Dunes State Park in Indiana.

EASTERN REDCEDAR .... *Juniperus virginiana* L.

Eastern redcedar is a small to medium-sized tree 40 to 50 feet high. The crown is dense and narrowly pyramidal, in some situations, columnar. The tapering bole terminates in a deep root system. Redcedar has the ability to grow under varying climatic conditions. It is slow growing and has a medium life span. BARK: 1/8 to 1/4 inch thick, reddish-brown, fibrous and exfoliates lengthwise in strips, exposed surfaces often ashy-gray. LEAVES: two types—one scale-like opposite, 1/16 inch long, in 4-sided branchlets, dark green; the other, bluish-green needles up to 1/3 inch long. FLOWERS: dioecious, yellowish staminate

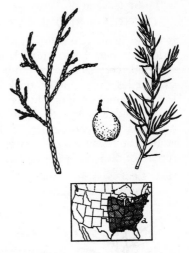

Fig. 29. Juniperus virginiana.

cones 1/3 inch long; pistillate cones inconspicuous. FRUIT: 1/4 inch in diameter, dark blue, glaucous bloom at maturity.

Redcedar occurs in pure stands generally originating on abandoned farmlands as a pioneer. It usually occupies dry sites, but can grow well on moist soils. It is common on limestone outcrops and other shallow soils. Redcedar is very intolerant and in pioneer succession is succeeded by various hardwoods. It occurs in several mixed types where it is associated with loblolly, shortleaf and Virginia pines, post oak, chestnut and red oaks, red maple, sweetgum, and dogwood. In these associations, it is soon replaced by more tolerant species. Understory vegetation is variable due to the wide range in soil and climate; some of the more common species are blackberry *Rubus* **spp.**, hawthorn, plum, greenbriar *Smilax* **spp.**, and persimmon. The fruits are eaten by many songbirds, turkey, grouse, quail, fox and opossum. Deer browse the new shoots. Fire is the worst enemy of eastern redcedar as the thin bark and spreading root system near the ground surface are injured by even light surface fires. Few insects damage redcedar. Wood rots do considerable damage, particularly in the South. Annosus rot works on the sapwood. Galls, called "cedar apples," *Gymnosporangium juniperi-virginianae* are conspicuous features. Eastern redcedar is the bridging host for apple rust. Its principal use is for fence posts, "cedar chests" and closet linings. It is planted for ornamental and shelterbelt purposes. The largest living eastern redcedar of record is 12 feet 2 inches in circumference, 76 feet high with a crown spread of 45 feet. It is growing near Roganville, Texas. Eastern redcedar is the State Tree of Tennessee.

SOUTHERN REDCEDAR, *Juniperus silicicola* (Small) Bailey, is found in the Coastal Plains as shown at "a" on the map. It has reddish-brown bark, thin, fibrous and shreddy. Leaf twigs are rounded, very slender, usually pendant. Leaves are scale-like 1/16 inch or less in diameter, dark blue-green; the "berry" 3/16 inch or less in diameter, dark blue. In contrast to eastern redcedar, southern redcedar is found on swampy sites. It is used for the same purposes as its counterpart of dry sites. The largest living specimen is 10 feet 2 inches in circumference, 50 feet high with a crown spread of 50 feet. It is growing near Pensacola, Florida.

10a. **Leaf bases remaining on the branches and roughening them** 11

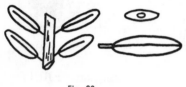

Fig. 30.

Fig. 31.

10b. **Leaf bases dropping with leaves, stems comparatively smooth** 12

11a. **Leaves stalked, flattened and appearing 2-ranked. Fig. 30. THE HEMLOCKS** 16

11b. **Leaves sessile, more or less 4-sided spreading in all directions. Fig. 31. THE SPRUCES** 17

12a. **Leaves stalked, flattened, winter buds pointed, not resinous. Fig. 32.**

DOUGLAS-FIR ....
..................*Pseudotsuga menziesii* (Mirb.) Franco **var.** *menziesii*

Douglas-fir is one of the monarchs of the western forests. It is a large tree, up to 300 feet in height. It is second in size only to the Bigtrees. It occurs in two forms which are now distinct, the Coastal form and the Rocky Mountain form. The differences in superficial characteristics are principally color of the crown and size of the cones. The growth requirements of each, however, are significantly different. The Coastal form is fast growing and long lived. BARK:

Fig. 32. Pseudotsuga menziesii.

smooth on young stems becoming thick, 6 to 24 inches, and divided
into thick irregular reddish-brown ridges separated by deep irregular fissures. LEAVES: needle-like 3/4 to 1 1/4 inches long, yellow-
green, soft and flattened, grooved above, persistent 5 to 8 years.
FLOWERS: monoecious, solitary, staminate bright red; pistillate
reddish. FRUIT: a cone, 4 inches long, pendant, brown, with 3-
lobed fork-like bracts.

Douglas-fir occurs on a variety of soils but makes its best growth
on well drained soils, slightly on the alkaline side. Glacial outwash
soils and soils of volcanic origin are preferred. The tree is anchored
by a well developed wide spreading root system. Douglas-fir is
considered as intermediate in tolerance. When compared with many
of its associates, however, it is intolerant. It occurs in pure stands
and is a major component of several forest types where it is associated with Sitka spruce *Picea stitchensis,* western hemlock *Tsuga
heterophylla,* Port-Orford-cedar *Chamaecyparis lawsoniana,* ponderosa pine and redwood *Sequoia sempervirens.* It is generally
recognized as a subclimax species in association with the more
tolerant species. Coastal Douglas-fir stands are quite dense in
younger ages, not opening up for understory plants and shrubs
until pole size or even later. The more common understory species
in the northern stands are Oregon grape *Mahonia aquifolium,* red
whortleberry *Vaccinium parvifolium,* box blueberry *Vaccinium ova-
tum,* oval-leaf whortleberry *Vaccinium ovalifolium,* salmonberry
Rubus spectabilis, rhododendron *Rhododendron* **spp.**, and vine
maple *Acer circinatum.* In southern Oregon and northern California,
various species of soapbloom *Ceanothus* **spp.** and bearberry *Arctostaphylos uva-ursi* occur under Douglas-fir. During early ages,
heavy rainfall and windthrow are damaging. The Douglas-fir beetle
and a flat headed borer may become serious. Some of the more
serious losses from disease are heart rots from *Fomes* and *Polyporus*
species. Animal damage runs high in regeneration areas where
black-tail deer and elk browse heavily on seedlings and saplings.
Douglas-fir represents a high percentage of standing timber in the
western forests; the lumber from the species is likewise widely
used. Sawtimber, plywood, and pulpwood are the most common
uses. Douglas-fir forests rate high in watershed protection. The
dense crown cover and deep root system protect against soil movement and retain moisture necessary for decomposition of litter and
soil enrichment. During regeneration and the mature years,
Douglas-fir forests are attractive to wildlife. Unfortunately, at times,
wildlife can be extremely damaging.

The largest living Coastal Douglas-fir of record is 45 feet 5 inches
in circumference, 221 feet high with a crown spread of 61 feet. It
is growing in the Olympic National Park in Washington. Douglas-
fir is the State Tree of Oregon.

ROCKY MOUNTAIN DOUGLAS-FIR ....
.... *Pseudotsuga menziesii* var. *glauca* (Beissn.) Franco

Rocky Mountain Douglas-fir (south and east of black line on map Fig. 32) does not reach the heights and diameters of its Coastal counterpart. It rarely exceeds 130 feet in height and is slower growing and shorter lived. It is more drought resistant than the Coastal form but makes its best growth on moist sites. It occurs pure or predominant over restricted portions of its range and in this type, it is considered to be climax. It is the principal species in several other mixed types where it is associated with larch *Larix occidentalis*, ponderosa pine, grand fir *Abies grandis*, lodgepole pine, western white pine and white fir. The place in the succession of the mixed types with which Douglas-fir is associated is not clear. They appear to be more subclimax in nature than anything else. The principal points of identification of the Rocky Mountain form are the cones, which are up to 3 inches long and the blue-green foliage of the crown. Where the two forms are intermixed, there may be some difficulty in identification. Some of the more common understory species in the northern portion of its range are Greene Mountain ash *Sorbus scopulina*, bristly black currant *Ribes lacustre*, big whortleberry *Vaccinium membranaceum*, alpine bilberry *Vaccinium uliginosum*, and myrtle boxleaf *Pachistima myrsinites*. In the central portion of the range they are, true mountain mahogany *Cercocarpus montanus*, Fendler's soapbloom *Ceanothus fendleri*, wax currant *Ribes cereum*, chokeberry *Prunus virginiana melanocarpa*, big sage *Artemisia tridentata*, common serviceberry *Amelanchier alnifolia*, and rock spirea *Holodiscus dumosus*; in the southern part, New Mexican locust *Robinia neomexicana*, Rocky Mountain maple *Acer glabrum* and creambush *Holodiscus discolor ariaefolius*. The majority of these species furnish pallatable browse for deer, elk, and livestock. The contribution of Rocky Mountain Douglas-fir to the lumber, plywood, and pulpwood markets is in the same proportion as the Coastal form. The species is subject to many of the same enemy problems as the Coastal form. Dwarf mistletoe *Arceuthobium douglasii* is recognized to be one of the most damaging diseases of the Rocky Mountain variety. The Douglas-fir beetle and spruce budworm have occurred in epidemic proportions.

The largest Rocky Mountain Douglas-fir of record and living is 19 feet 8 inches in circumference, 130 feet high and is growing near Boise, Idaho.

12b. **Leaves sessile. Winter buds obtuse, resinous. Cones erect.
Figs. 34-36** 13

13a. **Leaves flat and grooved above, usually rounded and often notched at apex** 14

13b. Leaves usually 4-sided, blue-green. Fig. 33.

NOBLE FIR ....*Abies procera* Rehd.

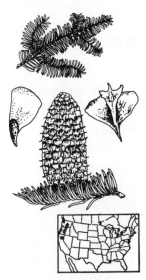

Noble fir is essentially a tree of the
mountains growing for the most part in
the Canadian Life Zone between 3,000
and 8,800 feet. It is the largest of the
western balsam firs and very probably
the longest lived. It has a moderately
rapid growth rate. Heights of 400 feet are
not uncommon and trees of this height
are about 400 years old. BARK: 1 to 2
inches thick, gray and smooth for many
years with prominent resin blisters,
eventually becoming darker and deeply
fissured and broken into thin, nearly
rectangular plates. LEAVES: 1 to 1 1/2
inches long, needle-like, blue-green, and
about equally 4-sided. FLOWERS:
monoecious, staminate reddish-purple;
pistillate scattered on upper branches.
FRUIT: a cone, 4 to 6 inches long, cylindrical, greenish-brown to purple, bracts
exserted.

Fig. 33. *Abies procera.*

Noble fir is intolerant and unlike other firs does not persist as
a subdominant component in established stands. It is one of the
more intolerant climax species and requires almost total light for
reproduction. Noble fir does not commonly occur in pure stands
except in small scattered even-age groups. Usually it is found growing with Douglas-fir, western white and lodgepole pines, white fir,
Engelmann *Picea engelmannii* and Sitka *Picea sitchensis* spruces.
It is a minor component of five forest cover types. Associated shrubs
are rusty menziesia *Menziesia ferruginea,* several whortleberries
Vaccinium **spp.,** woolly raspberry *Rubus lasiococcus,* Myrtle pachistima *Pachistima myrsinites* and several species of wild currant *Ribes*
spp. Dense stands characteristic of the types in which noble fir
occurs are not conducive to luxuriant understory. Nevertheless,
these types furnish a significant amount of desirable habitat in the
summer range of deer and elk. Noble fir is an important lumber
and plywood species. It is also planted in urban areas as an ornamental. Occurring as it does at higher altitudes, the types in which
it is associated are important watershed protective cover. Fire is
damaging to noble fir as it has a thin bark. Not too many insects
damage the species. Probably at this time, the noble fir bark beetle
Dendroctonus nobilies would be considered the worst pest. The
balsam woolly aphid is known to attack noble fir. Fungus is not
too much of a problem with vigorous, younger trees. Older trees,

however, are susceptible to Indian paint fungus, brown trunk rot, and red brown butt rot. The largest noble fir of record and living is 28 feet 4 inches in circumference, 278 feet high with a crown spread of 47 feet. It is growing in the Gifford Pinchot National Forest in Washington. The speculative age of this tree is estimated at 600 to 700 years.

14a. Leaves dark green and shiny above, cones purplish **15**

14b. Leaves pale blue or glaucous above, cones 3 to 5 inches long, often green or yellow (occasionally purplish). Fig. 34.

WHITE FIR .... *Abies concolor* (Gord. & Glend.) Lindl.

Fig. 34. Abies concolor.

White fir is an important tree in western United States. It attains its best development in the Sierras where it reaches heights of 130 to 150 feet. The Rocky Mountain trees are much smaller, rarely getting over 100 feet high. The root system is shallow and the long slender, tapering bole is clear for at least half to two-thirds of its length. In old trees, the crown may be dome-like, indicating little if any height growth. It grows at a moderate rate and has a medium life span. BARK: 4 to 7 inches thick on mature trunks, silvery blue to gray, broken into deep furrows, flattened ridges. Young stems are covered with resin blisters. LEAVES: needle-like, flattened and whitish on both sides, blunt, 2 to 3 inches long. FLOWERS: monoecious, staminate cones elongated, hanging from the underside of the lower limbs; pistillate small cones, standing erect on upper branches. FRUIT: cones 3 to 5 inches long, light olive green to purple, bracts shorter than the scales, wings of seed rose tinted. White fir is a species of middle elevations. It does occur in pure stands but not over large areas. It is usually associated with Douglas-fir, ponderosa pine, and sugar pine *Pinus lambertiana*. White fir is very tolerant from seedling to maturity and is a formidable competitor with its associated species. It is considered climax and occurs in climax types over the greater part of its range. Shrubs associated with white fir in the Coastal part of its range are Sierra gooseberry *Ribes roezlii*, snowberry *Symphoricarpos* spp., several species of *Ceanothus* spp., Sierra chinkapin *Castanopsis sempervirens*. In stands in the interior portion of its range, elder *Sambucus* spp., wild currant and gooseberry *Ribes* spp., Fendler ceanothus *Ceanothus fendleri*. White fir types are attractive to deer when open enough to produce a good source of browse. Where the type borders grassland meadows, the browse is usually plentiful and utilized by big game and livestock. Young trees are easily killed by fire; in the older stands, thick bark insulates against heat and fir can withstand some fire. Several bark beetles and defoliators attack white fir. Bole rot, trunk rot, and butt rot fungi extensively damage white fir. White fir is commonly cut for lumber and plywood. It makes a handsome ornamental tree. The largest white fir living of record is 27 feet 8 inches in circumference, 179 feet high with a crown spread of 34 feet. It is growing near Meridan, California.

15a. Bract of the cone much longer than the cone scales. Leaves mostly emarginate. Fig. 35.

FRASER FIR ....*Abies fraseri* (Pursh) Poir.

Fraser fir is a tree of medium proportions, not exceeding 70 feet in height. It is slender with a conical crown. This fir is confined to the higher elevations in the southern Appalachians above 4500 feet and 3000 feet in the Allegheny highlands of West Virginia. It is usually found on the drier sites. It makes rather rapid growth, but is short lived. BARK: gray, smooth with resin blisters. LEAVES: needle-like 1/2 to 1 inch long, blunt, arranged spirally on the stem, whitish beneath. FLOWERS: monoecious, staminate, cones reddish-yellow; pistillate, yellow-green with scales broader than long. FRUIT: an erect cone 2 to 3 inches long, seed

Fig. 35. Abies fraseri.

wide winged, bract longer than the scale. Fraser fir occurs either pure or in association with red spruce. The type, either pure or in mixture is climax for the site. Shrubs associated with Fraser fir are rosebay and Catawba rhododendrons, witch hobble *Viburnum alnifolium,* mountain maple, mountain ash, red-osier dogwood *Cornus stolonifera* and blueberries *Vaccinium* **spp**. The dense stands are not conducive to understory development but wherever these occur there is attractive environment for deer, grouse, and many song birds. The greatest use of Fraser fir is for ornamental uses, boughs for Christmas decorations and lumber when sold along with red spruce. It is thin barked and susceptible to fire. The shallow root system makes windthrow possible. Fraser fir is subject to the same insect pests and rots that attack balsam fir. The most dramatic danger at this time is from the balsam woolly aphid. The largest living Fraser fir of record is 7 feet 9 inches in circumference and is growing in the Great Smoky Mountains National Park in Tennessee.

15b.   Bract of the cone shorter than the cone scale or occasionally slightly longer; acute. Fig. 36.

BALSAM FIR .... *Abies balsamea* (**L.**) Mill. **var.** *balsamea*

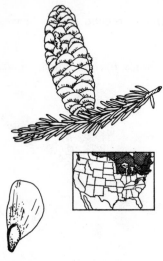

Fig. 36. Abies balsamea.

Balsam fir is a medium-sized tree 40 to 60 feet high and has a dense, dark green pyramidal crown ending in a slender spire-like tip. It is the most symmetrical of the northeastern conifers. Balsam fir is typically a cold climate species and requires abundant moisture for best growth. It grows rather fast but is short lived. BARK: 1/2 inch thick, on young trees dull green, then with grayish patches smooth except for raised resin blisters; it eventually becomes rich brown breaking up into scaly plates. LEAVES: needle-like, flattened, dark green above with 2 silvery strips below, 3/4 to 1 1/2 inches long, often sharp pointed, fragrant. FLOWERS: monoecious, staminate yellow, tinged with purplish red; pistillate, yellow-green. FRUIT: a cone 2 to 4 inches long, tinged with purple.

Balsam fir is very tolerant and is a component of types which are late subclimax or climax. It occurs pure in swamps and is considered climax on these sites. It does better growth-wise in association with spruce where it occurs on better drained sites. On higher sites, it is associated with red spruce, yellow birch, sugar maple, beech, paper birch, and aspen. In some of these associations, it is subclimax. Some understory species which occur in balsam fir stands are beaked hazel *Corylus cornuta*, hobblebush *Viburnum alnifolium*, mountain ash, blueberries *Vaccinium* **spp.**, raspberries *Rubus* **spp.**, mountain maple, and striped maple. Since balsam fir stands provide protection from snow during winter months, they are valuable as deer yards. Grouse are attracted to these stands in winter as well as summer. Because of its thin bark, balsam fir is easily killed by fire. It is subject to windthrow on the shallow, wet sites. Two insects are causing considerable damage to balsam fir;

they are spruce budworm and balsam woolly aphid. A damaging fungus *Stereum sanguinolentum* enters the tree through stubs and broken branches. Balsam fir is one of the most important pulpwood species in the northeast. There are two botanical varieties recognized—*Abies balsamea* var. *balsamea*, which is the one described in the body of the material; the other, *Abies balsamea* var. *phanerolepis* Fern., which is an infrequent occupant of the northeastern part of the range. It has the same silvical characteristics as *A. balsamea* var. *balsamea*. The major distinguishing characteristic is the bracts which are longer than the cone scales. The largest living specimen of balsam fir of record is 7 feet in circumference, 116 feet high with a crown spread of 33 feet. It is growing in the Porcupine Mountains State Park, Michigan.

16a. Cones less than 1 inch long; their scales about as wide as long. Fig. 37.

EASTERN HEMLOCK ....*Tsuga canadensis* (L.) Carr.

Eastern hemlock is a medium-sized tree usually 60 to 80 feet in height, although in the southern Appalachians, it does attain heights of 150 feet. The crown is pyramidal and the branches slender and drooping. It is an exceedingly graceful tree in the open as well as in the forest community. It grows at a moderate rate and is long lived. BARK: flaky on young trees, soon becoming broken into wide, flat ridges. On old trees, it is deeply furrowed. Freshly cut surfaces often show purplish streaks. LEAVES: needle-like, flat 1/4 to 3/4 inch long and 1/16 inch wide, dark green above and light green below with 2 silvery strips which are bands of stomata. FLOWERS: monoecious, staminate light yellow; pistillate pinkish-green. FRUIT: a cone 1/2 to 1 inch long, brown, seeds 1/16 inch long with wings twice as long as the seed.

Fig. 37. Tsuga canadensis.

Eastern hemlock is found on a great variety of soils, but it is on moist cool sites that it reaches best growth. Hemlock usually occurs in small groups and produces a distinctive environment within the stand. Except for these small groups, hemlock does not occur in pure stands. It is a common component of a number of forest types where it is associated with white pine, red spruce, yellow birch, yellow-poplar, sugar maple, beech, black cherry, and northern white-cedar. It is remarkably tolerant and a component of climax or near-climax types. Some of the more common understory species associated with hemlock are mountain ash, mountain sweet pepper bush *Clethra accuminata,* hawthorn, poison sumac and pawpaw. Animal damage is high where other vegetation is sparse. White-tail deer will browse young trees and porcupines and rabbits create wounds by gnawing on the bark. Two loopers defoliate hemlock. It is relatively free of disease but heart rot and several other rots will occasionally cause damage.

Hemlock is used for lumber and is very resistant to rot and termites. Sills found in mountain cabins, built over 100 years ago, are still sound. It is also used for plywood and paneling. Due to the dense, low spreading branches little understory exists in the hemlock groups. The crown is favorite nesting sites for a veery, several warblers, and junco. In streamside zones, shade from the spreading crowns contributes to cool water. It is a handsome ornamental either pruned or allowed to grow normally. The largest living hemlock of record is 19 feet 9 inches in circumference, 98 feet high with a crown spread of 69 feet. It is growing in the Great Smoky Mountains National Park in Tenneessee. Eastern hemlock is the State Tree of Pennsylvania.

16b. Cones more than 1 inch long, their scales much longer than wide. Fig. 38.

CAROLINA HEMLOCK .... *Tsuga caroliniana* Engelm.

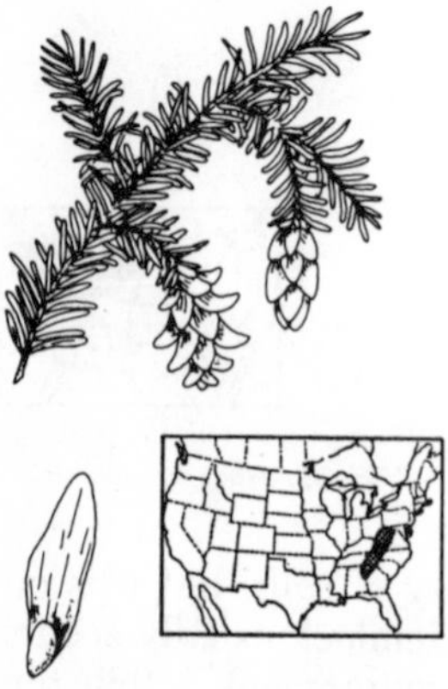

Fig. 38. Tsuga caroliniana.

Carolina hemlock is a relatively rare tree of the upper slopes of the Appalachians from Virginia to Georgia. In overall appearance, it closely resembles Eastern hemlock within which range it grows. There are differences in cones, leaves and flowers. BARK: dark and much furrowed in older trees. LEAVES: needle-like, flat, 1/3 to 3/4 inch long, with rows of whitish stomata below, shining and dark green above. FLOWERS: monoecious, purple. FRUIT: a cone, brown, 1 to 1 1/2 inches long. Seeds born on the scales have a large wing about 1/6 inch long. The silvical and environmental characteristics of Carolina hemlock are similar to Eastern hemlock. The largest Carolina hemlock living and of record is 9 feet and 9 inches in circumference, 101 feet tall with a crown spread of 54 feet. It is growing at Linville Falls, North Carolina.

17a. Twigs pubescent brown; cone scales stiff and rigid at maturity. Cones less than 2 inches long, oval 18

17b. Twigs glabrous; cones cylindric 19

18a. Leaves blue-green, covered with whitish bloom; cones persisting for several years. Fig. 39.

BLACK SPRUCE ....*Picea mariana* (Mill.) B.S.P.

Black spruce is a medium-sized
tree averaging 50 to 70 feet in
height, on occasion it may get as tall
as 90 feet. It has a long tapering bole
and a pyramidal crown. BARK: dark
brown, flaky. LEAVES: stiff, 1/4 to
1/2 inch long, often curved, bluish-
green. F L O W E R S: monoecious,
staminate with reddish anthers.
FRUIT: brown cones 3/4 to 1 1/2
inches long, remaining on tree for
two or three years.

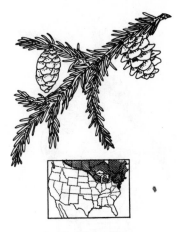

Black spruce occurs in cool bogs
for the most part, but in the northern portion of its range, it is found
on dry slopes. It makes its best
growth on the margins of peatland.

Fig. 39. *Picea mariana.*

Black spruce is a tolerant, slow
growing conifer of medium longevity. When growing in association
with other conifers or hardwoods, it acts as a subclimax species.
In bogs where it occurs in pure stands, it is considered to be climax.
It is one of the first pioneer trees to invade the sedge mat in filled-
lake bogs. Black spruce is a major component of several forest types
and is associated with white spruce, jack pine, balsam fir, tamarack,
northern white-cedar, and black ash. In acid bogs, heaths are the
characteristic ground cover. Some of the more common are blueberries and cranberries *Vaccinium* spp., Labrador tea *Ledum* spp.,
dwarf birch *Betula pumila*, several alders *Alnus* spp., beaked hazelnut *Corylus cornuta* along with a profusion of mosses and lichens.
Black spruce stands are valuable winter deer yards. They were the
choice habitat in the northeast of the woodland caribou. Black
spruce is used for lumber and pulpwood and is one of the more
common Christmas trees on the market. In bogs it is extremely vulnerable to flooding. Trees whose roots are submerged for 30 to 40
days are often killed. Crown and surface fires readily kill black
spruce. The shallow root system is poor anchor against windthrow.
Black spruce is relatively free of rots. It sustains frequent damage

from the spruce budworm and spruce beetle. Snowshoe hares de-
bark seedlings and saplings. The largest living black spruce of
record is 4 feet 4 inches in circumference, 94 feet high with a crown
spread of 20 feet. It is growing in Superior National Forest in
Minnesota.

**18b. Leaves yellow-green without whitish bloom; cones falling at
end of first season. Fig. 40.**

RED SPRUCE ....*Picea rubens* Sarg.

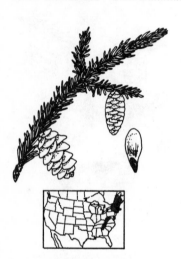

Fig. 40. Picea rubens.

Red spruce is an important northeastern conifer; it is characteristic of
mountainous regions of northern
New York, New England, and the
crests of the Appalachians southward. It is a tall slender tree with a
conical crown and rather straggly
appearance. It is long lived but slow
growing. BARK: reddish-brown,
scaly, on older trunks. LEAVES:
needle-like, 1/2 to 3/4 inch long,
dark yellow-green, not tufted but
scattered around the stem. FLOW-
ERS: staminate dark red; pistillate
oblong. FRUIT: a cone 1 1/4 to 2
inches long, chestnut brown at maturity, falling during the first winter.
The seed is about 1/8 inch long with
a wing 1/4 inch long.

Red spruce attains its best development in the higher parts of
the southern Appalachians where air is humid and rainfall plentiful.
Here there is a longer growing season than elsewhere in its range.
It does not do well on poorly drained soils. Red spruce is considered
a tolerant conifer and is climax in the Appalachians and Ontario,
but subclimax throughout the remainder of its range. Red spruce
does not commonly occur in pure stands, but it is a major component of several forest types where it is associated with yellow
birch, sugar maple, balsam fir, Fraser fir, white pine, paper birch,
and others. Some of the more important understory species are
witch-hobble *Viburnum alnifolium,* mountain ash, striped maple,
mountain maple, beaked hazel *Corylus cornuta,* speckled alder, low
bush blueberry *Vaccinium angustifolium,* and red raspberry *Rubus
idaeus.* The principal enemies of red spruce are wind due to its
shallow root system, several insects including the spruce budworm
and eastern spruce beetle, as well as wood rotting fungi of *Fomes*
and *Polyporus.* All occasionally damage red spruce. It is used com-

mercially for lumber and pulpwood. Deer, grouse, and many woodland rodents are attracted to red spruce lands. Song birds find the
type favorable for nesting and feeding. It affords good winter protection and food during critical periods. The largest living red
spruce of record is 13 feet 10 inches in circumference, 106 feet high
with a crown spread of 45 feet. It is growing in the Great Smoky
Mountains National Park, Tennessee.

19a. **Leaves 3/4 to 1 1/2 inches long** **20**

19b. **Leaves 1/2 to 3/4 inch long, highly glaucous. Cones 1 to
       2 inches long, scales rounded not ragged. Fig. 41.**

WHITE SPRUCE .... *Picea glauca* (Moench) Voss

White spruce is one of the most
important and widely distributed
conifers in United States and
Canada. It is a handsome tree
with a conical crown reaching
from almost ground level to the
top of the stem. It reaches heights
of 70 to 100 feet. It is a long-lived
slow-growing species. BARK: thin
and flaky, reddish-brown, some
exposed areas may be silvery
gray. LEAVES: needle-like, blue-
green and glaucous. They are 1/3
to 3/4 inch long and somewhat
incurved. FLOWERS: staminate
reddish-yellow; pistillate reddish-
green. FRUIT: a cone 1 1/2 to
2 inches long, light brown color,
scales thin and flexible.

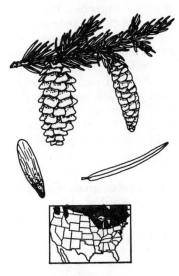

Fig. 41. Picea glauca.

White spruce is one of the
hardiest conifers and grows on a
variety of soils and elevations from sea level to almost 5000 feet.
A considerable part of the species range outside the United States
is within the permafrost zone in northern Canada. White spruce
is classed as tolerant to shade and will survive suppression for 40
to 50 years and still respond to release. Its place in succession varies
but is basically climax. In New England, it is pioneer on abandoned
fields, elsewhere it occurs with both climax and subclimax types.
The fact that it is tolerant to shade and long lived indicates that
it possesses the characteristics to be a member of a more or less
stable, long-lived forest community. In the northern portion of its
range, the major understory species are mountain laurel and blueberries *Vaccinium* **spp**. In the eastern portion, striped and mountain

maples are common. In some areas, American cranberry bush *Viburnum trilobum,* alder buckthorn *Rhamnus alnifolia,* and beaked hazel *Corylus cornuta* are common.

Although white spruce occurs in pure stands, it is also a member of several important forest types where it is associated with black spruce, red spruce, balsam fir, jack pine, aspen, sugar maple, paper birch. White spruce is very susceptible to fire with its thin bark, long crown and superficial rooting habit. Needle litter, droppings from cones cut by squirrels and lichens on the trunk is a type of fuel that ignites easily and burns rapidly. A number of insects attack white spruce. Probably the most damaging are spruce budworm, European spruce sawfly, and eastern spruce beetle. It is remarkably free of fungus damage; probably heart rot is the most common damaging fungus. Red squirrels cut the leaders and ends of upper branches. Porcupine damage is frequent. It is an important lumber and pulpwood species throughout its range. It is commonly planted in urban areas as an ornamental. White spruce and its associated conifers are important "deer yard" types where snow protection during the winter months is so necessary for survival of white-tail and mule deer. Understory deciduous species for the most part are important deer browse. Grouse also take refuge in these types during the winter months. The largest living white spruce of record is 10 feet 9 inches in circumference, 101 feet high with a crown spread of 34 feet. It is growing in Luce County, Michigan.

20a. Leaves green. Cones 3 to 7 inches long. Cone scales rounded at tip. Fig. 42.

NORWAY SPRUCE ....*Picea abies* (L.) Karst.

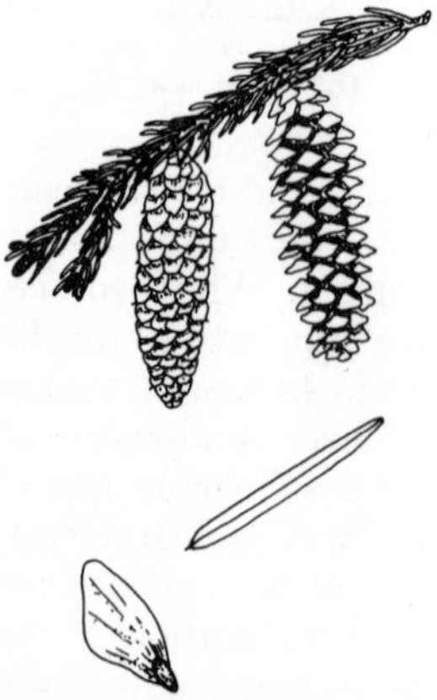

Fig. 42. Picea abies.

Norway spruce is a large conical tree with drooping branches. It attains heights of 70 to 90 feet. It is a native of northern and central Europe. BARK: thin and scaly, reddish-brown. LEAVES: needle-like 3/4 to 1 1/2 inches long, dark green and minutely pubescent. The needles are 4-sided and arranged spirally on the limbs. FLOWERS: are terminal or in the axils of the upper leaves; they are cone-like in shape. FRUIT: cones, cylindrical 4 to 7 inches long, light brown. The Norway spruce is widely planted as an ornamental, as a windbreak in the Central States, and for lumber.

20b. Leaves bluish green or silvery. Cones 2 1/2 to 4 inches long. Cone scales acute and ragged at tip. Fig. 43.

BLUE SPRUCE ....*Picea pungens* Engelm.

Blue spruce is never abundant in any part of its range. It attains heights of 80 to 120 feet. Branches are horizontal and arranged in whorls resulting in an extremely symmetrical bole. The conical sculptured crown and the silvery green foliage present an extremely handsome tree.

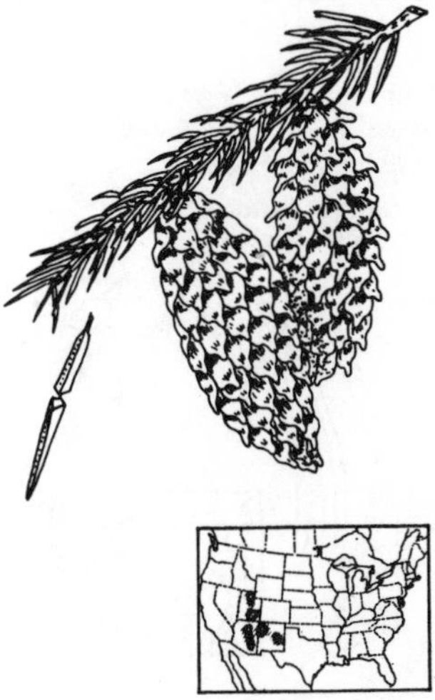

BARK: thin, gray, divided into ashy-gray loosely attached scales, with age becoming f u r r o w e d. LEAVES: needle-like about 1 inch long, 4-sided, blue-green to silvery gray, extending at right angles with the twig. FLOWERS: staminate, reddish-yellow; pistillate, pale green. FRUIT: a cone about 3 1/2 inches long, generally produced on the upper 1/3 of the crown.

Blue spruce is not a fast growing

Fig. 43. Picea pungens.

species and is moderately long lived. It has a deep root system which is valuable in holding it and the soils in place on steep slopes. It prefers moist sites. Blue spruce is tolerant and considered a subclimax species. It occurs in pure stands as well as a component in two other forest types. It is associated with aspen, several birches, lodgepole and ponderosa pines, willows and cottonwoods. Understory species are likewise variable; alders, sages *Artemisia* **spp.**, bitterweed *Purshia tridentata*, are some of the more common depending on site. The principal enemies are fire, spruce bark beetle and spruce budworm, several wood rotting fungi of both *Fomes* and *Polyporus* are damaging. The thin bark and low persistant branches make fire a particularly destructive enemy. The pallatable understory species and the adjacent grasslands are favorable range for livestock, mule and white-tail deer. Blue spruce is used for lumber, pulp and spruce gum. It is widely planted as an ornamental.

The largest living blue spruce of record is 15 feet 8 inches in circumference, 126 feet high with a crown spread of 36 feet. It is growing in the Gunnison National Forest in Colorado. Blue spruce is the State Tree of Colorado.

THE PINES: Genus PINUS

21a. Leaves in clusters of less than 5 22

21b. Leaves in clusters of 5; cones long stalked, their scales thin.
Leaves blue-green 21c

21c. Cones 3 to 8 inches long; EASTERN WHITE PINE. Fig. 44.

EASTERN WHITE PINE ....*Pinus strobus* L.

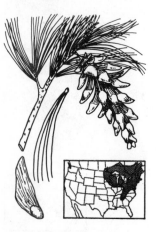

Fig. 44. Pinus strobus.

Eastern white pine is a large tree often attaining heights of 100 feet and over. The branches are arranged in whorls and may extend down the bole giving the younger trees a "bushy" appearance. It is moderately fast growing and long lived. BARK: thin and smooth on young trees becoming thick furrowed and deeply fissured with age. LEAVES: needle-like 3 to 8 inches long, bluish-green, arranged in bundles of 5. FLOWERS: monoecious, the staminate yellow; pistillate, purplish. FRUIT: a cylindrical cone 4 to 8 inches long. SEEDS: born on the scales of the cone and are winged.

Although white pine grows on a variety of soils within its range, best growth is attained on well drained sandy soils. It is a major component of 4 forest cover types and occurs as a minor assoicate in 14 others. Some of the more common associates are northern red, chestnut and scarlet oaks, white ash, hemlock, sugar maple, and many other northern and Appalachian species. Over its wide range, understory species are quite variable; some of the more common are blueberries *Vaccinium* **spp.**, maple viburnum *Viburnum acerifolium,* mountain-laurel, moosewood *Dirca palustris,* creeping snowberry *Gaulthera procumbens,* strawberry bush *Euonymus americana,* flowering dogwood, blackberry *Rubus* **spp.**, greenbriar *Smilax* **spp.**, and wild grape *Vitis* **spp**. White pine is considered intermediate in tolerance. Its place in succession is variable; as an "old field pine" in New England it is pioneer. On drier sites, it may be climax. In the deep coves of the Appalachians where it is invading dense subclimax hardwood stands, it appears as a long-lived intermediate species.

Major enemies are fire, white pine weevil, blister rust and recently annosus root rot. White pine is a valuable lumber tree and is used for pulp. It is frequently planted as an ornamental, even outside its range. White pine seed is eaten by about a dozen songbirds, grouse, quail, and turkey. Rodents cut the cones before they harden. Types in which white pine occurs are generally above average wildlife habitat.

The largest white pine of record is 17 feet 11 inches in circumference, 151 feet high with a crown spread of 48 feet. It is growing in the Brule River State Forest in Wisconsin. White pine is the State Tree of Maine and Minnesota.

21d. Cones 5 to 15 inches long. Fig. 45.

WESTERN WHITE PINE ....*Pinus monticola* Dougl.

Western white pine is a large tree reaching heights of 150 to 190 feet. Seedlings grow an exceptionally well developed tap root which makes the mature trees unusually windfirm. It makes rapid growth and is a long-lived species. The oldest white pine of record is 615 years old.

BARK: smooth, gray-green on the younger trees becoming dark gray and deep fissured, breaking into rectangular plates. LEAVES: 2 to 4 inches long, in bundles of 5, blue-green and glaucous. FLOWERS: monoecious, staminate, yellow; pistillate purple. FRUIT: a narrowly cy-

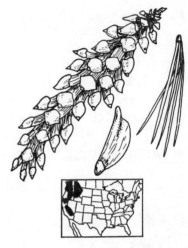

Fig. 45. Pinus monticola.

lindrical cone 5 to 15 inches long, stalked and often gently curved. SEEDS: 1/3 inch long with terminal wing 3/4 to 1 inch long.

Western white pine grows on a great variety of soils within its mountainous range. In the western portion, it occurs from sea level up to a variable limit of 2000 to 6000 feet. In the Rocky Mountains, it is generally found between 2000 and 6000 feet. It is rated as intermediate in tolerance and is a subclimax species. It occurs in pure stands and is an important component in 17 western forest types. It is more commonly associated with Douglas-fir, grand fir *Abies grandis*, western hemlock *Tsuga heterophylla*, larch *Larix occidentalis*, lodgepole pine, aspen and Engelmann spruce *Picea engelmannii*. Understory species are many and varied; Douglas maple *Acer glabrum* **var.** *douglasii*, red stem ceanothus *Ceanothus sanguineus*, bearberry *Arctostaphylos uva-ursi*, common snowberry *Symphoricarpos albus* and many others.

The principal enemies of western white pine are fire, to which it is rated as having intermediate resistance, white pine blister rust, heart rots, and annosus root rot. Its deep root system is valuable in holding mountain soil, affording watershed protection. The understory occurring in forest types where western white pine is present is important to wildlife. Most of the species are pallatable browse for deer, elk and moose, as well as bear and fur bearing animals. Western white pine produces high quality lumber and is frequently planted as an ornamental.

The largest western white pine of record and now living is 21 feet 3 inches in circumference, 219 feet high with a crown spread of 36 feet. It is growing near Elk River, Idaho. Western white pine is the State Tree of Idaho.

22a. Leaves most often in clusters of 3 (sometimes 5 in Pinus ponderosa and 2 in Pinus elliotii) 23

22b. Leaves most often in clusters of 2 (sometimes 3 P. echinata) 26

23a. Cones sub-terminal 24

23b. Cones lateral 25

24a. Cones 3 to 6 inches long, buds brown, leaves 8 to 11 inches long. Fig. 46.

PONDEROSA PINE ....*Pinus ponderosa* Laws. **var.** *ponderosa*

Ponderosa pine is the most widely distributed pine in North America. It is a large tree 150 to 200 feet in height and extremely long lived. As compared to other long-lived species, it makes better than average growth.

BARK: brown to black and deeply furrowed and on old boles becomes superficially scaly. LEAVES: needles 5 to 11 inches long, bundles of 3 sometimes 2, dark gray-green to yellow-green, flexible. FLOWERS: staminate yellow; pistillate dark red and in clusters or pairs. FRUIT: a cone 3 to 6 inches long, sessile and usually leaving a few scales on the twig when shed.

Fig. 46. Pinus ponderosa.

Ponderosa occurs in a sub-humid climate region where annual rainfall averages in the neighborhood of 10 inches. It grows on soils of volcanic and sedimentary origin, usually sandy and gravelly loams. Ponderosa is intolerant, but more tolerant than some of its associates such as western larch *Larix occidentalis*, but less than Douglas-fir and sugar pine *Pinus lambertiana*. It occurs in 20 forest types along with Douglas-fir, lodgepole pine, sugar pine and larch. A great variety of understory species occur with ponderosa pine; big sage *Artemisia tridentata*, bearberry *Arctostaphylos uva-ursi*, bitterbrush *Purshia tridentata*, black hawthorn, chokecherry, snowbrush *Cea-*

nothus velutinus, saskatoon serviceberry *Amelanchier alnifolia,* whitethorn soapbloom *Ceanothus cordulatus,* Sierra chinkapin *Castanopsus sempervirens,* quaking aspen, western snowberry *Symphoricarpos occidentalis* and Gambel oak *Quercus gambelii.*

In most types where ponderosa occurs, it is climax. In northern California and southern Oregon where it is associated with Douglasfir, it is subclimax. Ponderosa itself is not particularly attractive to wildlife but the understory species occurring along with it are. Mule deer, black-tail and white-tail deer and elk browse the preferred species. Many of the types are good livestock range.

In the Arizona and New Mexico portion of the range, a variety is recognized *Pinus ponderosa* var. *arizonica* (Engelm.) Shaw. It differs from Pinus ponderosa by having a smaller cone 2 1/2 to 3 1/2 inches long and needles mostly in bundles of 5. It occurs in this portion of the range between 6000 and 8000 feet. Both are important lumber and plywood trees.

Principal enemies are wild fire, western pine beetle, Blackhills beetle and several other bark beetles, the flat headed borer, annosus root rot and several other fungus infections follow the bark beetles into the bole. High deer populations in young sapling stands can be damaging as they browse heavily on the young growth. Ponderosa is exceedingly windfirm.

The largest ponderosa pine living and of record is 21 feet 6 inches in circumference, 223 feet high with a crown spread of 66 feet. It is growing in the Sierra National Forest in California. Ponderosa pine is the State Tree of Montana.

24b. Cones 6 to 10 inches long, buds white; leaves 8 to 18 inches long. Fig. 47.

LONGLEAF PINE .... *Pinus palustris* Mill.

Longleaf pine is one of the most distinctive of the southern pines. It is a medium-sized tree reaching heights of 80 to 120 feet. It has a normally short crown and branches with needles appearing in dense "tufts" near the end.

BARK: coarsely scaly orange-brown in color. LEAVES: 8 to 18 inches long in bundles of 3. FLOWERS: staminate yellow; pistillate dark red. FRUIT: a cone 6 to 10 inches long, when shed leaving a few of the basal scales attached to the branch. Cones are brown, weathering to ashy-gray. SEEDS: 1/2 inch long, wing 1 1/2 inches long, striped. BUDS: large, silvery and very conspicuous, especially on young seedlings in the grass.

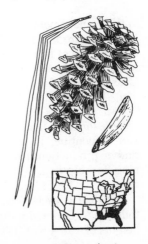

Fig. 47. Pinus palustris.

Longleaf grows in a humid climate in the Coastal Plains of the southeastern United States and on soils which are low in organic material, sandy and strongly acid. The sites are frequently "droughty." It makes rapid growth and is long lived. During the first two years, the seedling makes little height growth as this time is spent in putting down a tap root which in later life enables it to weather the summer droughts. This characteristic often gives an opportunity to other on-site species, which make early height growth, to over-top longleaf. Longleaf is remarkably intolerant and generally occurs in even-age, pure stands. Where it occurs on the same site with other species, the longleaf is in even-age groups. In addition to occurring as a pure or predominant type, it also appears in 5 other types associated in group-wise fashion with slash, short-leaf and loblolly pines, a number of oaks; turkey, bluejack, blackjack, southern red, scrub, myrtle and sweetgum. Occasionally several hickories occur with longleaf. The typical understory species are arrow-wood vibur-

num *Viburnum dentatum,* wax-myrtle *Myrica* **spp.**, gallberry *Ilex glabra,* yaupon, greenbriar *Smilax* **spp.**, sumacs *Rhus* **spp.**, bluejack, sand live and sand post oaks, hawthorns, pawpaws *Asimina* **spp.**, runner oak *Quercus pumila,* sawpalmetto *Serenoa* **spp.**, ground blueberry *Vaccinium myrsinites* and huckleberry *Gaylussacia* **spp.** Where longleaf occurs in pure stands, it is considered a primary association. Where fire is used

Fig. 47a. Typical "fire climax" in longleaf pine with an understory of flowering dogwood. (Miller Photo)

in the management of longleaf, a so-called "fire climax" has resulted. Not until fire is removed will succession progress in a normal fashion. The use of fire in longleaf stands develops an attractive environment for bobwhite quail and turkey, unique to the southeastern Coastal Plains. Legumes which follow fire respond well under longleaf. The seeds of these plants are good quail and turkey food. "Quail preserves" of the southeast, where wild birds are hunted, are on longleaf lands. Longleaf is a source of lumber, pulpwood, and turpentine. It is usually worked for naval stores along with timber production using the trees which would be removed in thinning for tapping. Many acres of longleaf lands are good cattle range.

Longleaf is exceptionally resistant to fire except in the first year following germination and later during the early sapling stage at heights of 1 to 4 feet. It is relatively resistant to insects and diseases.

Occasionally bark beetles, of which the black turpentine beetle is the worst offender, attack the tree. Fusiform rust, so common to the southern pines, is not a particular problem. In the seedling stage, longleaf is confronted with many hazards. The piney woods hogs root up and eat the seedlings; sheep nip off the buds. Brown spot needle blight *Scirrhia acicola* can be a problem to seedlings which are still "in the grass." Prescribed burning kills the fungus by the simple process of removing the needles, thus encouraging the growth of healthy foliage.

The largest longleaf living and of record is 10 feet 9 inches in circumference, 113 feet high with a crown spread of 40 feet. It is growing in Autauga County, Alabama.

24c. **Cones 1 1/2 inches long, leaves 1 1/2 inches long, twisted. Fig. 48.**

LODGEPOLE PINE ....*Pinus contorta* Dougl.

Lodgepole pine is a pine of variable characteristics and wide distribution throughout western United States. It is a medium-sized tree 70 to 90 feet high with a long, clear, slender bole and a short open crown. It is one of the most aggressive of the western conifers. Where it occurs on Pacific slope sites, it is often referred to as "shore pine" and on these sites it does not reach the size it attains elsewhere. The most important part of its range is east of the broken line—the Rocky Mountains. Lodgepole grows at an average rate and has a moderate life span. BARK: orange-brown, about 1/4 inch thick and covered by small thin loosely appressed scales. LEAVES: needle-like, 1 to 3 inches long in bundles of 2, dark green to yellow-green and often

Fig. 48. Pinus contorta.

twisted. They persist through 4 to 5 growing seasons. FLOWERS: staminate orange-red; pistillate, clustered or in pairs on stalks. FRUIT: a cone 3/4 to 2 inches long, occasionally opening at maturity but more often remaining closed. SEEDS: 1/6 inch long with mottled black wings 1/2 inch long. A stand of lodgepole may have both open and serotinous cone bearing trees.

Lodgepole is intolerant of shade. It occurs pure in the interior at middle elevations and is also represented in 11 other forest cover types. At higher elevations, it is a minor component with Engelmann spruce, subalpine fir, red fir, and whitebark pine. At middle elevations, it occurs in minor numbers with interior Douglas-fir, larch, ponderosa pine, western white pine, Rocky Mountain juniper and aspen. At the lower elevations in the interior, it occurs with Jeffery pine. Ecologically, lodgepole stands may be grouped into two categories; it is subclimax where it occurs in pure stands brought about by fire. These are virtually stable communities. It occurs as a transitional species when there are appreciable amounts of advance reproduction of other species, or it occurs in limited sized groups within stands of climax species which are longer lived, such as western larch *Larix occidentalis.* There is a large number of understory species associated with lodgepole pine where it grows in open fashion, and where grasslands merge with the forest. Many lodgepole stands are too dense for development of an understory. The more common species are bitter cherry *Prunus emarginata,* serviceberry *Amelanchier* **spp.**, snowberry *Symphoricarpos* **spp.**, whortleberry *Vaccinium myrtillus* and *scoparium,* myrtle boxleaf *Pachistima myrsinites,* soapbloom *Ceanothus* **spp.**, and mountain alder *Alnus tenufolia.*

The most serious enemies of lodgepole are the two pine beetles which inflict heavy damage in stagnated stands. A terminal weevil, leaf miners and sawflies and the spruce budworm cause defoliation. Dwarf mistletoe causes a large but undetermined amount of growth loss. There are several stem rusts and heart rot fungi which cause some damage. Because of its relatively thin bark, the tree is more susceptible to fire than some of its associates. It is subject to windfall due to its shallow rooting habit. Porcupines do considerable damage to trees over 4 inches d.b.h.

Lodgepole is used commercially for mine timbers, railroad ties, posts, and pulpwood. The understory species occurring with lodgepole where it grows open enough to support growth are generally good browse for mule and white-tail deer and elk. On steep sites where it grows in dense stands, it does a good job of holding the soil in place. There are two record specimens of lodgepole—one 21 feet 2 inches in circumference, 91 feet high with a crown spread of 36 feet growing in the Stanislaus National Forest, California; the other 19 feet 8 inches in circumference, 110 feet high with a crown spread of 37 feet. It is growing in the San Bernardino National Forest, California. Lodgepole pine is the State Tree of Wyoming.

25a.   Leaves 8 to 12 inches long, in clusters of 2 and 3. Cones 2 to 6 inches long with short stalks. Fig. 49.

SLASH PINE ....*Pinus elliottii* Englm. *var. elliottii*

Slash pine varies from 90 to 100 feet in height. It is a fast growing southern pine of moderate longevity and is the most popular species for pulpwood planting in the Coastal Plains. It is well adapted to flatwoods soils but makes its best growth on moister pond margins. BARK: even on young trees, is deeply furrowed,

becoming plated with thin papery surface scales. LEAVES: needles 8 to 12
inches long, glossy dark green and in
bundles of 2, infrequently 3. FLOW-
ERS: staminate dark purple; pistillate
pinkish. FRUIT: a cone 2 to 6 inches
long, stalked, persistent over winter
and until mid-summer. The scales are
armed with sharp prickles. SEEDS:
1/4 inch long with wing 1 inch long,
thin.

Fig. 49. Pinus elliotii.

Slash pine occurs as a pure type and is a major component of
4 mixed types where it is associated with longleaf pine, mixed hardwoods, cabbage palmetto and tupelo. It is a minor associate in 7
additional types where it occurs with loblolly and pond pines,
Atlantic white-cedar, sweetbay, and red maple. Understory species
occurring with slash pine are moisture loving species such as buckwheat-tree, swamp cyrilla, yaupon, dahoon, and loblolly-bay. Slash
pine is intermediate in tolerance and occurs in the subclimax
forests along with other similar mid-tolerant species. It is more
tolerant, aggressive, and faster growing than longleaf pine. It is
not as resistant to fire in seedling and early sapling stages as longleaf. Beyond these sizes, it can withstand fire as well as longleaf,
when grown in the same crown class. Its enemies are red heart, red-
brown butt rot and annosus root rot. Black turpentine and other
bark beetles frequently become damaging.

Slash pine is one of the more popular pines for use as lumber,
plywood, and pulpwood. It is fast growing and is not too difficult
to grow from planted seedlings. Unless grown in too dense stands,
the understory species are suitable quail and turkey food and cover.
Songbirds and quail eat the slash pine seeds. Buckwheat-tree and
yaupon are palatable deer browse.

The largest living slash pine of record is 11 feet 8 inches in circumference, 120 feet high with a crown spread of 32 feet. It is
growing near Manor, Georgia.

25b. Leaves 6 to 8 inches long, cones 1 to 3 1/2 inches long, sessile. Fig. 50.

LOBLOLLY PINE ....*Pinus taeda* L.

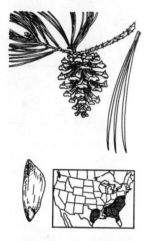

Fig. 50. Pinus taeda.

Loblolly is a fast growing pine reaching heights of 120 feet, with an open spreading crown. It is a species of average life span. BARK: on young trees is scaly and quite dark, becoming furrowed and broken into brownish blocks. LEAVES: needle-like 6 to 9 inches long in bundles of 3, sometimes 2, yellow-green and often twisted. FLOWERS: staminate yellow; pistillate yellow. Active through March to May. FRUIT: a cone, reddish-brown, prickly, 3 to 6 inches long.

Loblolly occurs in pure stands and is a major component in two additional forest types where it is associated with shortleaf pine and mixed hardwoods. It is a minor associate in 11 other types. Its associates are many; Virginia pine, longleaf and slash pines, sweetgum, yellow-poplar, southern red, white, laurel, willow, water and scarlet oaks, hickories, persimmon, red maple, and eastern redcedar. There is a great variety of understory species occurring with loblolly pine; some of the more common species are waxmyrtle *Myrica cerifera*, pepperbush *Clethra alnifolia*, gallberry, several viburnums *Viburnum* **spp.**, hawthorn, sweetshrub *Calycanthus* **spp.**, sparkleberry, blueberries *Vaccinium* **spp.**, greenbriars *Smilax* **spp.**, and grape *Vitis* **spp.** Many sites have a good development of legumes in the ground cover.

Loblolly pine is considered intolerant. It is less tolerant than oaks and more tolerant than slash and longleaf. It is pioneer on old fields which progress toward subclimax oak-hickory mixtures. Early invaders along with loblolly are sweetgum, yellow-poplar, and tupelo. These are replaced by oaks, hickories and other more tolerant species. Hardwood replacement species can be kept out of loblolly pine stands by the use of summer fires. Too frequent fire will eliminate loblolly and other species as well.

Principal enemies of loblolly pine are fusiform rust, heart and butt rot of the *Fomes* and *Polyporous* species. Stands often become centers of infestations by southern pine beetles. Loblolly pine cannot stand crown fire or hot ground fires.

Fig. 50a. The red-cockaded woodpecker *Dendrocopus borealis*, is among the rare and endangered species in the United States. Its habitat is confined to the southern coastal plains which are over-mature and subject to red-heart rot. Loblolly, slash and longleaf are commonly used species. (Photo courtesy Kirkley-Perkins)

Loblolly is one of the more popular southern yellow pines for lumber, plywood, and pulpwood. It has been used widely in erosion control in old eroded fields which have been abandoned for agriculture. The seeds are eaten by a number of songbirds, quail and turkey. The red-cockaded woodpecker nests and feeds largely in over-mature trees which have red-heart rot. These trees seem to have a series of beetles and grubs which are the preferred food of the woodpecker. Quail, turkey, fox squirrel, and white-tail deer find the associated species and understory vegetation attractive habitat.

The largest living loblolly pine of record is 14 feet 1 inch in circumference, 155 feet high with a crown spread of 72 feet. It is growing at Urania, Louisiana.

25c. Leaves 3 to 5 inches long. Cones 1 to 3 1/2 inches long, sessile. Fig. 51.

PITCH PINE ....*Pinus rigida* Mill.

Pitch pine is medium sized attaining heights of 100 feet and greatly varying in form and appearance. Sometimes oddly shaped and shrubby but on better sites it attains a tall pine-like bole. It grows at a medium rate and is short lived. It is one of the few species of pine to sprout. BARK: very scaly at first then becoming deeply furrowed into flat plates which are brownish-yellow. LEAVES: needles 3 to 5 inches long in bundles of 3, yellow-green and stiff, somewhat twisted. FLOWERS: staminate in short crowded spikes yellowish-green; pistillate, clustered on stout short stems light green tinged with red. FRUIT: a cone 2 to 3 inches long, persistent for many

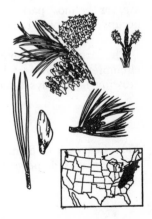

Fig. 51. Pinus rigida.

years, scales armed with sharp recurved prickles. Seed are borne on the scales and are a dull black to mottled gray, triangular in shape.

Pitch pine is usually restricted to the less fertile soils within its range. It is capable of persisting on extremely dry and unfavorable sites. It does make good growth on the better sites and becomes a well-shaped tree. It is an intolerant, pioneer species. It occurs pure and is an associate in 12 other forest types. It occurs with a large number of pine and hardwood species, the most common of which are red, Virginia, shortleaf, and white pines; a large number of oaks such as black, southern red, scarlet, bear, chestnut, post, blackjack, northern red, and various hickories, red maple, and eastern hemlock. Understory species are likewise varied, but the more common are blueberries *Vaccinium* **spp.**, huckleberries *Gaylussacia* **spp.**, mountain-laurel, dwarf chinkapin oak *Quercus prinoides,* sheep laurel *Kalmia angustifolia,* leatherleaf *Chamaedaphne calyculata,* staggerbush *Lyonia mariana,* and swamp azalea *Rhododendron viscosum.*

The principal enemies of pitch pine are wild animals, deer and rabbits, wind and snow. Several fungi attack pitch pine and it has many insect pests, sawflies, pitch pine looper, tip moths, pine beetles, webworm and leaf miners. Defoliators frequently take heavy damage in pitch pine stands. With the ability to sprout, fire does not eliminate pitch pine and is largely responsible for the pure pitch pine type. One hot fire can eliminate non-sprouting competitors. Pitch pine is used for lumber, pulp, and posts. It has limited use as landscape planting. The seed is used in limited amounts by songbirds, grouse, and turkey. The understory species occurring with it are, for the most part, good fruit and food producers. Whitetail deer occupy pitch pine range.

The largest pitch pine living and of record is 8 feet 3 inches in circumference, 97 feet high with a crown spread of 36 feet. It is growing near Mays Landings, New Jersey.

25d. **Leaves 6 to 8 inches long, cones 2 to 2 1/2 inches, remaining closed, persistent. Fig. 52.**

POND PINE ....*Pinus serotina* Michx.

Pond pine is a medium-sized tree found in swamps and wet lands of the Coastal Plains. It is similar in many respects to pitch pine. It makes average growth and is short lived. BARK: dark red-brown, irregularly divided into small plates on the surface, into thin scales. LEAVES: needles 6 to 8 inches long in bundles of 3 and on occasion 4, slender gently twisting, dark yellow-green. FLOWERS: monoecious, staminate, crowded in spikes, dark orange; pistillate, clustered or in pairs on stout stems. FRUIT: a cone 2 to 2 1/2 inches long, broad at the base and rounded at the apex, scales armed with deciduous prickles, serotinous and often remaining closed on the branches for several years.

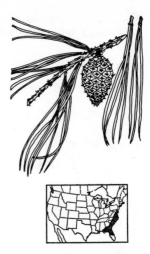

Fig. 52. Pinus serotina.

Occuring as it does in swamps of high organic matter, it is the principal pine of the east coast pocosins or "swamp on the hill." It occurs in pure stands and is a component in eight additional types. It is associated with other moisture loving conifers and hardwoods, slash and loblolly pines, Atlantic white-cedar, pondcypress, red maple, sweetbay, and swamp tupelo. Common understory species are gallberry, southern bayberry, saw palmetto *Serenoa repens,* and greenbriar *Smilax laurifolia.* Pond pine is an intolerant early subclimax species. Although fire and heat are helpful in opening cones for release of seed, the site on which pond pine grows does not favor too wide use of fire. Peat may be ignited, thus burning roots and killing the tree. Fire for regeneration of the species, under proper water levels and moisture conditions, appears to be indicated. Pond pine is subject to fusiform rust, red heart and insect damage from southern pine beetles. The understory vegetation is attractive to deer and bear. Its principal commerical use is lumber and pulpwood. In many wet areas, such as the pocosins, drainage is taking place which results in conversion from pond pine to loblolly pine. The largest living pond pine of record is 7 feet 5 inches in circumference, 86 feet high with a crown spread of 30 feet. It is growing near O'Neil, Florida.

26a. Cones terminal or subterminal 2 to 2 1/2 inches long, their scales without prickles. Leaves 5 to 6 inches long. Fig. 53.

RED PINE ....*Pinus resinosa* Ait.

Fig. 53. Pinus resinosa.

Red pine is one of the more distinctive of the northern conifers. Its symmetrical oval crown with dark green foliage appears much different than its associates, jack pine and eastern white pine. It is a sturdy tree reaching 100 feet in height. It grows at a moderate rate and is long lived. BARK: on young trees f l a k y, orange-red becoming broken into flat, scaly reddish-brown plates. LEAVES: needles, 4 to 6 inches long in bundles of 2, dark green. F L O W E R S: monoecious; staminate dark purple; pistillate, short stalked and scarlet. FRUIT: a cone 1 1/2 to 2 1/2 inches long, chestnut brown and unarmed.

Red pine grows in cool climate, under moderate rainfall patterns and on acid soils of good drainage and aeration. It is considered a more or less stable species on the driest sites where it is associated with jack pine. On the more moist sites, it is subclimax. Red pine occurs in pure stands extensively over much of its range. In three other forest types, its associates are jack pine, white pine and red maple, northern red oak, bigtooth aspen and quaking aspen. Red pine has an intersting understory of Canada blueberry *Vaccinium canadensis*, striped maple, Jersey tea *Ceanothus americana*, sand cherry *Prunus* **spp.**, lowbush blueberry *Vaccinium angustifolium*, bearberry *Arctostaphylos uva-ursi*, and American hazel *Corylus americana*. With this type understory, wildlife use is good; deer, grouse, and squirrel.

Its principal enemies are fire, a number of insects, weevils, tussock moth, tip moth, loopers and webworms, annosus root rot and other rots of the bole and roots. Porcupine damage occasionally runs high. Even though it occurs in areas of modest rainfall, it will suffer from drought. In early years, it is not as windfirm as some of its associates. It may sustain wind damage. It is used commercially for lumber, boxes, crates, and pulpwood. Within its range, it is a popular ornamental. The largest red pine living and of record is 9 feet 9 inches in circumference, 112 feet tall with a crown spread of 64 feet. It is growing near Watersmeet, Michigan.

26b. Go to 27

27a. Cones symmetrical 28

27b. Cones incurved, leaves less than 2 inches long. Fig. 54.

JACK PINE ....*Pinus banksiana* Lamb.

Jack pine is a medium-sized, thin foliage tree sometimes reaching heights of 70 to 80 feet. It makes rapid growth and is short lived. BARK: thin, dark brown, and irregularly broken into scaly ridges. LEAVES: needles 1 to 1 1/2 inches long and in bundles of 2, yellow-green, flat to slightly concave on the inner surface and frequently twisted. FLOWERS: staminate in loose clusters, yellow; pistillate, dark purple. FRUIT: a cone 1 1/2 to 2 inches long, slender, incurved not readily opening. It is serotinus opening at high temperatures.

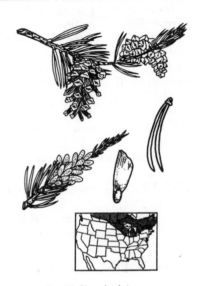

Fig. 54. Pinus banksiana.

Natural stands of jack pine are confined to soils of the podzol region which are dry sandy or gravelly. It can exist on poor sites but does well on the better soils. It occurs pure or predominant over much of its range. It is a major component in 3 forest types where it is associated with paper birch, black spruce, and aspen. It is a minor component in 7 other types where it occurs with white spruce, northern pin oak, red pine, white spruce, and balsam fir. Common understory species are blueberries *Vaccinium* spp., bearberry *Arctostaphylos uva-ursi*, sand cherries *Prunus* spp., green alder *Alnus* spp., American hazel *Corylus americana*, rhodora *Rhododendron canadensis*, and buffalo berry *Shepherdia canadensis*. Jack pine is an intolerant pioneer species and occurs on burned lands where there is little competition.

The principal enemies of jack pine are spring fire, sleet accompanied by strong winds, sawflies, budworm, tussock moth, rust gall, and needle cast. Deer browse heavily on young trees, either killing them or greatly

Fig. 54a. Typical jack pine nesting habitat of the Kirkland's Warbler. (Photo courtesy U. S. Forest Service)

reducing growth. Porcupines damage a high percentage of trees above 3 inches d.h.b. Jack pine makes usable lumber in the larger diameters, but it is more valuable in smaller diameters as pulpwood where it can be grown on a shorter rotation.

In the central part of Michigan, young dense stands of jack pines 6 to 8 feet tall with lower branches reaching the ground is the nesting habitat of the rare Kirkland's Warbler. These dense stands are maintained in this condition by burning at the proper frequency and under favorable moisture. The area is unique in that it is the only place the Kirkland's Warbler is known to nest.

The largest living jack pine of record is 6 feet 6 inches in circumference, 91 feet high with a crown spread of 21 feet. It is growing in the Superior National Forest in Minnesota.

28a. Leaves less than 3 inches long 29

28b. Leaves 3 inches or over in length 32

29a. Bark of medium-sized limbs orange-brown. Leaves 1 1/2 to 2 1/2 inches long, grayish-green. Fig. 55.

SCOTCH PINE ....*Pinus sylvestris* **L.**

An important lumber tree in Europe but has not proved to grow in good form in the United States. It grows from 75 to 100 feet high, but rarely straight with an open irregular top. BARK: smooth, becoming fissured at the lower portion of the bole. Orange-red color of the upper branches is distinctive. LEAVES: needles 1 to 3 1/2 inches long in bundle of 2, dark green. FLOWERS: staminate yellow; pistillate green. FRUIT: a cone 1 to 2 1/2 inches long with short stalk, scales thickened rhombic with central tubercle, ripening in two years.

Fig. 55. Pinus sylvestris.

The principal use now of Scotch pine is for ornamental planting; can be pruned to eliminate the undesirable open crown. It is hardy in cold climates. It does not stand heat with the same efficiency. Although it does have some value for lumber, when trees are not too misshapen, it does pulp well wherever a market exists.

29b. Bark of medium-sized limbs pale gray or grayish-brown 30

30a. Leaves soft, slim, dark green. Fig. 56.

SPRUCE PINE ....*Pinus glabra* Walt.

Spruce pine is a medium-sized
tree ranging from 80 to 100 feet in
height. Branching is often drooping.
It grows at a moderate rate and is
short lived. BARK: dark brown on
young stems becoming gray on older
trees, furrowed with narrow ridges
that are scaly on the surface.
LEAVES: needles, 2 to 3 inches long
in bundles of 2, gray-green. FLOW-
ERS: staminate, orange-brown; pistillate, pale green tipped with red
tints. FRUIT: a cone, reddish-brown,
1 1/2 to 2 inches long in clusters of
2-3. Spruce pine occurs scattered on
moist sandy loam intermediate between the moist bottomlands and
the dry sandy ridges. It is frequently
a minor associate with such trees as
swamp chestnut oak, cherrybark oak,

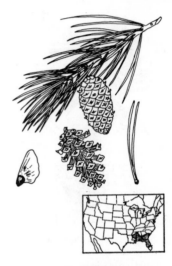

Fig. 56. Pinus glabra.

white ash and several hickories, Atlantic white-cedar and pond pine.
Understory species occurring with spruce pine are buttonbush,
roughleaf dogwood, hawthorn, possumhaw, loblolly-bay and buckwheat-tree. It is more tolerant than other southern yellow pines but
compared with the associated hardwoods, it is intolerant and is a
subclimax species.

It is moderately resistant to fire and is subject to bark beetles,
heart rot and root rots. It is used for lumber and pulpwood. The
forest types in which it occurs are good habitat for deer, turkey,
squirrel, bear, and many small mammals.

The largest living spruce pine of record is 12 feet 10 inches in
circumference, 92 feet tall with a crown spread of 81 feet. It is
growing near Tallahassee, Florida.

30b. Leaves not as in 30a **31**

31a. Leaves stout, gray-green, 1 1/2 to 2 1/2 inches long, buds very resinous. Fig. 57.

VIRGINIA PINE ....*Pinus virginiana* Mill.

Fig. 57. Pinus virginiana.

Virginia pine is a medium-sized pine usually not over 30 to 50 feet in height and has a limby bole. It grows at a moderate rate and is short lived. BARK: dark brown, thin when young becoming scaly. LEAVES: needles, gray-green 1 1/2 to 3 inches long in bundles of 2, usually twisted. FLOW-ERS: staminate in crowded clusters orange-brown; pistillate, pale green tinged with red. FRUIT: a cone, 2 to 3 inches long dark red-brown, scales with stout prickles.

Virginia pine occurs on low quality sites within its range. As a pioneer, it grows in pure stands on abandoned fields. It is a major component in 3 forest types and is associated with shortleaf pine and southern red oak. It is a minor component in 9 types occurring with black, scarlet and chestnut oaks, loblolly and shortleaf pines, eastern redcedar, maple and hickory. It grows in dense stands permitting little understory vegetation to occur. Where

Fig. 57a. Often regarded as a scrub species, Virginia Pine on its proper site makes better growth than other species might make on the same site. This is a high quality stand after the first commercial thinning. (Miller Photo)

there are openings, flowering dog-wood, hawthorn, blueberries *Vaccinium* spp. and greenbriar *Smilax* spp., are commonly found. Vir-ginia pine is an intolerant transi-tion species to a mixed hardwood subclimax.

Having a thin bark, as com-pared to other southern pines, it does not withstand fire success-fully. Its principal enemies are heart rot, pitch canker, bark bee-tles, pine sawfly and pales weevil which feeds on young seedlings. When it reaches sizes for lumber it is cut commercially, but it is in greater demand for pulpwood as the wood is dense and produces good fiber.

The seeds are eaten by songbirds and quail. The dense stands are attractive escape cover for deer.

The largest living Virginia pine of record is 7 feet 6 inches in circumference, 80 feet high with a crown spread of 48 feet. It is growing near Hollis, North Carolina.

31b. Leaves slender, blue-green, 2 to 3 inches long, twisted. Fig. 58.

SAND PINE ....*Pinus clausa* (Chapm.) Vasey

Sand pine is a small tree from 20 to 30 feet high occurring on light, sandy, infertile deposits of marine sand and clay. BARK: on upper portion of bole it is smooth becoming plated on the older portion. LEAVES: needles in crowded clusters of 2, between 2 and 3 inches long, slender, usually twisted and dark blue-green in color. FLOWERS: staminate in elongated loose spikes, yellow; pistillate, clustered and long stalked. FRUIT: sessile cone, armed with short prickles. Serotinous, remaining unopened on the branches for several years, on the central Florida Ocala sites. West Florida sand pine cones open more readily.

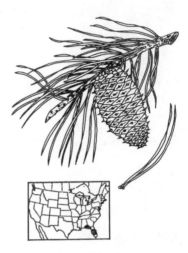

Fig. 58. Pinus clausa.

In the central Florida portion of its range, sand pine occurs in pure stands as a pioneer resulting from fire. In the west Florida sites, it is a more tolerant subclimax often invading oak stands. It occurs in but two types, pure and with longleaf and slash pines. It is associated with several understory shrub oaks which bear acorns prolifically; Chapman oak *Quercus chapmanii,* sand live oak, live oak, scrub oak, rosemary *Ceratiola ericoides,* and scrub palmetto *Sabal etonia.* Sand pine is not highly susceptible to diseases but mature trees are subject to heart rot and southern pine beetles. Central Florida sand pine with the closed serotinous cones requires the use of fire to regenerate. At any other times, fire will kill sand pine. It is used commercially for pulpwood. Due to the large number of mast bearing oaks under the sand pine, it is a valuable type for deer and turkey. Some of the best white-tail deer populations in Florida are in the sand pine forests.

The largest living sand pine of record is 6 feet 11 inches in circumference, 91 feet high with a crown spread of 36 feet. It is growing in the Ocala National Forest in Florida.

31c. Leaves stiff and twisted, bright green, 1 to 3 inches long. Exotic and cultivated as a shrub or small tree. Fig. 59.

SWISS MOUNTAIN PINE ....*Pinus mugo* Turra

Fig. 59. Pinus mugo.

Swiss mountain pine is an introduced species, coming from central and southern Europe. It was introduced in 1779. It is a shrub or low tree, sometimes reaching a height of 30 to 40 feet. The branches are crowded and stout. BARK: gray often in scaly angular plates. LEAVES: bright green 1 to 3 inches long and in bundles of 2. FLOWERS: staminate, yellow; pistillate, greenish. FRUIT: a cone 1 to 2 1/2 inches long, sessile, gray with prickly scales. Since it grows close to the ground, is fully branched and bears foliage year-round, it is a good ornamental for hedge planting and screening. It can be pruned successfully by pruning the "candles" in half, thus producing a more dense foliage.

32a. Cones without scales. Exotic and cultivated as an ornamental. Fig. 60.

AUSTRIAN PINE ....*Pinus nigra* Arnold

Fig. 60. Pinus nigra.

Austrian pine is a native of Southern Europe. It was introduced in the United States in 1759. It is a tall tree, rapid growing with branches in regular whorls, similar to white pine. It reaches heights of 90 to 150 feet and d.b.h. from 18 inches to 36 inches. BARK: broad ridged and dark gray. LEAVES: needles 3 to 5 inches long, stout, dark green and in bundles of 2. FLOWERS: staminate, yellow; pistillate, green. FRUIT: a cone 2 to 3 inches long, often born in pairs. It is widely planted for ornamental purposes, especially in the middle west and Prairie States. It is variable in nature and there are a number of varieties now in the United States.

32b. Cone scales armed with spines 33

33a. With stout spine at tip of cone scale. Cones 3 to 5 inches long. Fig. 61.

TABLE-MOUNTAIN PINE ....*Pinus pungens* Lamb.

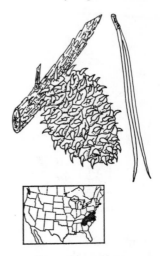

Table-mountain pine is a small tree attaining heights of 60 feet. It is similar in many ways to pitch pine but more limited in occurrence. It is slow growing and short lived. BARK: on the lower part of the bole broken into irregularly shaped plates with loose, thin, dark brown scales on the surface and on the branches. LEAVES: 1 1/2 to 2 1/2 inches long, in clusters, usually twisted, dark blue-green. FLOWERS: staminate in elongated spikes, yellow; pistillate, clustered, long stalked and green. FRUIT: a cone, several in a cluster, 2 to 3 inches long, each scale armed with a sturdy spine.

Fig. 61. Pinus pungens.

Table-mountain pine occurs sparingly on dry, rocky slopes as a minor component in 3 forest types where it is associated with Virginia, pitch and shortleaf pines, chestnut, black, blackjack, post and scarlet oaks, several hickories and sweetgum. It is an intolerant member of subclimax types. Blueberries *Vaccinium* **spp.**, tree sparkleberry, flowering dogwood, hawthorn, greenbriar *Smilax* **spp.**, and grape *Vitis* **spp.** are common understory species. It is susceptible to fire, fusiform rust and pitch canker.

Wherever it attains merchantable sizes, it is cut for lumber along with other southern yellow pines. Since it will occupy dry, steep slopes, it is preferable to hardwoods such as some of the scrub oaks for soil protection. Pine needles do not oxidize as rapidly as hardwood litter, thus affording at least a minimum of site protection.

Table-mountain pine seeds are eaten by songbirds but are less attractive than other species with which it occurs. Habitat in these forest types is suitable for turkey, deer, and squirrel.

The largest living table-mountain pine of record is 5 feet 6 inches in circumference, 81 feet high with a crown spread of 39 feet. It is growing at Penn State University, Mont Alto, Pennsylvania.

33b. With only a small prickle at tip of cone scale. Cones 1 1/2 to 2 1/4 inches long. Leaves 2 to 5 inches. Fig. 62.
SHORTLEAF PINE ....*Pinus echinata* Mill.

Fig. 62. Pinus echinata.

Shortleaf pine is one of the common southern yellow pines. It grows to heights of 80 to 100 feet and is one of the few pines that sprout. BARK: nearly black on small trees becoming reddish-brown with age, furrowed and broken into irregular flat plates. LEAVES: needles 3 to 5 inches long, blue-green, in bundles of 2, occasionally in 3. FLOWERS: staminate, light purple; pistillate, pale rose. FRUIT: a cone, brown, 1 1/2 to 2 1/4 inches long, nearly sessile and persistent for several years, sometimes with deciduous prickles.

The ability of shortleaf to grow on a great variety of soils partly accounts for its wide distribution. Best growth is attained on fine sandy or silt loams with good internal drainage. It does not tolerate soils of high calcium or high acidity. It is intolerant but can persist in very dense stands as long as it gets overhead light. Shortleaf occurs as a pure type and is a major component in 3 types where it is associated with a mixture of oaks, white, scarlet, blackjack, black, post and southern red, Virginia and loblolly pines and hickories. It is a minor component in 15 other types where it occurs with bear, chestnut and northern red oaks, eastern redcedar, white pine, mockernut hickory and various other species over its wide range. It acts as a pioneer when it takes over abandoned agricultural lands, but is an intolerant subclimax species. Some of the more common understory species which occur with shortleaf are blueberries *Vaccinium* **spp.**, dogwood, hawthorn, sweetshrub *Calycanthus americana*, tree sparkleberry, grape *Vitis* **spp.**, greenbriar *Smilax* **spp.**, sumac *Rhus* **spp.**, and elderberry *Sambucus* **spp.**

The principal enemies are southern pine beetles, Nantucket tip moth, and pales weevil. Shortleaf is quite fire resistant and windfirm. The seeds are eaten by a large number of songbirds and quail. Fruit and seeds of the wide variety of understory species provide good habitat for turkey, squirrel and white-tail deer. Shortleaf is one of the leading pines for quality southern pine lumber, plywood and pulpwood.

The largest living shortleaf of record is 13 feet 10 inches in circumference, 127 feet high with a crown spread of 50 feet. It is growing near Sandy Creek, Texas. Shortleaf pine is considered the State Tree of Arkansas.

THE BROADLEAVES

1a. Leaves alternate (only one at each node). Fig. 63. 2

Fig. 63.

1b. Leaves opposite (two at each node) or whorled (three or more at each node). Fig. 64 166

Fig. 64.

2a. Leaves simple. Fig. 65a 3
2b. Leaves compound. Fig. 65b 137

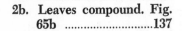

a   b

Fig. 65.

3a. Leaves with pinnate veins (principal veins arising along the mid rib) or with only a mid rib. Fig. 66 4

Fig. 66.

3b. Leaves with at least three heavy veins (mid rib counts as one) arising at the base of the blade (palmately veined). Fig. 67 ..122
4a. Leaves entire (margin smooth, not at all cut). Fig. 67a....... 5

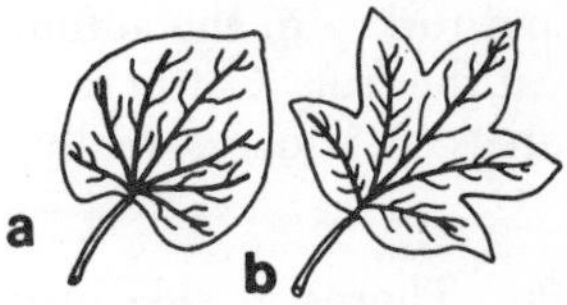

a   b

Fig. 67.

4b. Leaves with margins cut, notched or lobed. Fig. 68 29
5a. Branches with thorns; sap milky 6
5b. Without thorns, sap not milky 7

Fig. 68.

6a. Thorns terminal and sometimes axillary. Leaves tapering at base. Fig. 69.

GUM BUMELIA ....

.... *Bumelia lanuginosa* (Michx.) Pers. **var.** *lanuginosa*
Gum bumelia is a small tree, occasionally a shrub, ranging from 20 to 25 feet high to 70 and 80 feet in height. Branches armed with

spines. There are three varieties frequently encountered. While there are differences in leaves and branches, the differences in range are probably the best means to differentiation. BARK: 1/2 inch thick, deeply fissured, brown tinged with red. LEAVES: narrowed at the base, rounded at the tip, shiny, dark green above, rusty brown below (except in albicans). FLOWERS: minute, greenish-white; in axillary umbels. FRUIT: an oval berry on a slender drooping stalk, about 1/3 inch long; black when ripe in autumn and falling at that time. BUD: scales rusty tomentose. B. *lanuginosa* **var.** *albicans*

Fig. 69. Bumelia lanuginosa var. lanuginosa.

("b" on range map) differs in that the under side of the leaves are silvery white hairy. B. *lanuginosa* **var.** *rigida* ("c" on range map) differs in being smaller, more inclined toward shrubbiness, narrower leaves, more spinescent branches. Occurs in the open woods and glades; seems to prefer rocky, dry soils. The fruit is taken by quail and turkey in the autumn. Deer occasionally browse the leaves and eat the fruit. Cattle will browse the twigs on winter range. In urban areas, it is occasionally planted as an ornamental.

6b. Thorns at side of axillary buds. Leaves not tapering at base. Fruit a greenish ball, 2 inches or more in diameter. Fig. 70.

OSAGE-ORANGE .... *Maclura pomifera* (Raf.) Schneid.

A small tree with branches armed with stout thorns. Attains heights of 60 feet when crowded by other trees; in the open, it rarely makes this height. It is fast growing and short lived. BARK: orange-brown, peeling into strips. LEAVES: simple, broad-ovate to oblong turning bright yellow in fall. FLOWERS: dioecious, very small, greenish; male in racemes, female sessile in dense globular heads. FRUIT: large green ball, turning yellow when ripe, juice milky. BUD: scales brown with milky sap.

Planted extensively as a shelter-belt and hedgerow, particularly in the southern Plains areas. The wood is naturally durable and makes good fence posts. It is a source of a yellow dye. The fruits are readily eaten by fox squirrels. The seeds, a small part of the diet of quail. Twigs may be browsed by cattle where other more palatable material is lacking. The largest Osage-orange of record and living is 19 feet 4 inches in circumference, 66 feet high with a crown spread of 70 feet. It is growing near Carmichael, Maryland.

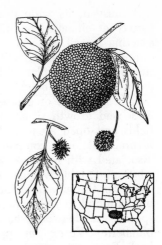

Fig. 70. Maclura pomifera.

7a. Twigs with complete stipular rings at each node, with large tulip-shaped flowers **8**

7b. Twigs without stipular rings **14**

8a. Leaves square cut or with a large notch at end. Fig. 71.

YELLOW-POPLAR ....*Liriodendron tulipifera* **L.**

A handsome tree of the forest often attaining heights of 200 feet. The trunk is tall, straight and remarkably free of branches on the lower portion. The root system is deep and wide spreading. It is commonly found on well drained soils. Yellow-poplar is considered to be a fast growing, long-lived species. BARK: thin and scaly on young trees becoming interlaced with rounded furrows, ashy-gray. Inner bark bitter and aromatic. LEAVES: decidu-ous, 4 to 6 inches across, shining green above, lighter below. Mostly 4-lobed margin. FLOWERS: large, showy tulip-like, petals pale green marked with orange; stamens and pistils nu-merous, spirally arranged. FRUIT: brown, cone-like about 2 1/2 to 3 inches long, ripening in early fall. Seed a samara 1 1/2 inches long. BUDS: terminal with 2 outer scales, flattened, glabrous; leaf scars nearly circular; bundle scars numerous scattered in an irregular ellipse.

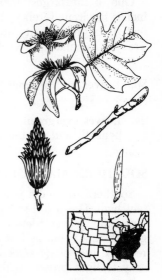

Fig. 71. Liriodendron tulipifera.

Because of its wide distribution, yellow-poplar grows under a variety of climatic conditions. For good growth yellow-poplar is exacting in soil and moisture requirements. It prefers moist, well drained, loose textured soils. Coves in the Appalachians are choice sites for yellow-poplar. Yellow-poplar is an intolerant species but its fast growth in height makes it appear more tolerant, as it can usually grow out of competition. It occurs in pure stands, mostly in second growth situations. It is characteristically found in old fields and open areas within the forest where site and soils are favorable. It is a component of several forest types where it is associated with hemlock, white oak, northern red oak, sweetgum, white pine, loblolly pine, and several hickories. Yellow-poplar is a species of the subclimax forest. An understory of considerable variation is found in yellow-poplar stands. Some of the more important species are dogwood, hawthorn, hobblebush *Viburnum alnifolia*, blueberries *Vaccinium* **spp.**, blackberries *Rubus* **spp.**, strawberry bush *Euonymus americanus*, buffalo nut *Pyrularia pubera*, elderberry *Sambucus canadensis*, wild grape *Vitis* **spp**. Yellow-poplar is remarkably free of disease, probably the most common is the canker caused by *Nectria magnoliae*. Occasionally insects become a problem, some of which are tulip gall fly, tulip tree scale, and a timber beetle. Because of extremely thin bark, yellow-poplar in the seedling-sapling stages is very susceptible to fire. Deer will browse heavily on young seedlings. Yellow-poplar is an important lumber tree for cabinet work, interior paneling, plywood, and pulpwood. It is rated high in humus building capacity. The fruits are eaten by squirrel, the shoots by deer.

One of the largest living yellow-poplars of record is 24 feet 3 inches in circumference, 110 feet high with a crown spread of 119 feet. It is growing at Amelia, Virginia. Yellow-poplar is the State Tree of Indiana and Kentucky.

8b. Leaves with normal pointed tips 9

9a. Leaves evergreen, with heavy coat of rust colored pubescence beneath and on buds. Fig. 72.

SOUTHERN MAGNOLIA ....*Magnolia grandiflora* **L.**

Southern magnolia is a medium-sized tree, commonly 60 to 100 feet high. Has a tall straight bole and pyramidal crown. Its persistent shiny leaves identify it among other trees of the forest. Its growth rate is not as fast as yellow-poplar but faster than southern red oak, two of its associates. It has a moderate life span. BARK: gray to light brown, scaly. LEAVES: shining bright green above and rusty pubescent beneath; falling after their second winter. FLOWERS: 6 to 8 inches in diameter, showy white, fragrant, filaments purple. FRUIT: 3 to 4 inches long, cone-like, rusty brown, white tomentose when young. BUDS: terminal, 1 to 1 1/2 inches long, pale or rusty tomentose; lateral, smaller; twigs rusty tomentose.

Southern magnolia grows best in moist well drained soils located along streams or near swamps in the Coastal Plains. Although considered to be a bottomland species, it will not withstand inundation for any great length of time. Southern magnolia does not grow in pure stands but is associated with several moist land species; beech, sweetgum, yellow-poplar, southern red oak, white oak, cherrybark oak, and hickories. It is a moderately intolerant species occurring in climax types. Understory vegetation associated with southern magnolia are the species found in bottomland types, not subject to extended overflow. Some of the

Fig. 72. Magnolia grandiflora.

more common are American beautyberry *Callicarpa americana,* trumpet creeper *Campsis radicans,* buckwheat-tree, swamp cyrilla, honeysuckle *Lonicera japonica,* and greenbriar *Smilax* **spp.**

Southern magnolia has very few insect enemies. Neither does fungi do any significant damage. Fire is a hazard, although a wild fire may not kill the trees, it usually opens wounds in the bole through which rot and stain can enter. The species is used for lumber, paneling and cabinet work. It is a popular ornamental throughout its range. The fruits are taken by squirrel, turkey and quail as well as yellow-bellied sapsucker, towhee, red-eyed vireo, and red-cockaded woodpecker. Deer on occasion will browse the twigs and leaves. The understory vegetation is of more importance in southern magnolia stands for game than the tree itself. The largest living southern magnolia of record is 21 feet 10 inches in circumference, 72 feet high and a crown spread of 71 feet. It is growing at the Lighthouse Hotel, Biloxi Mississippi. If it fell in hurriance Camille in 1969, an older record tree is 18 feet in circumference, 99 feet high with a crown spread of 71 feet. It is growing near Baton Rouge, Louisiana. Southern magnolia is the State Tree and Flower of Mississippi and Louisiana.

9b. Leaves deciduous, or only partly evergreen **10**

10a. Flowers greenish or yellowish. Leaves thin, rounded or cuneate at base. Leaf-buds silky. Fig. 73.

CUCUMBERTREE ....*Magnolia acuminata* **L. var.** *acuminata*

Cucumbertree is a medium-sized tree 80 to 90 feet high with a straight, clear, slightly buttressed bole, pyramidal crown and a deep, wide-spreading root system. Its growth is slower than yellow-

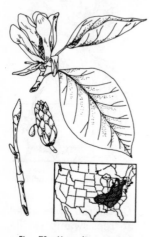

poplar and faster than beech, two of its associates and it has a moderate life span. BARK: dark brown, furrowed and covered with numerous thin scales, flaky. LEAVES: entire, deciduous, 7 to 10 inches long, 2 inches wide, dark green above and paler below. FLOWERS: 2 to 3 inches long, green to greenish-yellow, bell-shaped. FRUIT: 2 to 3 inches long, glabrous, dark red when ripe. BUDS: terminal, 1/2 to 3/4 inch long, silvery silky; lateral, smaller. Leaf scars horseshoe-shaped, bundle scars 5 to 9. Twigs moderately stout.

Cucumbertree is usually found on moist, deep fertile soils of loose texture, with other hardwoods. It makes its best growth in the southern Appalachians.

Fig. 73. Magnolia acuminata.

Cucumbertree is intolerant and does not occur in pure stands. It is a minor component of several subclimax types where it is associated with hemlock, yellow-poplar, beech, and sugar maple. The understory vegetation varies, but these are some of the important common species: flowering dogwood, mapleleaf viburnum *Viburnum acerifolium*, witherod *Viburnum cassinoides*, hawthorn, blueberries *Vaccinium* **spp.**, blackberries *Rubus* **spp.**, wild grape *Vitis* **spp.**

Cucumbertree is not subject to significant damage by insects or fungi. Fire does damage by opening the bole to inroads of insects and disease. Cucumbertree is used for paneling, cabinet work and furniture, frequently being mixed in with yellow-poplar. It is planted widely as an ornamental. It is attractive for nesting birds as cover; squirrels will eat the fruits. The high quality of understory found in the types where cucumbertree occurs is the basis for good wildlife habitat. The largest living cucumbertree of record is 18 feet 4 inches in circumference, 125 feet high with a crown spread of 60 feet. It is growing in the Great Smoky Mountains National Park, Tennessee.

The YELLOW CUCUMBERTREE *M. acuminata* **var.** *cordata* (Michx.) Sarg. is a smaller tree, native of central North Carolina

to central South Carolina and central Georgia. It is rare and local
in distribution. It has been rather widely planted. Its flowers are
yellow and more conspicuous than *M. acuminata var. acuminata.*

10b. Flowers white, large **11**

11a. Leaves cordate at base **12**

11b. Leaves tapering at base **13**

**12a. Leaves 1 to 3 feet long; white pubescent beneath. Buds to-
       mentose. Fig. 74.**

BIGLEAF MAGNOLIA ....*Magnolia macrophylla* Michx.

Bigleaf magnolia has rounded, wide spreading top, reaching to
60 feet in height. It is an infrequent species of the Piedmont Plateau
and upper Coastal Plains. Its growth
is not as rapid as either cucumbertree
or southern magnolia. BARK: thin,
light gray. LEAVES: 1 to 3 feet long,
bright green and smooth above, whitish
pubescent below. FLOWERS: creamy
white with a rose center, 10 to 12
inches or more in diameter. FRUIT:
2 to 3 inches long, rose colored when
ripe. BUDS: terminal, covered with
thick white snowy tomentum, 1 3/4 to
2 inches long, lateral brownish, pubescent, 1/8 to 1/4 inch long.

Bigleaf magnolia occurs in sheltered
valleys in deep rich soil, is intolerant
and does not occur in large numbers.
It makes its best growth in moist sites
along with other moist land species;
yellow-poplar, beech, sweetgum, and
southern red oak. Since it is so uncommon, it does not play an important role
in wildlife habitat. It is susceptible to

Fig. 74. Magnolia macrophylla.

fire and has no important insect or fungi problems. When cut for
lumber, it goes for the same products as other magnolias. The largest living bigleaf magnolia of record is 6 feet 7 inches in circumference, 59 feet high and has a crown spread of 64 feet. It is growing near Baltimore, Maryland.

SOULANGE'S MAGNOLIA *Magnolia X soulangiana* Soul, is an
import hybrid (M. denudata X liliflora.) Japan. It is commonly

planted as an ornamental. Its principal difference from other native magnolias is that the flowers, which are 4 to 6 inches across, are usually purplish or rose on the outside and white within. It is a large shrub or small tree.

12b. Leaves auriculate (ear-like lobes at base), glabrous. Leaf-buds glabrous. Fig. 75.

FRASER MAGNOLIA .... *Magnolia fraseri* Walt.

Fraser magnolia is a medium-sized tree seldom exceeding 45 to 50 feet in height. Has a wide spreading crown. BARK: thin, smooth and dark brown. LEAVES: 10 to 20 inches long and 5 to 8 inches wide, smooth, dark green above, lighter below. FLOWERS: 10 to 12 inches in diameter, pale yellow and fragrant. FRUIT: 4 to 5 inches long, bright red. BUDS: terminal, 1 1/2 to 2 inches long, glabrous, purple; axillary, minute.

Fig. 75. Magnolia fraseri.

Fraser magnolia occurs along the stream valleys within its range. It is intolerant and grows at a somewhat faster rate than other magnolias. It is associated with other moist site species such as yellow-poplar, sweetgum, red maple, loblolly pine, sycamore, southern red oak. It does not suffer significant damage from insects or fungi. With its thin bark, it is susceptible to fire. The fruits are eaten by squirrels. Where large enough to cut, it goes along with other magnolia lumber for panels, cabinet and furniture. It is a popular ornamental in urban areas. The largest living Fraser magnolia is 8 feet 4 inches in circumference, 65 feet high with a crown spread of 50 feet. It is growing near Philadelphia, Pennsylvania.

PYRAMID MAGNOLIA .... *Magnolia pyramidata* Bartr.

Pyramid magnolia is a small tree 20 to 30 feet high, having a restricted range in the Coastal Plains from South Carolina to Mississippi and southeastern Louisiana. It grows in the same type sites as Fraser magnolia but can be identified by the blunt point of the leaf. The largest living pyramid magnolia of record is 2 feet 3 inches in circumference, 51 feet high with a crown spread of 19 feet. It is growing near Bristol, Florida.

13a. Leaves 1 to 2 feet long; light green beneath; leaf-buds glabrous. Fig. 76.

UMBRELLA MAGNOLIA .... *Magnolia tripetala* L.

Umbrella magnolia is a small tree, 30 to 40 feet high with a straight or often inclining trunk, stout contorted branches at right angles with the trunk give the crown a wide spreading appearance. The branchlets are green at first then turning bright reddish-brown. Umbrella magnolia has a medium growth rate and is short lived. BARK: 1/2 inch thick, smooth and light gray in color, occasionally marked by many small bristle-like excrescences. LEAVES: deciduous, 12 to 20 inches long, at first pubescent below. FLOWERS: white 8 to 10 inches in diameter, malodorous. FRUIT: 2 1/2 to 4 inches long, dark red when fully ripe. BUDS: terminal, purple, glabrous, covered with a glaucous bloom, about 1 inch long, axillary, the color of the branch.

It occurs in deep rather moist rich soil along the mountain streams and swamps. Widely distributed but not occurring in numbers in any one place. It is intolerant but in the rich, moist soils will stand more shade than other intolerants. It oc-

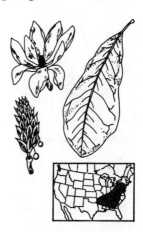

Fig. 76. Magnolia tripetala.

curs along with other subclimax species such as red maple, sweet birch, yellow-poplar and sweetgum. Common to the types, in the understory are dogwood, hawthorns, strawberry bush *Euonymus americanus*, blackberries *Rubus* **spp.**, and wild grape *Vitis* **spp.** This understory is attractive to grouse, turkey and deer, as well as the many forest rodents, squirrel and chipmunks. Where the bole is straight and clear of limbs, umbrella magnolia is used for lumber, furniture, and paneling, just the same as the other species of magnolia. Umbrella magnolia is not subject to significant damage by either insects or fungi. Its thin bark makes it susceptible to damage from fire. The largest living umbrella magnolia of record is 4 feet 9 inches in circumference, 50 feet high with a crown spread of 41 feet. It is growing near Cashiers, North Carolina.

13b. Leaves 3 to 6 inches long, glaucous beneath. Leaf-buds pubescent. Fig. 77.

SWEETBAY .... *Magnolia virginiana* L.

Sweetbay is a slender tree up to 75 feet high, usually shorter. Small short branches form a narrow round-topped head. Branches become glabrous in their second year. BARK: thin, smooth and gray colored. LEAVES: bright green upper side, whitish beneath, 4 to 6 inches long, deciduous in the northern portion of the range, falling in autumn; in the southern portion not falling until the appearance of new leaves in the spring. FLOWERS: 2 to 3 inches across, white and fragrant. FRUIT: 2 inches long, red. Seeds oval, flattened. BUDS: covered with fine silky pubescense, the terminal 1/2 to 3/4 inch long.

Sweetbay is a native of the southern Coastal Plains; it occupies swamps and wet lands, not wet enough for pondcypress and its associates, but too wet for dryland species. It is considered intolerant and medium in growth rate. Sweetbay occurs in transitional types which are neither climax or truly subclimax. It is associated with other moist land species such as sweetgum,

Fig. 77. Magnolia virginiana.

swamp tupelo, red maple, laurel oak, water hickory, and buckwheat tree ("titi"). There is a multitude of understory species, due to the moist growing conditions. Some of the more common are swamp cyrilla, hollies *Ilex* **spp.**, greenbriar *Smilax* **spp.**, Virginia willow *Itea virginica,* possum-haw *Viburnum nudum,* swamp fetterbush *Leucothoe racemosa,* and dahoon. This habitat is attractive as winter range for deer and southern black bear. Sweetbay does not have any significant insect or fungi pests. With its thin bark, it is susceptible to fire damage. When occurring in diameters large enough to make a sawlog, it is cut and sold along with other magnolia logs. It is used in urban areas for ornamental planting. The largest living sweetbay of record is 9 feet 6 inches in circumference, 80 feet high with a crown spread of 58 feet. It is growing near Magnolia, Texas.

14a. Leaves evergreen (some leaves on wood of previous season), thick and leathery **15**

14b. No leaves on wood of previous season **20**

15a. Bark aromatic. Leaves 4 to 5 inches long, pointed at both ends, bright green above, paler on the underside, wood red. Fig. 78.

REDBAY ....*Persia borbonia* (L.) Spreng.

Redbay is a shapely tree 60 to 70 feet high, the crown is well rounded and dense. BARK: 1/2 to 3/4 inch thick, dark red and irregularly furrowed. LEAVES: deciduous during the second year, thick and leathery, bright green above, whitish below, 3 to 4 inches long. FLOWERS: creamy white, about 1/8 inch long. FRUIT: 1/2 inch long, fleshy with single seed, dark blue or nearly black. BUDS: coated with rufous tomentum, 1/4 inch long.

Redbay occurs scattered or in small groups in the Coastal Plains along streams and swamps in rich moist soil. It is occasionally found growing on sandy ridges as an understory species with longleaf pine. Redbay is moderately tolerant and considered a subclimax species. On moist sites, it is associated with red maple, sweetgum, blackgum, water tupelo and swamp cyrilla. On sandy sites, bluejack oak, sand live oak, longleaf pine and yaupon. Redbay does not have any significant insect or fungi enemies.

Fig. 78. Persia borbonia.

It can withstand fire and when properly used, fire stimulates seed germination and induces a growth of palatable sprouts. Redbay, together with some of its palatable associates, is good deer browse. Quail eat the seeds. The lumber is used for cabinet work and paneling. The leaves, when dried, are the "bay leaves" of gourmet cookery. The largest living redbay of record is 8 feet 6 inches in circumference, 53 feet high with a crown spread of 50 feet. It is growing near Conroe, Texas.

15b. Bark not aromatic 16

16a. Leaves pointed at top, smooth; winter buds scaly 17

16b. Leaves usually blunt at tip, wedge-shaped at base 18

17a. Leaves 3 to 4 inches long, light yellow-green beneath. Winter
      buds naked. Fig. 79.

MOUNTAIN-LAUREL ....*Kalmia latifolia* L.

Mountain-laurel is a small tree rarely 30 to 40 feet high, more
commonly seen as a flowering understory shrub in the eastern hardwood forests. The trunk is short and contorted with stout diverging
branches. Often occupies hundreds of square yards of ground space
under the forest canopy. BARK: thin, dark brown and tinged with
red. Older stems becoming furrowed and separating into long narrow ridges. LEAVES: evergreen, thick, dark green above, yellowish-
green beneath. FLOWERS: 1 to 1 1/2 inches across, white, pink

or rose; borne in many flowered corymbs. FRUIT: a woody capsule about
1/4 inch across. BUDS: formed before
midsummer in the axils of the leaves
just below those producing inflorescence. At maturity about 1 inch long
and 1/2 inch wide, light green, covered
with glandular white hairs, when falling marking the base of the shoots with
conspicuous broad scars.

Mountain-laurel grows in a variety
of sites, from moist to some of the
driest. It is very tolerant and stands
shade well. It forms almost impenetrable thickets in parts of its range. It is

Fig. 79. Kalmia latifolia.

a member of subclimax types and
would undoubtedly be a component of
climax types, due to its tolerance. It is
associated with the following tree species; northern red oak, scarlet
oak, yellow-poplar, white oak, white pine, beech, sugar maple and
sourwood. Understory species with which it is associated are greenbriar *Smilax* spp., smooth hydrangea *Hydrangea arborescens*, rosebay rhododendron, witch hazel, blueberries *Vaccinium* spp., and
cinnamon clethra *Clethra acuminata*. Dense thickets of mountain-
laurel are good escape cover for grouse during moult and nesting
sites for turkey and grouse. The high oak composition of forests in
which it occurs provides food for squirrel, deer, turkey and grouse.
Although mountain-laurel itself is supposed to be poisonous to deer,
they do take some of it without apparent bad effects. Mountain-
laurel may be killed by fire, but it sprouts freely. It is remarkably
free of insects and diseases. Most of the mountain-laurel present
in forests is too small to use for any commercial product and con-
sequently is not cut. At one time, the burls were tried as a replacement for Italian briar for pipes. Taste was not favorable and the
attempt was dropped. Mountain-laurel is a popular ornamental

shrub in urban areas. The largest living mountain-laurel of record
is 3 feet 6 inches in circumference, 25 feet high with a crown spread
of 45 feet. It is growing in the Great Smoky Mountains National
Park in Tennessee.

**17b. Leaves 4 to 12 inches long, green on both sides. Winter buds
scaly. Fig. 80.**

ROSEBAY RHODODENDRON ....*Rhododendron maximum* **L.**

Rosebay rhododendron is a common shrub or small tree of the
mountainous regions of the South. It rarely exceeds 40 feet in
height. It has a short crooked often prostrate trunk and stout contorted branches forming a round head. BARK: thin, light red-brown,
broken on the surface into small thin appressed scales. LEAVES:
evergreen, shiny dark green above, 4 to
12 inches long. FLOWERS: showy
white, about 1 1/2 inches across.
FRUIT: woody capsule, reddish-brown,
1/2 inch long. BUDS: leaf buds conic,
dark green, axillary or terminal on barren shoots, 1 to 1 1/2 inches long.

Occurs in the majority of eastern
mountain forests, more common in hardwood than coniferous types. Rosebay
rhododendron is very tolerant of shade
and is a component of subclimax types.
It is associated with northern red, white,
scarlet and black oaks, yellow-poplar,
white pine, hemlock, and basswood.
Typical understory species in these types
are blueberries *Vaccinium* **spp.**, mountain-laurel, greenbriar *Smilax* **spp.**, buffalo nut *Pyrularia pubera*, blackberries
Rubus **spp.**, hobblebush *Viburnum alnifolium.*

Fig. 80. Rhododendron maximum.

Rosebay rhododendron does not appear to have any significant
insect pests or diseases. It is susceptible to fire, but readily sprouts
when burned. It is widely planted as an ornamental. Except for
limited use of the figured burls for pipes, it has little commercial
value. Contrary to some published material, rosebay rhododendron
is commonly browsed by white-tail deer in the Appalachians without dire consequences. On many heavily populated deer ranges, it is
the most palatable remaining browse. Ruffed grouse use the buds
and occasionally leaves and twigs. Dense thickets furnish good
escape cover during moult. Mast from oaks with which it is associated furnish high quality wildlife habitat. The largest living rosebay rhododendron is 4 feet 9 inches in circumference, 18 feet high

with a crown spread of 18 feet. It is growing in the Nantahala National Forest in North Carolina.

Locally in the southern mountains, CATAWBA RHODODEN-DRON *Rhododendron catawbiense* Michx. is a large shrub or small tree occurring upwards from 3000 feet elevation. It is a showy species and has the same growth characteristics as rosebay rhododendron. It does, however, have a purple flower. It is not as tolerant as rosebay and thrives on open slopes and ridgetops away from the shade of the forest. On ridgetops, it is associated with red spruce, chestnut oak, white pine, Fraser fir. The common species along with it in the understory are mountain-laurel, minnie-bush *Menziesia pilosa,* flame azalia *Rhododendron calendulaceum,* hobblebush *Viburnum alnifolium,* witherod *Viburnum cassinoides* and cinnamon clethra *Clethra acuminata.* Where it occurs in thickets, it is good escape cover for grouse during moult. Catawba rhododendron has no commercial value except appeal to beauty.

18a. Leaves with veins scarcely showing on underside; flower racemes terminal. Fig. 81.

BUCKWHEAT-TREE ....*Cliftonia monophylla* (Lam.) Britton

Buckwheat-tree is a small tree, occasionally 40 to 50 feet high. The trunk is often crooked and inclining. The clear bole is short, from 10 to 15 feet, from there it divides into stout ascending branches. BARK: dark red-brown with fine scales; branches reddish for first 2 or 3 years. LEAVES: evergreen, 1 1/2 to 2 inches long, bright green above, paler below. FLOWERS: fragrant, white or rose colored, appearing in February or March. FRUIT: 2 to 4 winged capsules about 1/4 inch long with usually 3 brown seeds. Ripens in August and September. BUDS: about 1/4 inch long.

Occurs in swamps and wet lands throughout its range not subject to overflow. Does not tolerate salt and does not occur in the swamps near sea waters. Is an understory species, and of medium tolerance. It is considered to be a component of transitional types and is associated with slash pine, pondcypress,

Fig. 81. Cliftonia monophylla.

blackgum, sweetbay, swamp tupelo, red maple, and swamp cyrilla. Common understory species are yaupon, dahoon, red bamboo *Smilax Walteri* and Virginia willow *Itea virginica.* Buckwheat-tree does not seem to have any insect or fungus enemies.

Fire will "prune" it back and make it sprout freely. It is a source of excellent honey, "titi" honey is a delicacy long to be remembered. The swamp types in which it occurs are excellent winter deer range. Palatable understory species are abundant. The largest living buckwheat-tree of record is 5 feet 6 inches in circumference, 30 feet high with a crown spread of 21 feet. It is growing near Crooked Creek, Florida.

18b. Netted veins plainly evident on underside of leaves 19

19a. Leaves glabrous, flowers as pictured, white or rose, in lateral racemes. Fig. 82.

SWAMP CYRILLA ....*Cyrilla racemiflora* **L.**

A slender tree, occasionally 30 to 40 feet high, with a stout eccentric trunk dividing several feet above the ground into numerous wide-spreading branches. In some respects, it resembles its associate, buckwheat-tree. BARK: thin, with bright red-brown scales. LEAVES: 2 to 3 inches long, usually deciduous, fall colors are orange or red. In the deep South, leaves may be persistent until the following summer. FLOWERS: in racemes, white or rose. FRUIT: 2-seeded brown capsule about 1/16 inch long. Ripens August or September. BUDS: about 1/8 inch long.

Fig. 82. Cyrilla racemiflora.

As its name indicates, it is a swamp species. It thrives best on acid soils in full sunlight. It does not compete well with other understory species common to the types in which it occurs. It is one of the earlier subclimax species to be crowded out. It is associated with slash pine, pondcypress, blackgum, sweetbay, swamp tupelo, red maple, and buckwheat-tree. Understory species are yaupon, dahoon, greenbriar *Smilax* **spp.**, and Virginia willow *Itea virginica*. Swamp cyrilla seems to be free of insects and fungus. It is "pruned" back by fire. In unburned stands, it is replaced by other bays, hollies, titis and pines. It is an important deer browse when shoots are tender, leaves are also eaten. It is about on a par with buckwheat-tree so far as palatability is concerned. It furnishes good winter range and escape cover for deer as well as bear. Its flowers are a source of "titi" honey.

19b. **Leaves pubescent when young; flowers bell-shaped, white. Fig. 83.**

TREE SPARKLEBERRY ....*Vaccinium arboreum* Marsh.

A tree, 20 to 30 feet high, with short crooked trunk, slender more or less contorted branches forming an irregular rounded-topped head. BARK: reddish-brown. LEAVES: evergreen in the southern portion of its range, deciduous in the north, 1 to 3 inches long, tips rounded and margins revolute, shining dark green above, lighter below. FLOWERS: white on long slender stalks in loose, leafy-bracted racemes, March and May FRUIT: black, about 1/4 inch in diameter, dry pulp and hard stone-like seeds. May remain on the branches over winter. BUDS: obtuse, with chestnut-brown scales often persistent on the base of the branchlet throughout the season.

Fig. 83. Vaccinium arboreum.

Tree sparkleberry is found in sandy or rocky woods, thickets and clearings. It is one of the blueberries that grows well in slightly alkaline soils. It is only a minor component of the forest types in which it occurs. Some of the overstory associates are southern red oak, post oak, loblolly pine, shortleaf pine, white oak, scarlet oak. Understory associates are dogwood, sweetleaf *Symplocos tinctoria,* greenbriar *Smilax* **spp.**, blackberry *Rubus* **spp.**, grapes *Vitis* **spp.** Tree sparkleberry is intolerant of shade and is a subclimax species. There do not appear to be any significant enemies of tree sparkleberry. Fire does not improve the bearing of blueberries in tree sparkleberry. The hard and very close grained wood of tree sparkleberry is occasionally used for tool handles. The fruit is usually too dry to be very palatable. Deer browse the twigs and the intensity of this use varies from one point to another within its range. Fruits are taken by bear, opossum, fox, raccoon, skunk and grouse, quail and turkey. The largest living tree sparkleberry is 2 feet in circumference, 28 feet high with a crown spread of 24 feet. It is growing near Tallahassee, Florida.

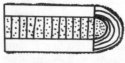

Fig. 84.

20a. **Pith solid but with diaphragms. Fig. 84.** **21**

20b. **Pith either diaphragmed or solid but not both** **22**

**21a. Leaves 10 to 12 inches long; two ranked (in 2 rows on twig);
with a disagreeable odor. Fig. 85.**

PAWPAW ....*Asimina triloba* (**L.**) Dunal

A shrub or low tree, sometimes 30 to 40 feet high, with a straight
bole and small spreading branches. It is the most northern representative of the Custard-apple family, a group of woody species
usually found in the tropics. BARK:
smooth, dark, marked by large ash-
colored blotches. LEAVES: at first
pubescent, becoming glabrous at maturity, 6 to 12 inches long. FLOW-
ERS: deep purple, 1 to 1 1/2 inches
across. FRUIT: a banana-like berry,
3 to 5 inches long and 1 to 2 inches
in diameter. Large flattened seeds.
The fruit is edible in autumn. BUDS:
1/8 inch long, flattened, and clothed
with rusty brown hairs.

It is an occasional tree on deep,
rich, moist soils. The only part of the
range in which it occurs abundantly
is in the Delta of the Mississippi
River. Here it is associated with
cherrybark oak, swamp chestnut oak,
hickories, Delta post oak, and Shu-

Fig. 85. Asimina triloba.

mard oak. Understory species are devils-walkingstick, stiffcornel
dogwood *Cornus stricta,* dwarf palmetto *Sabal minor,* arrowwood
Vibrunum dentatum and possumhaw *Viburnum nudum.* Pawpaw
is a tolerant species in subclimax types. It does not appear to have
any significant insect and disease problems. It is susceptible to fire
damage and occurs in forest types where fire is very damaging.
The fruit is eaten by opossum, raccoon, squirrel, bear and turkey.
The largest living pawpaw is 3 feet 2 inches in circumference, 41
feet high with a crown spread of 27 feet. It is growing near Smith
Mills, Kentucky.

**21b. Leaves 2 to 5 inches long, not two ranked. Figs. 160 and
161. THE TUPELOS** 83

**22a. Pith 5 angled when viewed in
cross section; leaves usually with
bristle at tip. Fruit an acorn. Fig.
86a. THE OAKS (in part) 54**

**22b. Pith cylindrical or nearly so. Fig.
86b.** 23

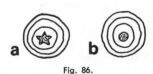

Fig. 86.

23a. Underside of leaves and the young stems covered with
silvery-white scurfy scales. Leaves 2 to 3 inches long. Flowers
yellow covered with silvery scales. Fig. 87.

RUSSIAN OLIVE .... *Elaeagnus angustifolia* L.

Russian olive is a small tree or shrub, deciduous, and sometimes
spiny, the branchlets are silvery-white. It attains heights up to 20
feet. It is a native of Europe and western Asia and is now estab-

lished widely in the West and particularly in the northwest. It appears to
be hardy to droughts. BARK: shiny,
smooth. LEAVES: lanceolate or oblong
lanceolate, 2 to 3 inches long, light
green above, silvery below. FLOW-
ERS: golden yellow inside, 1 to 3 in
the axils of the leaves, fragrant, June.
FRUIT: oval, about 1/2 inch long on
very short stalks; yellow, covered with
silvery scales.

Russian olive is planted as an ornamental in yards and parks. It is a good
plant for soil cover in western areas.
Fruit clings to the plants through most
of the winter thus making it available.

Fig. 87. Elaeagnus angustifolia.

It is an important food for cedar wax-
wing, robin and evening grosbeak.
Twigs and foliage are both taken by elk and deer. In eastern United
United States, Autumn Olive *Elaeagnus umbellata* is widely planted
for wildlife food and cover in strips and hedges. It is a shrub, rarely
over 12 feet high. The leaves are not as long as *E. angustifolia* and
are broader. The berries are good grouse and turkey food.

23b. Not as in 23a 24

24a. Twigs of 2 or 3 years, bright green, shiny. Leaves entire or
2 or 3-lobed. Readily told by the odor of its bark, leaves and
roots. Fig. 88.

SASSAFRAS ....*Sassafras albidum* (Nutt.) Nees

Sassafras is a small tree, not more than 40 feet high, aromatic, with short stout more or less contorted branches spreading at right angles and forming a narrow open flat-topped crown. BARK: red-brown, deeply furrowed, twigs bright green. LEAVES: three shapes on the same tree; some oval, some with two lobes—mitten shaped, others with three lobes. They are 4 to 5 inches long. FLOWERS: clustered, greenish-yellow, open with the unfolding of the leaves in the spring, April. FRUIT: oblong, dark blue or black; shining berry containing but one seed. BUDS: usually solitary, twigs bright green, 1/4 to 3/8 inch long.

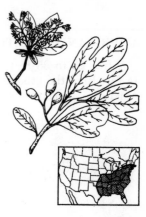

Fig. 88. Sassafras albidum.

Sassafras grows best in open woods on moist well drained sandy loam soils. However, it is a pioneer species on abandoned fields and on dry ridges and upper slopes, especially following fire. Although considered to be a tolerant species, when it becomes overtopped in mixed stands it is one of the first species to die. Its major associate is persimmon. These two species are pioneers on abandoned fields; they are temporary giving way to mixed hardwood types. Many such sites in the southeast have been planted to commercial crops of pine. Sassafras is associated with other species, such as elm, eastern redcedar, sweetgum, hickory and pawpaw. In older stands, it is associated with ash, sugar maple, yellow-poplar and oaks. It may be found in the understory of stands of aspen and northern pin oak. It is associated with other understory species such as dogwood, hawthorn, American hornbeam, eastern hophornbeam, red maple, and sourwood. Sassafras is susceptible to fire damage at all ages. Mistletoe and 19 species of fungi attack sassafras. Trees on poor sites often have trunk and stem cankers of *Nectria*. At least 15 species of insects attack sassafras. Except for small local outbreaks, damage is relatively unimportant. Wood products of sassafras are posts, rails, and an aromatic oil from the roots. The fruit is eaten by quail, turkey and many song birds, fruit and buds by squirrels, twigs and foliage by white-tail deer. The largest living sassafras of record is 17 feet 3 inches in circumference, 100 feet high with a crown spread of 68 feet. It is growing near Owensboro, Kentucky.

25a. Leaves tapering to a point at their tip 26

25b. Leaves usually rounded or slightly notched at their tip. Fig. 89.

AMERICAN SMOKETREE ....*Cotinus obovatus* Raf.

A tree 25 to 35 feet high with a straight trunk, dividing 12 to 14 feet from the ground into several erect stems, widely branched. American smoketree probably reaches its greatest numbers in the

Edwards Plateau of Texas. BARK: thin, furrowed, light gray. LEAVES: 3 to 6 inches long, thin, glabrous or sometimes pubescent beneath. FLOWERS: dioecious, green, very small in large open panicles, greenish-yellow at first, becoming purplish. FRUIT: drupe-like, 1/8 inch long, seeds flat. BUDS: buds and leaf scars small, the edges of the scars showing minute folds or wrinkles; twigs shiny, when freshly cut aromatic with a pleasant fruity odor.

It occurs in rocky soils of limestone origin, bluffs and dry slopes. It occurs in the "oak shinneries" of the Edwards Plateau associated with Mohr oak, *Quercus mohriana*, American plum, live oak, and holly *Ilex* **spp**. It is used for fence posts and orange dye. The largest living smoketree of record is 2 feet 6 inches in circumference, 33 feet high with a crown spread of 18 feet. It is growing in the Dawes Arboretum near Newark, Ohio.

Fig. 89. Cotinus obovatus.

26a. Petioles (leaf stems) very slender, 1 to 2 inches long. Fig. 269. ALTERNATE-LEAF DOGWOOD 183b

26b. Petioles heavier and usually short 27

27a. Branchlets without terminal bud; fruit fleshy 28

27b. Branchlets with a terminal bud; flowers in catkins, fruit dry. Fig. 90.

CORKWOOD ....*Leitneria floridana* Chapm.

Corkwood is a small tree or shrub sometimes up to 20 feet high, with slender
straight trunk above a swollen, gradually
tapering base. Spreading branches form a
loose, open crown. BARK: thin, brownish
gray. LEAVES: 4 to 6 inches long, pubescent both sides; petioles 1 to 2 inches long.
FLOWERS: dioecious, in catkins, staminate 1 to 1 1/2 inches long; pistillate shorter. FRUIT: a dry flattened drupe. BUDS:
terminal, broad, conic 1/8 inch long, coated
with pale tomentum and long persistent at
base of the branch; lateral scattered, ovoid,
flattened. Within its limited range, it occupies borders of swamps and brackish muddy shores of the Gulf Coast. The wood is
soft, exceedingly light, more so than cork
and frequently used as floats on fishing
nets.

Fig. 90. Leitneria floridana.

**28a. Leaves smooth, shining. Fruit, tomato shaped, smooth, 3/4
to 2 inches in diameter. Very astringent before frost. Fig. 91.**

COMMON PERSIMMON ....*Diospyros virginiana* **L.**

Persimmon is a small tree, occasionally
50 to 60 feet high. It has a short trunk,
spreading branches forming a broad
round-topped crown. Its rate of growth
is slow and it is short lived. BARK: almost
black and separated into thick nearly
square blocks. LEAVES: 4 to 6 inches
long, dark green and shining above, paler
beneath. FLOWERS: yellowish or cream
white, bell shaped, appear in spring, May.
FRUIT: pulpy, round, orange-colored
berry when ripe, 1 inch or more in diameter with 4 to 12 flat oblong seeds. Ripens
after first good frost. Very puckery while
green. BUDS: terminal bud lacking, bud
scales 2, greatly overlapping, twigs often
velvety.

Fig. 91. Diospyros virginiana.

Persimmon is found in a wide variety of sites but grows best on
terraces of larger streams and first bottoms of the Mississippi River.

Frequently it occurs on old fields and dry soils as a pioneer where it rarely gets large enough to be considered a commercial tree. In these situtaions, its growth is very slow and short lived. Intolerant persimmon does not occur in pure stands. Its most common associate is sassafras. In this type, it is a pioneer species and is eventually displaced by other hardwoods. On bottomland sites, it is more tolerant and associated with subclimax sweetgum, Nuttall oak, willow oak, sugarberry, American elm, green ash, overcup, and water hickory. Common understory species are swamp privet *Forestiera acuminata*, roughleaf dogwood, hawthorns, shining and smooth sumacs. On dry sites persimmon is intolerant; on the moist bottomland soils it can persist in the understory for many years. A number of insects attack persimmon but normally do no serious harm. A fungus disease which causes wilt, kills many trees and is characterized by sudden wilting of the leaves, followed by defoliation. Persimmon is susceptible to fire but although the stems may be killed, the roots will sprout vigorously. The wood of persimmon is valuable in the trade for shoe lasts, shuttle blocks and golf club heads. The fruit is eaten by about every animal in the forest, many songbirds, and turkey. Deer will browse the twigs, foliage and eat the fruit. The largest living persimmon of record is 13 feet in circumference, 80 feet high with a crown of 74 feet. It is growing near Johnson, Indiana.

28b. Leaves dull, hairy. Fruit, apple-like with fuzzy covering. Fig. 92.

QUINCE ....*Cydonia oblonga* Mill.

Quince is a native of Asia and was brought to this country for orcharding and production of fruit for preserves. It is a shrub or small tree, rarely over 30 feet high. The crooked branches give the crown a round-topped appearance. BARK: dark. LEAVES: 2 to 4 inches long, tomentose beneath, turning yellow late in the fall. FLOWERS: white or pinkish 1 1/4 to 2 inches across. FRUIT: apple-like pome, green turning yellow when ripe, covered with fuzz. Quince is grown chiefly for its fruit.

Fig. 92. Cydonia oblonga.

29a. Lateral veins straight and parallel, or nearly so, at least part of them ending in the teeth or lobes. Fig. 93 30

Fig. 93.

29b. Lateral veins not straight and parallel. Fig. 94 78

30a. Leaves and buds in two distinct rows on the stem 31

30b. Leaves and buds not in two rows on the stem 51

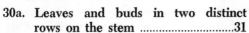

Fig. 94.

31a. Leaf blades unequal at their base (the 2 sides not symmetrical) Fig. 95a 32

31b. Leaf blades nearly equal at base. Fig. 95b 40

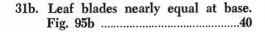

a   b

Fig. 95.

32a. Axillary buds on stalks. Flowers appearing in late fall with ripening of fruit of previous year. Fig. 96.

WITCH-HAZEL ....*Hamamelis virginiana* L.

A tree occasionally 20 to 25 feet high with a short trunk and spreading branches forming a broad, open crown. It is considered to be a slow growing short-lived species. A second species occurs only in the Ozark region of southern Missouri as a shrub, Vernal Witch-hazel *Hamamelis vernalis* Sarg. BARK: thin, broken into scales, light brown. LEAVES: unequal at base; dull green, lighter below; 4 to 6 inches long. FLOWERS: opening in late fall. Petals strap shaped and bright yellow; sepals, orange-brown. FRUIT: ripening during late fall of second year, 1/2 inch long, brown. BUDS: greenish-yellow or tan colored, covered with fine pu-

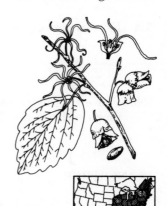

Fig. 96. Hamamelis virginiana.

bescence, sometimes with a pair of small inconspicuous scales near the base; stipules deciduous.

Witch-hazel ocurs in forest openings, along streams and occasionally on rocky banks. It is moderately tolerant and is a minor species in many moist site types, most of which are subclimax. It

is associated with gray birch, white ash, white, red, and burr oaks, beech, sweet birch, balsam fir and American elm. In the understory, downy serviceberry, flowering dogwood, and mapleleaf virburnum *Viburnum acerfolium*. Witch-hazel is not known to be susceptible to significant insect or fungi damage. It is susceptible to fire. It is used for ornamental planting and for medicines. The fruits are used by grouse and wild turkey. The bark, foliage and seeds by squirrel and rabbit.

Fig. 96a. WITCH-HAZEL. Current year flowers and second year fruit. (Miller Photo)

Deer browse on the twigs and foliage. In general, its wildlife value is rather average. The largest living witch-hazel of record is 1 foot 1 inch in circumference, 39 feet high with a crown spread of 30 feet. It is growing near Franklin, Michigan.

32b.   Buds sessile; leaves mostly doubly serrate 33

33a.   Flowers perfect, before the leaves or in autumn; fruit winged 34

33b.   Flowers partly unisexual appearing with the leaves; fruit a rough surfaced nut. Fig. 97.

PLANERTREE ....*Planera aquatica* Gmel.

A tree 30 to 40 feet high with a short trunk and rather slender spreading branches forming a low open crown. It is considered slow growing and short lived. BARK: inner bark red-brown, partly covered with large gray or light brown scales. LEAVES: 2 to 2 1/2 inches long, dull dark green above, paler below; veins yellowish. FLOWERS: inconspicuous, appearing with the leaves in early spring. Staminate develop along the branches; pistillate in the leaf axils. FRUIT: an oblong drupe about 1/2 an inch long with irregular soft projections.

It is a tree of the low country and prefers sites covered with water for a portion of the year. Such sites are similar to the lower Mississippi River bottom lands and widely distributed swamps and deep sloughs. It is moderately tolerant and an associate of many wet land types where it grows along with water tupelo, baldcypress, slash pine, water oak, black willow and overcup oak. It is a minor subclimax species of wet types. Understory associates are swamp privet *Forestiera acuminata,* buttonbush, supple-jack *Berchemia scandens,* wild rose *Rosa carolina,* and possumhaw viburnum *Viburnum nudum.*

Fig. 97. Planera aquatica.

Fire is a major enemy when the bottomlands are dry enough to burn. There are no significant insects or fungi which damage the planertree. It is occasionally used for anchoring fishing nets and for posts of a temporary nature. It is not a durable wood. Planertree has very little attraction to wildlife, but the forest types in which it occurs are good habitat for deer, bear, turkey, squirrel, and waterfowl wintering grounds. The largest living planertree is 8 feet 4 inches in circumference, 77 feet high with a crown spread of 47 feet. It is growing near Chattahoochie, Florida.

34a. **Flowers appearing in early spring before the leaves** 35

34b. **Flowers appearing in autumn, twigs with wings or cork** 39

35a. Leaves very rough above; buds downy, reddish-brown; inner bark slippery; no cork wings on twigs. Flowers on short stems. Fig. 98.

SLIPPERY ELM ....*Ulmus rubra* Muhl.

Slippery elm is a medium-sized tree 60 to 70 feet in height. It resembles the American elm in many ways but can best be identified by the character of the crown. The twigs have a tendency to be ascending and this feature gives individuality to slippery elm, as the crown resulting from this growth is graceful and broad. Slippery elm is considered to be a relatively fast grower and long

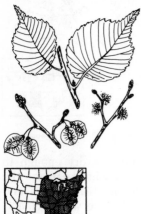 lived. BARK: dark reddish-brown, coarsely scaly on older trunks. The inner bark is mucilaginous and medicinal. LEAVES: 5 to 7 inches long; often creased along the midrib; hairy on the underside. FLOWERS: small reddish-brown, appearing before the leaves in the spring, March and April. FRUIT: flat, winged hairy seeds, maturing in early spring. BUDS: lateral, dark chestnut-brown to almost black, pubescent; flower buds larger, often with an orange tip.

Slippery elm makes its best growth on the moist, rich soils of lower slopes, streambanks, river terraces and bottomlands. It does, however, occur on much

Fig. 98. Ulmus rubra.

drier sites, particularly those of limestone origin. Most of the range of slippery elm is within 500 to 1800 feet above sea level. It is a common but scattered tree. It occurs in several major forest types where it is associated with black ash, red maple, northern red oak, basswood, white oak, silver maple, American elm and black walnut. On the moist sites, there is an abundance of understory species; blackberry *Rubus* spp., gooseberries *Ribes* spp., several dogwoods, grape *Vitis* spp., elderberries *Sambucus* spp., American bittersweet *Celastrus scandens* and hawthorns. Slippery elm has the ability to persist even under shade, although growth is reduced to a minimum. This characteristic permits slippery elm to be a member of the more stable types, although the majority of the types in which it occurs are transitional or subclimax. Slippery elm is susceptible to fire, particulary as it opens wounds through which fungus can enter. Slippery elm has its share of insect and fungus pests. The most serious at this time is the Dutch elm disease. The value of slippery elm to wildlife is not great; purple finches eat the seeds, fox and red squirrels eat the buds and seeds. Deer will, on occasion, browse the twigs and foliage. Its large crown is attractive to nesting song-birds. The wildlife value of the types in which it occurs is very high, as high quality food plants are numerous in the understory. Lumber is the principal use of the tree in the commercial market. It is planted as a shade tree in many towns. Elms are high in humus building capacity. The largest living slippery elm of record is 21 feet 2 inches in circumference, 116 feet in height with a crown spread of 101 feet. It is growing in Henderson, Kentucky.

The WYCH ELM *Ulmus glabra* Huds. with leaves much rough-ened above but with smooth buds and no slippery bark is cultivated in various forms.

35b. **Leaves smooth or at most somewhat roughened above. Flow-ers on longer stems** **36**

36a. **At least some of the branches with wing-like ridges, or twigs with short hairs. Fig. 99** **37**

36b. **Not as in 36a** **38**

37a. **Branchlets with broad corky wings. Fruit with narrow wings. Leaves 1 to 3 inches long. Fig. 99.**

WINGED ELM ....*Ulmus alata* Michx.

Winged elm is a medium-sized tree with a rounded top attain-ing heights of 80 feet. Normally it is a rather small tree with a spreading crown. It is moderately fast growing with medium lon-gevity. BARK: thick, light brown, on branches expanding into wing-like ridges. LEAVES: when mature thick, dark green and smooth above, lighter and pubescent beneath, 1 to 3 inches long. FLOWERS: small, drooping from fasicles. FRUIT: winged, brown, ripen-ing before leaves. BUDS: slender, 1/8 inch long, dark chestnut-brown, acute but not sharp, with glabrous scales.

Winged elm is found on a great va-riety of soils. It does fairly well on dry as well as rich moist sites. Its best de-velopment is on bottomlands and ter-races where it grows only as scattered trees in mixture with other hardwoods. It is not major component of any forest type, but it occurs in varying amounts in several major types. It is associated with

Fig. 99. Ulmus alata.

eastern redcedar, hickory, sugarberry, American elm, green ash and black, white, red, chestnut and cherrybark oaks. Common understory species are American holly, dogwood, supplejack *Berche-mia scandens*, greenbriar *Smilax rotundifolia*, blackberry *Rubus* **spp.**, and grape *Vitis* **spp**. Winged elm is relatively intolerant and is a temporary component of subclimax types. Winged elm's thin bark makes it susceptible to fire damage. It is attacked by several serious pests; Dutch elm disease and a virus of the phloem tissue. Also, it is attacked by many kinds of insects, defoliators, bark beetles, borers and sucking insects. Most of this damage occurs to shade trees. It is commercially cut for lumber and goes along with other elms. Elms are high in humus building capacity. Winged elm itself is not an important wildlife food tree. The types in which it occurs are for the most part favorable habitat. Deer, squirrel, turkey and waterfowl in the winter are attracted to these types. The largest living winged elm of record is 11 feet 1 inch in circumference, 93 feet in height with a crown spread of 81 feet. It is growing on the Morehouse College campus, Atlanta, Georgia.

37b. Branches often with corky wings. Fruit with broad wings. Leaves 2 to 5 inches long. Fig. 100.

ROCK ELM ....*Ulmus thomasii* Sarg.

Rock elm, so called because of its extremely hard tough wood, is a medium-sized tree straight and well balanced, reaching heights of 100 feet. It is intermediate in rate of growth. BARK: branches

sometimes with cork wings. LEAVES: dark green above, pale pubescent beneath, margin coarsely serrate, 3 to 6 inches long. FLOWERS: in racemes; anthers purple. FRUIT: winged, ripening when leaves are about half grown. TWIG AND BUDS: twigs light reddish-brown, glabrous or slightly puberous; buds downy ciliate.

Rock elm often occurs on rocky ridges, limestone outcrops and streambanks. It attains its optimum development on moist, well drained sandy loams or silt loams in mixture with better hardwoods. It varies in tolerance at certain periods in its life. During its younger years as a seedling or sapling, it can withstand suppression for a number of years and still recover. Older trees are more light demanding. In general, the species is rated as intermediate in tolerance. It is a minor component of two major forest types which are climax. Its major associates are sugar maple, beech, yellow birch, American elm and red maple. Others are American basswood, white ash, butternut, slippery elm, red oak, and white spruce. Under-

Fig. 100. Ulmus thomasii.

story shrubs commonly associated with rock elm include prickly ash, beaked hazel *Corylus cornuta,* blackberry *Rubus* **spp.**, round-leaf dogwood *Cornus rugosa,* red-osier dogwood *Cornus stolonifera,* American bittersweet *Celastrus scandens,* grape *Vitis* **spp.**, hawthorn, several elders *Sambucus* **spp.**, and nannyberry. As a member of the elm genus, it is attacked by many different insects but it is not a particular host of any specific insect. Although there are no specific referneces, Phloem necrosis and Dutch elm disease undoubtedly attack rock elm. It is susceptible to fire. Its tough wood is used for containers, dairy and poultry supplies and planted as a shade tree. Elms are high in humus building capacity. Generally the wildlife value of elms is low, seeds and buds are used by at least 8 species of songbirds, grouse, pheasant and turkey. White-tail deer browse the twigs and foliage. Understory vegetation of the associations in which it occurs is valuable to turkey, grouse and white-tail deer. The largest living rock elm of record is 11 feet 1 inch in circumference, 99 feet high, with a crown spread of 59 feet. It is located in Swope Park, Kansas City, Missouri.

38a. Buds and fruit smooth. Leaves 4 to 6 inches long. Fig. 101.

AMERICAN ELM ....*Ulmus americana* var. *americana* L.

American elm is perhaps one of the most symmetrical and beautiful trees in the United States. Surely more streets have been named after it. It is a large tree with spreading branches arching above. It is a relatively fast growing and long-lived tree frequently reaching heights of 125 feet. BARK: light gray, rough, flaky, ridged. LEAVES: oval, parallel veined, abruptly pointed, sharply serrate, dark green, clear yellow in autumn; 3 to 6 inches long. FLOWERS: in drooping clusters. Calyx green tinged with red above the middle; anthers bright red, April. FRUIT: on long pedicels or stems in crowded clusters, ripening as the leaves unfold. One seed, entirely surrounded by wing. TWIG AND BUD: twigs and buds brown, sometimes slightly pubescent. Buds acute but not sharp-pointed.

American elm is commonly found in wet flats and bottomland sites. It can, however, do well on better drained soils and makes its best growth on these sites.

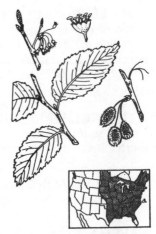

Fig. 101. Ulmus americana.

It rarely occurs in pure stands but grows in association with black ash, red maple, silver maple, sugarberry, green ash, sycamore and pecan. It is a major component of four forest cover types and a minor component of 22. It is commonly found in subclimax and climax types. In the majority of the types in which it occurs, it is associated with understory species, greenbriar *Smilax* **spp.**, blackberry and dewberry *Rubus* **spp.**, elder *Sambucus canadensis,* hawthorn, and sumac *Rhus* **spp**. It is intermediate in tolerance among the hardwoods with which it is associated.

American elm is attacked by many kinds of defoliators, bark beetles, borers and sucking insects. These are not considered serious in forest trees. In shade and ornamental elms, they do serious damage. Dutch elm disease has made serious inroads on American elm. Strains resistant to the disease are the best hope for elms in the future. Phloem necrosis is another serious problem in both shade and forest trees. Fire damage is not a major problem but it is not resistant to spring and summer fires. The wood is used for containers, furniture and caskets. It is extensively planted as a shade tree across the United States. Elms are high in humus building capacity. The American elm crown is a favorite nesting site for the Baltimore oriole. Its seeds are eaten by 9 species of songbirds, grouse, pheasant, prairie chicken, and turkey. White-tail deer browse the twigs and foliage. Understory species associated with elm provide additional wildlife food and cover. The largest American elm of record and living is 24 feet 7 inches in circumference, 160 feet high with a crown spread of 147 feet. It is growing near Trigonia, Blount County, Tennessee. American elm is the State Tree of Massachusetts.

The FLORIDA ELM *Ulmus americana* var. *floridana* (Chapm.) Little, a southern variety, is the only recognized variety. (See range map line a.) Due to lack of winter hardiness, American elm has developed several geographical races. The largest living Florida elm of record is 7 feet 4 inches in circumference, 66 feet tall with a crown spread of 36 feet. It is growing in Manatee County, Florida.

The ENGLISH ELM *Ulmus procera* Salisb. often planted in the United States appears in various forms. The leaves and fruit have shorter stems than the American elm. Leaves are 2 to 3 inches long.

38b.   **Leaves 3/4 to 2 inches long, numerous, usually singly serrate. Smooth on both sides. Twigs brittle. Fig. 102.**

SIBERIAN ELM ....*Ulmus pumila* **L.**

A tree with broad rounded top and somewhat hanging twigs. Frequently to 75 feet high. Is a native of Eastern Siberia and China. BARK: gray and furrowed. LEAVES: 3/4 to 2 inches long, usually with single teeth; dark green. FLOWERS: small, in axils of leaves. FRUIT: winged.

Siberian elm is recommended as a street tree for arid regions. It has a tendency to brittleness and to break up badly in storms or ice and sleet. The species is commonly but incorrectly called CHINESE ELM. The largest living Siberian elm of record is 17 feet 4 inches in circumference, 80 feet high with a crown spread of 75 feet. It is growing at Bath, New Hampshire.

Fig. 102. Ulmus pumila.

39a. Leaves rough above, soft pubescent below; bud-scales covered with hair. Fig. 103.

CEDAR ELM ....*Ulmus crassifolia* Nutt.

A round topped tree reaching 80 feet in height. It is one of the southern small-leaved elms, fast growing and short lived. BARK: light brown tinged with red; sometimes 1 inch thick. LEAVES: leathery, 1 to 2 inches long, dark green above turning bright yellow in the fall. FLOWERS: August to October, on slender pedicels. FRUIT: 1/3 to 1/2 inch long; ripening September to November. TWIGS AND BUDS: twigs bear two corky wings which are only about half as wide as those of winged elm; buds, chestnut-brown puberulous on the outer surface, bright red.

Cedar elm occurs on a wide variety of soils ranging from the dry limestone hills of Texas to the deep bottomland soils of the southern bottomlands. It does not occur in pure stands but is a minor component in

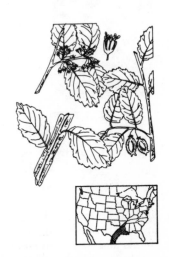

Fig. 103. Ulmus crassifolia.

four major forest types. It is associated with ashe-juniper, Mohr and Durand oaks in Texas, but with more moisture loving species such as sweetgum, Nuttall oak and willow oak, sugarberry, American elm and green ash in the bottomland portion of its range. It is a relatively intolerant species occurring in subclimax types. Over the major part of its range, it is associated with such understory species as hawthorn, greenbriar *Smilax* **spp.**, buttonbush, elder *Sambucus* **spp.**, and blackberry and dewberry *Rubus* **spp**. It is subject to the same insect damage as other elms. It also is susceptible to Dutch elm disease and phloem necrosis. Fire will cause butt scars to the thin bark. It is cut commercially when it is large enough to make a log. When it is sold, it goes along with other elm. Elms are high in humus building capacity. Seeds are eaten by several songbirds, grouse and turkey. White-tail deer will browse the foliage and twigs if hard put. The largest living cedar elm of record is 8 feet 2 inches in circumference, 94 feet high with a crown spread of 50 feet. It is growing near Oletha, Texas.

39b. Leaves glabrous above, bud-scales glabrous. Fig. 104.

SEPTEMBER ELM ....*Ulmus serotina* Sarg.

A broad topped tree 50 to 60 feet high with pendulous branches often forming a broad handsome head. It is one of the southern

elms which grow in minor numbers in several of the hardwood types. BARK: 1/4 to 3/8 inch thick, light brown. LEAVES: 2 to 4 inches long, yellow-green, covered with white hairs when young, later smooth and thin. FLOWERS: in many flowered racemes in September. FRUIT: 1/2 inch long, fringed with long silvery hairs. TWIGS AND BUDS: twigs, with 2 or 3 corky wings; buds, dark chestnut-brown, glabrous, sometimes 3/4 inch long when fully developed.

It occurs on moist soils in smaller stream and major river bottoms. It does not occur in pure stands but is mixed with other hardwoods many of which are elms. It is intermediate in tolerance

Fig. 104. Ulmus serotina.

and occurs in four forest types, which are subclimax. Its associates are northern red oak, hickory, sweetgum, beech, sugar maple, silver maple and American elm. Common understory species are pawpaw, hawthorn, hazel *Corylus* **spp.**, possumhaw, hydrangea *Hydrangea arborescens,* and greenbriar *Smilax* **spp**.

September elm has the same enemies of all elms. The most serious of which are Dutch elm disease and phloem necrosis. With its thin bark, it is susceptible to fire. When large enough to make a sawlog, it is cut and sold along with other elm species. It is widely planted as a shade tree. Songbirds eat the seeds, deer will browse on foliage and twigs when hard pressed for food. The understory shrubs and vines associated with the types in which it occurs are more important for wildlife than the tree itself.

The largest September elm of record and living is 6 feet 2 inches in circumference, 77 feet high with a crown spread of 42 feet. It is growing near Glenwood, Arkansas.

CHINESE ELM *Ulmus parvifolia* Jacq. has smooth leaves and flowers in the fall but does not have winged branches.

40a. **One fairly large simple serrate tooth for each lateral vein in which it ends** **41**

40b. **Not as in 40a** **43**

41a. **Leaves with slender points on the teeth, often incurving. Leaves usually more than twice as long as wide. Bark rough** **42**

41b. **Leaves without slender points at tips, usually less than twice as long as wide. Bark smooth, light gray. Several 3-sided nuts born in the spiny fruit. Fig. 105.**

AMERICAN BEECH ....*Fagus grandifolia* Ehrh.

Beech is one of the most distinctive and common trees of the eastern hardwood forest. In the open, it has a short stocky bole with a wide spreading crown; under forest conditions a clear massive trunk and smaller crown are developed. It attains heights of 100 feet or more. It is considered to be slow growing and long lived. BARK: bluish-gray, very smooth and thin. LEAVES: 3 to 6 inches long; dark green above and paler beneath. Margin remotely serrate with sharp, incurved teeth. FLOWERS: male, in globular heads about 1 inch in diameter; female, in pairs. FRUIT: a very prickly bur about 3/4 inch long containing several brown, 3-sided nuts. (Fig. 5) TWIGS AND BUDS: stipule scars long and narrow, nearly encircling the twig; buds lance-

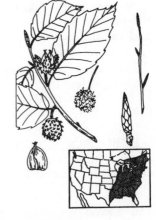

Fig. 105. Fagus grandifolia.

shaped with about 8 or more visible scales; twigs tough, at first brown, later gray.

American beech occurs on a wide variety of soils from sandy loams of the northeast to the alluvial bottoms of the larger river valleys. It is more abundant on the cooler and moister northern slopes than on southern slopes. Beech is a major species in 4 major forest types, and is associated with a large number of other species. Some of the principal associates are sugar maple, yellow birch, American basswood, black cherry, southern magnolia, eastern white pine, red spruce, several hickories and oaks. Beech is a tolerant climax species. Some of the more important understory associates are buffalo nut *Pyrularia pubera*, blueberries *Vaccinium* spp., blackberries and dewberries *Rubus* spp., hobblebush *Viburnum alnifolium*, strawberry-bush *Euonymus americanus*, greenbriar *Smilax* spp., and dogwoods. Because of its thin bark and large surface roots, beech is highly vulnerable to fire. Several bark diseases and rot fungi damage and sometimes kill the tree. The most serious insect pest is the beech scale. Several defoliators occasionally damage beech. Beech is used for lumber, furniture, and containers. It is planted for shade and ornamental purposes. Beech is medium in humus building capacity. The nuts are eaten by a dozen or so songbirds, grouse, pheasant, turkey, rodents, and the mammals; white-tail deer browse the twigs, foliage and eat the nuts as well. The understory associated with beech types is valuable wildlife food and cover.

Fig. 105a. The smooth bark of beech is a challenge to woodland artists. (Miller Photo)

The largest living beech of record is 20 feet 6 inches in circumference, 55 feet high with a crown spread of 78 feet. It is growing in Jamaica Plain, Massachusetts. Another co-champion is 12 feet 9 inches in circumference, 144 feet high with a crown spread of 96 feet. It it is growing near Three Oaks, Michigan.

EUROPEAN BEECH *Fagus sylvatica* L. with fewer veins and larger teeth is frequently planted. There are several varieties, one of which has purple leaves.

42a.   Leaves green on both sides. Spiny fruit containing 2 or 4 nuts. Large trees. Fig. 106.

AMERICAN CHESTNUT ......*Castanea dentata* (Marsh.) Borkh.

Demise of the American chestnut resulting from the chestnut blight *Endothia parasitica* is one of the greatest botanical catastrophes within the memory of man. In the past 40 to 50 years, one of the most important American forest trees has been exterminated from its range. Ability to sprout vigorously from the stump has helped it exist in spite of continued attacks of the fungus. Where it may still occur in remote areas out of its normal range, it is a tall straight tree occasionally reaching 100 or more feet in height. It was a fast growing, long-lived tree. BARK: dark brown, broad flat ridges. LEAVES: coarsely serrate with pointed, sharp teeth, smooth and green on both sides. FLOWERS: monoecious, the long slender whitish catkins opening in mid-summer. Female, on the new wood,

Fig. 106. Castanea dentata.

rather inconspicuous. FRUIT: prickly bur, nuts 2 to 3 in each involucre, flattened on one or both sides, very sweet. TWIGS AND BUDS: twigs olive green tinged with yellow; buds, chestnut-brown, glabrous.

a   b

Fig. 106a-b. (a) Once a ruling monarch of the Blue Ridge, this remaining chestnut has but two living limbs. (b) Evidence of vigorous sprouting ability. Here are four separate series of sprouts originating from the roots of this chestnut stump. The largest living sprout is 5 inches d.b.h. and is not yet infected. (Miller Photos)

American chestnut was a tolerant tree of climax forest types occuring in the Appalachian Mountains and Ohio River valley. It was a source of income to people living within its range—bark for tanning, nuts for the table and as lumber is one of the most durable hardwoods. The many sound chestnut rail fences still standing are mute testimony to its durability. Even as "sound wormy" cut from the dead air seasoned trunks, it is still in great demand for cabinet wood. When present sprouts get large enough to bear fruit, it is eagerly taken by squirrel and other rodents. The foliage and twigs are browsed by white-tail deer. The largest living chestnut of record in 1964, was 15 feet 8 inches in circumference, 90 feet high with a crown spread of 64 feet. It is growing in Oregon City, Oregon—a long distance from its natural range which possibly accounts for its still being alive.

42b. Underside of leaves densely covered with white hairs. Spiny fruit producing only one nut. A shrub or small tree. Fig. 107.

ALLEGHENY CHINKAPIN ..*Castanea pumila* var. *pumila* Mill.

A small tree rarely reaching heights over 50 feet. It is round topped with slender spreading branches. The Ashe chinkapin,

Castanea pumila var. *ashei* Sudw., is a variety which occurs in the Coastal Plains portion of its range. (See map south of black line at "a".) BARK: light brown, tinged with red. LEAVES: 3 to 5 inches long; bright yellow-green above and silvery pubescent beneath. FLOWERS: monoecious; male in catkins eventually 4 to 6 inches long; female, on smaller catkins with some male flowers. FRUIT: a prickly bur 1 to 1 1/2 inches in diameter with single nut. TWIGS AND BUDS: grayish wooly.

Fig. 107. Castanea pumila.

The Allegheny chinkapin is an infrequent component of three major forest types and occurs on heavier, dry soils and moist flats. Understory species associated with it are dogwood, yaupon, hawthorn, blackberry *Rubus* spp. Common overstory tree species are post, black, bear, white and red oaks, hickory. It has a relatively thin bark and is susceptible to fire damage. It has the same insect pests as many of the hardwoods, defoliators, and bag worms. Fungi cause rot of the trunk. It is not too susceptible to the chestnut blight, probably because of its rare occurrence as compared with the chestnut. Commercially, it is used for posts and

occasionally ties. Although the fruit
is palatable, it occurs so infrequently
that it cannot make up any major
amount of the diet of the red and
fox squirrel.

The largest chinkapin living as of
record is 14 feet 3 inches in circumference, 43 feet high with a crown
spread of 45 feet. It is growing in
Daingerfield State Park, Texas.

Fig. 107a. Typical fruit of Allegheny
chinkapin. (Miller Photo)

43a. Lateral veins ending in only a part of the teeth or lobes. 44
43b. Lateral veins not ending in any of the marginal teeth ....
................................DOWNY SERVICEBERRY. See Fig. 151.
44a. Bark smooth, bluish-gray, with projecting ridges on the trunk
and larger branches. Staminate catkins not in evidence during
the winter. Fig. 108.

AMERICAN HORNBEAM ....*Carpinus caroliniana* Walt.

A bushy tree rarely over 40 feet high, with a short fluted trunk,
long slightly zigzag slender tough spreading branches pendulous
toward the ends. It is a slow growing long-lived tree. BARK: thin,
close, greenish-gray with heavy rounded ridges. LEAVES: ovate-
oblong, pointed, sharply double serrate, blue-green above, yellow-
green below, 2 to 4 inches long. FLOWERS: male catkins over 1
inch long; female catkins less than 1 inch long; styles scarlet.
FRUIT: single involucre-like bract; small ovate nut. BUDS: two
distinct sizes; both types somewhat angled; scales without evident
striations or lines.

It occurs in moist soils in the smaller creek bottoms and steep
slopes facing these bottoms. It is a very tolerant subclimax species
and occurs as an understory in hardwood mixtures. It is slow growing and short lived. It is associated with
northern red oak, sweetgum, mockernut hickory, bur oak, sugar maple
and basswood. In the understory,
it is associated with hophornbeam,
alder, redbud, sumac *Rhus* **spp.**, elder
Sambucus canadensis, and greenbriar
Smilax **spp**. Its thin bark makes it readily susceptible to fire. It does not have
any outstanding insect pests or fungus.
The wood is tough and when cut commercially is used for handle stock and
wedges. It is of secondary importance

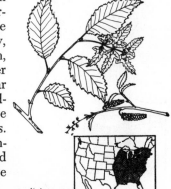

Fig. 108. Carpinus caroliniana.

to wildlife. Seeds, buds and catkins are eaten by grouse, pheasant and quail. A few songbirds eat the seeds. Squirrels and other rodents will eat the seeds and twigs and the foliage is browsed by white-tail deer. Two trees share the honors as to size, one is 7 feet 7 inches in circumference, 42 feet high with a crown spread of 30 feet. It is growing in the Great Smoky Mountains National Park in North Carolina. The other is also 7 feet 7 inches in circumference, 42 feet high but with a crown spread of 50 feet. It is growing in North Lawn Cemetery, Canton, Ohio.

44b. **Large branches without projecting ridges. Staminate catkins appearing in late summer and conspicuous throughout the winter** 45

45a. **Bark of trunk brownish, with fine scales and furrows. Usually twisted spirally, fruit hop-like. Fig. 109.**

EASTERN HOPHORNBEAM *Ostrya virginiana* (Mill.) K. Koch
A small tree, occasionally 40 to 50 feet tall, with a short trunk and long slender branches drooping at the end. In the open it develops a round crown. It has a medium rate of growth and is

Fig. 109. Ostrya virginiana.

Fig. 109a. Typical bark of eastern hophornbeam. (Miller Photo)

short lived. BARK: gray, shreddy appearing with shaggy plates curving away from trunk. LEAVES: dull yellow-green, lighter beneath, 3 to 5 inches long. FLOWERS: male catkins 2 inches long when unfolding; female catkins about 1/4 inch long. FRUIT: hoplike, seed enclosed in a bladdery elipsoid bag. BUDS: marked by fine longitudinal striations.

It occurs on a variety of sites ranging from moist, fertile soils to sandy sites. Hophornbeam is an intolerant species occurring as a minor understory component in three major subclimax forest types. It is associated with such tree species as sugar maple, beech, yellow birch, basswood, American elm and hickory. In the understory, it grows along with American hornbeam, redbud, alder, sumac *Rhus* **spp.**, elder *Sambucus canadensis*, bittersweet *Celastrus scandens*, and grape *Vitis* **spp**. It is susceptible to damage by fire. Insects and fungi are not too serious unless they occur in epidemic proportions. Its tough wood is used for handles and implements where strength is required but not demanding large diameter logs. Seeds are eaten by at least three species of songbirds, buds and catkins by grouse, seeds and buds by both red and fox squirrel. Whitetail deer browse on the twigs and foliage. Hophornbeam is not a valuable food tree for wildlife, rather the understory species with which it is associated are attractive.

The largest living hophornbeam of record is 9 feet 6 inches in circumference, 70 feet tall with a crown spread of 57 feet. It is growing near Winthrop, Maine.

45b. **Bark of various colors usually splitting into thin paper layers. Seeds numerous, borne in scaly catkins** **46**

THE BIRCHES: Genus BETULA

There are about 40 species of birches, widely distributed from the Arctic to the southern states. Several species have attractive white bark and are used for ornamental planting in the cooler climates. The foliage and twigs are browsed by moose, elk, whitetail and mule deer, as well as reindeer. Grouse eat the catkins and buds. Birches are rated high in humus building capacity.

46a. **Leaves with 9 to 11 pairs of veins; bark of twigs with wintergreen flavor; fruiting catkins sessile or nearly so** **47**

46b. **Leaves with 5 to 9 pairs of veins; bark or twigs usually bitter; fruiting catkins with stems** **48**

47a. Bark dark brown, not separating into layers; leaves heart-shaped or rounded at base, shining above. Fig. 110.

SWEET BIRCH ....*Betula lenta* L.

Sweet birch is a medium-sized tree with graceful somewhat hanging branches. It develops a long, clear bole reaching total heights of 50 feet or more. It has a moderate growth rate and is moderately long lived. BARK: dark brown with reddish tinge, thin; bark and leaves aromatic. LEAVES: dark green and dull above, lighter beneath, 3 to 6 inches long. FLOWERS: male catkins from previous summer, 3 to 4 inches long in bloom; female, about 3/4 inch long. FRUIT: cone-like, 1 to 1 1/2 inches long; bearing many seeds. TWIGS: slender, light reddish-brown; terminal buds absent, lateral buds lustrous, sharply pointed, chestnut brown, spurs numerous on old growth.

Fig. 110. Betula lenta.

Sweet birch occurs over a wide range of soils and altitudes. It makes its best growth in the moist protected northerly or easterly slopes throughout its range. Rarely, if ever, does sweet birch occur in pure stands. It is a minor component in 11 forest types. In these it is associated with white pine, northern red oak, white ash, hemlock, sugar maple, yellow birch, black cherry, basswood, yellow-poplar, and beech. in the understory it is associated with buffalo-nut *Pyrularia pubera*, elder *Sambucus canadensis*, blueberries *Vaccinium* **spp.**, mountain-laurel, rosebay rhododendron, mapleleaf viburnum *Viburnum acerifolium*, hobblebush *Viburnum alnifolium* and witherod *Viburnum cassinoides*.

Sweet birch is rated between intolerant and intermediate and is a minor species in both climax and subclimax types. It suffers from ice and snow damage in the northern portion of its range. Several fungi attack living sweet birch trees causing defective boles but rarely death. There are several leaf-feeding insects which infest sweet birch. Fire is highly damaging to sweet birch because of its thin bark. It is cut commercially for lumber, paneling and drugs. Due to its occasional abundance on rocky mountains in the northeast, it has been suggested that it may be valuable for soil protection. Seeds, buds, and catkins are eaten by grouse, prairie chicken and at least 7 species of songbirds; twigs and foliage browsed by white-tail and mule deer, elk and moose. Beaver and porcupine eat the bark and wood. Sweet birch, together with the common understory species, results in a valuable habitat for wildlife.

The largest living sweet birch of record is 15 feet 2 inches in circumference, 70 feet tall with a crown spread of 87 feet. It is growing near New Boston, New Hampshire.

47b. Bark yellow or silvery-white, separating into thin layers. Leaves dull above. Fig. 111.

YELLOW BIRCH ....*Betula alleghaniensis* Britton

Yellow birch is the most important member of the native birches. It is a medium-sized tree with a broad round topped crown up to 100 feet tall. The bole terminates in a wide spreading shallow root system. It is fast growing with a medium life span. BARK: young stems silvery-gray to orange, on old trunks reddish-brown. LEAVES: smooth, dull green, paler beneath, 2 to 5 inches long. FLOWERS: male catkins, when expanded 3 to 4 inches long; female about 3/4 inch long. FRUIT: erect, cone-like 1 to 1 1/2 inches long. TWIGS AND BUDS: twigs slender, yellowish-brown to dark brown, aromatic; buds acute but not sharp to the touch, often appressed along the lower half, often hairy.

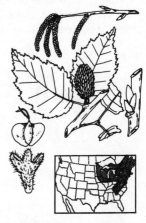

Fig. 111. *Betula alleghaniensis.*

Yellow birch occurs on a variety of sites, mostly on those of good moisture and in the southern portion of its range on steeper slopes but northerly in aspect. It is the most tolerant of the eastern birches and is a component of many subclimax associations. It does not occur pure, but is an integral member of three major forest types; in these it is associated with hemlock, sugar maple, beech, red spruce. It is an associate in 17 forest cover types, where it occurs with a large number of mixed hardwoods. Its typical understory associates are striped maple, mountain maple, hobblebush *Viburnum alnifolium,* American fly honeysuckle *Lonicera canadensis* and beaked hazel *Corylus cornuta.* The thin bark of young birch is highly flammable and rot may follow fire damage. Birches are subject to infestation by the bronze borer, two-leaf feeders, a skeletonizer, gypsy moth, and a sawfly. It is infected frequently by several species of fungi. It is girdled by mice, rabbits and porcupines. Yellow birch is cut commercially for lumber, flooring, paneling and cabinet work. Yellow birch sprouts are rated as a first quality deer browse; the buds and catkins are eaten by grouse and squirrel and at least 7 species of songbirds. This species with its typical understory is the heart of a high quality wildlife habitat. The largest living yellow birch of record is 14 feet 1 inch in circumference, 90 feet tall with a crown spread of 64 feet. It is growing in the Great Smoky Mountains National Park, Tennessee.

48a. Bark light reddish-brown. Fruiting catkins erect. Fig. 112.

RIVER BIRCH .... *Betula nigra* L.

River birch is the only member of the birches which occurs at low elevations in the south. It is a medium-size tree, 70 to 80 feet high. The trunk often divides 15 to 20 feet high into several arch-

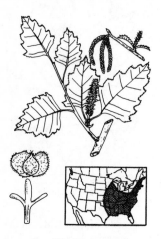

Fig. 112. *Betula nigra.*

ing branches. The branchlets are drooping. It makes rapid growth and is short lived. BARK: orange-red or greenish-brown, peeling in thin layers. LEAVES: dark green above, paler beneath, acute at both ends, irregularly serrate; 2 to 4 inches long. FLOWERS: male catkins when extended 2 to 3 inches long; female about 1/2 inch long, March, April. FRUIT: cone-like, 1 to 1 1/2 inches long, bearing many tiny winged nuts. Ripens in May or June. TWIGS AND BUDS: twigs reddish-brown, slender, usually pubescent; buds terminal lacking, laterals acute.

River birch is confined to the moist soils at the edge of creeks and rivers, often occurring in pure stands and con-

fined to a narrow strip. The species is widespread on sites within its range. It is a tree of medium tolerance occurring in subclimax types. It is a component of 4 major forest types where it is associated with sycamore, red maple, black willow, cottonwood, American elm, pecan, boxelder and sugarberry. Understory species common in these types are elder *Sambucus canadensis,* palmetto *Sabal minor,* possumhaw, sumac, poison ivy *Rhus radicans* and French mulberry *Callicarpa americana.*

The thin barked trunk with highly flammable papery scales is susceptible to fire. The usual insect enemies of birches attack river birch, bronze borer, leaf feeders, skeletonizer, gypsy moth and a sawfly. It is infected by several species of fungi. It is cut commercially for pulpwood, lumber and planted along stream banks for control of erosion. The seeds are eaten by at least 7 songbirds and several rodents. The southern beaver girdles the bole and white-tail deer browse the twigs and foliage of young sprout growth.

The largest living river birch of record is 13 feet 6 inches in circumference (2 feet from the ground), 85 feet tall with a crown spread of 95 feet. It is growing near Germantown, Pennsylvania.

48b. Bark of trunk and larger branches white; fruiting catkins hanging or spreading **49**

49a. Bark not easily separable into thin layers. Fig. 113.

GRAY BIRCH ....*Betula populifolia* Marsh.

Gray birch is the smallest of the northeastern tree birches. It attains a height of 40 feet. The bole is limby with a shallow root system. The crown is open and irregularly shaped. It is considered to be a fast growing, short-lived species. BARK: thin, chalk-white. LEAVES: shiny dark green, 2 1/2 to 3 inches long. FLOWERS: male catkins, 2 1/2 to 4 inches when expanded; female catkins about 1/2 inch long. FRUIT: cone-like about 3/4 inch long, producing many winged nutlets. TWIGS AND BUDS: twigs, slender, lenticels warty; buds terminal wanting, laterals ovoid, gummy.

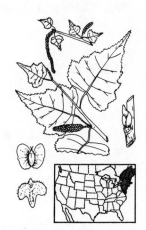

Fig. 113. Betula populifolia.

Gray birch occurs on the poorest of sterile soils principally on abandoned farmlands and burned over lands. It may pioneer in pure stands widely spaced on old farmlands. Usually it occurs with other primary species—red maple, eastern redcedar, pin cherry, paper birch, and quaking aspen. It is an intolerant pioneer. Understory species associated with gray birch are blueberries *Vaccinium* **spp.**, dewberry *Rubus* **spp.**, greenbriar *Smilax bona-nox,* and St. John's wort *Ascyrum* **spp.** Although it fol-

Fig. 113a. Pioneer gray birch on an abandoned rocky pasture in New England. (Miller Photo)

lows fire in succession, it is easily killed by fire due to its thin bark and shallow root system. It is subject to damage by the usual insect enemies of birch, the bronze borer, leaf skeletonizers, gypsy moth and sawfly. Several species of fungi, mostly polyphores, infect the bole. The catkins and seeds are taken by sharp-tailed and ruffed grouse, redpoll and pine siskin. Moose, hare, and white-tail deer browse the twigs and foliage. Porcupines and beavers eat the woody tissue. If the diameter is large enough, it is frequently cut for pulpwood.

The largest living gray birch of record is 7 feet 3 inches in circumference, 60 feet tall with a crown spread of 51 feet. It is growing near Clarksville, Maryland.

49b. Bark peeling into thin layers **50**

50a. Cultivated. Leaves of various forms. Twigs often hanging. Fig. 114.

EUROPEAN BIRCH .... *Betula pendula* Roth

Fig. 114. Betula pendula.

A medium-sized tree frequently reaching heights of 60 feet. Spreading branches, drooping. It is short lived and was originally imported from Europe as a cultivated species. BARK: chalky-white marked with black expanded lenticels. LEAVES: rather deeply cut with fine serrations, some varieties very much cut; 2 to 3 inches long. FLOWERS: staminate catkins clustered, sessile, 1 inch long, expanding to 3 inches, 1/8 inch thick; pistillate catkins, slender, cylindric, 1/2 inch long, May. FRUIT: numerous small winged seeds in cone-like bodies.

The European birch is suited for dry and poor soils as well as boggy sites. It is useful as a nurse tree for more valuable species.

50b. Leaves ovate. Scales of the catkins glabrous. Fig. 115.

PAPER BIRCH ....*Betula papyrifera* Marsh. var. *papyrifera*

Paper birch with its varieties has a transcontinental range. The varieties are primarily separated on the basis of range: *Betula papyrifera* **var.** *commutata* (Reg.) Fern., Western paper birch; *Betula papyrifera* **var.** *cordifolia* (Reg.) Fern., mountain paper birch, are the most common varieties.

It is a medium-sized tree, reaching heights of 50 to 75 feet. The crown is pyramidal and relatively open. The often curved bole ends in a shallow root system. BARK: smooth, creamy-white with long dark horizontal lenticels. LEAVES: dull dark green above, yellow-green beneath, 2 to 4 inches long. FLOWERS: male catkins, in winter 3/4 to 1 1/4 inches long, expanding to 4 inches long; female 1 to 1 1/4 inches long. FRUIT: about 1 1/2 inches long. TWIGS AND BUDS: twigs, slender, dull reddish-brown to orange-brown, lenticellate; buds, terminal lacking, lateral ovoid, acute, gummy and covered with chestnut brown scales.

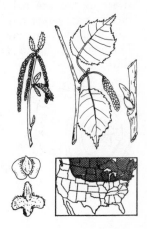

Fig. 115. Betula papyrifera.

Paper birch is a fast growing species with with a medium life span. It is a cold climate species and can tolerate wide variations in precipitation pattern. It makes its best growth on sandy, well drained soil, however, is common on shallow, stony soils and even in peat bogs. The variety *cordifolia* is found on bog soils more often than other varieties. Paper birch does occur in pure stands. It is however more often associated with white, red and black spruces, jack pine, balsam fir, white pine, yellow birch, beech and white ash. It is an integral component of 5 major forest types and a minor component of 23 eastern and 3 western types. It is an intolerant pioneer and in natural succession lasts but one generation, then replaced by more tolerant species. In the Lake States, it is a common temporary component of the climax White Spruce-Balsam Fir-Paper Birch Type. Understory species with which it is associated are blueberries *Vaccinium* **spp.**, hobblebush *Viburnum alnifolium,* bunchberry *Cornus canadensis,* dewberries *Rubus* **spp.**, wild lily-of-the-valley *Maianthemum canadense,* bearberry *Artostaphylos uva-ursi,* and moosewood *Dirca palustris.*

Mortality is heavy throughout the life of paper birch. It is so intolerant that crowding will result in death by suppression. If it makes it through the early years, it may be infested by the birch borer or forest tent caterpillar. Several rots are damaging. Fire, which is responsible for the establishment of many paper birch stands, is also one of the most serious enemies of established stands. Its thin bark and shallow root system is not adequate protection against heat. It is cut commercially for toothpicks, spools and other turned articles as well as pulpwood and is planted as an ornamental. The wildlife use is confined to northern species, among which are sharp-tailed, spruce, and ruffed grouse, which feed on catkins, buds and seeds; the redpoll and pine siskin on seeds; browsing and wood-eating animals such as moose, hares, porcupine and beaver. White-tail deer often browse young stands to the point of damage. Under-story species are palatable deer browse. The largest living paper birch (var. *papyrifera*) is 10 feet 11 inches in circumference, 96 feet high with a crown spread of 93 feet. It is growing at Lake Leelanau, Michigan. Paper birch is the State Tree of New Hampshire.

Fig. 116.

51a. Pith in cross-section five-angled, buds not stalked. Fig. 116 53

51b. Buds stalked, pith three-angled 52

THE ALDERS: Genus ALNUS

Most species of alder do not attain a size and shape which would make them desirable as commercial wood products. They do, how-ever, play an important role in the forest associations where they occur. Their contribution is similar to legumes in agriculture, as they are nitrogen-fixing plants. Where they are associated with ash, sweetgum, yellow-poplar, pine, spruce, sycamore, poplar and Douglas-fir, they substantially improve the growing environment. When growing in streamside zones, they contribute to cool water.

52a. Flowers occurring in fall, veins arching, pistillate catkins one to three in each bud. Fig. 117.

SEASIDE ALDER .... *Alnus maritima* (Marsh.) Muhl.

A small tree occasionally reaching 30 feet in height. Small spreading branches form a narrow, round topped crown. Has a straight bole. It grows rather fast and is short lived. BARK: thin, smooth, light brown tinged with gray. LEAVES: shining dark green with numerous pale glandular dots below. FLOWERS: catkins appear in July and mature in August or September. Pistillate, one to three in each bud. FRUIT: matures following midsummer, seeds nut-like. TWIGS AND BUDS: twigs, moderately stout, reddish or tinged with red; buds, stalked, dark red, scurfy pubescent.

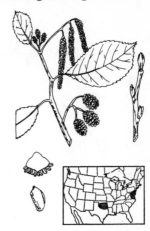

It occurs along banks of streams and ponds. Often in pure stands as a swamp. It may be associated with willows, river birch, sweetgum, and red maple as an understory component. In the understory, it is associated with button bush, greenbriar *Smilax* **spp.**, trumpet creeper *Campsis radicans*, honeysuckle *Lonicera japonica*, and hawthorn. It starts out as

Fig. 117. Alnus maritima.

a young seedling and sapling, moderately tolerant, becoming more intolerant with age. Alder is relatively free of insect damage, but occasionally tent caterpillars, sawflys and bark beetles damage the tree. Heart rot is not uncommon. Fire is damaging as it has a thin bark. Since the species rarely gets to commercial size, it is not commonly cut for lumber. In event it is taken, it is thrown in with other soft hardwoods being cut on the location. Alders get about the same wildlife usage as the birches to which they resemble in flowers and fruit. The seeds are taken by redpolls, siskins, and goldfinches. Buds and fruits are eaten by grouse. White-tail deer browse the twigs and foliage. Woodcock find the moist sites under alder productive worming areas.

The largest living seaside alder of record is 3 feet 6 inches in circumference, 78 feet high with a crown spread of 50 feet. It is growing in Rock Creek Park, Washington, D. C.

52b. **Flowers occurring in spring, several pistillate catkins in each bud, lateral veins straight. Fig. 118.**

EUROPEAN ALDER ....*Alnus glutinosa* (**L.**) Gaertn.

Introduced from Europe and Africa. Has a rounded crown and reaches heights of 70 feet. The young growth is very glutinous. The dark foliage remains green until late autumn. It grows well in swampy soils. BARK: gray, lightly furrowed. LEAVES: 2 to 5 inches long, glabrous dull dark green above. FLOWERS: male catkins, 2 to 3 inches long; female 1/2 inch long. FRUIT: cone-like with many wingless seeds.

' Occurs mostly in the same range as seaside alder on the east coast. Although it was originally imported for charcoaling, it is now used for ornamental and wet land plantings. Prior to plastics, its wood was used for spools, wooden shoes and wooden ware. The largest living European alder of record is 5 feet 8 inches in circumference, 69 feet high with a crown spread of 47 feet. It is growing in Morton Arboretum, Lisle, Illinois.

Fig. 118. Alnus glutinosa.

52c. Flowers appearing in spring; bark with prominent linear transverse whitish lenticels. Fig. 119.

SPECKLED ALDER ....*Alnus rugosa* (Du Roi) Spreng.

A small spreading tree, more often a shrub with many stems. When growing in a tree form, it attains heights of 25 to 30 feet. It is fast growing and short lived. BARK: brown to blackish-gray

marked with whitish linear lenticels up to 1/4 inch long. LEAVES: 2 to 4 inches long, finely and regularly serrulate, green beneath and pubescent on the veins. FLOWERS: male catkins 1 to 1 1/2 inches long; female 1/2 inch long. FRUIT: cone-like on thick stalks or sessile. TWIGS AND BUDS: twigs nearly glabrous,, stipules oval; buds with 2 or 3 subequal scales.

Occurs along stream banks and on margins of ponds. Often in pure stands in swamps. It is intolerant and grows in association with hazel alder, red-osier dogwood, several willows and red maple. In the understory, it is associated with green-brier *Smilax* **spp.**, cranberry *Vaccinium* **spp.**, hawthorn, and buttonbush. Alder is

Fig. 119. Alnus rugosa.

relatively free of insect pests. Occasionally bagworms and tent caterpillars will defoliate several of the trees in a stand. Some species of *Fomes* cause rot in the stems. Fire is damaging as it has a thin bark. Since it usually is below commercial sizes it is not an important timber tree. Its greatest contribution is probably the shade it affords trout streams, thus keeping temperatures down. The moist sites on which speckled alder grows is good feeding grounds for woodcock as worms seem to be plentiful. Fruits are eaten by grouse and deer browse the twigs and foliage.

The largest living speckled alder is 2 feet 6 inches in circumference, 50 feet high with a crown spread of 23 feet. It is growing along the Holland-Ottawa Beach Road, Ottawa County, Michigan.

52d. Flowers occurring in spring, lenticels on bark either obscure or dark and short. Fig. 120.

HAZEL ALDER .... *Alnus serrulata* (Ait.) Willd.

Is a small shrubby species closely resembling speckled alder. It does reach heights of 30 feet in the southern portion of its range. Like the other shrubby alder, it grows fast but is short lived.

BARK: brown, marked by dark short lenticels. LEAVES: 2 to 4 inches long, simply serrulate with a wavy margin. FLOWERS: male catkins 1 to 1 1/2 inches long; female 1/2 inch long. FRUIT: cone-like, scales persistent, short stalked or sessile. TWIGS AND BUDS: twigs nearly glabrous, stipules oval; buds with 2 or 3 subequal scales, more ovoid and smaller than speckled alder.

Occurs along streams, ponds and frequently grows in pure stands in swamps and low wet areas. It is intolerant and grows in association with red maple, willows, swamp cottonwood, and river birch. Understory associates are buttonbush, greenbriar *Smilax* **spp.**, roughleaf dog-

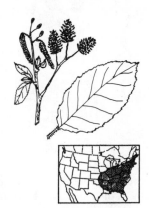

Fig. 120. Alnus serrulata.

wood, hawthorn, planertree, trumpet creeper *Campsis radicans,* and morning-glory *Ipomoea* **spp.** Hazel alder is relatively free of insect damage. Bag worms and tent caterpillars frequently defoliate. *Fomes* are troublesome rot producers. Fire is damaging as the species has thin bark. It is usually too small to be considered a timber tree. It shades streams, thus holding down water temperatures. In the southern portion of its range, wintering songbirds eat the fruits and buds. Woodcock winters in Louisiana and other southern states near alder thickets for the earthworms found there. White-tail deer browse the twigs and foliage. The largest living hazel alder of record is 1 foot 5 inches in circumference, 40 feet tall with a crown spread of 22 feet. It is growing near Shreve, Wayne County, Ohio.

52c. Flowers occurring in spring, bark roughened by minute wart-like excrescences. Growing on the west coast. Fig. 121.

RED ALDER ....*Alnus rubra* Bong.

Red alder is essentially a coastal species rarely found more than 75 miles inland. It is the most important single hardwood in the northwest. Although it is dwarfed in size by the towering conifers with which it is associated, it is still a good sized tree ranging from

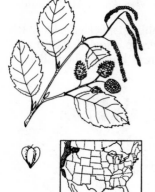

Fig. 121. Alnus rubra.

80 to 130 feet in height. In dense stands it develops a clear, symmetrical slightly tapered bole, with a shallow spreading root system. Open grown trees often have a crown extending to the ground. It is fast growing and short lived. BARK: grayish-white to blue-gray at the surface on large trees breaking up into large flat plates; inner bark bright reddish-brown. LEAVES: 3 to 6 inches long, doubly serrate, dark green and glabrous above, paler and rusty pubescent on the midrib and principal veins below. FLOWERS: preformed, the male catkins 1 1/4 to 1 1/2 inches long. FRUIT: cone-like, long stalked, 1/2 to 1 1/4 inches long. TWIGS AND BUDS: slender, bright red to reddish-brown, somewhat 3-angled on fast growing shoots; terminal buds 1/3 to 2/3 inch long, stalked, covered by 2 or 3 red, scurfy pubescent scales; lateral slightly smaller.

Red alder grows in a humid and superhumid climate on soils varying from gravel and sand to clay. Alder contributes both to physical and chemical improvement of soil. Its litter decomposes rapidly forming a mull humus with subsequent improvement in soil structure. It is capable of nitrogen fixation by organisms contained in the root nodules. Best stands of alder occur below 1500 feet elevation. It occurs pure or predominant and is a major component in four forest types. Pure stands are confined to lower elevations and stream-bottoms, flats and lower slopes. Associated with red alder are Sitka spruce *Picea sitchensis,* western hemlock *Tsuga heterophylla,* white spruce, birch, black cottonwood *Populus trichocarpa,* and several willows *Salix* **spp.** There is a well developed understory in which typical species are Pacific red elder *Sambucus* *callicarpa,* blackbead elder *S. melanocarpa,* blueberry elder *S. cerulea,* salmonberry *Rubus spectabilis,* American devilsclub *Oplopanax horridus,* rusty menziesia *Menziesia ferruginea,* red whortleberry *Vaccinium parvifolium,* creambush *Holodiscus discolor,* and vine maple *Acer circinatum.*

Alder is an intolerant pioneer species. When growing in pure stands, most trees that fail to make the dominant and codominant crown classes quickly die. Damage by fire is unusual because dry inflammable debris is scarce under a red alder stand. The bark, though thin, is sufficiently fire resistant to protect the tree from light surface fires. Often red alder serves as a fire break to protect adjacent conifer stands from fire damage. During its early years, 40 years or so, it is exceptionally free from disease and other damaging agents. White heart rot and cankers do attack young trees causing deformation and stunted growth. Tent caterpillars, sawflies, beetles and borers likewise kill weakened trees. Red alder is the leading commercial hardwood of the Pacific Northwest, being used principally for furniture stock. Except for browsing on twigs and foliage by deer and elk, red alder itself is not an outstanding wildlife species but the understory species with which it is associated are.

The largest living red alder of record is 13 feet 9 inches in circumference, 92 feet tall with a crown spread of 54 feet. It is growing in Polk County, Oregon.

53a. **Leaves with sharply pointed even teeth; fruit prickly, enclosing one or more nuts. CHESTNUT, ETC. See Figs. 106 and 107.**

53b. **Fruit an acorn (nut with cup-like base). Leaves round lobed or sharp lobed or entire with bristle tip at end of leaf and lobes. Staminate flowers in catkins. Fig. 122 ....54**

53c. **Trees not as in 53a or 53b 76**

THE OAKS: Genus QUERCUS

Oaks are a widely distributed and variable group. In the eastern portion of the United States they are the most common component of hardwood types. The "Checklist of trees of the United States" lists 58 native species, 1 naturalized and 69 accepted hybrids. Oaks are basic to high quality, multiple species, wildlife habitat. The fact that the acorns of white oaks mature in one season, while those of red oaks take two seasons, provides a partial "built in" protection against total mast failure in any one year. They display some of the most brilliant autumn color. Most of the oaks produce valuable wood products. Scarlet oak was one of the first invaders of chestnut sites as that species disappeared from blight. Oaks of the white group are rated medium in humus building capacity, those of the black group, low.

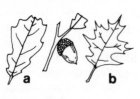

Fig. 122.

54a. Leaves or their lobes bristle tipped; acorns maturing at end of second season; cups lined with silky hairs. THE RED OAKS. Fig. 122b 55

54b. Leaves and their lobes rounded without bristle tips; acorns ripening the first year; cups without silky hairs. THE WHITE OAKS. Fig. 122a 67

55a. Leaves entire, oblong or lanceolate; 3 to 6 times as long as wide. Fig. 123 56

55b. Leaves more or less deeply lobed on sides. Fig. 122b 61

55c. Leaves wider above the middle, often with 3 to 5 lobes on this outer region 59

56a. Leaves pubescent or tomentose on underside 57

56b. Leaves glabrous 58

57a. Leaves dark green, pubescent below. Fig. 123.

SHINGLE OAK ....*Quercus imbricaria* Michx.

Shingle oak is a medium-sized tree with a handsome rounded crown often reaching heights of 75 to 100 feet. Its rate of growth is medium with medium longevity. BARK: dark brown to nearly black; on trunk, deeply fissured. LEAVES: narrow, oblong, thickish, smooth and shining above; downy beneath. Entire, 3 to 6 inches long, spine at tip. Turn brown and remain on tree during the winter. FLOWERS: male, long yellowish catkins in early spring; female, green, small. FRUIT: solitary acorns, or 2 to 3 together, stemmed, nut brown about 1/2 inch long and 1/3 enclosed in the flatish cup of small scales, reddish-brown, matures the second season. TWIGS AND BUDS: twigs slender, dark green to greenish-brown, glabrous; buds, terminal

Fig. 123. Quercus imbricaria.

1/8 inch long, sharp pointed, covered with pubescent light brown scales; lateral, similar but smaller.

Shingle oak occurs on a variety of sites ranging from the dry uplands and ridges to moist soils along streams and hillsides. It is associated with southern red, scarlet and live oaks, but reaches its best development in composition with pin, willow and overcup oaks. It is of medium tolerance and when occurring on dry sites, it is probably in a climax association. On moist sites, however, it is subclimax. Wherever it occurs, it does not make up a major portion of the composition. The variable understory on dry sites is composed of hawthorn, blackberry *Rubus* **spp.**, sumac *Rhus* **spp.**, greenbriar *Smilax* **spp.**; on the moist sites, honeysuckle *Lonicera japonica*, poison ivy *Rhus radicans*, elder *Sambucus canadensis*. Fire is a serious hazard to the thin barked shingle oak. Insects and disease are not too harmful. When cut for lumber, it goes along with the other "red oaks" being cut from the same area. The acorn is small enough to be attractive to turkey and squirrels. Quail, if on the same range, will eat acorn pieces from squirrel feeding but the nut is just a little large for quail to take without some form of reduction. When grown along rivers, waterfowl, mallard and woodduck mostly eat the acorns during overflow. Deer find the acorns palatable.

The largest living shingle oak of record is 18 feet 1 inch in circumference, 80 feet high with a crown spread of 80 feet. It is growing in Wayne County, Ohio.

57b. Leaves pale bluish-green, white, tomentose below. Fig. 124.

BLUEJACK OAK .... *Quercus incana* Bartr.

Bluejack oak is a small tree with irregular crown usually 15 to 20 feet in height. The thick rigid branchlets are coated at first with a dense hoary tomentum of fascicled hairs, soon becoming glabrous. It is slow growing and short lived. BARK: to 1 1/2 inches thick, covered with square blackish scales 1 to 2 inches long. LEAVES: 2 to 5 inches long; rarely 3-lobed at apex. FLOWERS: staminate catkins 2 to 3 inches long, red and yellow. FRUIT: very abundant, nut 1/2 inch long. BUDS: ovoid, acute, with numerous rather loosely imbricated bright chestnut-brown scales ciliate on the margins, often 1/4 inch long, born on vigorous branches.

Fig. 124. Quercus incana.

Blujack oak occurs on sandy barrens and dry upland ridges in the Coastal Plains. It is intolerant and grows in sparse stands where shade is not a problem. Where it occurs it is the size of other understory species. Types in which it occurs are transitional, follow fire, heavy grazing, or heavy cutting. It occurs in three forest cover types where it is associated with longleaf pine, turkey oak, southern red oak, persimmon and hickory. Understory species are yaupon, American beauty berry *Callicarpa americana,* hawthorn, and lance-leaf greenbrier *Smilax smallii.* Due to the lack of moisture on sites occupied by bluejack, there is not a great development of understory vegetation.

There are no significant insect or fungi enemies of bluejack oak. Fire used year after year in the same area for control of understory vegetation or production of grass will eventually eliminate bluejack oak. There is little commercial use made of this species, occasionally it is cut for temporary fence posts. Its greatest contribution is acorns for the wildlife living in this bleak environment. It bears prolifically each year. Within a quail range it is a valuable food supply. Fox squirrel will visit the trees and eat the acorns but are messy eaters and many small crumbs of the acorn are left—these are taken by quail. White-tail deer also eagerly eat bluejack acorns.

The largest bluejack living and of record is 6 feet 2 inches in circumference, 51 feet high with a crown spread of 52 feet. It is growing near Fairfield, Texas.

58a. Leaves lanceolate, green on both sides, falling in autumn. Fig. 125.

WILLOW OAK ....*Quercus phellos* **L.**

Willow oak is a medium-sized tree, 80 to 100 feet high. Open grown trees are very distinctive with dense oval crowns and bright

green leaves. Forest grown trees are less developed but still have a full rounded crown. It makes moderately rapid growth on good sites and is long lived. On poor waterlogged sites, it goes to pieces rather rapidly. BARK: reddish-brown, somewhat roughened. LEAVES: shiny and light green above, paler and sometimes pubescent beneath, 2 1/2 to 5 inches long. FLOWERS: male catkins 2 to 3 inches long; female, small with bright red stigmas. FRUIT: sessile or short stocked acorns, 1/2 inch or less in length, single or in pairs, rarely 3's. TWIGS AND BUDS: twigs, slender, glabrous, red to reddish-brown; buds, terminal 1/8 inch long,

Fig. 125. Quercus phellos.

sharp pointed covered by chestnut-brown scales paler on the margin, lateral, similar but smaller.

Willow oak grows on many alluvial sites. Its growth rate and quality are affected by soil and site factors. Site quality decreases from the higher to the lower topographic positions. On upland flats with poor drainage willow oak is usually of poor quality. It is an important tree in two forest types, where it is associated with laurel oak, sweetgum, and Nuttall oak. It is a minor component in four other types where it is associated with loblolly pine, overcup, cherrybark oak, sugarberry, American elm, green ash and water hickory. Typical understory species found in these types are swamp privet *Forestiera acuminata*, roughleaf dogwood, hawthorn, American hornbeam, greenbriar *Smilax* **spp**. and buttonbush.

Willow oak is intolerant but responds well to release if not too long suppressed. It is a subclimax species. It is highly susceptible to damage by fire. Seedlings and saplings are easily killed and mature trees are scarred, resulting in rot entering the bole. Bark and trunk borers do considerable damage as do occasional twig galls. Trunk cankers and heart rot are common. Acorns are subject to weevil damage. Lumber cut from willow oak goes in the trade along with red oak. Due to its dense crown and bright green leaves, it is planted widely as a shade tree. It is especially valuable as squirrel, deer, and turkey food. During overflow, mallard and woodducks feed on the acorns. Quail can eat the small acorns as well as several songbirds.

The largest living willow oak of record is 21 feet 2 inches in circumference, 118 feet high with a crown spread of 106 feet. It is growing in Queenstown, Eastern Shore, Maryland.

58b. Leaves usually widest at upper half, falling in late winter. Fig. 126.

LAUREL OAK ....*Quercus laurifolia* Michx.

Laurel oak is a medium-sized tree, rarely attaining heights in excess of 90 feet. It has a dense round topped crown. Laurel oak grows rapidly and matures in about 50 years, a short-lived species. Its rapid growth, however, makes it valuable as an ornamental. BARK: deeply ridged and dark. LEAVES: 3 to 4 inches long; shiny green above, less shiny and paler below. FLOWERS: male catkins 2 to 3 inches long; stigmas of female flowers dark red. FRUIT: mostly solitary, sessile or nearly so; flat saucer-shaped cup; nut nearly black, 1/2 inch long. TWIGS AND BUDS: twigs, slender, dark red, glabrous; buds, terminal 1/10 to 1/8 inch long, acute, covered with lustrous red-brown scales; lateral buds similar but smaller.

Laurel oak usually occupies well drained, sandy soil with good water capacity. It occurs along the edges of rivers swamps and in rainwater flats that are only rarely flooded. Occasionally it moves into dry sandy ridges. It is the key species in one major forest cover type and an associate in ten others.

Its principal associates are willow, Nuttall, live and scrub oaks, longleaf pine, loblolly pine, baldcypress and water tupelo. It is one of the more tolerant oaks and occurs in a large number of transitional and subclimax hardwood and pine-hardwood types. Growing as it does in good moisture conditions, the understory is made up of a large number of species such as Virginia sweetspire *Itea virginica,* swamp cyrilla, sweet pepper bush *Clethra alnifolia,* dahoon, possumhaw, and two greenbriars *Smilax walteri* and S. *laurifolia.*

Fig. 126. Quercus laurifolia.

Laurel oak is highly susceptible to damage by fire. The thin bark is killed by even light ground fires. Heart rots are common in areas subjected to fire. Not much is known about the diseases and insects harmful to laurel oak. It is, however, an alternate host for the fusiform rust of southern pine. The alternate stage does not harm the oak host. When there was a market for fuel wood, it was cut for that purpose. Its principal use now is a shade tree for which it is admirably suited, with rapid growth and a dense rounded crown. The small acorn is eagerly taken by waterfowl, turkey, quail, songbirds, rodents and other mammals; the twigs and foliage by whitetail deer.

The largest living laurel oak of record is 14 feet 3 inches in circumference, 69 feet high with a crown spread of 77 feet. It is growing in Brookgreen Gardens, South Carolina.

59a. Leaves shed in their first autumn or winter **60**

59b. Leaves retained until their second summer or autumn. Fig. 127.

MYRTLE OAK ....*Quercus myrtifolia* Willd.
   A small round topped tree rarely over 40 feet in height. Short or rarely long spreading branches and slender branchlets. Frequently intricately branched as a shrub. Is slow growing and short lived. BARK: smooth, dark, thin. LEAVES: shining dark green above, yellow-green to orange-brown below, 1/2 to 2 inches long, rusty hairs in the axils of the veins. FLOWERS: whitish pubescent

catkins about 1 1/2 inches long, stamens 2 or 3. FRUIT: solitary or in pairs, 1/4 to 1/2 inch long in saucer-shaped cup. TWIGS AND BUDS: twigs, red or dark gray pubescent during first year becoming darker and glabrous; buds, with closely imbricated dark chestnut-brown puberulous scales.

Myrtle oak occurs on dry sandy ridges except when it is associated with cabbage palmetto next to marshes. It is a moderately tolerant species of transitional and subclimax forest types. It is a minor component of 5 forest cover types. In these it is associated with sand pine, longleaf pine, scrub, blackjack, sand live, and laurel oaks. It is one of the chief associates with sand pine in the "Big Scrub" in Florida. The understory species in the types are variable; yaupon, dune holly, gallberry *Ilex glabra*, wax myrtle *Myrica pumila* and sumac Rhus **spp**. It does not have

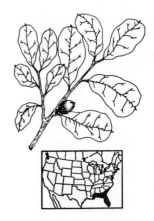

Fig. 127. Quercus myrtifolia.

any significant insect or fungi pests. Fire damages the thin bark, often killing the tree. It is a non-commercial species. The acorn is taken by wild turkey, deer and squirrel. Where quail are present, they will use the acorn pieces dropped by rodents. The large number of other scrub oak associates in the sand pine type make it a valuable deer range. They seem to bear acorns in abundance.

The largest myrtle oak living of record is 3 feet 7 inches in circumference, 21 feet high with a crown spread of 36 feet. It is growing in Ft. Clinch State Park, Florida.

60a. Leaves wedge-shaped at base, variable. Fig. 128.

WATER OAK ....*Quercus nigra* **L.**

Water oak is a medium-sized tree up to 60 to 70 feet in height with a tall slender bole and symmetrical rounded crown. It is rapid growing with moderate longevity. BARK: light brown, rather smooth but eventually with rough, wide scaly ridges. LEAVES: dull bluish-green, paler below, size variable, but usually 2 to 4 inches long. Margin may be entire, 3-lobed or pinnately lobed. FLOWERS: male catkins, 2 to 3 inches long; stigmas of female flowers red. FRUIT: solitary or paired, nut 1/2 inch long, black, often striate, minutely tomentose, resting in a thin saucer-like cup. TWIGS AND BUDS: twigs, slender, dull red, glabrous; buds, ter-

minal 1/8 to 1/4 inch long, sharp pointed with reddish-brown
scales; lateral, similar but smaller.

Water oak grows on a variety of bottomland soils and on some
upland sites. Upland trees are usually
defective and of poor quality. Best
sites are alluvial bottoms on silty or
loamy better drained ridges. It is a
component of 7 forest cover types. The
principal associates in these types are
loblolly, longleaf and slash pines, mixed
hardwoods, chestnut and cherrybark
oaks, sweetgum, pecan, American elm
and sugarberry. Understory species are
variable but include swamp privet
Forestiera acuminata, roughleaf dogwood, hawthorn, American hornbeam,
possumhaw, trumpet creeper *Campsis
radicans,* and greenbriar *Smilax* spp.

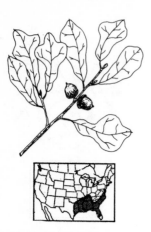

Fig. 128. Quercus nigra.

Water oak is an intolerant subclimax
species. Growth is limited by fire, insects and disease. It is very susceptible
to fire at all ages. A number of insects attack water oak, the most
damaging are bark scarrers and trunk borers. Trunk canker and
heart rot cause cull in commercial products. The small acorns are
eagerly taken by squirrel, turkey, quail, deer and songbirds. In
overflow bottomland sites, mallards, pintails and wooducks feed
on the acorns. Water oak is widely planted as a shade tree.

The largest water oak living and of record is 20 feet 3 inches in
circumference, 77 feet tall, with a crown spread of 100 feet. It is
growing near Center, Texas.

**60b. Leaves rounded at the base with brown tufts of hairs on
underside. Fig. 129.**

BLACKJACK OAK ....*Quercus marilandica* Muenchh.

Blackjack oak is a small poorly formed tree rarely reaching
heights over 30 to 40 feet. The crown is composed of short stout
contorted branches giving it an irregular appearance. It is slow
growing and short lived. BARK: nearly black and deeply ridged.
LEAVES: variable, 5 to 7 inches long, shallowly 3-lobed at apex,
thick and dark green above, yellowish pubescence below. FLOW-
ERS: male catkins, hairy 2 to 4 inches long; female, hairy with dark
red stigmas. FRUIT: 3/4 inch long, about half enclosed in thick
bowl-shaped cup with loose reddish-brown scales. TWIGS AND
BUDS: twigs, stout, scurfy-pubescent; buds, rusty, wooly.

Blackjack oak is characteristic of dry sterile soils where it is associated with a variety of pine and hardwoods. Usually occurring in open mixtures, it is an intolerant oak and a component of transitional and subclimax types. In 11 forest types its principal associates are post, black and southern red oaks, mockernut hickory, redcedar, longleaf and loblolly pines. Understory species vary widely; some of the more comon are yaupon, hawthorn, gallberry *Ilex glabra,* dwarf huckleberry *Gaylussacia dumosa* and bluejack oak. It rarely attains commercial sizes, so if not cut for fuel, it has very little commercial value. It withstands fire rather well, due to its thick bark. Insects and fungi do not appear to damage blackjack to any significant degree. It is a valuable wildlife species

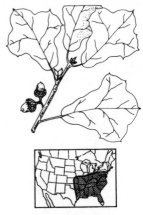

Fig. 129. Quercus marilandica.

in many of the sites where it occurs. Due to its moderate resistance to fire, it is about the only mast producing hardwood left where fire is used in pine types for understory control. Acorns from blackjack, together with the herbaceous understory resulting from the fire, provide a rather valuable wildlife environment. Turkey, deer, and squirrel find the habitat favorable to their needs on blackjack sites.

The largest blackjack oak living and of record is 11 feet 6 inches in circumference, 47 feet high with a crown spread of 76 feet. It is growing near Wakita, Oklahoma.

61a. Leaves whitish or grayish on underside 62

61b. Leaves green on both sides 63

62a. Leaves 3 to 11 deeply lobed, large tree. Fig. 130.

SOUTHERN RED OAK ....*Quercus falcata* Michx. **var.** *falcata*

Southern red oak is one of the common upland southern oaks. It is a medium-sized tree reaching heights of 80 to 90 feet, with a deep root system and a short bole and rounded crown. Its rate of growth is considered medium for average longevity. BARK: broadly ridged, pale to darker brown. LEAVES: 5 to 9 inches long, shape either shallowly 3-lobed at apex or more or less deeply 5 to 7 lobed; the terminal lobe much longer than the laterals; shiny dark green above and with pale or rusty pubescence beneath. FLOWERS: male, hairy catkins 3 to 5 inches long; female, pubescent with dark red stigmas. FRUIT: solitary or paired, nut 1/2 inch long, orange-brown, sometimes striate, enclosed 1/3 or less in a thin shallow cup. TWIGS AND BUDS: twigs, dark red, pubescent; buds, terminal 1/8 to 1/4 inch long, acute reddish-brown; lateral, similar but smaller.

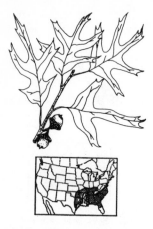

Southern red oak is characteristically an upland tree occurring on dry sandy or clay soils. Along streams and fertile bottoms it attains its best growth. Southern red oak is found in 13 forest cover types. It is a major component of two types where it is associated with Virginia and shortleaf pines. It is also associated with loblolly pine, beech, southern magnolia, scarlet oak, sweetgum, black gum and several hick-

Fig. 130. Quercus falcata.

ories. Understory species found in these types are such as azalea *Rhododendron* **spp.**, sweetshrub *Calycanthus floridus*, dogwood, blackberry *Rubus* **spp.**, greenbriar *Smilax* **spp.**, sweetleaf *Symplocos* **spp.**, and sumac *Rhus* **spp.** Southern red oak is intermediate in tolerance and is a member of transitional and subclimax forest types. It is susceptible to fire because of its thin bark. Cankers and rot are common and it is susceptible to oak wilt. Trees attacked by this fungus may die within a month or two after the first symptoms become visible. It is cut for flooring lumber and used widely in the southeast as a shade tree. The acorns are eaten by deer, turkey, squirrel, quail and many songbirds.

The largest living southern red oak of record is 22 feet 1 inch in circumference, 90 feet tall with a crown spread of 115 feet. It is growing in Como, Mississippi.

62b.   Leaves 5 to 11 lobed, but more shallowly than in 62a. Fig. 131.

CHERRYBARK OAK ....*Quercus falcata* **var.** *pagodaefolia* Ell.

Cherrybark oak is a more massive tree than southern red oak. It often attains heights of 100 to 130 feet. It is fast growing and reaches ages of 90 to 120 years in vigorous condition. BARK: smooth, soon with narrow, flaky or scaly ridges. LEAVES: more uniformly lobed than southern red oak, not so variable. FLOWERS: similar to southern red oak. FRUIT: similar to southern red oak.

Except for the leaves and bark, cherrybark oak closely resembles southern red oak. It is considerably different in growth habits and site. Cherrybark oak occurs widely on best loamy sites in the first bottoms and well drained terraces of the major rivers of the South. It has an excellent growth rate. It is intolerant and occurs in two major forest cover types. It is the major component in Swamp Chestnut Oak-Cherrybark Oak Type, where it is associated with other oaks, white ash, hickories, blackgum, southern magnolia and yellow-poplar. With a preponderance of tolerant species, the type is considered to be climax. Typical understory species are about the same as for southern red oak on the moister sites. The wildlife value is the same, as cherrybark oak is a good producer of

Fig. 131. Quercus falcata var. pagodaefolia.

acorns. It is cut widely for flooring and other lumber. It, like southern red oak, is suceptible to fire. It has the same insect and fungus pests.

The largest living cherrybark oak of record is 24 feet 1 inch in circumference, 110 feet tall with a crown spread of 80 feet. It is growing near Cumberstone, Maryland.

62c. Small tree 18 to 20 feet high. Leaves usually with 5 lobes. Fig. 132.

BEAR OAK .... *Quercus ilicifolia* Wangenh.

Bear oak is a small tree occasionally 18 to 20 feet high with slender spreading branches forming a round topped head. It is slow growing and short lived. BARK: dark brown, smooth, thin. LEAVES: shiny dark green above, pale beneath turning yellow to scarlet in the fall; 2 to 5 inches long. FLOWERS: male catkins, red or greenish, 4 to 5 inches long; female flowers red. FRUIT: acorns born in pairs and very numerous, 1/2 inch long and enclosed for about half its length in a cup abruptly enlarged above the stalk-like base. TWIGS AND BUDS: twigs, wooly; buds, about 1/8 inch long, dark chestnut-brown.

Bear oak occurs on dry sites within its range. It is pure or predominant in but one forest type. It is associated with pitch, white and shortleaf pines, chinkapin, scarlet oak, black oak, black locust, red maple, and sassafras. Understory species: dwarf chinkapin oak

Quercus prinoides, blackberry *Rubus* **spp.,** blueberry *Vaccinium* **spp.,** and hawthorn. Bear oak is intolerant and temporary following heavy cutting and repeated fire. It has no commercial value. It is not particularly susceptible to insects or fungi. With its thin bark, it is susceptible to fire damage. Deer, turkey, and rodents make good use of the mast.

The largest bear oak living and of record is 4 feet in circumference, 60 feet tall with a crown spread of 75 feet. It is growing in the Dawes Arboretum, Newark, Ohio.

Fig. 132. Quercus ilicifolia.

63a.   Leaves usually dull on upper side; 7 to 11 lobes. Acorns large, cup 3/4 to 1 inch across. Fig. 133.

NORTHERN RED OAK .... *Quercus rubra* **L.**

Northern red oak usually grows to be 70 to 100 feet tall. Under forest conditions, it prunes up well and develops a columnar bole. In the open, it tends to have a short bole and bushy crown. It is rapid

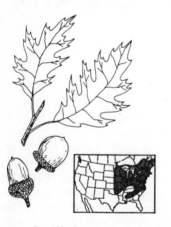

growing and moderately long lived. BARK: smooth on young stems and upper portion of bole, otherwise dark gray and roughened. LEAVES: 4 to 8 inches long, margin with 7 to 11 toothed lobes, dark green above, paler beneath. FLOWERS: male catkins, pubescent, 4 to 5 inches long; female, flowers with red scales and stigmas, appears in May and June. FRUIT: solitary or paired, short stalked, ripening second year, nut 1/2 to 1 inch long in either deep narrow or flat saucer-shaped cup, covered with reddish scales. TWIGS AND BUDS: twigs, moderately stout, greenish-brown to reddish-

Fig. 133. Quercus rubra.

brown, glabrous; buds, red to reddish-brown, the scales near the tip silky.

Northern red oak grows in soils ranging from clay to loamy sands and from deep stone-free to shallow rocky soils. Positions on the slope are important in favoring growth of red oak. Northerly and easterly aspects when accompanied by good soil conditions are good sites. Northern Red Oak is the type name for pure stands of this tree or when it is predominant. It is a major associate in 5 forest types where it is in composition with white pine, white ash, basswood, mockernut hickory, sweetgum, yellow-poplar, white oak. In addition it occurs in 20 other types. Tree associates of red oak are very numerous; they include 4 ashes, 2 aspens, 3 birches, 2 cherries, 3 elms, 2 firs, 5 hickories, 3 maples, at least 12 oaks, 7 pines, 2 spruces and many more single species. Some of the important but variable understory species are flowering dogwood, redbud, service-berry, greenbrier *Smilax* **spp.**, hydrangea *Hydrangea arborescens,* rosebay rhododendron, mountain-laurel, witch-hazel, hobblebush *Viburnum alnifolium* and many others. Some of the trees and shrubs associated with northern red oak are most colorful in spring when in flower and again in fall with brilliant foliage. Northern red oak is intermediate in tolerance and is a component of subclimax and climax cover types. Fire rarely kills red oak but does scar it, per-mitting decay to enter. Oak wilt and canker are two troublesome pests. Many insects attack red oak but are rarely of killing pro-portion. It is probably the most important commercial red oak. It is widely planted as a shade tree. The acorns are eaten by deer, turkey, grouse, squirrel and other rodents; understory species aug-ment this diet with berries and forage. The types in which northern red oak is a major component are valuable wildlife habitat.

The largest northern red oak living and of record is 26 feet 4 inches in circumference, 78 feet tall with a crown spread of 104 feet. It is growing in Ashford, Connecticut.

63b. Leaves shiny, acorns smaller **64**

64a. Leaves usually pubescent below, buds pointed and hairy. Inner bark orange. Fig. 134.

BLACK OAK ....*Quercus velutina* Lam.

Black oak is a medium-sized tree 50 to 60 feet high and is one of the most common of the eastern upland oaks. It has large spread-ing branches and a narrow open crown. It has a moderate growth rate and long life span. BARK: dark brown and rough, very thick on old trees, has a bright orange or yellow inner bark showing through the furrows. LEAVES: 6 to 8 inches long, 7 to 9 lobes which are again divided, many bristley tips. FLOWERS: male cat-

kins 4 to 6 inches long; stigmas of female flowers bright red.
FRUIT: solitary or in pairs, the nut 3/4 to 1 1/4 inches long,

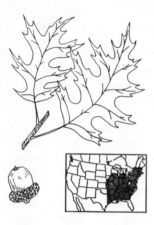

enclosed in a thick saucer-shaped cup to about 1/2 its length. It ripens in the second year. TWIGS AND BUDS: twigs, slender to moderately stout, grayish-brown, glabrous; buds, grayish, wooly.

Black oak is commonly found on dry sandy or rocky ridges, upper slopes and heavy glaciated hillsides. It makes its best growth on lower slopes and coves. Young trees characteristically develop long tap roots which is perhaps why they thrive well on dry sites. Black oak will grow on dryer sites than either white or northern red oak, but it does not do well on dry blackjack sites. Black oak grows in pure stands as well as being an associate tree in a great many

Fig. 134. Quercus velutina.

forest types throughout its wide range. It commonly occurs with hickories, post, scarlet, southern red, blackjack, chestnut, white and northern red oaks. In the southern portion of its range, it is found with shortleaf and loblolly pines and sweetgum. Black oak is a chief tree in two major forest types and it is a component in 16 other types. Black oak is intermediate in tolerance; more tolerant than yellow-poplar and less tolerant than white oak, hickory, elm and blackgum. It is a subclimax and transitional species. Its wide range covers a large number of understory species; some of the more common of which are azalea *Rhododendron* **spp.**, flowering dogwood, strawberry bush *Euonymous americanus*, greenbrier *Smilax* **spp.**, possumhaw, blackberry *Rubus* **spp.**, sumac *Rhus* **spp.**, and grape *Vitis* **spp.** It is one of the principal lumber producing red oaks; the bark has been a source of tannin. It is widely planted as a shade tree. The chief cause of defect in black oak is decay associated with fire scars. Heart rot generally spreads slowly into the tree. Oak wilt is an important disease of black oak and oaks dieback within a few weeks after symptoms of infection first become evident. The acorns are taken by deer, turkey, grouse, squirrel, and other rodents. More than 20 songbirds are attracted to types with black oak. The majority of types in which black oak occurs are considered to be good wildlife habitat.

The largest black oak living of record is 22 feet 3 inches in circumference, 125 feet tall with a crown spread of 85 feet. It is growing near Warrensville Heights, Ohio.

64b. Leaves with large tufts of rusty hairs in axils of veins below; winter buds covered with rusty pubescence; inner bark reddish. Fig. 135.

TURKEY OAK ....*Quercus laevis* Walt.

Turkey oak is a small tree rarely exceeding 50 feet in height with stout spreading more or less contorted branches forming a broad open irregular shaped crown. It is considered to be a slow growing oak and short lived. BARK: 1/2 to 1 inch thick, dark gray, red inside. LEAVES: 3 to 5 or rarely 7 lobed, 3 to 10 inches long, yellowish-green. FLOWERS: reddish catkins 4 to 5 inches long. FRUIT: about 3/4 inch broad and 1 inch long. It is enclosed in a thin bowl-shaped cup. TWIGS AND BUDS: twigs, stout, usually glabrous; buds, up to 1/2 inch long, tapering, rusty pubescent above the middle.

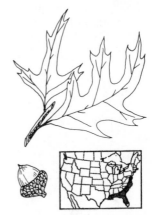

Fig. 135. Quercus laevis.

Turkey oak occupies dry barren sandy ridges and hammocks of the Coastal Plains. It is a minor component in 4 forest cover types where it is associated with sand pine, longleaf pine, a number of scrub oaks, southern red oak, persimmon and sassafras. Understory vegetation is variable and in Florida where it is growing with sand pine in the "Big Scrub" its chief understory species are the shrub oaks, Chapman oak *Q. chapmanii* and sand live oak common to the type and myrtle oak; elsewhere yaupon, gallberry, wax myrtle, sumac *Rhus* **spp.**, dewberry *Rubus* **spp.**, and greenbrier *Smilax* **spp**. It is an intolerant oak occurring in subclimax and transitional types following fire and heavy cutting. It does not appear to have any significant insect or fungi enemies. It suffers damage from fire as the top is killed back. Sprouting from the root collar then follows. In this manner, turkey oak stays in composition. Turkey oak has little if any commercial value. It is a major component of wildlife habitat; acorns are taken by deer, turkey and squirrel. Quail will pick up the bits dropped by rodents. It and its associates are heavy producers of acorns. About 10 species of songbirds frequent types in which turkey oak occurs.

The largest living turkey oak of record is 8 feet in circumference, 63 feet tall with a crown spread of 50 feet. It is growing in the Ocala National Forest in Florida.

64c. Leaves glabrous on both sides but sometimes with tufts of hair on underside 65

65a. Cup of acorn much broader than high 66

65b. Cup of acorn deep; leaves 5 to 9 lobed, the lobes with teeth. Fig. 136.

SCARLET OAK .... *Quercus coccinea* Muenchh.

Scarlet oak is a medium-sized tree 70 to 80 feet high. It grows rapidly, matures early, and is moderately long lived. BARK: brownish, with rather fine fissures, often flaky on the upper branches. LEAVES: deeply divided 3 to 6 inches long, very shiny, bright green above, paler beneath, sometimes with pubescence on veins,

turning brilliant scarlet in the fall. FLOWERS: male catkins glabrous, 3 to 4 inches long, bright red; female flowers 1/2 inch long, bright red. FRUIT: solitary or paired, the nut 1/2 to 1 inch long, reddish-brown often with concentric rings near the apex, 1/3 to 1/2 enclosed in a deep bowl-shaped cup. TWIGS AND BUDS: twigs, slender, reddish-brown, glabrous; buds, terminal, often obtuse, whitish pubescent only toward the tip; lateral, similar but smaller.

Scarlet oak is found on a wide variety of soils. It is the typical upland oak on ridges, upper and middle slopes.

Fig. 136. Quercus coccinea.

Although its successional position is not well defined, scarlet oak is probably a climax tree on dry sites. It is one of the most intolerant of the oaks and does not stand suppression. It is able to maintain its position in the many forest types in which it occurs because of its rapid early growth rate and ability to withstand droughty conditions. Scarlet oak was successful in taking over many of the sites formerly occupied by American chestnut in which position it is considered to be subclimax. Scarlet oak is a component of 15 forest cover types. It is described as pure or predominant in the Scarlet Oak Type, elsewhere it is associated with a large number of other oaks and hardwoods. When growing in mixtures, it is associated with black, southern red, chestnut, white and post oaks, several hickories, pitch, shortleaf, and Virginia pines, blackgum, sweetgum, black locust. Other minor associates are northern pin oak, white pine, northern red oak. It has a well developed understory. Some of the more common species are mountain-laurel, sourwood, blueberries *Vaccinium* **spp.**, buffalo nut

Pyrularia pubera, rosebay rhododendron, American elder *Sambucus canadensis,* blackberry *Rubus* **spp.,** mapleleaf viburnum *Viburnum acerifolium,* hobblebush *Viburnum alnifolium,* flowering dogwood, and several hawthorns. Because of its thin bark, scarlet oak is very susceptible to fire damage. If not killed, it is usually butt scarred so that sap and heart rots enter. It is susceptible to oak wilt, several cankers, canker worms, forest tent caterpillar, and the chestnut borer. It is cut commercially for lumber and is widely planted as a shade tree. It is one of the most brilliant fall colored oaks. Scarlet oak acorns are choice food for deer, turkey, grouse, squirrels and other rodents. At least 15 species of songbirds take the acorns. Understory berries and forage are likewise important wildlife food and cover.

The largest living scarlet oak of record is 15 feet 9 inches in circumference, 102 feet tall with a crown spread of 110 feet. It is growing at Swarthmore, Pennsylvania. Scarlet oak is the official tree of the District of Columbia.

65c. Cup of acorn deep. Leaves 5 to 9 lobed with yellowish axillary pubescence beneath. Fig. 137.

NUTTALL OAK .... *Quercus nuttallii* Palmer

Nuttall oak is a medium-sized tree 70 to 90 feet tall with a vigorous well developed crown. It is fast growing and early maturing but goes to pieces soon after maturity.
BARK: dark gray-brown, smooth, on older trees broken into broad flat ridges. LEAVES: 4 to 8 inches long, usually 5 to 7 lobed, separated by deep sinuses, dark green above, paler below, glabrous except for axillary tufts. FLOWERS: male catkins, slender, 6 to 7 inches long; female with bright red stigmas; 1/2 inch long. FRUIT: solitary or clustered, nut 3/4 to 1 1/4 inches long, reddish-brown, often striate, 1/4 to 1/2 enclosed in a deep, thick cup. TWIGS AND BUDS: twigs, moderately slender, gray-brown, glabrous; buds, 1/4 inch long with numerous gray-brown, glabrous or slightly downy scales.

Fig. 137. Quercus nuttallii.

Nuttall oak grows well in heavy, poorly drained, alluvial clay soils in the first bottoms of the Mississippi Delta region. It is the chief component of one forest type and a minor species in 5 others. It is associated with willow, overcup oak, sugarberry, American elm, green ash, sycamore, water hickory, baldcypress and water tupelo. Understory species are roughleaf dogwood, hawthorn, swamp privet *Forestiera acuminata,* button-bush, planertree, common greenbrier *Smilax rotundifolia,* poison ivy *Rhus radicans.* It is an intolerant subclimax species. It is subject to damage from large grubs, beetles and borers. Few diseases seriously effect Nuttall oak. It is a popular commercial species and is sold as a red oak. On sites where it grows it is probably the highest quality hardwood available. Acorns are eaten by deer, tur-key, squirrel and waterfowl. The understory species with their berries and forage are components of a high quality wildlife habi-tat. The bottomland forests in which Nuttall oak occurs are widely known for abundant game populations.

The largest living Nuttall oak is 12 feet 3 inches in circumfer-ence, 120 feet tall with a crown spread of 82 feet. It is growing in Clay County, Mississippi.

**66a. Leaves differing on upper and lower branches. Acorns taper-
        ing with a shallow cup. Fig. 138.**

SHUMARD OAK .... *Quercus shumardii* Buckl. **var.** *shumardii*

Shumard oak is one of the largest of the southern red oaks; it frequently attains heights of 100 to 125 feet. It has a long clear symmetrical bole above a slightly but-tressed base and a moderately shallow root system. The crown is usually open and spreading. It is moderately fast growing and has about the same life span as its associate cherrybark oak. BARK: light brown tinged with red. LEAVES: 6 to 8 inches long, lustrous, dark green and smooth above, paler beneath, axillary tufts on underside. FLOWERS: male catkins slender, 5 to 7 inches long; female with bright red stigmas 1/2 inch long. FRUIT: solitary or in pairs, nut, 3/4 to 1 1/4 inches long, enclosed at the base in a thick, shallow saucer-shaped cup. TWIGS AND BUDS: twigs, slender to moder-ately stout, gray to grayish-brown and glabrous; buds, usually smooth, rarely downy, straw-colored.

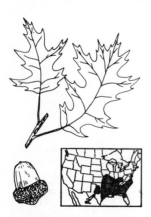

Fig. 138. *Quercus shumardii.*

In the southern forests, Shumard oak grows on well drained soils and terraces, colluvial sites and bluffs adjacent to large or small streams. It is also found in Coastal Plains hammocks but rarely on first bottom sites. It does not occur pure but rather as an occasional individual or in small groups in mixtures with several major types. It is associated with swamp chestnut oak, cherrybark oak, ashe juniper, Mohr's oak, post oak, black oak, white oak, several hickories, and white ash. Shumard oak is intolerant and needs full light for satisfactory regeneration. It is one of the prominent southern oaks in subclimax oak-hickory communities. On moister sites, understory species are well developed and numerous; they are red buckeye, flowering dogwood, witch-hazel, hawthorn, possumhaw, smooth sumac *Rhus glabra,* Carolina basswood, greenbrier *Smilax* spp., and red mulberry.

Shumard oak is susceptible to wilts and leaf diseases. No insects are associated specifically with Shumard oak but attacks often come from defoliators, borers, scales, galls, and leaf miners. Although its thick bark is some protection from ground fires, scars result in rot entering the bole. It is one of the more important commercial red oaks and is used for flooring and furniture. The acorn is eaten by deer, turkey, squirrel and other rodents. Where rainfall floods Shumard sites, waterfowl also utilize the acorns. Songbirds consume large quantities. In association with Mohr's oak and ashe juniper, Shumard acorns are an important source of food for the deer herd in that particular locality. One variety of Shumard is recognized, namely TEXAS OAK, *Quercus shumardii* var. *texana* (Buckl.) Ashe. This tree has a limited range in Texas (see map at "a"). It may be distinguished from Shumard by its smaller size and smaller acorns in addition to differences in range.

The largest living Shumard oak of record is 16 feet 4 inches in circumference, 130 feet tall with a crown spread of 107 feet. It is growing on Noxubee National Wildlife Refuge, Mississippi.

66b. Leaves 5 to 7 rarely 9 lobed, acorns somewhat elongated, cup deep. Fig. 139.

NORTHERN PIN OAK ....*Quercus ellipsoidalis* E. J. Hill

Northern pin oak is a medium-sized tree 60 to 70 feet high with many forked branches ascending above and often pendulous, lower on the bole forming a narrow oblong crown. It is relatively slow growing and short lived. BARK: brown with shallow furrows. LEAVES: deeply divided, bright green above, paler beneath, 3 to 5 inches long. FLOWERS: male catkins reddish, 1 1/2 to 2 inches long; female flowers in groups of 2 or 3, red. FRUIT: solitary or in pairs, short stalked, the nut ellipsoidal, chestnut-brown and often striate, enclosed for 1/3 to 1/2 of its length in cup-shaped cap. TWIGS AND BUDS: twigs, slender covered at first with matted pale hairs bright reddish-brown; buds, about 1/8 inch long, red-brown, lustrous, outer scales ciliate on the margins.

Northern pin oak is more commonly found on dry upland soils and occupies very small range in comparison with other native oaks. It occurs pure or predominant in the Northern Pin Oak Type. It is associated in four other forest types. Its associates are white, black, scarlet and northern red oaks, jack pine, red pine, white pine, bur oak, and several hickories. It is moderately intolerant and a component of subclimax associations. In parts of eastern Minnesota, pure northern pin oak may form an edaphic climax on poor sandy soils. It is subject to fire damage but there are no significant insect or fungi pests associated with northern pin oak. It is cut occasionally for lumber but is not an important commercial tree. Its symmetrical long crown makes it an attractive shade tree. Due to relatively small size of the acorn, it is eaten by a large number of songbirds, quail, grouse, turkey, deer, and squirrel.

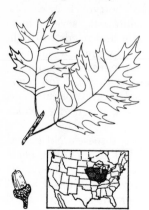

Fig. 139. Quercus ellipsoidalis.

The largest living northern pin oak of record is 10 feet 9 inches in circumference, 78 feet high with a crown spread of 82 feet. It is growing in the Menominee Indian Reservation, Shawano County, Wisconsin.

66c. Leaves 5 to 7 inches long, deeply lobed. Acorns globose, cup shallow saucer-shaped. Fig. 140.

PIN OAK .... *Quercus palustris* Muenchh.

Pin oak is a medium-sized tree 70 to 80 feet high; it has a shallow root system and a bole more or less studded with small top branches which do not prune off readily. The crown of open grown trees is pyramidal with slightly drooping lower branches which presents a pleasant appearance. It is relatively short lived. BARK: grayish-brown, smooth, eventually becoming scaly. LEAVES: with wide deep cuts, bright green and lustrous above, pale and glabrous below except for axillary hairs, 3 to 5 inches long. FLOWERS: male, catkins hairy 2 to 3 inches long; stigmas bright red. FRUIT: solitary or clustered, the nut 1/2 inch long, light brown and enclosed only at the base in a thin saucer-like sessile cup. TWIGS AND BUDS: twigs, slender lustrous reddish-brown; buds, terminal, 1/8 inch long, lateral smaller.

Pin oak makes good growth on wet sites and on heavy soils with poor internal drainage. On these soils, or flats, pin oak commonly grows in nearly pure stands. On deeper, better drained, but heavily textured bottomland soils, pin oak grows in association with other trees. In bottomland soils of lighter texture, it is seldom found in pure stands. Periodic flooding does not harm the tree but permanent flooding can kill pin oak in 2 to 3 years. Where pin oak occurs in other than even-aged pure stands, its chief associates are sweetgum, red maple, overcup oak, elms, green ash, bur oak, hackberry, and honey locust. Less frequent associates are cherrybark oak and river birch. Pin oak is intolerant; it is less tolerant than elm, hackberry and ash but more tolerant than cottonwood and willow. It is considered a subclimax tree. Typical understory species are trumpet creeper *Campsis radicans,* hawthorn, American holly, possumhaw, dewberry and blackberry *Rubus* **spp.***,* grape *Vitis* **spp.***,* and several greenbriers *Smilax* **spp.**

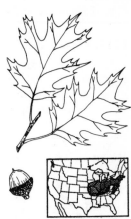

Fig. 140. Quercus palustris.

Because of its thin bark, it is more susceptible to fire injury than many other oaks. Although pin oak occurs on moist sites where fires do not frequently occur, during the fall conditions are often ideal for severe fire and at this time fires kill trees up to sawtimber size. Pin oak may possibly be susceptible to the oak wilt. There are several cankers that appear on pin oak, but are not serious. There are no important insect enemies of pin oak except possibly some of the wood borers. It is cut for lumber, flooring, and structural uses. Its symmetrical crown recommends it as an ornamental tree. The small acorn is especially attractive to a large number of songbirds, quail and turkey. Its most important wildlife adaptation is in waterfowl management where artificial shallow flooding of pin oak flats during fall and winter makes available the abundant small acorns for waterfowl, mallards, pintails and woodducks. This type of management is called "greentree reservoir management" and popular throughout the Mississippi Flyway. It is so called because the temporary flooding does not kill the trees which would be the case with permanent inundation.

The largest pin oak living and of record is 19 feet 10 inches in circumference, 110 feet tall with a crown spread of 85 feet. It is growing in Carrollton, Missouri.

67a. Leaves pinnately lobed. Fig. 146 72

67b. Leaves not lobed 68

69a.   Leaves evergreen, very thick and leathery. Fig. 141.

LIVE OAK ....*Quercus virginiana* Mill. **var.** *virginiana*

Live oak is usually a medium-sized tree 40 to 50 feet high. The short and enlarged buttressed trunk may divide into three or four wide spaced horizontal branches. The crown is closed, round topped and may spread in open grown trees up to 125 feet across.

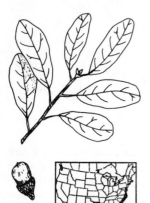

Fig. 141. *Quercus virginiana.*

Its rate of growth is rather variable and it is considered to be a long-lived species. BARK: dark brown with reddish tinge, slightly furrowed. LEAVES: evergreen, thick and leathery, dark, glossy green above, paler and often with white pubescence below. FLOWERS: hairy catkins light yellow, 2 to 3 inches long; stigmas of female flowers bright red. FRUIT: usually in clusters of 3 to 5 on a stem of varying length. The nut is about 3/4 inch long, ellipsoidal, dark brown to nearly black, 1/3 enclosed in a turbinate cup. TWIGS AND BUDS: twigs, slender, brown to ashygray; buds, 1/16 inch long with chestnut-brown scales, whitish on the margins.

Live oak grows in a wide variety of soils; it is present in nearly every habitat in northern Florida from hammocks to sand hills and occurs across the Coastal Plains to Louisiana and Texas. It is resistant to salt spray and is reported to tolerate salinities as high as 2.2 percent, providing drainage is good. Live oak thus is a climax type in coastal Louisiana, along the east coast and on the outer banks of North Carolina. It also occurs as a minor species in 4 cover types where it is associated with post oak, black oak, ashe juniper, Mohr's oak. Where it occurs in the subtropical zone, it is associated with southern magnolia, sweetbay, red bay. Understory vegetation associated with live oak is variable. In the climax community, its principal associates are bayberry *Myrica* **spp.**, yaupon, tree sparkleberry; in other types, dahoon, titi, devilwood *Ozmanthus americanus*, leatherwood *Dirca palustris*, American holly, hawthorn, Carolina jasmine *Gelsemium sempervirens*, and honeysuckle *Lonicera japonica*. In the northern part of its range, live oak assumes dominance only near the coast where it is free from suppression of other broadleaf trees which have a greater sensitivity to salt spray. Once established in a favorable habitat, it is very tenacious and withstands competition. Live oak is highly susceptible to fire. Its thin bark is readily killed even by a light ground fire. Where it grows as a shade tree, it is relatively free from insects and disease. Occasionally leaf blister causes defoliation. Several borers may damage the tree. Spanish moss *Tillandsia* **spp**. may accumulate in great abundance and reduce the amount of light reaching the interior and lower portions of the crown. The wood is exceedingly strong and one of the heaviest of the native woods. In the days of wooden ships, it was the prime tree to be cut for ribs and other hull parts. The present market is rather limited as it does not have a clear bole suitable for saw logs. It is a popular shade tree within its range. The small acorns are eaten by many songbirds native and wintering in the live oak range. Quail, turkey, squirrel and deer eat the acorns. The understory species associated with most of the types are excellent berry producers and forage species. They are an important supplement to live oak mast.

The largest live oak living of record is 35 feet in circumference, 78 feet tall with a crown spread of 168 feet. It is growing near Hahnville, Louisiana. Live oak is the State Tree of Georgia.

Two varieties of live oak are distinguished: SCRUB LIVE OAK *Quercus virginiana* var. *fusiformis* (Small) Sarg. This is a small, shrubby, small-leaved tree with a small fruit. It occupies dry limestone ridges and flat topped hills in a restricted area in southern Texas, the Edwards Plateau and southwestern Oklahoma. The other, SAND LIVE OAK *Quercus virginiana* var. *geminata* (Small) Sarg. is also a small tree but often having two acorns on the end of each stalk as compared to one in the case of *Q. virginiana* var. *virginiana*. It occurs along with live oak from southeastern North Carolina to southern Florida, Mississippi and southeastern Louisiana.

69b. Leaves deciduous within the first year. Fig. 142.

DURAND OAK ....*Quercus durandii* Buckl.

Durand oak is a medium-sized tree 60 to 90 feet high with a tall trunk and comparatively small branches. Upper branches ascend forming a dense round topped handsome head. BARK: very light gray and thin. LEAVES: thin, shiny dark green above 6 to 7 inches long occasionally 3-lobed. FLOWERS: in hairy catkins, 3 to 4 inches long. FRUIT: in pairs or solitary, 1/2 to 2/3 inch long, barely enclosed at the base in the thin shelled saucer-shaped cup. TWIGS AND BUDS: twigs, slender pale gray-brown, covered when they first appear with fascicled hairs soon becoming glabrous and darker; buds, dark chestnut-brown, rounded scales, ciliate on the margins.

Durand oak infrequently occurs east of the Mississippi River scattered on rich limestone prairies, low hammocks and minor river bottoms. West of the Mississippi River and in central Texas, it occurs on dry limestone hills. It occurs

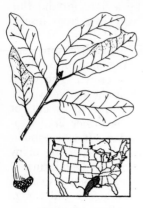

Fig. 142. Quercus durandii.

frequently enough to be considered a component of one forest type, the Ashe-Juniper Type of Texas. Here it occurs with live oak, cedar elm, hackberry, Shumard oak, and Mohr's oak *Quercus mohriana*. Understory vegetation commonly associated with Durand oak is yaupon, large gallberry, hawthorn, flowering dogwood, greenbrier *Smilax* spp. Durand oak is not an especially valuable commercial tree. Its principal use, due to its handsome shape, is as a shade tree. Thin bark renders it susceptible to fire. There are no outstanding insect or fungi pests attacking Durand oak. Acorns are eaten by deer, turkey, squirrel and a number of native and wintering songbirds. The acorn is a little too large for quail but they will follow rodent users and pick up pieces.

The largest Durand oak living and of record is 16 feet 6 inches in circumference, 139 feet tall with a crown spread of 69 feet. It is growing in the Noxubee National Wildlife Refuge in Mississippi.

70a. Fruit stems longer than the leaf stems. Leaves wedge-shaped at the base, whitish beneath, usually widest beyond the middle. Fig. 143.

SWAMP WHITE OAK ....*Quercus bicolor* Willd.

Swamp white oak is a medium-sized tree 60 to 70 feet high, frequently with a poorly formed bole and irregular crown. BARK: young stems and small branches smooth, reddish or purplish-brown; trunk deeply furrowed into flat scaly ridges. LEAVES: shining dark green above, white pubescent below, 5 to 6 inches long. FLOWERS: staminate, hairy catkins 3 to 4 inches long; stigmas bright red. FRUIT: acorn maturing the first year, usually paired and on slender stalks 1 1/2 to 4 inches in length. TWIGS AND BUDS: twigs, straw-brown, dull; buds, terminal 1/16 to 1/8 inch long, orange-brown, glabrous.

Swamp white oak is commonly found on wet soils having a hardpan and in areas subject to flooding in lowlands, swamps, and meadows. It occurs in three major forest types where it is associated with basswood, black ash, several hickories, pin oak, red maple, silver maple, sweetgum, sycamore, American elm, and northern red oak. Swamp white oak is intermediate in tolerance and is a subclimax species. Understory vegetation associated with the types are elder-berry *Sambucus* **spp.**, dewberry and blackberry *Rubus* **spp.**, boxelder, red-osier dogwood *Cornus stolonifera*, hazel nut *Corylus americana* and several willows *Salix* **spp**. Swamp white oak is relatively free from serious pests, either insects or disease. While its commercial quality may not be the highest, it does occur in rather large numbers in certain areas. It is harvested and used along with other white oaks. The acorn is rather large and therefore is not as easily utilized as other smaller nuts. Deer eat swamp white oak acorns. Woodpeckers can reduce them to pieces which probably results in some songbird use as well. Squirrel and other rodents have no problem as it

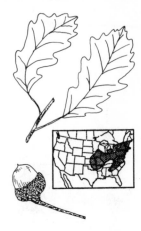

Fig. 143. Quercus bicolor.

is a good meal. Understory species occurring in the types along with swamp white oak provide good browse, berries and nuts for wildlife.

The largest swamp white oak living and of record is 18 feet 1 inch in circumference, 60 feet high with a crown spread of 107 feet. It is growing near Johnstown, New Jersey.

70b. Fruit stems about as long or shorter than the leaf stems. Acorns 1 inch or more in length 71

70c. Fruit sessile or nearly so, less than 1 inch long. Fig. 144.

CHINKAPIN OAK ....*Quercus muehlenbergii* Engelm.

Chinkapin oak is rare over most of its range and has but little commercial value. It is a medium-sized tree averaging 60 to 80 feet in height. Is a fast growing tree with a moderate life span. BARK: ashy-gray, more or less rough and flaky. LEAVES: green on upper surfaces, coarsely serrate, silvery beneath, 4 to 7 inches long. FLOWERS: staminate, in hairy yellowish catkins, 3 to 4 inches long; female flowers with heavy coat of white hairs. FRUIT: sessile or short stalked, solitary or in pairs, nut 1/2 to 1 inch long, with a thin bowl-shaped cup. TWIGS AND BUDS: twigs, slender, orange-brown; buds, terminal 1/8 inch long, orange-brown, lateral similar and smaller.

Chinkapin oak is rare over much of its wide range. Occurrence and abundance appear to be related more to soil reaction and texture than to other properties. It is usually restricted to well drained uplands and often occurs on limestone outcrops. In the southern part of the range, it is found along streams in limestone regions. In general it is associated with physiographic features which effect soil drainage, aeration and leaching. It is rarely a predominant type and is a common component of but one forest type, Post Oak-Black Oak. It is found in several other types in minor numbers. Throughout its range, it grows in stands containing white and black oaks, sugar maple, hickory, black cherry, cucumber tree, butternut, black walnut, shortleaf pine and eastern redcedar. Any species with such a wide range as chinkapin oak has a variable understory; some of the more common species are downy serviceberry, pawpaw, bittersweet *Celastrus scandens,* redbud, American elder *Sambucus canadensis,* maple leaf viburnum *Viburnum acerifolium,* summer grape *Vitis aestivalis,* greenbrier *Smilax* **spp.**, hawthorn, fringetree, and flowering dogwood. It is intolerant of shade, becoming more so with age. Despite its tolerance rating, it is regarded as a climax tree on droughty soils. On moist sites, it is subclimax. Chinkapin is subject to oak wilt, several insect pests, and damage by fire. It occurs too infrequently to be important commercially. Wherever it attains commercial size, it is sold along with other white oaks. It has a high wildlife value. Many songbirds eat the acorns, as well as deer, squirrel and other rodents, turkey and grouse. The bark is known to be eaten by beaver. Understory species are moderately valuable berry, seed and forage producers.

Fig. 144. Quercus muehlenbergii.

The largest living chinkapin oak of record is 21 feet 2 inches in circumference, 71 feet high with a crown spread of 87 feet. It is growing in Ross County, Ohio.

71a. Teeth of leaves acute; fruit short stemmed, nearly sessile. Leaves often silver-white on underside. Fig. 145.

CHESTNUT OAK ....*Quercus prinus* L.

Chestnut oak is a medium-sized tree 50 to 60 feet high, well formed with a massive straight trunk and narrow crown. BARK: brown to nearly black, on older trees very deeply and coarsely furrowed. LEAVES: 4 to 8 inches long, large and coarsely crenate, yellowish-green and lustrous above, paler and often fine pubescent below. FLOWERS: male, slender catkins 3 to 4 inches long; female with a dark red stigma. FRUIT: single or paired, stalked, nut 1 to 1 1/2 inches long, although commonly smaller, very lustrous, enclosed at the base from 1/2 to 1/3 of its length in a thin cup. TWIGS AND BUDS: twigs, orange to reddish-brown; buds, terminal 1/4 inch long covered with chestnut-brown scales.

Fig. 145. Quercus prinus.

Chestnut oak grows on dry sandy or gravelly soils, but reaches its maximum size in well drained coves and bottom sites. It is found in 13 forest types and is a major tree in 2. Here it is associated with white pine, scarlet oak, black, and white oaks, pitch pine, blackgum, sweet-gum, and red maple. It frequently occurs in pure stands on dry rocky ridges. In other forest types, it is associated with red pine, white pine, hemlock, eastern redcedar, northern red oak, and shortleaf and Virginia pines. Its growth rate is slow and it has a moderate life span. It is intolerant and although reproduction tends to persist under overhead shade, the tops will die back and resprout repeatedly unless they are released. It is considered a subclimax species. Understory vegetation associated with chestnut oak include highbush blueberry *Vaccinium corymbosum,* lowbush blueberry *Vaccinium angustifolium,* dwarf chinkapin oak *Quercus prinoides,* mountain-laurel, rosebay rhododendron, azalea *Rhododendron* **spp.,** service-berry, flowering dogwood, greenbrier *Smilax* **spp.,** and grape *Vitis* **spp.** It is susceptible to oak wilt, leaf blight and several decay fungi. It seems to be resistant to borer attacks but is susceptible to attacks from the ambrosia beetle. It is subject to fire scar and subsequent rots. As a prolific sprouter much of the present second growth stands are from sprout origin. It is sold as white oak and used for furniture and other lumber. The acorns are large but nevertheless are eaten by squirrel, deer, turkey, and grouse. The abundant berries and forage of the understory provide a high class wildlife habitat.

The largest living chestnut oak of record is 22 feet 3 inches in circumference, 95 feet high with a crown spread of 108 feet. It is growing in Easton, Maryland.

72a. Cup of acorn shallow 73

72b. Cup of acorn deep with ragged edge; leaves white below with fine matted hairs 74

73a. Leaves glabrous on underside; deeply cut into 3 to 9 lobes. Large tree with closely furrowed light gray bark. Fig. 146.

WHITE OAK .... *Quercus alba* L.

White oak is the most important species of the white oak group. It is a large tree 80 to 100 feet high and in the open is character-

ized by a short stocky bole and wide spreading crown. Under forest conditions, it develops a tall straight bole with a short crown. It has a deep root system. Is moderately slow growing and long lived. BARK: light ashy-gray variable in appearance, on young trees often broken into small vertically aligned blocks, scaly on the surface, sometimes deeply fissured. LEAVES: dark green above, slightly paler below, 5 to 9 inches long. FLOWERS: long yellowish male catkins to 3 inches long; female flowers bright red. FRUIT: solitary or paired, short stalked, nut 1/2 to 3/4 inch long, enclosed for about 1/4 of its length in a light chestnut brown bowl-like cup. TWIGS AND BUDS: twigs, moderately stout, purplish-gray to greenish-red; buds, terminal, 1/8 to 3/16 inch long, glabrous.

Fig. 146. *Quercus alba.*

White oak grows on a wide range of soils and sites. It reaches its best development in coves and higher bottomlands where the soil is deep and moist with good drainage. It grows on all upland aspects, slope positions and ridge tops within its range except extremely shallow soil on rocky ridges, poorly drained flats and wet bottomland. It is associated with many other hardwoods. White oak is the major component of 3 forest types with hickory, yellow-poplar and northern red oak. It is a minor component of 24 other types where it is associated with several hickories, other oaks, basswood, white ash, black cherry, sweetgum, white, shortleaf, Virginia, and loblolly pines, beech, sugar maple and southern magnolia. Over its wide range it occurs with a great variety of understory species. Some of the more common are fringetree, cinnamon clethra *Clethra acuminata,* flowering dogwood, hawthorn, strawberry bush *Euonymus americanus,* smooth hydrangea *Hydrangea arborescens,* buffalo

nut *Pyrularia pubera,* rosebay rhododendron, blackberry and dewberry *Rubus* **spp.,** American elder *Sambucus canadensis,* several
viburnums *Viburnum* **spp.,** greenbrier *Smilax* **spp.,** and summer
grape *Vitis* **spp.** White oak is generally considered intermediate in
tolerance. When associated with other oaks and hickories in the
central and southern portion of its range, it is a climax tree. In
the north on good sites, it is often succeeded by sugar maple. In
sheltered moist coves it may be succeeded by beech and other more
tolerant species, thus reacting as subclimax.

Several insects attack white oak. It is susceptible to heart rot
resulting from fire, cankers and shoe string root rot. It is used
commercially as lumber, flooring, furniture and paneling. The
mixed oak-hickory types in which it occurs are among the finest
wildlife environment within its range. The large number of berry
producing species and forage provide an additional source of food
and cover for wildlife. Acorns are eaten by deer, turkey, grouse,
squirrel, and other rodents, as well as a large number of songbirds.
Early settlers and Indians used ground white oak acorns as meal
for food. The largest living white oak of record is 27 feet 8 inches
in circumference, 95 feet tall with a crown spread of 165 feet. It is
growing in the State Park at Wye Mills, Maryland. White oak is
the State Tree of Connecticut, Maryland, and West Virginia.

The ENGLISH OAK *Quercus robur* L. is an import cultivated
in the United States. There are many cut leafed, yellow leafed and
other sport variations. It differs from white oak in that its bark,
while furrowed, is not scaly. It is a native of Europe, northern
Africa and western Asia.

**73b. Leaves pubescent beneath, rather coarsely and deeply 5-
lobed. Smaller trees, bark reddish-brown. Fig. 147.**

POST OAK ....*Quercus stellata* Wangenh. **var.** *stellata*

Post oak is a small to medium-sized tree 40 to 50 feet high. It
has a characteristic gnarled and twisted appearance in the crown.
It is slow growing and of medium longevity. BARK: reddish-brown
with deep fissures and broad ridges. LEAVES: thick and somewhat
leathery, 4 to 6 inches long, margin usually deeply 5-lobed, the
two middle lobes squarish and nearly opposite giving the leaf a
cruciform appearance. Dark green with scattered stellata-pubes-
cence above, tawny tomentose below. FLOWERS: male catkins,
yellow 3 to 4 inches long, stigmas bright red. FRUIT: solitary or
paired, nut 1/2 to 2/3 inch long, sometimes slightly striped, enclosed for about 1/3 its length in a bowl-shaped cup. TWIGS AND
BUDS: twigs, somewhat tomentose; buds, terminal about 1/8 inch
long, covered with chestnut-brown pubescent scales.

Post oak grows in a wide variety of soils and on many sites. Commonly on gravelly or sandy uplands of low organic content. Typical sites are rocky ridges and sandy outcroppings on southern exposures. It is characteristic of sites that are alternately water logged

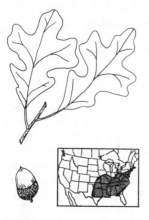

and hard and dry as found in the Alabama and Mississippi flatwoods and some of the heavier soils of the central states. It is the major tree of one forest cover type, Post Oak-Black Oak, occurring on dry uplands and ridges throughout all but the most eastern part of its range. In some areas, it replaces short-leaf pine after repeated wildfires. In the southwest, post oak often becomes the predominant tree of the Post Oak-Black Oak Type. It is less common in the northeast but is found in at least 13 other forest types where it is associated with scarlet, chestnut and southern red oaks, eastern redcedar, shortleaf, Virginia, loblolly, longleaf, and slash pines.

Fig. 147. Quercus stellata.

Occuring as it does over a wide range the understory is quite variable. Some of the more common species are shining sumac, smooth sumac, gum bumelia, hawthorn, yaupon, redbud, rusty black haw, greenbrier *Smilax* **spp.**, wild grape *Vitis* **spp.**, blackberry and dewberry *Rubus* **spp.**, poison ivy *Rhus radicans* and French mulberry *Calicarpa americana*.

Post oak is intolerant and because of its slow height growth is often over topped by other species. It is subclimax. Post oak is subject to most of the insects and diseases common to oaks. Sand post oak *Quercus stellata* **var.** *margaretta* is often infected by the gall wasp. Wilts and chestnut blight infect post oak. Acorns are heavily infested by weevils. It is susceptible to fire and subsequent rot infection. It is used commercially along with other white oaks, although not a high quality species. The forest types in which it occurs have either a high proportion of mast producing oaks which make them important or it is one of the few mast producers among non-mast species, then it becomes important to deer, turkey, squirrel and other rodents. Many songbirds spend their winter in the post oak range.

The largest post oak living and of record is 17 feet in circumference, 86 feet tall with a crown spread of 42 feet. It is growing near Hartwell, Georgia.

SAND POST OAK *Quercus stellata* **var.** *margaretta* (Ashe) Sarg. is a common variety of the Coastal Plains from Virginia to Texas. The lobes of the leaves are more rounded and less cruciform than those of post oak. Acorn cup sales are sometimes thinner and the winter buds larger and more acute. The largest sand post oak living and of record is 5 feet in circumference, 41 feet tall with a crown spread of 51 feet. It is growing at Fort White, Florida.

74a. Nut enclosed in the cup or nearly so. Leaves narrower than bur oak. Fig. 148.

OVERCUP OAK ....*Quercus lyrata* Walt.

Overcup oak is a medium-sized tree attaining heights of 50 to 75 feet. It is often poorly formed with a short twisted bole and large open crown with relatively few branchlets. It is slow growing and medium longevity. BARK: light gray with large irregular plates or ridges frequently with a twisted appearance. LEAVES: 6 to 10 inches long, variable, dark green and glabrous above, green and nearly glabrous or silvery white downy below. FLOWERS: male catkins hairy, light yellow, 3 to 6 inches long; female flowers pale. FRUIT: 1/2 to 1 inch long, 2/3 to almost entirely enclosed in a deep cup, unfringed margin. TWIGS AND BUDS: twigs, slender and gray; buds, terminal about 1/8 inch long covered with light chestnut-brown somewhat tomentose scales. Stipules are often persistent near the tip of the twig.

Fig. 148. Quercus lyrata.

Overcup oak is a bottomland tree commonly found on the lower poorly drained sites of first bottoms and terraces. It is common in sloughs and backwater areas, but infrequently grows on better sites. It is the principal tree in the Overcup Oak-Water Hickory Type. Here it is associated with willow oak, Nuttall oak, American elm, cedar elm, green ash, sugarberry, persimmon and red maple. It is a component in 4 other types. Overcup oak is rather tolerant as compared to other oaks. It can stand overtopping for many years. It is climax in the low backwater flats. On the better sites it is subclimax. Understory species generally associated with overcup are swamp privet *Forestiera acuminata,* hawthorn, roughleaf dogwood, buttonbush, planertree, possumhaw, smooth sumac, peppervine *Ampelopsis arborea,* honeysuckle *Lonicera japonica,* greenbrier *Smilax* spp., and grape *Vitis* spp. Overcup oak has high trunk borer damage which is a serious defect. Bark pocket and the flat head borer in overflow areas may degrade the species to a non-commercial level. No other serious defects are found in overcup oak. Heart rot follows fire and many trees have been damaged. Large overcup oaks are fairly fire resistant. It is sold along with other white oaks in the trade providing it does not have too many blemishes. The large acorn is a favorite food of deer and bear in the overflow country. Squirrel and other rodents eat the large nut and many songbirds and ground feeders profit from their droppings. Understory species are productive of berries, nuts and forage.

The largest overcup oak living and of record is 16 feet 7 inches in circumference, 110 feet tall with a crown spread of 56 feet. It is growing near Simpson, Louisiana.

74b. Nut at maturity about half exposed from cup. Leaves enlarged and toothed beyond middle. Fig. 149.

BUR OAK ....*Quercus macrocarpa* Michx.

Bur oak is a medium-sized tree 70 to 80 feet high with massive trunk and broad crown. It is relatively slow growing and moderately long lived. BARK: dark brown deeply furrowed. LEAVES: thin, when mature bright green and shining above; whitish pubescence beneath; 5 to 9 inches long. FLOWERS: male catkins slender,

2 to 6 inches long; calyx yellowish. FRUIT: variable in size but usually 3/4 to 1 1/2 inches long, cup covering more than half of the nut and the edge of the cup is heavily fringed. TWIGS AND BUDS: twigs, stout, yellowish-brown, usually pubescent, often with conspicuous corky ridges; buds, terminal, tawny pubescent.

Bur oak is one of the most drought resistant oaks. It occurs on dry exposed sandy plains and on loamy slopes of south and west exposures. It occurs in the subclimax prairies of the mid-west. In bottomlands of the central states and southward, bur oak is frequently found on moist flats and hammocky topogra-

Fig. 149. Quercus macrocarpa.

phy in both first and second bottoms. Because of its adaptability to a wide range of soil and moisture conditions, it is an associate with a great number of other trees. It occurs pure or predominant forming the Bur Oak Type where it is associated with northern pin oak, northern red oak, black oak, basswood. It is an associate in 5 other forest types. In the bottomlands, it is associated with American and slippery elms, shellbark hickory, hackberry and eastern cottonwood. On dryer sites, it grows in mixed stands with bitternut hickory and other dry site species. Understory vegetation is especially abundant in bur oaks stands of the plains region and some of the species are American hazel nut *Corylus americana,* corral berries *Symphoricarpos orbiculatus,* smooth sumac, hawthorn, western snowberry *Symphoricarpos occidentalis,* and the prairie crabapple. Bur oak is intermediate in tolerance. On prairie edges, bur oak is pioneer but it may be a climax tree with hickory on extremely dry southern aspects and stony soils. Bur oak is seldom attacked by insects but June beetles are occasionally pests. Defoliators often slow growth. Oak wilt is less serious on bur oak than other members of the oaks. Several root rots, cankers and die back may be serious at times. The larger bur oaks are resistant to fire. It cannot withstand flooding. It can withstand city smoke better than most oaks. Bur oak is cut for lumber wherever it occurs in merchantable sizes. Acorns are eaten by deer, hares, squirrels and other rodents, turkey, grouse, and a large number of songbirds.

The largest bur oak of record is 20 feet 9 inches in circumference, 122 feet tall with a crown spread of 107 feet. It is growing in Algonac, St. Clair County, Michigan. Although Illinois statutes refer to "the native oak" as the State Tree, it is generally accepted that bur oak is the species intended.

75a. **Branches with sharp pointed spines, single or branched. Small apple-like fruit with bony center. THE HAWTHORNS, see 103a, Fig. 183a-i.**

75b. **Without sharp pointed spines, carpels not bony** 76

76a. **Flowers in racemes; winter buds long. Fruit small, blue or black. See 78b, Fig. 151.**

76b. **Flowers in umbels; no thorns but sometimes with stunted branches. Fruit apple-like** 109

77a. Leaves in two rows on the stem 78

77b. Leaves not in two rows on the stem 79

78a. Leaves with double serrations on lobes or teeth in which the veins end, bark separating into papery sheets. Fig. 150. See 46, THE BIRCHES.

Fig. 150.

78b. Lateral veins not ending in the serrations. Fig. 151. Leaves with densely white tomentose.

DOWNY SERVICEBERRY...
....*Amelanchier arborea* (Michx. f.) Fern.

A tree up to 40 feet in height, with small erect and spreading branches forming a narrow round topped crown, often a shrub. The early spring flowers are showy in an otherwise bleak forest

landscape. It is slow growing and short lived. BARK: smooth, ashy-gray. LEAVES: when young folded lengthwise and brownish-purple, 2 1/2 to 4 inches long. When unfolding covered with silvery white tomentum. FLOWERS: very showy, large drooping, white, five petaled, appear before or with leaves, April. FRUIT: attached to elongated pedicels, crimson or purplish, weak tasting, 1/4 inch in diameter, ripens in June-July, falls early. TWIGS AND BUDS: twigs, first covered with long white hairs soon becoming glabrous, bright red-brown, have a faint bitter almond taste; buds, green, tinged with brown, second scale less than half the length of the bud.

Fig. 151. Amelanchier arborea.

Serviceberry occurs in open woods, rocky slopes and bluffs throughout its range. For the most part, it is found below the intermediate crown class and in the understory. It is sufficiently tolerant to withstand overhead shade and is a subclimax species. In tall timber where it occurs in the understory, it receives light from the side. It is associated with northern red, scarlet, and black oaks, yellow-poplar, loblolly and shortleaf pines, several hickories and sweet birch. In the understory, flowering dogwood, hydrangea *Hydrangea arborescens*, deerberry *Vaccinium stamineum*, hobblebush *Viburnum alnifolium*, and grape *Vitis* spp. Serviceberry does not appear to have any serious insect or fungi pests. Occasionally the tent caterpillar will infest it for a season. It is susceptible to fire damage. Serviceberry ranks with persimmon as being one of the heaviest woods in North America. It has been used for tool handles and other small articles. It makes a beautiful cabinet wood, but hard to work. Although the fruit has a weak taste when eaten raw, when cooked in pies, muffins and puddings, they add a pleasing flavor. The fruits are sought by thrushes and many other songbirds. They are important wildlife food during the early summer. Squirrels and other rodents, even bear, eat the fruits. Deer browse on the foliage and twigs.

The largest downy serviceberry now living is 9 feet 9 inches in circumference, 72 feet tall with a crown spread of 48 feet. It is growing near Standish, Michigan.

78c. Lateral veins not ending in the serrations. Leaves glabrous. Fig. 152.

ALLEGHENY SERVICEBERRY .... *Amelanchier laevis* Wieg.

A small tree sometimes 30 to 40 feet tall with small spreading branches forming a narrow round topped crown. This and the downy serviceberry are often called Sarviceberry which probably comes from modification of the term *Sorbus,* the name applied to a fruit known to the Romans and resembling that of Amelanchier. The accepted common name is Serviceberry. It is slow growing and short lived. BARK: dark reddish-brown, divided by shallow fissures into narrow ridges and covered by small persistent scales. LEAVES: as in *A. arborea,* but glabrous and smaller, 2 to 2 1/2 inches long. FLOWERS: very showy, large, drooping, white, appearing when the leaves are nearly half grown. FRUIT: purple or nearly black, 1/3 inch in diameter, succulent and sweet, ripens in June-July. TWIGS AND BUDS: twigs, slender, reddish-brown at first then dull grayish-brown, with small dark lenticels; buds, 1/2 inch long, green tinged with red, scales ciliate with silky white hairs, sometimes 1 inch long when fully grown.

Fig. 152. Amelanchier laevis.

The Allegheny serviceberry is found in cool ravines and hill sides. It is most abundant in the forests of the Appalachian region. It occurs mostly as an understory species but frequently reaches the intermediate crown class. It is a subclimax species and intermediate in tolerance. Forest types in which it occurs are predominantly composed of northern red oak, scarlet oak, black oak, white pine, Virginia pine, yellow-poplar, beech, buckeye and silverbell. In the understory; flowering dogwood, mountain-laurel, azalea *Rhododendron* spp., rosebay rhododendron, blueberry *Vaccinium* spp., greenbrier *Smilax* spp. and grape *Vitis* spp. Allegheny serviceberry does not appear to have any serious insect or disease problems. It is susceptible to fire. It so rarely attains commercial size that it is not considered an important tree by the wood-using industries. It has the same wood characteristics as downy serviceberry. Berries are eaten by grouse, turkey and about 20 songbirds. Large and small mammals eat the fruit and twigs. Deer, in particular, browse on the twigs and foliage.

The largest Allegheny serviceberry of record is 4 feet 10 inches in circumference, 61 feet high with a crown spread of 39 feet. It is growing at East Lansing, Michigan.

ORIENTAL SERVICEBERRY *Amelanchier asiatica* (Sieb. & Zucc.) Endl., an import from Asia, is frequently cultivated on lawns and in parks.

79a. Leaves evergreen, except in 80d. Fruit a berry-like drupe. THE HOLLIES 80

79b. Leaves not evergreen 81

THE HOLLIES: Genus ILEX

Hollies are small trees and shrubs which are either—evergreen, with thick leathery leaves and spines in varying degrees or; deciduous, with thin leaves and without spines. The fruit is a well known brilliant berry-like drupe often used in Christmas decorations. The bright green leaves and showy fruits make festive the eastern winter forest.

80a. Leaves with spiny teeth, drupe red. Fig. 153.

AMERICAN HOLLY ....*Ilex opaca* Ait. var. *opaca*

American holly is the largest of the native hollies frequently attaining heights of 30 to 50 feet. The bole is rather short and in

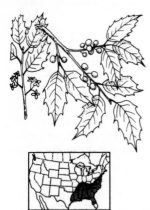

Fig. 153. Ilex opaca.

the open the crown is well formed and bushy. It is slow growing and long lived. BARK: light gray, with wart-like roughenings. LEAVES: evergreen, retained for several years, dull yellow-green, lighter below, 2 to 4 inches long. FLOWERS: male in 3 to 10 flowered cymes; female in groups of 1 to 3. FRUIT: globose or elongate drupe about 1/3 inch in diameter with 2 to 3 roughened seeds; usually bright red, ripening in fall and retained through winter.

American holly occurs on sites ranging from dry to moist. It is tolerant of salt water spray. It makes its best growth in deep, moist bottomlands. It is a minor component in several forest types where it is associated with longleaf and slash pines, southern red oak, sweetgum, southern magnolia, red maple, and hackberry. Principal understory species with which it is associated are hawthorn, large gallberry, green-brier *Smilax* **spp.**, grape *Vitis* **spp.**, elder *Sambucus* **spp.**, and sumacs. It is very tolerant of shade and is a climax species. American holly does not appear to have any serious insect pests or diseases. It is susceptible to injury from fire. As a timber tree, American holly is certainly of secondary importance. It does make attractive paneling. The drupes are used by at least 20 species of songbirds, most extensively thrushes, mockingbirds, robins, catbirds, bluebirds and thrashers. Game birds, grouse, turkey, and quail use the berries extensively as do small mammals. White-tail deer browse the twigs and young foliage.

The largest American holly of record is 13 feet 4 inches in circumference, 53 feet high with a crown spread of 61 feet. It is growing near Hardin, Liberty County, Texas. American holly is the State Tree of Delaware.

DUNE HOLLY *Ilex opaca* **var.** *arenicola* (Ashe) Ashe is a variety of holly which grows in northern and central Florida. It is similar to American holly in fruit and leaves.

80b. Leaves entire, leathery, drupe red or yellowish. Fig. 154.

DAHOON ....*Ilex cassine* **L.**

Dahoon is a small tree or shrub rarely exceeding 25 feet in height. The branches at first are coated with silky pubescence. It is slow growing and short lived. It sprouts profusely. BARK: thin, dark gray, thickly covered by roughened lenticels. LEAVES: 1 1/2 to 4 inches long, leathery with down-like hairs beneath, persistent. Some may be finely serrate above the middle. FLOWERS: numerous, small, white in umbel-like clusters, usually on new growth, May and June. FRUIT: bright to dull red or yellow, globose drupe, up to 3/4 inch in diameter, four nutlets, fruit persists until spring. TWIGS AND BUDS: twigs, slender, finely hairy, the first few years; leaf scars cresent-shaped, bundle scars solitary.

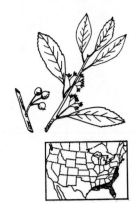

Dahoon occurs in moist sites and wet areas. It is only a minor component of any of several forest types. It is associated with southern red oak, Nuttall oak, sweetgum,

Fig. 154. Ilex cassine.

slash pine, pond pine, willow, and sugarberry. In the understory, it grows along with hawthorn, possumhaw, greenbrier *Smilax* **spp.**, elder *Sambucus* **spp.**, and roughleaf dogwood. It is very tolerant and is considered a climax species. Highly susceptible to fire with its thin bark; fires cause multiple root sprouts to appear following killback of the crown. It is not attacked by insects or disease to any significant degree. It has no commercial value as it rarely reaches commercial sizes. Its range is in the wintering grounds of many songbirds and the "berry" which is available until spring provides an important food supply. Thrushes, mockingbirds, robins, catbirds, bluebirds and thrashers more commonly use the "berries." Turkey, grouse, quail and many small mammals depend on the berries. Deer browse the twigs and foliage.

The largest dahoon of record is 1 foot 10 inches in circumference, 31 feet high with a crown spread of 19 feet. It is growing at Perry, Florida.

80c. Leaves coarsely crenulate-serrate, drupe red. Fig. 155.

YAUPON ....*Ilex vomitoria* Ait.

A small much branched tree up to 25 feet in height often with a slender inclining trunk. In Texas the Big Thicket is the largest remaining stand of pure or predominant yaupon known. It covers

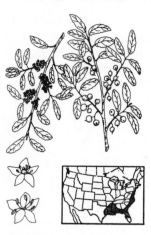

thousands of acres and in many places is all but impenetrable. Yaupon is a ready sprouter but once the root energy is used it becomes a slow grower. It has medium longevity. BARK: thin, light red-brown with tiny scales. LEAVES: shining dark green above, pale below, 1/2 to 2 inches long. FLOWERS: small and white in nearly sessile clusters on branches of previous year; monoecious but occasionally dioecious. FRUIT: about 1/4 inch in diameter, scarlet, maturing in October and persisting into winter, four pale amber seeds. TWIGS: puberulous during the first season, then glabrous and pale gray.

Fig. 155. Ilex vomitoria.

Yaupon prefers moist sandy soils but does well on dry sites. It grows well in the open and thrives in fully stocked pine stands. Its tolerance permits it to make good growth and produce berries even under dense crowns. It is a minor component of subclimax and transitional associations. Yaupon occurs as a minor component in 6 forest cover types. Where it occupies dry sites, it is associated with post, black, turkey, blackjack, sand post and bluejack oaks. On moist sites with slash pine, pond pine, black gum, swamp tupelo and red maple. Typical understory species are loblolly-bay, swamp cyrilla, titi, and dahoon. Hot or frequent fires will eliminate yaupon but fires of lesser intensity stimulate sprouting. Yaupon does not appear to have any serious insect pests or diseases. It does not attain commercial sizes frequently enough to be considered an important lumber tree or for any other wood products. It has the ability to stand heavy use by browsers and "hedges" well. Optimum use is about 40 percent of annual growth. Due to its ability to withstand browsing, it is an important deer browse species on the sites where it occurs. The "berries" are also taken by many songbirds. It is one of the important berry producing species in southern wintering grounds and is heavily used. Turkey and quail eat the berries.

The largest yaupon of record is 3 feet 10 inches in circumference, 32 feet high with a crown spread of 37 feet. It is living near Devers, Texas.

80d. Leaves remotely crenate, 1 1/4 to 3 inches long, deciduous, fruit orange to scarlet. Fig. 156.

POSSUMHAW ....*Ilex decidua* Walt.

A small tree up to 30 feet tall with stout spreading branches. It grows relatively fast, but is short lived. BARK: thin, light brown, roughened by wart-like excrescences. LEAVES: 1 1/4 to 3 inches long, in crowded groups at the end of short branchlets, thick, firm and deciduous, smooth on the upper side, lower sometimes pubescent on the ribs. FLOWERS: small, whitish, March to May. FRUIT: a globose drupe, orange to scarlet 1/3 inch in diameter, ripens in early fall. TWIGS: gray, with warty-appearing lenticels.

Possumhaw occurs along streams and around ponds. It is a minor component wherever it occurs. Tree species which are more commonly found with possumhaw are willow, water, Nuttall and laurel oaks, sweetgum, sycamore and American elm. In the understory it grows along with buttonbush, planer-

Fig. 156. Ilex decidua.

tree, smooth sumac, poison ivy *Rhus radicans*, dewberry and blackberry *Rubus* **spp.**, and greenbrier *Smilax* **spp**. It is intermediate in tolerance and a subclimax species. It can be reduced to ground level by fire but sprouts well. There do not appear to be any significant insect pests or diseases. The "berries" are eaten by many species of songbirds which winter in the hardwood bottoms where possumhaw occurs. Turkey and quail are regular users. Succulent sprout growth following fire is readily browsed by deer but older stems do not appear to be as palatable.

The largest possumhaw of record is 1 foot in circumference and 24 feet high with a crown spread of 9 feet. It is growing in Big Oak Tree State Park in Missouri.

80e. Leaves spiny, serrate above the middle 1 1/2 to 3 inches long. Fruit shiny black. Fig. 157.

LARGE GALLBERRY ....*Ilex coriacea* (Pursh) Chapm.

Usually a shrub less than 10 feet high but occasionally becomes a small tree up to 15 feet with a trunk 2 to 3 inches in diameter. Is fast growing and short lived. BARK: gray with blackish streaks.

LEAVES: 1 1/2 to 3 inches long, glaucous beneath, tips acute and short, sharp spines are sparingly borne on the leaf edge from about midpoint to tip, evergreen. FLOWERS: small and white, April-May. FRUIT: a shiny black drupe, smooth, soft and pulpy, ripens in fall. TWIGS: slender, green to gray, smooth or slightly hairy.

In the Coastal Plains, large gallberry grows scatteringly in the shade or open woods along streams and swamps as well as in upland sites with sandy acid soils. It is tolerant and a subclimax species. Tree species with which it is associated are longleaf, slash, and loblolly pines, bluejack oak, live and turkey oaks. Understory species: bayberry *Myrica cerifera*, huckleberry *Gaylussacia dumosa*, Jerseytea *Ceanothus americanus*, hawthorn, slimleaf pawpaw *Asimina angustifolia*, and sawpalmetto *Serenoa repens*. Stems are easily killed by fire but root stalks sprout rapidly folowing a burn. It has no commercial value. Large gallberry is one of the most highly preferred browse plants within its range. It furnishes palatable browse for deer throughout the year. Game birds and animals, as well as songbirds, use the fruits less than the other hollies.

Fig. 157. Ilex coriacea.

81a. Pith solid 82

81b. Pith not solid, diaphragmed, fruit a 4-winged samara. Fig. 158.

CAROLINA SILVERBELL ....*Halesia carolina* **L.** **var.** *carolina*

A small tree rarely over 40 feet high, round-crowned. Has an average rate of growth and life span. BARK: reddish-brown, somewhat ridged. LEAVES: pubescent, dark yellowish-green, pale beneath, 3 to 6 inches long. FLOWERS: bell-shaped about 1/2 inch long, white, sometimes tinged with rose. FRUIT: 1 1/2 inches long, 4-winged. TWIGS AND BUDS: twigs, bark on older twigs shreddy; buds, ovoid, acute.

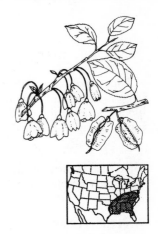

Occurs on wooded slopes and banks of streams and is usually a species of less than intermediate crown class. It is tolerant and subclimax. As a minor species in forest types it is associated with loblolly, shortleaf, and white pines, southern red oak, several hickories, red maple, serviceberry, blackgum and white oak. The understory varies but some of the more common species are blackberry and dewberry *Rubus* **spp.**, American elder *Sambucus canadensis*, hawthorn, sweetleaf *Symplocos tinctoria*, blueberries *Vaccinium* **spp.** It is sus-

Fig. 158. Halesia carolina.

ceptible to fire damage but does not appear to have any serious problem with insects and disease. Occasionally the tent caterpillar will infest selected trees, slowing growth for a season. Occasionally it reaches diameters large enough for sawtimber, it then is cut and is used for paneling and possibly some cabinet work. The seeds are not attractive to birds or animals. For some reason, in parts of the mountains of North Carolina it is chosen by gray squirrel as a den tree in preference to other normally used tree species present on the site.

The largest Carolina silverbell living and of record is 11 feet 1 inch in circumference (at 18 inches), 50 feet high with a crown spread of 52 feet. It is growing in Wyndmoor, Pennsylvania.

The MOUNTAIN SILVERBELL *Halesia carolina* var. *monticola* Rehd. occurs in a much restricted range in the mountains of North Carolina, Tennessee, Georgia, Arkansas, and southeastern Oklahoma. For the most part it appears as the Carolina silverbell. It does have larger flowers 2 inches long and fruit up to 2 inches in length. The largest mountain silverbell living and of record is 11 feet 9 inches in circumference and is growing in the Great Smoky Mountains National Park, Tennessee.

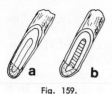

Fig. 159.

82a. Without diaphragms. Fig. 159a 84

82b. With prominent diaphragms in pith. Fig. 159b. 83

THE TUPELOS: Genus NYSSA

The tupelos are native to the southeastern United States. The bark is rough and furrowed into scaly ridges and in black tupelo, blocky in appearance. The fruit is a drupe with sour taste. Black tupelo is rated as medium in soil humus building capacity.

83a. Leaves usually dentate. Carpelate flowers solitary, fruit one inch or more long. Fig. 160.

WATER TUPELO .... *Nyssa aquatica* **L.**

Water tupelo is a medium-sized tree 80 to 90 feet tall with a narrow pointed crown. The bole is buttressed at the base tapering rapidly to a long clear length and lower limbs. It has a moderate rate of growth and long life span. BARK: dark brown roughened with small scales. LEAVES: thick, shining dark green, pale and somewhat downy beneath, 5 to 7 inches long. FLOWERS: small greenish white; male in spherical clusters; female solitary, early spring. FRUIT: drupe one inch long on long stem, dark purple. TWIGS AND BUDS: twigs, rather stout, reddish-brown; buds, terminal, yellowish and somewhat rounded, 1/16 to 1/8 inch in diameter. Leaf scars rounded, bundle scars 3.

Fig. 160. Nyssa aquatica.

Water tupelo is nearly always found on alluvial soils ranging in texture from plastic clay to silt loam. It grows on low flats or sloughs and in deep swamps on the floodplains of alluvial streams. It is a major component of 6 forest types where it is associated with baldcypress, longleaf and slash pines, black willow, swamp cottonwood, red maple, overcup oak, water oak, and water hickory. Understory

species commonly associated with water tupelo are swamp privet
Forestiera acuminata, buttonbush, planertree, supplejack *Berch-
mia scandens,* buckvine *Ampelopsis arborea,* poison ivy *Rhus radicans,* poison sumac, blackberry and dewberry *Rubus* **spp**. It is
intolerant but will respond to release. It is considered to be a subclimax swamp species. Fire is a major enemy of water tupelo. Any

major changes in water level sharply
decreases growth and may cause death.
The tree is seldom bothered by insects.
Little information is available on diseases of water tupelo. It is an important lumber tree and is used as paneling, wooden ware and pallets. Tupelo
honey is an important product. The
fruits are eaten by woodduck, turkey,
deer and bear. Fleshy portions of the
fruit are eaten by a large number
of songbirds; robins, mockingbirds,
thrushes, thrashers and starlings are
among the prominent users. Deer will
browse the twigs and foliage.

Fig. 160a. Typical water tupelo site,
frequently under water, buttress bole,
scaly ridged bark. (Miller Photo)

The largest water tupelo living and
of record is 13 feet 10 inches in circumference, 70 feet tall with a
crown spread of 48 feet. It is growing in the Alabama-Coushatta
Indian Village near Livingston, Texas.

**83b.   Leaves mostly entire; fruit less than 3/4 inch long, carpellate
flowers in clusters of 2 to 14. Growing on uplands in dry to
moist sites. Fig. 161.**

BLACK TUPELO ....*Nyssa sylvatica Marsh.*

Black tupelo is divided into two distinct and commonly recognized varieties—typical black tupelo *Nyssa sylvatica* **var.** *sylvatica* and swamp tupelo
Nyssa sylvatica **var.** *biflora* (Walt.)
Sarg. Black tupelo is a medium-sized
tree up to 60 to 80 feet tall with a
rounded crown and blocky appearing
bark. It is adaptable to varying site
conditions. It differs from water tupelo
in sites, smaller leaves, smaller fruit,
twigs more slender and bark characteristics. It has a moderate growth rate
and longevity. BARK: thick, light
brown, deeply fissued and squarish.
LEAVES: shinging dark green above,

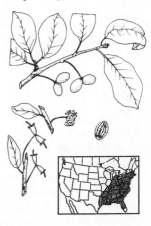

Fig. 161. Nyssa sylvatica.

somewhat pubescent beneath, 3 to 5 inches long. FLOWERS: male in clusters of numerous flowers; female 2 to a few in a cluster. FRUIT: drupe about 1/2 inch long, dark blue, 1 to 3 on each stem. TWIGS AND BUDS: twigs, slender, reddish-brown; buds, scaly, bundle scars 3.

Black tupelo grows in the uplands and alluvial stream bottoms throughout its range. It does well on better drained light textured soils and on high flats of silty alluvium. It is adapted to a wide variety of sites ranging from creek bottoms to altitudes of 3,000 feet in the Appalachian Mountains. It does not dominate in any major forest types but is an important component of 29 types. In the northeast and central forest region, it is associated with post, black, scarlet, bear, chestnut and white oaks, eastern redcedar and white pine. In the southern forest region with shortleaf, Virginia, loblolly, longleaf and slash pines, beech, southern magnolia, sugarberry, Atlantic white-cedar, pondcypress, red maple and swamp tupelo. Black tupelo is of medium tolerance and is a subclimax species. Typical understory species associated with black tupelo are eastern redbud, American hornbeam, eastern hophornbeam, bayberry *Myrica* **spp.**, mountain-laurel, dogwood, sourwood, hawthorn, and greenbrier *Smilax* **spp.** It is susceptible to fire damage. Several insects, leaf miners, tent caterpillar and cankers occasionally attack tupelo. Black tupelo is used for furniture, implements, and paneling. The flowers are a source of honey. Fruit is eaten by turkey, grouse and quail; the flesh by many songbirds. Squirrel and other rodents eat the fruit and buds. Sprout growth is a prime deer browse.

The largest black tupelo living and of record is 16 feet and 1 inch in circumference, 130 feet tall with a crown spread of 65 feet. It is growing at the Noxubee National Wildlife Refuge in Mississippi.

83c. Leaves mostly entire, oblanceolate, fruit less than 3/4 inch long and a distinctly ribbed pit. Growing in swamps and estuaries of the Coastal Plains.

SWAMP TUPELO ....*Nyssa sylvatica* var. *biflora* (Walt.) Sarg.

Swamp tupelo is a medium-sized tree 50 to 70 feet tall with a thin rounded crown. Growth rate is moderate and a medium life span. The bark is similar to black tupelo, the leaves are narrower and oblanceolate. The fruit pit has prominent ridges more so than black tupelo. The principal difference between black and swamp tupelos is site. Swamp tupelo develops best in the coves and low swamps of the southeast (see range map below heavy line, Fig. 161) and on the wetter bottomland soils ranging from highly organic muck soils to heavy clays in ponds and sloughs. Swamp tupelo

a   b

Fig. 161a-b. (a) Comparison of tupelo seeds. Ribbed seed on left is swamp tupelo. Smoother on right, black tupelo. (b) Typical swamp tupelo site. Periodically inundated but less frequently than water tupelo, buttress bole and "blocky" bark. (Miller Photos)

occurs pure or predominant in one major forest type. It is a component in 10 other forest types. Its associates are slash, longleaf, loblolly pines, red maple, pondcypress, Atlantic white-cedar, baldcypress and water tupelo. Swamp tupelo is intolerant and subclimax. Typical understory species are pawpaw, buckwheat-tree (titi), swamp cyrilla, yaupon, dahoon, swamp privet *Forestiera acuminata,* and redbay. It is particularly susceptible to fire damage when swamps dry out enough to burn. It has about the same insect and fungus problems as the other tupelos. It is cut for lumber and probably much of the so-called "black tupelo" on the market comes from swamp tupelo. Fruit is eaten by waterfowl, wild turkey, deer and bear. The fruit and buds are eaten by squirrel and other rodents, fleshy portion of the fruit by numerous songbirds. The twigs and foliage are browsed by deer.

The largest living swamp tupelo of record is 7 feet in circumference, 86 feet tall with a crown spread of 38 feet. It is growing at Brookgreen Gardens, Murrells Inlet, South Carolina.

84a. **Buds with more than one scale** 94

84b. **Buds wholly covered with one scale. Staminate and carpellate flowers on separate trees, both in catkins. Fig. 162 to 172** 85

THE WILLOWS: Genus SALIX

The Genus Salix comprises a large number of species which range from the arctics to the tropics. They are most numerous in the arctic and cold temperate regions. Thirty-eight native species and four naturalized species are accepted as trees in the "Check list of trees of the United States." For the most part, willows are found on "new" land such as water margins, dunes and sandbars. With the exception of one species, they are not important as a source of wood products. They are however useful in erosion control as they stabilize stream banks and newly formed sandbars. Principal wildlife use is by moose and elk in the colder regions. They are all intolerant pioneers.

85a. Twigs either erect or drooping but not "weeping" **86**

85b. Twigs long and hanging limply suspended. Fig. 162.

WEEPING WILLOW .... *Salix babylonica* **L.**

A small tree which may attain heights of 60 feet. Long hanging branches nearly reach the ground. It is a native of China. Like

most willows it is fast growing and short lived. It hybridizes with both crack and white willows. BARK: gray and ridged. LEAVES: smooth, dark green above, pale beneath, 3 to 6 inches long, small stipules. FLOWERS: slender catkins about 1 inch long. FRUIT: small brown seeds with many whitish hairs for flight.

This species is often confused with other "weeping" willows of which there are about 7. Its principal use is as an ornamental. It is hardy only in the southern portion of the United States. It is adapted to moist soil and tolerant of city smoke. Roots invade sewers. The largest weeping willow living and of record is 19 feet 4 inches in circum-

Fig. 162. Salix babylonica..

ference, 96 feet tall with a crown spread of 106 feet. It is growing in Detroit, Michigan.

86a. Leaves with very short petiole or sessile, usually pale yellowish-green, very narrow, stamens 2. Fig. 163.

SANDBAR WILLOW .... *Salix interior* Rowlee

A small slender tree rarely over 50 feet in height. Is fast growing and short lived. BARK: smooth, dark brown slightly tinged with red. LEAVES: yellowish-green, stipules small, 2 to 6 inches long. FLOWERS: dioecious; male catkins yellowish, 1 to 2 inches long; female catkins with 2 stamens to each flower, April and May. FRUIT: capsules in catkins containing seed covered with long tangled hairs.

Occurs on sand bars, mud flats, alluvial banks of streams, margins of lakes, ponds and sloughs. Generally it occurs pure and dense stands. It is associated with silver maple and cottonwood. Lesser vegetation with which it is associated is cocklebur *Xanthium* **spp.**, sumpweed *Iva ciliata*, morning-glory *Ipomoea* **spp.** and several sedges *Carex* **spp.** It is an intolerant pioneer species. Sandbar willow is useful as a soil binder and prevents much washing and erosion along streams and flats. It does not appear to have any serious insects or diseases. In the Alaskan portion of its range, it is browsed heavily by moose.

The largest sandbar willow of record and living is 1 foot 5 inches in circumference, 32 feet tall with a crown spread of 12 feet. It is growing near Utica, Michigan.

Fig. 163. *Salix interior.*

86b. Petioles 1/4 inch or longer **87**

87a. Twigs bright or reddish-yellow, glaborous. Leaves glaucous beneath, stamens 2. Fig. 164.

GOLDEN WILLOW ....*Salix alba* **var.** *vitellina* (L.) Stokes

A medium-sized tree with spreading branches and whitish foliage. Attains heights of 50 to 70 feet and is fast growing and short lived. It is native to Europe and introduced in the United States. BARK: dark gray, rough, with scaly ridges; twigs yellow, brittle at base. LEAVES: glabrous, dark green above, whitish beneath, narrowed at base, 2 to 5 inches long, stipules short. FLOWERS: dioecious, narrow cylindric catkins 2 1/2 to 3 inches long, early spring. FRUIT: light red-brown in narrow-ovoid capsules, seeds covered with tangled hairs.

Golden willow is planted as an ornamental in moist climates in the United States. It has escaped and naturalized in wet ground along streams. It is one of the basket willows and has been used for shelterbelts in the north. It has been

Fig. 164. *Salix alba* var. *vitellina.*

used for charcoal. The WHITE WILLOW *Salix alba* **L.** is similar to the golden willow but has olive-brown to green branchlets. It grows under the same conditions as the golden willow.

The largest golden willow living of record is 30 feet 7 inches in circumference, 58 feet tall and with a crown spread of 96 feet. It is growing near Commerce, Oakland County, Michigan.

87b. Not as in 87a **88**

88a. Leaves with white pubescence beneath, stamens 2. Fig. 165.

BEBB WILLOW ....*Salix bebbiana* Sarg.

A bushy tree occasionally 25 feet in height with stout ascending branches forming a round crown. Is a northern species, fast grow-

ing and short lived. BARK: olive-green or gray with reddish tinge, thin. LEAVES: thick, smooth dull green, bluish or silvery-white beneath with brownish pubescence. FLOWERS: dioecious, catkins yellowish or reddish. FRUIT: brown with whitish hairs.

Occurs along streams, swamps and open wooded forest margins where moisture is ample. It occurs in pure stands and may be associated with other northern species. It is useful in erosion control and is an intolerant invader of new sites. It is a pioneer species. Bebb willow does not appear to be damaged by insects or diseases. Due to its thin bark it is highly susceptible to fire. It is browsed by moose and white-tail deer. Buds are

Fig. 165. Salix bebbiana.

eaten by grouse; the bark, buds and wood by beaver, hare, rabbit and squirrel.

The largest living Bebb willow is 2 feet in circumference 31 feet tall with a crown spread of 18 feet. It is growing near Maple City, Michigan.

88b. Leaves green above, stamens 2, scale of flowers persistent..89

88c. Scales of flowers deciduous **90**

89a. Leaves acute, broader than in 89b; catkins sessile; ovary pubescent. Fig. 166.

PUSSY WILLOW ....*Salix discolor* Mühl.

A small tree with stoutly ascending branches rarely reaching heights over 25 feet, crown round. Is a fast growing and short-lived species. BARK: light brown tinged with red. LEAVES: dark green above, glaucous white beneath, 2 to 5 inches long, stipules conspicuous but falling away early. FLOWERS: dioecious, erect catkins 1 to 2 inches long and 1/2 inch in diameter, thickly covered with silky white hairs appearing as fur; very early. FRUIT: capsules narrow with long point.

Pussy willow occurs in moist sites and banks of streams and lakes. It is associated with other willows, cottonwood, and silver maple. Is tolerant and a pioneer species. Lesser vegetation associated with it—morning glory *Ipomoea* **spp.**, cocklebur *Xanthium* **spp.**, and several species of sedge *Carex*. It normally

Fig. 166. Salix discolor.

grows in pure or predominant numbers. Is not subject to serious insects or diseases. Fires will kill it back to the root. It is low quality deer browse but is gnawed by rodents. Pussy willow is planted as an ornamental and occasionally used for charcoal. The largest living pussy willow of record is 4 feet 2 inches in circumference, 32 feet high with a crown spread of 31 feet. It is growing in Checupinqua Woods, Chicago, Illinois.

The pussy willow sold in shops and planted as an ornamental shrub or small tree is probably the import from Europe and Asia known as Goat Willow, *Salix caprea* L.

89b. Leaves acuminate, lanceolate; catkins with short stalks, ovary glabrous. Fig. 167.

MISSOURI RIVER WILLOW ....*Salix eriocephala* Michx.

A tall straight tree often reaching heights of 50 feet. The spreading branches form a narrow open crown. It is fast growing but has a life span longer than the majority of other willows. BARK: light gray, thin and smooth. LEAVES: glandular serrate 4 to 5 inches long, often silvery white below. FLOWERS: in February, male catkins 1 1/2 inches long and nearly 1/2 inch thick; female 3 to 4 inches long when mature. FRUIT: reddish-brown, long pointed, narrow.

Missouri River willow occurs in the alluvial soils following the larger rivers within its range ("a" on map). In most sites it is either pure or predominant. Where it is growing with other species, they are cottonwood, other species of willow and silver maple. Lesser vegetation is morning-glory *Ipomoea* **spp.**, cocklebur *Xanthium pensylvanicum,* poke *Phytolacca americana,* and ragweed *Ambrosia artemisiifolia.* It is an intolerant and pioneer species. Fire will kill the bole. It does not seem to be attacked by any serious insects or diseases. It is useful for erosion control. This species, peachleaf, and sandbar willows all play important roles in holding soil on river banks. The wood because of its relative permanence when in contact with the soil, is used for fence posts. It furnishes some browse for deer. Rodents eat the shoots.

Fig. 167. Salix eriocephala.

The BALSAM WILLOW *Salix pyrifolia* Anderss. has more oval leaves with considerable red on the leaves, winter buds are bright scarlet. It is a rather common shrub but only occasionally a tree. See map Fig. 167 for range "b".

90a. Petioles and stipules with glands. Twigs and leaves shiny. Fig. 168.

SHINING WILLOW .... *Salix lucida* Mühl.

A small tree occasionally reaching 25 feet in height. Has erect branches forming a broad round topped symmetrical crown. It is fast growing and short lived. BARK: thin, dark brown. LEAVES: shining dark green above, paler with yellowish midrib below, finely serrate margin, 2 to 6 inches long. FLOWERS: dioecious, catkins erect; stamens 5. FRUIT: long acute, retained after liberating the hairy seed.

Fig. 168. Salix lucida.

Shining willow occurs on banks of streams and swamps usually in pure stands though not over wide areas. Where it is growing with other species, they may be alder, balsam, and other willows. Understory species are sparse; red-osier dogwood, *Cornus stolonifera,* blueberries *Vaccinium* **spp.** and several sedges *Carex*. It is an intolerant pioneer species. It is killed by hot fires. It does not appear to be affected by any significant insects or diseases. It has no commercial value, but is often planted as an ornamental. It is browsed by deer and moose and gnawed by rodents.

The largest shining willow living and of record is 5 feet 9 inches in circumference, 58 feet high with a crown spread of 51 feet. It is growing in Traverse City, Michigan.

90b. No glands on petioles or stipules **91**

91a. Twigs very brittle, stamens 2, capsules narrow conic. Fig. 169.

CRACK WILLOW .... *Salix fragilis* L.

A native of Europe, was planted and escaped from cultivation in the United States. For a willow it is a large tree often attaining heights of 80 feet. The twigs are very brittle, thus the name. It is fast growing and short lived. BARK: gray and scaly. LEAVES: dark green above, slightly paler beneath, 3 to 6 inches long; serrations bearing glands. FLOWERS: dioecious, short catkins. FRUIT: capsules long, conical.

Crack willow, when escaped from cultivation, occurs along streams, swamps, and wet woods. It is associated with other pioneer species such· as cottonwood, other species of willows and silver maple. In the understory—cocklebur *Xanthium pensylvanicum*, dock *Rumex* spp., poke *Phytolacca americana,* and several sedges *Carex*. It is an intolerant pioneer of new and wet sites. When the

Fig. 169. Salix fragilis.

material is dry enough to burn it can be easily killed by fire. It does not appear to have any serious insect or disease enemies. During early colonial times it was used for charcoal. Presently it is planted as an ornamental. It is valuable in retarding erosion. It is browsed by deer and the bark and tips eaten by rodents.

The largest crack willow living and of record is 23 feet in circumference, 108 feet tall with a crown spread of 100 feet. It is growing near Utica, Michigan.

91b. Not as in 91a **92**

92a. Petioles, slender, 1/2 inch or more. Leaves pale beneath. Fig. 170.

PEACHLEAF WILLOW .... *Salix amygdaloides Anderss.*

A tree sometimes 60 to 70 feet high with a straight or slightly inclining bole and straight ascending branches. Frequently slightly drooping branches give it a "weeping" effect. It is fast growing and short lived. BARK: scaly, brown, somewhat tinged with red.

LEAVES: about 1 inch wide and 2 to 6 inches long, dark green above, paler beneath, stout yellow midrib and prominent veins. FLOWERS: dioecious, catkins on leafy branchlets, 2 to 3 inches long, scales yellow, appear with leaves. FRUIT: globose-conic capsules, light reddish-yellow.

Peachleaf willow occurs along alluvial muddy banks and low woods bordering the major rivers in its range. It is associated with other willows, silver maple and cottonwood. Invaders of the next successional stage are sycamore, river birch, and green ash. It is an intolerant pioneer and as the soils build, more tolerant species replace the intolerant pioneers. Understory species

Fig. 170. Salix amygdaloides.

are cocklebur *Xanthium pensylvanicum*, sumpweed *Iva ciliata*, ragweed *Ambrosia* **spp.**, and goldenrod *Solidago* **spp**. It is highly susceptible to damage by fire. Peachleaf willow does not appear to be seriously damaged by insects or diseases. Occasionally it is cut for lumber, charcoal and fuel. Deer browse the twigs and foliage. Rodents eat the bark and shoots. Its principal value is in erosion control and holding stream banks in place.

The largest peachleaf willow living and of record is 10 feet 6 inches in circumference, 55 feet tall with a crown spread of 78 feet. It is growing at Kasota Lake north shore, Minnesota.

92b. Petioles short; leaves lanceolate 93

93a. Leaves green on both sides, narrow. Fig. 171.

BLACK WILLOW .... *Salix nigra* Marsh.

Black willow is the tallest and largest of any native species of willow in the United States. It sometimes reaches heights of 120 feet, grows rapidly and is short lived. BARK: rough, thick, flaky, dark brown or nearly black. LEAVES: 3 to 6 inches long; light green and smooth above, paler and usually smooth beneath. FLOWERS: dioecious, yellowish catkins, April or May. FRUIT:

capsules in catkins, seed covered with hairs, ripens in June and July and is carried long distances by wind.

Black willow grows on almost any soil but its extensive shallow roots need an abundant and continuous supply of moisture during the growing season. It is common on river margins and batture land where it usually dominates the lower wetter and often less sandy soils. Black willow is the most common single species in the Black Willow Type, a pioneer type. It is also an associate species in 6 other types where it occurs with black spruce, river birch, sycamore, cottonwood, pondcypress, baldcypress and water tupelo. Typical understory species of the better sites are swamp privet *Forestiera acuminata*, buttonbush, planertree, and sandbar willow. Black willow is an intolerant pioneer and usually grows in dense, even-aged stands. Dieback from competition in this situation is very high. Hot fires will kill entire stands of black willow. Drought and water level changes cause serious mortality. Few insects attack black willow but leaf rust and fungus scab cause leaf and shoot destruction. In well stocked stands on good sites it becomes a respectable timber tree and is cut for lumber. Some use is made of it in particle board and pulp. Shoots are browsed by deer and rodents eat the bark and shoots. Sapsuckers feed on the inner bark and cause degrade in the lumber trade.

Fig. 171. Salix nigra.

The largest living black willow is 26 feet 1 inch in circumference, 85 feet tall with a crown spread of 79 feet. It is growing in Traverse City, Michigan.

93b. Leaves white beneath, wider than 93a. Fig. 172.

COASTAL-PLAIN WILLOW ....*Salix caroliniana* Michx.

A small tree 20 to 30 feet high with spreading branches, quite frequently a shrub. Grows rapidly and is short lived. BARK: dark brown, prominently ridged. LEAVES: bright green above; somewhat pubescent and whitish beneath, 4 to 7 inches long. FLOWERS: dioecious, catkins 3 to 4 inches long, scales yellow. FRUIT: capsules 1/4 inch long, seed carried by wind.

It occurs along gravel bars, sandy gravel beds and rocky banks of streams throughout its range. It is associated with other willows, cottonwood, silver maple and green ash. Common understory is ragweed *Ambrosia* **spp.**, goldenrod *Solidago* **spp.**, dewberry *Rubus* **spp.**, and greenbrier *Smilax* **spp.** It is an intolerant pioneer. It is

Fig. 172. Salix caroliniana.

the first woody species to invade the outer edges of gravel bars and rocks in the Ozarks. Susceptible to fire but has few enemies among insects and diseases. Is used occasionally for baskets, furniture and ornamental pieces. Deer will browse the shoots and foliage. Rodents eat the bark and shoots. It is valuable for erosion control.

The largest Coastal-Plain willow living and of record is 2 feet 8 inches in circumference, 46 feet tall with a crown spread of 21 feet. It is growing at Glenwood, Arkansas.

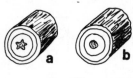

Fig. 173.

94a. Pith 5 angled in cross section. Fig. 173a 95

94b. Pith round or nearly so in cross section. Fig. 173b. ....
....103

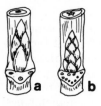

Fig. 174.

95a. Bundle scars 3 (Fig. 174a); teeth on leaf margins gland tipped 96

95b. Bundle scars several, scattered (Fig. 174b); no glands on leaves; buds clustered at tip of twigs. THE OAKS 54

THE POPLARS: Genus POPULUS

The genus Populus is widespread throughout the United States and goes under common names of aspen, poplar, and cottonwood. Poplars are fast growing and for the most part short-lived trees. Several imported poplars are planted as ornamentals. Roots of city dwelling poplars often become troublesome in stopping up sewers. Poplar leaves are rated high in humus building capacity. Buds, catkins, bark and foliage are used in varying degrees by wildlife.

96a. Leaf stem flattened on its side 97

96b. Leaf stem rounded; not noticeably flattened on sides 102

97a. Leaves coarsely toothed; winter buds tomentose or pubescent. Fig. 175.

BIGTOOTH ASPEN ....*Populus grandidentata* Michx.

Bigtooth aspen is a medium-sized tree 60 to 70 feet tall with a narrow rounded crown. It is a rapid growing short-lived species. BARK: thin, light grayish-green, dark at the base of older trees. LEAVES: with few incurved teeth; dark green above, paler below, 3 to 6 inches long. FLOWERS: dioecious, catkins hairy. FRUIT: light green, hairy, ripening early, scattered by wind. TWIGS AND BUDS: stout, dull, brownish gray; buds, grayish.

Fig. 175. Populus grandidentata.

Bigtooth aspen is most frequently found on well drained sandy soils. It occurs on sand, sandy loams, and less frequently on heavier textured loams and clays. Ordinarily it is a tree of the uplands but occasionally is found in the well drained flood plains of streams. Generally it occurs in pure stands or in combination with quaking aspen and balsam poplar. It is the major component of the Aspen Type and occurs in 14 other forest types. Its common associates are aspen, gray and paper birches and red maple. Others are jack pine, balsam fir, red pine, pin cherry, white pine, white and northern red oaks. Common understory associates are chokecherry, downy serviceberry, prairie willow *Salix humilis*, blueberries *Vaccinium* spp., blackberry *Rubus allegheniensis*, smooth sumac, dwarf bush-honeysuckle *Diervilla lonicera*. Common lesser vegetation is wintergreen *Gaultheria procumbens*, and eastern bracken *Pteridium latiusculum*. Bigtooth aspen is one of the most intolerant of deciduous forest trees. It is rarely found in other than even-aged stands and there in the dominant or codominant crown classes. It is a pioneer species. It has many natural enemies. Fire easily kills the thin barked tree. Forest tent caterpillars are perhaps among the most damaging insects but it has its share of defoliators, borers and galls. It is susceptible to several rot producing fungi. Cankers are common on bigtooth aspen. Its principal commercial use is for pulpwood. Yields of 30 cords per acre at 50 years are not uncommon. Grouse, prairie chicken and quail eat the buds and catkins. The purple finch and Abert towhee eat the buds. Beaver, hare, muskrat, porcupine, rabbits and squirrel eat the bark, buds and foliage. Deer, elk, moose and mountain sheep eat the twigs and foliage.

The largest bigtooth aspen living and of record is 17 feet 2 inches in circumference, 95 feet tall with a crown spread of 82 feet. It is growing near Walker, New York.

97b. Leaves not coarsely toothed 98

98a. Tree tall, narrow, spire-like; all branches ascending. Fig. 176.

LOMBARDY POPLAR ....*Populus nigra* **var.** italica Muenchh.

Lombardy poplar is a spire-like tree of rapid growth and ascending branches. It was introduced from Europe and is widely used

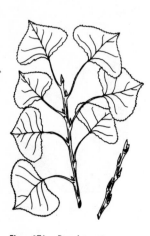

Fig. 176. Populus nigra var. italica.

for ornamental planting in the United States. It is short lived and subject to the European canker disease. It becomes troublesome when planted near sewers as its roots will enter pipes and stop the flow of sewage. BARK: dark gray on trunk, light gray on branches. Shallow furrows on trunk; smooth on branches. LEAVES: broader than long, shining green. FLOWERS: hanging male catkins, 1 to 3 inches long. FRUIT: cultivated trees all staminate, bearing no fruit. Lombardy poplar is a variety of black poplar.

BLACK POPLAR *Populus nigra* L. is also an introduced species. It is planted as an ornamental. It resembles the native cottonwood except that it lacks glands at the base of the leaf blade.

98b. Tree with spreading limbs; not spire shaped 99

99a. Tree slender with smooth greenish-white bark; winter buds glabrous; leaves finely serrate. Fig. 177.

QUAKING ASPEN ....*Populus tremuloides* Michx.

Quaking aspen is the most widely distributed tree of North America. It is medium sized 50 to 60 feet in height with a round topped crown and slender branches. It is fast growing and short lived. BARK: smooth, greenish-white, lower trunk rough and darker. LEAVES: roundish heart-shaped with a short sharp point, smooth on both sides. Flattened petiole 1 1/2 to 3 inches long. FLOWERS: dioecious, male catkins 1 1/2 to 2 1/2 inches long with soft gray hairs resembling "pussy willow" and sometimes confused with it. FRUIT: capsules in long catkins, seeds coated with tangled hair. TWIGS AND BUDS: twigs, slender, lustrous, reddish-brown; buds, terminal, conical, sharp pointed, sometimes very resinous.

Quaking aspen grows on a great variety of soils ranging from shallow rocky sites to loamy sands and heavy clays. Growth and development are strongly influenced by soil conditions; if moisture occurs between 18 inches and 5 feet below the surface it is considered favorable. Quaking aspen grows with a large number of species. It occurs pure or predominant in both eastern and western forest types. In the east, it is a major component with jack pine, white spruce, balsam fir, black spruce and paper birch. In the west with tamarack, lodgepole pine, ponderosa pine, white fir, blue spruce and Engelmann spruce. In the prairie provinces, balsam poplar, paper birch, white spruce, bur oak, pin cherry, American elm and boxelder. In Alaska, balsam poplar, paper birch and white spruce. Understory vegetation over such a wide range is quite variable. In the east, some of the more common species are beaked hazel *Corylus cornuta*, mountain maple, speckled alder, and several species of wild current and willow. In the prairie provinces add snowberry *Symphoricarpos* **spp.**, mooseberry *Viburnum pauciflorum*, red-osier dogwood *Cornus stolonifera* and Bebb willow. In Alaska add Scouler willow *Salix scouleriana*, and mountain cranberry *Vaccinium vitisidaea*. In the Rocky mountains the more common shrubs are mountain snowberry *Symphoricarpos oreophilus*, creeping mahonia *Mahonia repens*, Fendler woods rose *Rosa woodsi fendleri*, myrtle pachistima *Pachistima myrsinites*, and scarlet elder *Sambucus pubens*.

Fig. 177. Populus tremuloides.

In all of its range, quaking aspen is very intolerant. Its fast rate of growth and intolerance permit it to become dominant rapidly. It is an aggressive pioneer species and quickly invades burns and can hold the site in spite of repeated fires. Many factors cause injury or mortality. Big game animals may consume reproduction. Insects and diseases of aspen such as cutworms, shoot dieback, sawfly, cankers, leaf spot, and borers all damage quaking aspen from time to time. Quaking aspen is an important pulping species for paper and other digested products. It is regarded as a soil improver after forest fires. Its leaves are rated high in humus building capacity. Buds and catkins are eaten by grouse, (blue, ruffed, and sharp-tail), prairie chicken and quail. Several songbirds eat the buds. Fur and game mammals, beaver, hare, muskrat, porcupine, rabbit, and squirrel eat the bark, buds, and foliage. Deer (mule and white-tail), elk, moose and mountain sheep browse the twigs and foliage.

The largest quaking aspen living and of record is 11 feet 2 inches in circumference, 75 feet tall with a crown spread of 38 feet. It is growing near Cedar City, Utah.

99b. Buds sticky, often angular, leaves somewhat triangular 100

100a. Leaves with glands at apex of leaf stem; rounded or broadly wedge-shaped at base. Buds very resinous. Fig. 178.

BALSAM POPLAR ....*Populus balsamifera* L.

Balsam poplar is a fast growing medium-sized tree 60 to 80 feet tall with a narrow pyramidal crown. It grows rapidly and is short lived, but longer lived than either quaking aspen or bigtooth aspen.

BARK: gray on old trunk; on younger trees greenish-yellow. LEAVES: dark green above, pale beneath with reticulated veins, 3 to 6 inches long. FLOWERS: dioecious; male catkins 1 1/2 to 2 inches long; female 3 to 3 1/2 inches long. FRUIT: in catkins 8 to 12 inches long. Seeds light brown. TWIGS AND BUDS: twigs, moderately stout, reddish-brown, lustrous; buds, terminal, narrow conical, covered with 5 overlapping scales sealed by a fragrant amber-colored resin.

Balsam poplar usually occurs on low, often inundated, alluvial bottoms of river flats, sandbars and borders of lakes and swamps. In the eastern portion of its range, it occurs pure or associated with white spruce, balsam fir, paper birch, black ash, American elm and red maple. In the western portion of its range, it also occurs pure or associated with white spruce, several willows, Engelmann spruce and black cottonwood. Common understory shrubs are also grouped by regional distribution. In the eastern and northeastern aspen types; speckled alder, green alder *Alnus crispa,* red-osier dogwood *Cornus stolonifera,* mountain maple, bunchberry *Cornus canadensis,* red raspberry *Rubus idaeus* var. *canadensis* and American red current *Ribes triste.* In the western portion and Alaska; mooseberry *Vaccinium pauciflorum,* bearberry honeysuckle *Lonicera involucrate,*

Fig. 178. *Populus balsamifera.*

American cranberry bush *Viburnum trilobum*, western red raspberry *Rubus strigosus*, prickly rose *Rosa acicularis*, and mountain
cranberry *Vaccinium vitis-idaea* **var.** *minus.*

Balsam poplar is about equal in tolerance with quaking aspen
and paper birch. It is not as tolerant as black ash and red maple.
It will grow only in even-aged stands where it is in the dominant
or codominant crown classes. In the far northern portion of its
range, it is the first important species to invade sandbars and other
alluvium subject to overflow. It does not invade upland dry sites.
It is easily killed by fire in the young age classes but older and
more mature trees have thick protective bark. The tent caterpillar,
borers, weevil, and lace bugs all attack balsam poplar. Leaf spot,
leaf rusts, and heart rot are damaging to varying degrees. It is
commonly used for pulpwood. Buds and twigs are eaten by blue,
ruffed, sharp-tailed grouse and prairie chicken. Several songbirds
eat the buds. Beaver, hare, porcupine, rabbit and squirrel all eat
bark, foliage and buds. White-tail deer and moose browse twigs
and foliage.

The largest living balsam poplar of record is 11 feet 11 inches
in circumference, 89 feet tall with a crown spread of 78 feet. It is
growing at Cornell, Delta County, Michigan.

The BALM-OF-GILEAD POPLAR, a sterile clon of *Populus
balsamifera* **var.** *subcordata Hylander,* is often planted as an ornamental.

100b. Leaves without glands at apex of petiole **101**

**101a. Young leaves shining; square cut at base with rounded teeth.
Winter buds glabrous, twigs gray to reddish-brown. Fig.
179a.**

EASTERN COTTONWOOD ....
......................................*Populus deltoides* Bartr. **var.** *deltoides*

Eastern cottonwood is the most important member of the genus
in the east. It is a medium-sized tree 80 to 100 feet in height, is
fast growing and has a moderate life span. Many believe it to be
the country's fastest growing timber tree; it is not uncommon for
trees under natural conditions to grow 4 to 5 feet in height annually. The use of improved clones in plantations has resulted in
height growth of 8 to 10 feet each year. BARK: grayish-green,
rough and furrowed. LEAVES: glistening, broadly triangular as
the species name implies, petiole flattened. FLOWERS: dioecious,
in catkins 2 to 3 inches long; male catkins red. FRUIT: drooping,
in long catkins. TWIGS AND BUDS: twigs, gray to reddish-brown;
buds, glabrous.

Cottonwood requires an abundant and continuous supply of moisture throughout the growing season. On the Mississippi flood plains it makes its best growth. It does not do well on heavy clay flats but requires moist medium textured soils with good internal drainage. It occurs pure but may be associated with several other bottomland hardwoods but they will definitely be in the minority. It

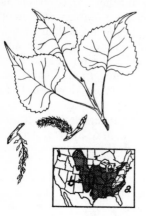

is a component in 6 other forest types where it is associated with black ash, American elm, red maple, bur oak, silver maple, Nuttall oak, willow oak, sycamore and black willow. Under cottonwood stands in the bottomlands the typical shrubs and vines are rough-leaf dogwood, swamp privet *Forestiera acuminata,* hawthorn, planertree, sumac, American elder *Sambucus canadensis,* greenbrier *Smilax rotundifolia,* trumpet vine *Campsis radicans* and buckvine *Ampelopsis arborea.* Cottonwood is more intolerant than any of its associates, except willow. It rarely succeeds itself unless a suitable seedbed has been prepared. It is a pioneer

Fig. 179. Populus deltoides.

species. Insects at times are damaging, leaf beetles, twig borers, root and stem borers and defoliating insects. Diseases do not seem to be important to growing cottonwood. At all ages cottonwood is susceptible to fire. It is an important lumber tree, for ground products and pulpwood. Buds and catkins are eaten by grouse and prairie chicken. Several species of songbirds eat the buds. Bark, foliage and buds are eaten by beaver, hare, rabbit, porcupine and squirrel. White-tail deer and moose browse the twigs and foliage.

The largest Eastern cottonwood living and of record is 30 feet 3 inches in circumference, 118 feet tall with a crown spread of 100 feet. It is growing near Perry, Iowa. Cottonwood is the State Tree of Kansas.

101b. Young leaves shining; square cut at base with rounded teeth. Winter buds minutely pubescent, twigs light yellow. Map 179b.

PLAINS COTTONWOOD ....
.................................*Populus deltoides* **var.** *occidentalis* Rydb.

Plains cottonwood occurs in the western portion of the range formerly attributed to eastern cottonwood (Range "b" Fig. 179). It is very similar in many respects. The best distinguishing characteristic is its region of growth. On the eastern limit it intermingles with eastern cottonwood. It is a medium-sized tree 60 to 90 feet tall with erect spreading branches forming an open crown. It is fast growing and short lived. Although it occurs in a region characterized by dry subhumid climate, cottonwood has definite requirements for moisture. Availability of moisture seems to be more important than soil texture. Plains cottonwood predominates on the level narrow bands of river flood plains and streams that cross the region. It is common in pure stands on riverbed sandbars and overflow lands along large rivers. It is an associate in three forest types where it grows along with bur oak, several willows, boxelder, slippery elm, red mulberry and silver maple. Common understory species are sandbar willow, coyote willow *Salix exigua*, red-osier dogwood *Cornus stolonifera*, indigo bush *Amorpha fruticosa*, coralberry *Symphoricarpos orbiculatus*, grape *Vitis* **spp.**, poison ivy *Rhus radicans*, smooth sumac and American plum. Plains cottonwood is intolerant and requires full sunlight for maximum growth. It usually occurs in pure, even-aged stands or in open well spaced mixtures. It is a pioneer species. It is quite free of insects and diseases. Occasionally some damage is sustained from leaf beetles, webworms, bagworms, sawflies, borers and even grasshoppers. The poplar canker and leaf rusts are the more common fungus enemies. Plains cottonwood is susceptible to fire. It is used for lumber, ground wood products and planted for shelterbelts. Buds are eaten by a number of songbirds. Bark, foliage, and buds by cottontail and swamp rabbits. Mule and white-tail deer browse the twigs and foliage.

The largest Plains cottonwood living and of record is 29 feet 8 inches in circumference, 120 feet tall with a crown spread of 93 feet. It is growing in Hygiene, Colorado.

101c. A hybrid with only staminate catkins; main trunk usually continuing to tree top. Fig. 180.

CAROLINA POPLAR ....
..................*Populus Xcanadensis* (**Ait.**)**Sm.**

Carolina poplar is a large tree with upright ascending branches often reaching heights of 90 feet. It is a hybrid of eastern cottonwood and Lombardy poplar. It is extensively planted across the United States and spreads from cultivation by root-sprouts. It is fast growing, tolerant of city smoke and dust. It does get into trouble when planted near sewers as its roots will penetrate. BARK:

Fig. 180. Populus Xcanadensis.

gray, furrowed. LEAVES: shiny and smooth both sides, blades triangular, 3 to 4 inches long, pointed, the margins with curved teeth. FLOWERS: male only. FRUIT: none, as the trees are male.

102a. Twigs and underside of leaves with dense white hairs, often lobed. Fig. 181.

WHITE POPLAR ....*Populus alba* L.

A large, much branched wide spreading tree. Native of central Europe and planted across the eastern United States and adjacent Canada. It is fast growing and tolerant of city smoke. Its extensive root system is the source of much sewer stoppage. BARK: smoothish, whitish or light gray. LEAVES: 3 to 5 lobed, maplelike, 2 1/2 to 4 inches long, silvery-white and hairy. FLOWERS: catkins, long and drooping, eventually 3 to 4 inches long. FRUIT: two-valved, oblong capsules in catkins.

Fig. 181. Populus alba.

102b. Leaves not lobed, pale or rusty beneath, densely tomentose when young. Buds sticky. Fig. 182.

SWAMP COTTONWOOD ....*Populus heterophylla* L.

Swamp cottonwood is a medium-sized tree 60 to 90 feet tall with an open irregular shaped crown. It is fast growing and short lived. BARK: grayish-brown, prominently furrowed. LEAVES: when young thickly covered with tangled white hairs, smooth when older, 4 to 8 inches long. FLOWERS: dioecious, drooping catkins 2 to 3 inches long. FRUIT: ovoid capsules, 2 to 3 valved. TWIGS AND BUDS: twigs, moderately slender, brownish gray, with an orange pith; buds, stout.

Fig. 182. Populus heterophylla.

Swamp cottonwood is usually found on sites too wet and heavy textured for eastern cottonwood. It grows in shallow swamps, sloughs and very wet river bottoms where the water table remains at the surface of the soil for all but a few summer and early fall months. It occurs sparsely throughout its range. It is not a major species in any one forest type but is a minor component in 3 forest types where it is associated with baldcypress, water tupelo, black willow, green ash, water hickory, sycamore, red maple, persimmon and overcup oak. In the understory several species are common; planertree, buttonbush, swamp privet *Forestiera acuminata*, possumhaw, smooth sumac, and hawthorn. Swamp cottonwood is an intolerant pioneer species. Insects cause but minor damage to swamp cottonwood. Leaf beetles and borers occasionally do some damage. It is relatively free of disease. Fire causes considerable damage to trees of all ages as it scars the lower trunk, thus permitting entry of rot producing fungi. Swamp cottonwood is not as important commercially as other cottonwoods. Its form is usually poor with a short limby bole. Where the form is satisfactory it goes along with other cottonwood for the same uses. Due to its infrequent occurrence it does not play any large part in the food for wildlife. Where it does occur, it is utilized by songbirds, Carolina beaver, rabbit, squirrel and white-tail deer.

The largest living swamp cottonwood of record is 18 feet in circumference, 100 feet tall. It is growing in Franklin County, Ohio.

103a. **With true lateral thorns, fruit small, apple-like; with bony centers when ripe. Fig. 183.**

THE HAWTHORNS: Genus CRATAEGUS

More than 1200 species of Crataegus have been listed for the United States. They are extremely variable, hybridize readily and are difficult to classify. For the most part, hawthorns are intolerant, slow growing and short lived. Many sterile individuals do not bear fruit. Where they do they make a definite contribution as food, cover, and forage for wildlife. In the midwest their thorns are food storage points for shrikes. They stand browsing well and "hedge" rather than die. The fruits are eaten by wildlife and mankind as well. Red haw jelly is a choice spread in the central States. The species chosen as examples of the genus were selected because of regional distribution, common occurrence, published data of use and value to wildlife. Sargent's "Manual

Fig. 183. Typical hawthorn leaves, fruits and thorns. (Miller Photo)

of Trees of North America" and Steyermark's "Flora of Missouri" have been used as a guide to distinguishing characteristics. The diagramatic drawings of leaf outlines may be helpful in identification.

103a. (1) Nutlets without ventral cavity.

Veins of the larger leaves extending to the sinuses as well as the lobes.

Leaves mostly ovate, incised and often trilobate.

WASHINGTON HAWTHORN, *Crataegus phaenopyrum* (L. f.) Med. Scattered in open ground thickets and borders of woods. Flowers May-June. Grouse, turkey, songbirds, fox, rabbit, squirrel, white-tail deer. The largest Washington hawthorn is 3 feet 3 inches in circumference, 24 feet high with a crown spread of 20 feet. It is growing in Secrest Arboretum, Wooster, Ohio.

Fig. 183a. Crataegus phaenopyrum.

Leaves mostly broadly ovate, deeply incised, acute at apex, shallow rounded lobes, glabrous.

LITTLEHIP HAWTHORN, *Crataegus spathulata* Michx. Moist or fertile ground, thickets and open woods. Flowers, May. Turkey, fox, squirrel, white-tail deer.

Fig. 183b. Crataegus spathulata.

Leaves broad ovate, deeply incised lobes, pubescent.

PARSLEY HAWTHORN, *Crataegus marshallii* Eggl. Low, wet or alluvial ground, stands hedging well. Turkey, quail, songbirds, fox, white-tail deer. Flowers in May.

Fig. 183c. Crataegus Marshallii.

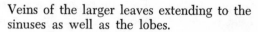

Veins of leaves running only to the point of the lobes.

Leaves firm, glabrous, bark rough.

MARGARET HAWTHORN, *Crataegus margaretta* Ashe. Thickets and rocky open ground. Fruit dark red or rusty orange. Flowers April-May. Grouse, prairie chicken, quail, turkey, songbirds, white-tail deer.

Fig. 183d. Crataegus margaretta.

Leaves of flowering branchlets mostly ovate, firm and glossy above.

COCKSPUR HAWTHORN, *Crataegus crus-galli* L. A large number of varieties. Thickets and rocky pastures, fruit remaining hard and dry. Grouse, turkey, songbirds, squirrel and white-tail deer. The largest living cockspur hawthorn is 6 feet 2 inches in circumference, 27 feet tall with a crown spread of 37 feet. It is growing near Orrville, Wayne County, Ohio.

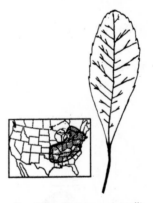

Fig. 183e. Crataegus crus-galli.

Leaves densely tomentose, especially when young, rounded at the base.

DOWNY HAWTHORN, Crataegus mollis Scheele. Open woods and along small streams. Fruit succulent and makes good jelly. Flowers in April. Grouse, prairie chicken, quail, squirrel, turkey and white-tail deer. The largest downy hawthorn is 8 feet in circumference, 50 feet tall with a crown spread of 62 feet. It is growing at Paris, Illinois.

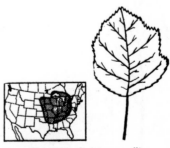

Fig. 183f. Crataegus mollis.

Leaves glabrous or slightly pubescent, fruit hard and dry remaining pruinose, flowers white hairy tomentum.

FROSTED HAWTHORN, *Crataegus pruinosa* (H. L. Wendl.) K. Koch. Rocky woods and thickets. Flowers late in April and May. Grouse, prairie chicken, quail, white-tail deer and squirrel.

Fig. 183g. Crataegus pruinosa.

103a. (2) Nutlets with longitudinal cavities on their ventral face.

Fruit short oblong, black, nutlets 5, obscurely ridged on back, thick.

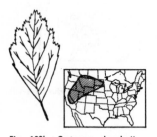

Leaves thick and lustrous above, coarsely serrate, usually lobed, spines numerous.

BLACK HAWTHORN, *Crataegus douglasii* Lindl. Banks of mountain streams and moist sites. Fruit large and edible, flowers in May. Grouse, mule and white-tail deer, songbirds. The largest living black hawthorn of record is 5 feet 1 inch in circumference, 40 feet tall with a crown spread of 20 feet. It is growing in Polk County, Oregon.

Fig. 183h. Crataegus douglasii.

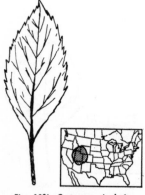

Leaves thin, dull bluish-green, finely serrate, spines few or wanting, long and slender.

RIVER HAWTHORN, *Crataegus rivularis* Nutt. Along streams and water courses, moist valleys at elevations of 3000 to 8000 feet. Not as tall as black hawthorn. Flowers in May. Grouse, mule and white-tail deer, elk. Hedges well.

Fig. 183i. Crataegus rivularis.

103b. Without true lateral thorn (some have dwarfed branches that are thorn-like) **104**

104a. With stipules or stipular scars **107**

104b. Without stipules or stipular scars **105**

105a. Leaves resinous dotted, aromatic when bruised. Fig. 184.

SOUTHERN BAYBERRY .... *Myrica cerifera* **L.**

A small tree occasionally reaching 40 feet in height. More frequently a shrub. As a tree it has a narrow round topped crown. It is normally slow growing and short lived. In the region where it grows, fire is frequently used in management of cattle range or pine forests. Under this treatment the plant is often killed back to the roots. From the root, regrowth is rapid. BARK: close fitting, smooth, light gray. LEAVES: yellowish-green with many minute dark glands above and bright orange glands below. FLOWERS: dioecious, staminate catkins 1/2 to 3/4 inch long; pistillate catkins shorter. FRUIT: covered with pale blue wax. Ripens in fall and remains on tree throughout winter.

Fig. 184. Myrica cerifera.

Southern bayberry is one of the most common understory woody plants of the southern coastal plains pinelands. It can tolerate dry sites, but makes its best growth in sandy swamps and on pond margins. It occurs as an understory component in several forest types where it is associated with longleaf, loblolly and slash pines, southern red oak and sweetgum. On the dryer sites; bluejack, blackjack and sand post oaks. In the understory it is associated with gallberry, tree sparkleberry, dwarf bayberry *Myrica pusilla*, shining sumac, and poison ivy *Rhus radicans*. It is an intolerant subclimax species. Southern bayberry does not appear to be subject to serious insects or diseases. Fire prunes it back to the ground, but following that it sprouts freely, producing more berries. Myrica contains volatile oils useful in the manufacture of candles, soaps, and deodorants. The berries are eaten by some 30 species of songbirds. Twigs and foliage are browsed by white-tail deer. Quail and turkey eat the berries.

The largest southern bayberry living and of record is 3 feet 9 inches in circumference, 32 feet tall with a crown spread of 33 feet. It is growing at Crestview, Florida.

The ODORLESS BAYBERRY *Myrica inodora* Bartr. found in the Coastal Plains from Florida, Mississippi and Louisiana has entire leaves and only rarely becomes a tree. The berries have the same wildlife attraction as southern bayberry.

105b. Leaves without resinous dots **106**

106a. Leaves persisting into their second year; flowers showy, fragrant. Fig. 185.

LOBLOLLY-BAY ....*Gordonia lasianthus* (L.) Ellis

A medium-sized tree 60 to 70 feet tall with a narrow compact crown. It is fast growing and short lived. BARK: dark red-brown, thick with deep parallel rounded ridges. LEAVES: dark green, leathery 4 to 5 inches long, turning scarlet and dropping during second year. FLOWERS: white, 2 1/2 inches in diameter, July to September, on heavy red pedicels, 2 to 3 inches long. FRUIT: 3/4 inch long; seeds winged.

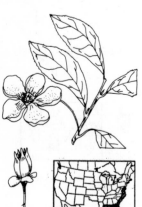

Loblolly-bay occurs in shallow swamps and wet lands in the Coastal Plains of the south and southeast. It is either in the intermediate crown class or understory in 6 major forest types. Here it is associated with slash pine, pondcypress, Atlantic white-cedar, swamp tupelo, black tupelo, sweetbay and red maple. In the understory; buckwheat-tree, swamp cyrilla, dahoon, yaupon and gumbo-limbo *Bursera simaruba*. It is a moderately intolerant, subclimax species. Loblolly-bay is not subject to any serious damage by insects or disease. It can be damaged by fire if the wet site in which it grows gets dry enough to burn. The reddish wood finishes well and is regarded as an attractive cabinet wood. Loblolly-bay itself does not have any particular attraction to wildlife.

Fig. 185. Gordonia lasianthus.

The largest loblolly-bay living and of record is 11 feet 10 inches in circumference, 94 feet tall with a crown spread of 54 feet. It is growing in the Ocala National Forest in Florida.

106b. Leaves deciduous, sour to taste. Fig. 186.

SOURWOOD ....*Oxydendrum arboreum* (L.) D.C.

Sourwood is a small tree 50 to 60 feet tall with a slender crown. It is an infrequent species in several hardwood types within its range. It is slow growing and short lived. BARK: reddish-gray, longitudinally furrowed, blocky scales on older boles. LEAVES: shining dark green 5 to 7 inches long, sour to the taste. Bright scarlet in the early fall. FLOWERS: in panicles, white, about 1/3 inch long, midsummer. FRUIT: a capsule to 1/2 inch long, turning upward when pollinated. TWIGS AND BUDS: leaf scars rounded, with a single bundle scar; buds, puberulous on margin and inner surface.

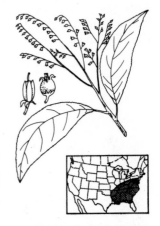

Fig. 186. Oxydendrum arboreum.

Sourwood occurs on well drained, acid soils found on slopes and ridges. It does not do well on lime base soils. It is not found in pure stands but is a minor component of 3 major forest types where it is associated with post, black, scarlet oaks, and a number of other upland oaks, shortleaf, loblolly, and pitch pines, several hickories and sweetgum. It is usually in the intermediate crown class rather than dominant or even codominant. Understory species commonly found with sourwood are azalea *Rhododendron* spp., elder *Sambucus canadensis,* mountain-laurel, tree sparkleberry, smooth hydrangea *Hydrangea arborescens,* blackberry *Rubus* spp., greenbrier *Smilax* spp., and blueberry *Vaccinium* spp. Sourwood is intermediate in tolerance and is a subclimax species. The only serious insect enemy is the sphinx moth whose caterpillars often defoliate young trees in late spring. Fire will induce profuse sprouting from the roots. Sourwood is occasionally used for attractive paneling. Sourwood honey is a prized product of the southeastern mountains. Twigs and foliage of sourwood are rated well as browse for white-tail deer, sprout growth higher than normal growth. Sourwood can withstand removal of 40 percent of current annual growth by browsing without seriously damaging the plant.

The largest sourwood living and of record is 7 feet 7 inches in circumference, 80 feet tall with a crown spread of 40 feet. It is growing in the Great Smoky Mountains National Park in Tennessee.

107a. Leaves with one or more disk-like, wart-like or tooth-like glands at base of blade or on outer end of petiole 111

107b. Without glands as mentioned in 107a 108

108a. Glands at tips of serrations on leaf margins. Fruit a spherical berry, about 1/3 inch through with 2 to 4 seeds, black when ripe. Fig. 187.

CAROLINA BUCKTHORN .... *Rhamnus caroliniana* Walt.

A small tree 30 to 40 feet in height with spreading unarmed branches. Slow growing and short lived. BARK: thin, light gray, with black blotches. LEAVES: dark yellow-green above, pale below, 2 to 5 inches long. FLOWERS: greenish-white in umbels. FRUIT: about 1/3 inch in diameter, black when ripe, with 3 to 4 hard seeds. TWIGS AND BUDS: twigs, puberulent at first then glabrous, stipules persistent; buds, naked, brownish.

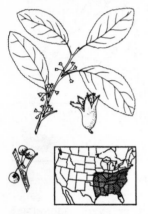

Carolina buckthorn is widely distributed and occurring on sites of good moisture and soils of calcareous origin, borders of streams and rich bottomlands. Usually in open woods. It is a minor component of many central and southern hardwood forest types where it is associated with redcedar, blackgum, pin oak, sweetgum, beech, southern magnolia and sycamore. It rarely, if ever, is above the intermediate canopy, more often in the understory. It is associated with other understory species such as dogwood, painted and dwarf buckeyes, hawthorn, American hornbeam, pawpaw,

Fig. 187. Rhamnus caroliniana.

and arrowwood *Viburnum dentatum.* It is medium tolerant and subclimax. Carolina buckthorn does not appear to have any serious problems with insects or diseases. Its thin bark is highly susceptible to fire. The only commercial use made of buckthorn is for ornamental plantings in cities. Fruit is eaten by a large number of songbirds; the greatest use probably is by the pileated woodpecker. Squirrels and other rodents eat the fruit. White-tail deer browse the twigs and foliage during the winter months.

The largest living Carolina buckthorn of record is 1 foot 3 inches in circumference, 16 feet high with a crown spread of 10 feet. It is growing in Dawes Arboretum, near Newark, Ohio.

The EUROPEAN BUCKTHORN *Rhamnus cathartica* L. has been introduced into the United States for ornamental purposes. Its leaves are less elongate, have only 3 or 4 lateral veins and are opposite on the stem.

108b. Serrations not gland tipped. Fruit apple-like **109**

109a. Leaves usually dull, irregularly dentate or serrate, sometimes lobed **110**

109b. Leaves glabrous and usually shiny, sharply and regularly serrate. Fruit usually pear-shaped. Fig. 188.

COMMON PEAR .... *Pyrus communis* L.

A small tree sometimes to 60 feet tall. Usually much smaller and kept that way by pruning for easier maintenance and greater fruit production. It is an import from Europe and Asia. BARK: dark, smooth. LEAVES: shining green, 2 to 4 inches long. FLOWERS: borne at the ends of short twigs of the preceding year, 3/4 to 1 1/2 inches broad, white or pinkish. FRUIT: many varieties, mostly edible. Branches often thorny. It is planted throughout the northeast and central states as a fruit tree.

Fig. 188. Pyrus communis.

110a. Leaves rounded or cordate at the base with whitish pubescence below and on petiole, fruit of various shapes and colors when ripe. Fig. 189.

COMMON APPLE .... *Malus pumila* Mill.

A medium sized tree with round crown and spreading branches. A native of Europe where it has been cultivated since ancient times. It was brought to the United States during colonial times. BARK: dark grayish-brown, flaky. LEAVES: pubescent and often wooly beneath, more or less glabrous above, 3 to 5 inches long. FLOWERS: white or light pink, 1 to 2 inches across; appearing with foliage or just before it. FRUIT: fleshy pome of many varieties due to cultivation. It and its varieties are planted throughout the United States for fruit production.

Fig. 189. Malus pumila.

110b. Leaves rounded at the base. Fruit shiny green, 3/4 to 1 1/2 inches in diameter. Fig. 190.

PRAIRIE CRAB APPLE ....*Malus ioensis* (Wood) Britton

A small tree 20 to 30 feet tall with stout spreading branches forming an open crown. It is slow growing and short lived. BARK: longitudinally fissured, the outer layer separating into long narrow persistent red-brown scales. LEAVES: villous pubescent; 1 to 2 inches long. FLOWERS: beautiful pink, 1 1/4 to 1 1/2 inches in diameter, May-June. FRUIT: Yellowish-green at maturity.

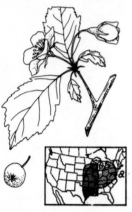

Fig. 190. *Malus ioensis.*

It is widely distributed in prairies, woods openings, pastures and bottomlands, frequently forming dense thickets. On prairies and pastures it is associated with hawthorn and coralberry *Symphoricarpus* **spp.**, grasses and sedges. For the most part it is considered to be tolerant of shade and a subclimax species. On prairies it would be considered a pioneer. Within forest types its associates are bur oak, northern pin oak, northern red oak, cottonwood and shellbark hickory. Prairie crab is definitely an understory species in these types. It does not appear to have any serious enemies except fire which does kill. The thin bark is little protection. There are no commercial uses for the wood but the fruit makes fine jellies. More than 20 species of songbirds, pheasant, grouse, turkey and quail as well as squirrels and other rodents eat the fruit. White-tail deer eat the fruit and browse the twigs and foliage. Dense thickets of prairie crab are good moulting cover for grouse and other game birds and nesting habitat for a number of songbirds.

The largest prairie crab living and of record is 2 feet 8 inches in circumference, 27 feet high with a crown spread of 28 feet. It is growing at Kansas City, Missouri.

The prairie crab has been described at least 13 times as a variety or additional species. The variations are great.

The SWEET CRAB APPLE *Malus coronaria* (L.) Mill. has been described as at least 24 species or varieties. It differs from the Prairie crab in having leaves glabrous at maturity. Its range is more eastern but overlapping and shown on the map at "a."

The SOULARD CRAB APPLE *Malus Xsoulardii* (Bailey) Britton is a natural hybrid of the apple *Malus pumila* and the prairie crab *Malus ioensis*. It is found in the middle western states.

110c. Leaves often wedge-shaped at base, glabrous at maturity, fruit flattened at end. Fig. 191.

SOUTHERN CRAB APPLE ......*Malus angustifolia* (Ait.) Michx.

A small tree 15 to 20 feet high with a short bole and wide spreading crown. It is slow growing and short lived. BARK: thin, dark reddish-brown, with narrow ridges and scales. LEAVES: 1 to 2 inches long, hoary-tomentose below when young but presently glabrous. FLOWERS: 1 inch in diameter, pink to rose-colored. FRUIT: 3/4 to 1 inch in diameter, yellowish-green.

Occurs in the Coastal Plains in forest types containing longleaf and loblolly pines, sweetgum, yellow-poplar, red maple and southern red oak. It is a member of the understory where it is associated with hawthorn, possumhaw, gallberry, greenbrier *Smilax* spp., and Virginia sweetspire *Itea virginica*. It is tolerant and subclimax. It does not appear to be subject to any significant insects or diseases. Fire will kill as the bark is very thin. This is one reason its numbers are

Fig. 191. Malus angustifolia.

low in Coastal Plains forests where fire has been used in management. The only commercial use of the tree is the fruit which makes delicious preserves. Fruit is eaten by a large number of songbirds, turkey, quail, squirrel and other rodents and white-tail deer.

The largest southern crab apple of record is 3 feet 3 inches in circumference, 40 feet high with a crown spread of 38 feet. It is growing at Columbia, South Carolina.

The SIBERIAN CRAB APPLE *Malus baccata* (L.) Borkh. is sometimes cultivated.

111a. Twigs usually red on top and green below although sometimes wholly red or green. Fig. 192.

PEACH ....*Prunus persica* Batsch

A small tree 15 to 30 feet high with wide spreading branches. Is an import from China. BARK: smooth, rather dark. LEAVES: 4 to 7 inches long, taper equally to both ends; petioles often red. FLOWERS: pink, appear before leaves 1/2 to 2 inches broad, scaly-bracted. FRUIT: clothed with velvety down, large stone, wrinkled, diameter 1 1/2 to 3 inches. There are a number

Fig. 192. Prunus persica.

of varieties, Nectarines and Flat peaches. There are a number of
pests in commercial orchards; sprays are widely used to control.
More recently a root rot has caused trouble.

The ALMOND *Prunus amyglatus* Batsch is a closely similar tree,
but is grown for the seed only, the flesh is thrown away.

111b. Twigs not red or green. Fruit a smooth drupe **112**

112a. Leaves folded lengthwise in the bud and when emerging;
petioles usually rather slender and long; fruit usually small
with rounded pits. THE CHERRIES **113**

112b. Leaves wrapped around each other in the bud and when
emerging; petioles tending to be short and stout; fruit
usually larger with somewhat flattened pits. THE PLUMS
....**117**

Fig. 193.

113a. Flowers and fruits in axillary
umbels (sometimes in corymbs,
in pensylvanica); blossoming
with or before the appearance
of leaves. Fig. 193a. **114**

113b. Flowers and fruit in racemes
at end of leafy branches. Fig.
193b **116**

THE CHERRIES: Genus PRUNUS

The genus Prunus is widely distributed in the cooler regions of
the United States; 22 species are listed in the "Check List." They
vary greatly in size from the large black cherry to some of the
small almost shrubby sizes. Lenticels in the bark are usually prominent on twigs and younger growth. Cherries are eaten by more
than 30 songbirds, grouse, turkey, prairie chicken and quail, squirrels and other rodents. Species of the genus Prunus are rated high
in humus building capacity.

113c. Flowers and fruit in terminal corymbs. Fruit about 1/4 inch,
black when ripe. Fig. 194.

MAHALEB CHERRY ....
....*Prunus mahaleb* **L.**

A small tree to 25 feet with a rounded crown. Foliage fragrant. Native of
southern Europe. BARK: brownish-
gray, rough. LEAVES: bright-green, 1
to 2 inches long. FLOWERS: white
1/2 inch across or smaller, May-June.
FRUIT: dark red when ripe in July,
1/3 inch in diameter. Planted as an
ornamental and stock for grafting.

**114a. Fruit usually 1/2 inch or more
in length** **115**

Fig. 194. Prunus mahaleb.

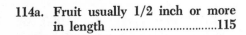

114b. Fruit about 1/4 inch, very sour. Fig. 195.

PIN CHERRY ....*Prunus pensylvanica* **L.f.**

A small tree 30 to 40 feet high with bitter aromatic bark, leaves,
and slender horizontal branches forming a more or less rounded
crown. It makes rather rapid growth
and is short lived. BARK: smooth purplish-brown. Lenticels very prominent.
LEAVES: shining green above, paler
below, 3 to 6 inches long. FLOWERS:
1/2 inch across, white. FRUIT: light
red, 1/4 inch in diameter, tart to the
taste. TWIGS AND BUDS: twigs, with
a rank disagreeable bitter-almond taste;
buds, small round and clustered.

Pin cherry is not exacting as to soil
requirements. It is a short lived pioneer
which invades clearcut or heavily
burned areas. It occurs in pure stands
as well as in composition with other
species. It is a component of 3 forest
types where it is associated with quaking aspen, bigtooth aspen, paper birch

Fig. 195. Prunus pensylvanica.

and red maple, northern red oak, yellow birch, red spruce and
Fraser fir. Due to the wide range of pin cherry, there is considerable variation in the understory species. Some of the more common

are mountain ash, beaked hazel *Corylus cornuta,* mountain maple, several alders, wild current *Ribes* **spp.**, and willows. It is not susceptible to many insects or diseases. Occasionally the bag worm will defoliate. It is susceptible to fire, but is a fire follower. It has no commercial value. As an invader it will take over badly burned sites and reduce soil movement. Grouse, pheasant, prairie chicken, turkey and 24 species of songbirds eat the fruits, as do squirrels and rodents. White-tail deer and moose browse the twigs and foliage.

The largest pin cherry of record is 5 feet 4 inches in circumference, 45 feet high with a crown spread of 38 feet. It is growing in the Great Smoky Mountains National Park in Tennessee.

CAROLINA LAURELCHERRY *Prunus caroliniana* (**Mill.**) **Ait.** differs from Prunus pensylvanica in having flowers and fruit in racemes which arise from axiliary buds of wood of the previous year. The cherries are about 1/2 inch in diameter. Note southern range on the map (Fig. 195). It is more demanding of moisture than pin cherry. The wilted leaves and twigs are not browsed heavily, if at all, due to the presence of hydrocyanic acid which makes them unpalatable and dangerous, especially to livestock. Deer seem to be able to eat moderate quantities without danger.

115a. Leaves glabrous, fruit sour. Fig. 196.

SOUR CHERRY .... *Prunus cerasus* L.

A low spreading tree with a rounded top to 30 feet tall. A native of Europe. BARK: older trees have thin curled scales leaving somewhat ridged inner bark, dark color. Twigs reddish-brown, smooth with prominent lenticels. LEAVES: 2 1/2 to 4 inches long, firm and thick, lustrous dark green above, paler beneath. FLOWERS: white, about one inch broad, appear before or with leaves. FRUIT: 1/2 inch in diameter (larger in cultivation), red, without bloom, juicy tart flesh with subglobose pit. Sour cherry is planted widely in the middle western states for fruit. The wood is not used commercially.

Fig. 196. Prunus cerasus.

115b. Leaves pubescent on underside, fruit sweet. Fig. 197.

MAZZARD (SWEET CHERRY) ....*Prunus avium* (L.) L.

A wide spreading tree at maturity to 75 feet tall. A native of Europe. BARK: smooth, reddish-brown, in layers like the birches. LEAVES: dull dark green above usually pubescent beneath, 4 to 6 inches long. FLOWERS: about 1 inch across, white, appearing with the leaves. FRUIT: flesh sweet, many varieties, yellow to dark red. The Mazzard is planted widely in the middle west and the Lake States as a fruit tree. The wood has been used for furniture and musical instruments. The largest living Mazzard cherry of record is 6 feet 1 inch in circumference, 30 feet tall with a crown spread of 50 feet. It is growing at Dayton, Ohio.

Fig. 197. Prunus avium.

116a. Leaves thickish with incurved teeth, glands on petiole elongated, tooth-like. Fig. 198.

BLACK CHERRY ....*Prunus serotina* Ehrh.

A medium-sized tree 50 to 60 feet high with a rounded crown. Growth is rapid for the first 40 to 50 years, after which it slows down. It is a tree of medium life span. BARK: rough, black and flaky. Branches reddish-brown with prominent lenticels. LEAVES: 2 to 5 inches long, thickish, serrate with incurved teeth. FLOWERS: small and white in long hanging racemes. Usually appear later than flowers of most trees. FRUIT: small reddish-black drupes in racemes, not edible. TWIGS AND BUDS: twigs, bitter-almond taste, older growth often with short spur shoots; buds, terminal, chestnut-brown with several visible scales.

Fig. 198. Prunus serotina.

Black cherry grows on a variety of soils throughout its range; it does best however on moist, fertile north and east facing lower slopes and in coves. It occurs in pure stands and mixtures with other hardwoods and conifers. In addition to the pure type, it occurs as a component in 10 forest types. It is associated with sugar maple, northern red oak, white oak, white pine, hemlock, beech, yellow birch, basswood and white ash. The understory is variable according to range. Some of the more common species are flowering dogwood, redbud, pawpaw, hydrangea *Hydrangea arborescens,* leatherwood *Dirca palustris,* mountain-laurel, rosebay rhododendron, and witch-hazel.

Black cherry is intolerant and a minor member of climax types. In these types it occurs either in even-aged pure groups or as a dominant in mixed stands. Were it not for its rapid early growth it could not maintain its position in climax environment. Black cherry has a number of enemies, tent caterpillar, borers and cambium-mining larvae. A number of fungi attack black cherry of the *Polyporus* and *Fomes* groups. Trees of all sizes are highly susceptible to fire. It has the ability to sprout following any but very hot and deep fires. Black cherry is used extensively in furniture and cabinet work. The cherries are eaten by grouse, quail, prairie chicken and pheasant, at least 30 songbirds. Small mammals also eat the fruit. Although the twigs and foliage contain cyanic acid and may be poisonous to deer and other browsers in wilted condition, white-tail deer appear to be able to eat the unwilted material without danger.

The largest black cherry is 23 feet 4 inches in circumference, 102 feet tall with a crown spread of 89 feet. It is growing in Lawrence, Van Buren County, Michigan.

116b. Leaves thinish with diverging teeth, glands on petiole usually rounded or disk-like. Fig. 199.

COMMON CHOKECHERRY ....*Prunus virginiana* L.

A small tree frequently a shrub 20 to 30 feet tall with irregular rounded crown. Bole often crooked and leaning. It is moderately

fast growing but short lived. BARK: grayish-brown, more or less mottled and rather smooth. LEAVES: thin, 2 to 3 inches long, dull dark green above, paler along veins beneath. Teeth somewhat spreading. FLOWERS: 1/4 to 1/3 inch across in cylindrical racemes, white, May. FRUIT: a raceme of drupes, almost black when ripe, with a very astringent taste. Kernels poisonous. BUDS: scales gray margin.

Occurs on moist soils along roads, fence rows and edges of woods. Common chokecherry rarely becomes a member of the dominant crown class in

Fig. 199. *Prunus virginiana.*

forest types but is a minor component of the understory. It occurs in several forest types where it is associated with pin cherry, aspens, paper birch, northern red oak and red maple. In the understory with hazelnut *Corylus americana*, bearberry *Arctostaphylos uva-ursi*, elder *Sambucus canadensis*, dewberry *Rubus* spp., and willows *Salix* spp. It is an intolerant pioneer species. It is not subject to any serious insect attacks or diseases. Tent caterpillars, borers and other defoliators take their toll from time to time. Both *Polyporus* and *Fomes* fungi attack the bole. It is susceptible to fire but sprouts prolifically from the root crown. It does not have any commercial value but does do a good job of erosion control on sites denuded by fire or logging. The cherries and some buds are taken by grouse, prairie chicken, pheasant and quail. Upwards of 25 songbirds eat the cherries. Foliage and twigs are a staple deer browse in the Lake States.

The largest common chokecherry living and of record is 5 feet 3 inches in circumference, 65 feet tall with crown spread of 53 feet. It is growing at Ada, Michigan.

117a. Flowers and fruit with very short stem; petiole 1/2 as long as leaf blade. Fig. 200.

APRICOT ....*Prunus armeniaca* L.

A small tree about 20 feet tall, rounded crown. Imported from China for fruit production. BARK: reddish, glabrous twigs. LEAVES: short-pointed, glabrous above, pubescent on veins beneath, conspicuous petioles, dark green. FLOWERS: pinkish or nearly white, 3/4 to 1 inch across, single and sessile, appear before foliage. FRUIT: one-seeded drupe, matures in August-September. Is planted for the fruit and has no other uses.

117b. Not as in 117a **118**

Fig. 200. Prunus armeniaca.

THE PLUMS: Genus **PRUNUS**

118a. Leaves abruptly acuminate. Fig. 201 ..**119**

118b. Leaves not at all or but gradually acuminate **121**

119a. Leaves dull, usually broad and thick, veins impressed **120**

Fig. 201.

119b. Leaves shining, firm, glabrous. Fig. 202.

WILDGOOSE PLUM ....*Prunus munsoniana* Wight & Hedr.

A small tree sometimes spreading into dense thickets with spreading branches and reaching heights of 20 to 30 feet. It is fast growing and short lived. BARK: thin and ridged. LEAVES: dark, shining green, paler beneath, with glands on serrations and on the petiole near the leaf blade. FLOWERS: 2 to 4 in umbels, about 3/5 inch across, white appearing when leaves are grown. FRUIT: red or reddish-yellow, 3/4 inch long; several cultivated varieties with larger fruit.

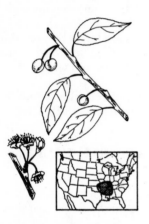

Occurs in moist and fertile soils in openings, pastures and along roadways. Does not occur as a part of a forest type, rather a "type" of its own, in thickets. In these areas it is associated with sumac *Rhus* spp., choke and pin cherries, elderberry *Sambucus canadensis,* and wild rose *Rosa* spp. It has few, if any, natural enemies. It will sprout following fire. It is an intolerant pioneer species. Foxes, bobcat, raccoon and bear are the principal users of the fruit. The thickets are fine nesting cover for songbirds and moulting and escape cover for game birds.

Fig. 202. Prunus munsoniana.

The largest living wildgoose plum of record is 4 feet in circumference, 14 feet tall with a crown spread of 30 feet. It is growing in Kansas City, Missouri.

The HORTULAN PLUM *Prunus hortulana* Bailey, with much the same range, differs from wildgoose plum in bearing a little larger and more globular plum. Its leaves are wider. Both of these species have been widely planted. When growing in the wild, the fruit is utilized the same as the wildgoose fruit.

Fig. 203. Prunus americana var. americana.

120a. Leaves sharp serrate; flowers white. Fig. 203.

AMERICAN PLUM .... *Prunus americana* Marsh. **var.** *americana*

American plum is a small tree, more frequently a shrub. As a tree it may reach 20 to 30 feet in height. It grows rapidly and is short lived. BARK: thin, dark brown with reddish tinge. LEAVES: dark green above, pale and smooth below. FLOWERS: in umbels of 2 to 5, calyx bright red; petals white with a claw. FRUIT: orange to bright red, 1 inch or less long. There are several cultivated varieties.

Fig. 203a. Prunus americana var. americana.

American plum occurs in rich soil along streams and wet lands. It grows in pure, even-age thickets in openings in the woodlands. It is intolerant and subclimax. It occurs as an understory in several types over its wide range. The more common types are those where it is associated with shin oak, live oak, Shumard oak, hackberry and holly. Typical associated understory species are elderberry *Sambucus canadensis*, the sumacs *Rhus* **spp.**, yaupon, possumhaw, hawthorn and greenbrier *Smilax* **spp.** American plum does not appear to suffer serious damage from insects or diseases. Several fruit-worms may attack the fruit, rendering it unfit for human consumption but not for wildlife. Its commercial value is in the field of fruit production. Fruits are eaten by fox, bobcat, raccoon and bear. Deer will also eat the fruits. Thickets are good escape cover for game birds and nesting sites for songbirds.

The largest American plum is 5 feet in circumference, 29 feet high with a crown spread of 33 feet. It is growing near Steyer, Maryland.

The INCH PLUM *Prunus americana* var. *lanata* Sudw., a variety of American plum, has a more restricted range and differs from it by the deep crimson fruit covered with glaucous bloom and the leaves pubescent below. The largest inch plum is 1 foot 10 inches in circumference, 26 feet tall with a crown spread of 24 feet. It is growing in the Ouachita National Forest in Arkansas.

203b. Prunus americana var. lanata.

The ALLEGHENY PLUM *Prunus alleghaniensis* Porter, likewise has a restricted range but has a purple fruit covered with glaucous bloom. Both species listed above receive the same type of wildlife usage.

Fig. 203c. Prunus alleghaniensis.

120b. Leaves obtusely serrate; flowers turning pink. Fig. 204.

CANADA PLUM ....*Prunus nigra* Ait.

A small tree 20 to 30 feet high with a broad rounded crown. It is fast growing and short lived. BARK: thin, light grayish-brown; in scales and layers. LEAVES: at first reddish and pubescent, becoming dull dark green above, under surface paler. Two large

glands at apex of petiole. FLOWERS: 1 1/4 inches across, white turning pink, in umbels, with red stems. FRUIT: orange-red when ripe, 1 to 1 1/4 inches long. Several cultivated varieties.

Occurs in the alluvial valleys of rivers and on limestone hills. Grows in pure even-age thickets along the borders of woods and roadways. Where it occurs in woodlands it is a species of the understory most frequently shrubby. It is associated with hawthorn, elder *Sambucus canadensis,* smooth and shining sumac, blackberry *Rubus* spp., and wild rose *Rosa* spp. It is an intolerant pioneer species. Canada plum does not appear to have any serious insect enemies or diseases. Fire will kill the stems but the

Fig. 204. Prunus nigra.

roots will sprout profusely. Fruits are eaten by fox, bobcat, raccoon, bear and some of the larger rodents. Deer will eat the plums. The wood is not used for commercial purposes, but the species is widely planted for fruit.

The MEXICAN PLUM *Prunus mexicana* S. Wats. differs from Canada plum in having sharply serrate teeth. Fruit is purple-red and more than an inch long. Its range (southern) is shown on the map. The largest living Mexican plum of record is 3 feet 9 inches in circumference, 24 feet tall with a crown spread of 36 feet. It is growing near Woodville, Texas.

121a. Leaves pubescent beneath but slightly pointed if at all. Cultivated. Fig. 205.

GARDEN PLUM ......*Prunus domestica* L.

A small tree strong growing with thick twigs; maximum height about 35 feet. Many forms due to cultivation. Imported from Asia and Europe. BARK: dark brown

Fig. 205. Prunus domestica.

or black, thick. LEAVES: simple, serrate, form varying with variety. FLOWERS: white or cream-color, 1 inch or less across, in small clusters appearing before or with the leaves. FRUIT: drupe of various sizes; color and palatability, variable. Often blue or purple. Covered with whitish bloom. Is cultivated for fruit and as an ornamental.

121b. Leaves glabrous when mature, lanceolate. Fig. 206.

CHICKASAW PLUM ....*Prunus angustifolia* Marsh.

A small tree with spreading branches 15 to 25 feet tall. Rarely in single specimens but more frequently in dense thickets. Extensively

naturalized and spread by Indians in prehistoric times. It is fast growing and short lived. BARK: rough, dark brown. LEAVES: shining bright green above, paler beneath, 1 to 2 inches long. FLOWERS: about 1/3 inch across in 2 to 4 flowered umbels. FRUIT: bright red, about 1/2 inch in diameter. Known as "sand plum" locally.

Occurs in even-aged thickets in pastures, fields, along fence rows, roads, and prairie streams. It is intolerant and a pioneer. Other shrubby species with which it is associated are cockspur hawthorn, elderberry *Sambucus canadensis*, smooth sumac, shining sumac, and other plums. Chickasaw plum does not appear

Fig. 206. Prunus angustifolia.

to have any serious enemies, except fire which kills back the stems. Sprouting occurs from the roots. The fruit is eaten by fox, bobcat, raccoon, bear, and deer. Squirrels and other rodents find the fruit palatable. Thickets are excellent escape cover and nesting habitat. The only use made of the tree is its fruit for eating and preserves.

122a. Stipules large leaving stipular rings on twig **123**

122b. Twigs without stipular rings, axillary buds not covered ..**124**

123a. Axillary bud wholly covered by base of petiole. Fig. 207.

AMERICAN SYCAMORE ....*Platanus occidentalis* L.

Sycamore is one of the largest eastern hardwoods commonly attaining heights in excess of 100 feet. It has a well developed

spreading crown. Is fast growing and has a moderate longevity.
BARK: trunk gray, breaking up into small scales, upper limbs
with large peeling scales, exposing smooth greenish-white bark.
LEAVES: with large stipules, yellow-greenish, 4 to 8 inches long.
FLOWERS: in hanging balls about 1/2 inch in diameter. FRUIT:
brown balls 1 inch in diameter on slender stems. Seeds an achene.

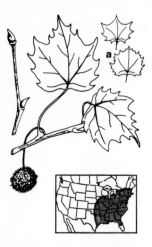

TWIGS AND BUDS: twigs, conspicuously zigzag. Terminal buds lacking;
lateral buds resinous with caplike outer
scale.

Sycamore occurs most frequently and
reaches its best growth on alluvial soils
along streams and in bottom lands.
Occasionally it is a pioneer tree in upland old-field sites. It most commonly
grows on flat land having a good supply of moisture. It may occur in pure
stands but its normal habit is in association with other species. It is the
major species in two forest types where
it is associated with river birch, pecan
and American elm. In four other types,
it is associated with black ash, northern red oak, mockernut hickory, sweetgum, silver maple and black willow.

Fig. 207. Platanus occidentalis.

Understory species commonly found in the bottomland types are
roughleaf dogwood, hawthorn, possumhaw, redbud, smooth sumac,
elder Sambucus canadensis and grape Vitis spp. Sycamore is considered intermediate in tolerance although in some instances it
appears to react to shade as an intolerant. It can compete success-
fully with cottonwood and willow. It occurs in types that are pioneer, subclimax and climax. It seems to react better in subclimax
and pioneer situations. Many insects feed on sycamore, but none
appear to be too damaging, except possibly on shade trees. Lace
bugs, borers, tussock moth, and others are commonly found on
sycamore. Few diseases cause loss. It is a windfirm species due to
its well developed root system. Sycamore is susceptible to damage
from fire. It is used widely for lumber, panels, furniture and pallets.
It does not have any significant wildlife use; purple finches use
the seed for food. Occasionally beaver and squirrel eat the bark
and wood. The largest American sycamore of record is 32 feet 10
inches in circumference, 80 feet tall with a crown spread of 102
feet. It is growing near South Bloomfield, Ohio.

The LONDON PLANE Platanus Xacerifolia (Ait.) Willd. is often
planted as an ornamental. The leaves are (usually) less lobed than
the native American sycamore. See Fig. 207a.

123b. Flowers borne within a pear-shaped hollow receptacle; leaves roughened on both sides with stiff hairs. Fig. 208.

COMMON FIG ....*Ficus carica* **L.**

A small tree to 30 feet high, frequently a shrub. It is an import from western Asia. BARK: smooth, purplish gray. LEAVES: 4 to 8 inches long, deciduous. FLOWERS: as pictured. Borne inside the receptacle which is later filled with seeds. FRUIT: the matured receptacle. Green or purplish when ripe. Highly valued. The common fig is grown for its edible fruit which is of considerable commercial importance; many pomological varieties are distinguished.

124a. Leaves and buds in two rows on the stem 125

124b. Leaves not 2-ranked 135

125a. Purplish-red flowers appearing before the leaves; leaves heart shaped, entire. Fig. 209.

Fig. 208. Ficus carica.

EASTERN REDBUD ....*Cercis canadensis* **L. var.** *canadensis*

Eastern redbud is a small slender tree 20 to 50 feet high with a flat or rounded crown. It grows rapidly and is short lived. BARK: grayish or red-brown, scaly. LEAVES: 3 to 5 inches long, heart shaped at the base, lustrous above, hairy in the axils of the veins beneath, bright yellow in the fall. FLOWERS: 1/2 inch long in sessile umbels; corolla pink-purple. Appearing before the leaves, April. FRUIT: pod 2 1/2 to 3 1/2 inches long; seed oblong, 1/4 inch long. TWIGS AND BUDS: twigs, dark reddish-brown, upper edge of leaf scar unevenly fringed; buds, small and obtuse.

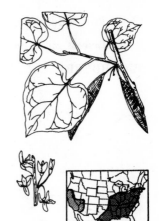

Eastern redbud occurs on moist slopes, stream bottoms and river bottoms as an understory component among larger trees. It occurs as an occasional species in forest types containing northern red, southern red, scarlet, black, Shumard, cherrybark and white oaks, several hickories, American

Fig. 209a. Cercis canadensis var. canadensis.

elm, yellow-poplar, and hackberry, loblolly, shortleaf, Virginia and white pines. Associated understory species are dogwood, hydrangea

Hydrangea arborescens, hawthorn, azalea *Rhododendron* **spp.**, elder *Sambucus canadensis,* smooth and shining sumac, and greenbrier *Smilax* **spp.** It is a tolerant subclimax species. Possibly in certain of the Oak-Hickory climax groups it becomes climax. Eastern redbud does not appear to have any serious insect or disease enemies. Fire will kill the stem and sprouting is not profuse. It has no commercial uses. Its particular value is in making the spring forest colorful and as a popular ornamental. It is not used to any significant extent by wildlife. The seeds, like many legumes, apparently are not palatable. The species is rated high in humus building capacity.

The largest eastern redbud of record is 9 feet 2 inches in circumference at 2 1/2 feet, 36 feet high with a crown spread of 39 feet. It is growing at Charleston, Missouri.

The TEXAS REDBUD, *Cercis canadensis* **var.** *texensis* (S. Wats.) Hopkins, has a more limited range, Fig. 209b. Leaves with more deeply lobed base, kidney shaped and less inclined to hairs in the axils of the veins on the underside.

Fig. 209b. Cercis canadensis var. texensis.

The CALIFORNIA REDBUD, *Cercis occidentalis* Torr., is similar to the eastern species. There should be no confusion as the ranges do not overlap. Fig. 209a.

125b. Leaves not entire **126**

126a. Pith with transverse partitions (see Fig. 159b) leaves tapering, sides unequal at base **127**

126b. Pith solid, without diaphragms (see Fig. 159a) **128**

127a. Leaves entire or nearly so. Fig. 210.

SUGARBERRY ....*Celtis laevigata* Willd.

Sugarberry is a medium-sized tree 60 to 80 feet tall with spreading and somewhat pendulous branches. It grows at a medium rate and is relatively short lived. BARK: pale gray, covered with numerous wart-like roughenings. LEAVES: smooth, dark green above, paler below, 1 1/2 to 3 inches long. FLOWERS: small yellowish-green, appearing with the leaves. FRUIT: a drupe 1/8 to 1/4 inch in diameter, yellow, orange or red when ripe. TWIGS: slender, at first light green turning reddish-brown during first winter; buds, chestnut brown wtih puberulous scales.

Fig. 210. Celtis laevigata.

Sugarberry occurs most commonly on clay soils of the broad flats and flood plains of the major southern rivers. It is found to a limited extent on upland sites. It rarely occurs in pure stands, but usually along with cottonwood, sweetgum, Nuttall, willow, overcup and water oaks, American elm, and water hickory. It is represented in 6 forest types. Common understory species are swamp privet, roughleaf dogwood, hawthorn, greenbrier *Smilax rotundifolia,* grape *Vitis* **spp.** and possumhaw. Sugarberry is moderately toler- ant and subclimax. The thin bark is poor protection against fire. There are no major insects or diseases which attack sugarberry. Locally, eastern mistletoe may cause damage. A number of scales attack the twigs. Leaf petiole galls are common. Where it grows without too much overstory, and the form is good, it is used for lumber, boxes, and furniture. It is planted as a shade tree and does well under adverse moisture conditions. The fruit is used by dove, quail, and turkey. About 25 species of songbirds eat the fruit; blue- bird, catbird, mockingbird and robin are notable in this respect. Squirrels and other rodents eat the fruits. White-tail deer occasion- ally browse the twigs and foliage. It is not however considered a staple browse species.

The largest sugarberry living and of record is 14 feet 2 inches in circumference, 78 feet tall with a crown spread of 50 feet. It is growing at Cumby, Texas.

127b. Leaves sharply serrate, rough. Fig. 211.

HACKBERRY ....*Celtis occidentalis* **L.**

A medium-sized tree 60 to 80 feet in height with many small branches. Frequently trees contain tangled bunches of twigs known as "witches brooms," a fungus disease. On good sites, growth is rapid. It is short lived. BARK: dark gray with characteristic warty appearance, deep- ly grooved. LEAVES: inequilateral, variegated green, surface glabrous. FLOWERS: appearing in May or soon after the leaves. FRUIT: fleshy, dark purple, matures in fall. TWIGS AND BUDS: slender, zigzag, reddish-brown; buds, small, closely appressed.

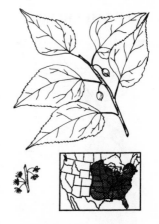

Hackberry can withstand a variety of climatic conditions and grows on a wide range of soils. It is basically a bottomland species but does occur on limestone outcrops. In western Nebras- ka, for instance, it grows on the north

Fig. 211. *Celtis occidentalis.*

side of sand dunes and in river valleys. It seldom occurs in pure stands but is prominent in the northern phase of the Sugarberry-American Elm-Green Ash forest type where it replaces sugarberry. It is a component in 6 other forest types where it is associated with sugar maple, basswood, post oak, black oak, bur oak, eastern red-cedar, Ashe-juniper and Mohrs oak. Understory species with which it is associated are eastern hophornbeam, sumac *Rhus* **spp.**, elder *Sambucus canadensis*, hawthorn, and grape *Vitis* **spp**. It is only moderately tolerant and under extended suppression develops very poor form. It is considered a subclimax species. Hackberry is host to a number of galls and several other insects. It is highly susceptible to fire damage. The most common disease is the "witches brooms." When occurring in good form, it is cut for lumber, furniture stock and boxwood. Hackberry fruit is a preferred food of fox squirrel and other woodland rodents. Yellow-bellied sapsucker, mockingbirds, robins and bluebirds along with about 20 other songbirds use the fruit. Turkey, grouse and prairie chicken use the fruits. Twigs and foliage are occasionally taken by white-tail deer.

The largest hackberry living and of record is 18 feet in circumference, 113 feet tall with a crown spread of 79 feet. It is growing near Wayland, Allegan County, Michigan.

PAPER-MULBERRY ....*Broussonetia papyrifera* L.

A medium-sized tree up to 50 feet tall with a wide rounded crown. Is an import from Asia. BARK: young trees smooth; old trees much roughened. LEAVES: variously lobed or without lobes, rough above, tomentose below; 3 to 8 inches long. FLOWERS: in spherical shaped catkins. FRUIT: red, about 3/4 inch in diameter. Has been planted as an ornamental and escaped to the wild. Wherever they grow, the fruit is eaten by many songbirds; in the wild, by turkey, grouse and quail. Squirrel and other rodents eat the fruits.

Fig. 212. Broussonetia papyrifera.

130a. Leaves rough above, pubescent beneath. Fig. 213.

RED MULBERRY ....*Morus rubra* **L.**

Red mulberry is a medium-sized tree 50 to 60 feet tall with a round compact crown. It is relatively fast growing but short lived. BARK: rough and gray; separating in strips. LEAVES: large heart-shaped, some of the leaves deeply lobed, hairy beneath in contrast with leaves of white mulberry which are smooth. FLOW-ERS: drooping yellowish-green catkins, May. FRUIT: berry-like, long, dark purple, delicious; ripe in July.

Occurs in rich soils in the foothills of the southern Appalachians up to 2000 feet altitude. It is an infrequent component of several forest types and is associated with yellow-poplar, northern red, white, scarlet, chestnut and black oaks, several hickories, sweetgum, black-gum, and red maple. Understory species consist of azalea *Rhododendron* **spp.**, mountain-laurel, blueberry *Vaccinium* **spp.**, mapleleaf viburnum *Viburnum*

Fig. 213. Morus rubra.

acerifolium, hobblebush *Viburnum alnifolium*, grape *Vitis* **spp.**, greenbrier *Smilax* **spp.** and sumac *Rhus* **spp.** Red mulberry is tolerant and subclimax. It does not appear to be subject to significant attacks by insects or disease. Fire will kill the bole if hot. Red mulberry does not sprout well following fire damage. The wood is used locally for fence posts, furniture, interior finish, and cooperage. It is planted as a shade tree. For folks who enjoy songbirds, this is a fine tree to have in the yard. In the wild its fruit is eaten by about every wild creature, songbirds, game birds, squirrel and other rodents. White-tail deer will eat the fruits although they do not particularly care for the foliage and twigs as browse. Red mulberry is considered outstanding in humus building capacity. The largest red mulberry living and of record is 15 feet 7 inches in circumference, 56 feet tall with a crown spread of 87 feet. It is growing at Fremont, Sandusky County, Ohio.

130b. Leaves smooth on both sides, thin. Fig. 214.

WHITE MULBERRY ....*Morus alba* **L.**

A medium-sized tree 60 to 70 feet tall with a wide spreading crown and smooth branches. Was imported from China to feed silkworms. BARK: dark brown tinged with red and divided into irregular elongated plates. LEAVES: thin, more or less deeply

Fig. 214. Morus alba.

lobed, occasionally double serrate; glabrous beneath in contrast with red mulberry. FLOWERS: appear with unfolding of leaves, staminate in a spike 2 to 2 1/2 inches long, narrow. FRUIT: matures in June or July, 1/2 to 1 1/2 inches long, rather tasteless. The wood is used to some extent in boat building and for fence posts. Some use in fruit country is made by planting white mulberry to attract birds away from more valuable fruit.

The BLACK MULBERRY, *Morus nigra* L., originally from Persia is also planted. It is apparently not as hardy as the white mulberry.

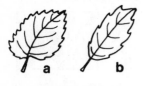

Fig. 215.

131a. Leaf blade unequal in size at base. Fig. 215a 132

131b. Leaves symmetrical. Fig. 215b. THE BIRCHES 46

THE BASSWOODS: Genus TILIA

132a. Leaves wholly glabrous except on veins and in their axils 133

132b. Leaves pubescent or hairy beneath 134

133a. Leaves comparatively large (4 to 6 inches) with tufts of hairs in axils. Fig. 216.

AMERICAN BASSWOOD ....*Tilia americana* L.

American basswood is a medium-sized tree normally ranging from 70 to 80 feet in height and occasionally attaining heights in excess of 100 feet. It has a large spreading crown and straight bole.

It is deep rooted, fast growing and moderately long lived. BARK: light brown, deeply furrowed, inner bark very tough. LEAVES: inequilateral, dark dull green above, yellow-green below, 5 to 6 inches long. FLOWERS: yellowish-white, in drooping clusters, fragrant, May and June. FRUIT: berry-like, dry, rounded pod with short, thick brownish wool, attached in clusters to leafy bract, which carries them in the wind. TWIGS AND BUDS: twigs, slender, zigzag; buds, terminal wanting, lateral, mucilaginous, stout, divergent.

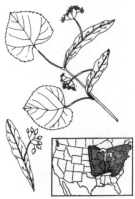

Fig. 216. Tilia americana.

American basswood is exacting in site requirements. It prefers sandy loams, loams and silt loams. Sites must be moist but not wet. It is a major component of two forest types, Sugar Maple-Basswood and Northern Red Oak-Basswood-White Ash. It occurs in 14 other forest types where it is associated with paper birch, white pine, hemlock, yellow birch, black cherry, sugar maple, American elm, beech, yellow-poplar and white oak. Understory species are quite variable; some of the more common are eastern hophornbeam, hornbeam, azalea *Rhododendron* spp., mountain-laurel, blueberries *Vaccinium* spp., wild current *Ribes* spp., blackberry *Rubus* spp., hawthorn, greenbrier *Smilax glauca*, and grape *Vitis* spp. American basswood is considered to be a tolerant species which becomes a major component in more stable long-lived communities. Basswood is susceptible to fire. Several diseases are associated with basswood. There are no limiting insect pests; cankerworms, gypsy moth, leaf caterpillar and borers along with a host of leaf feeding species give trouble from time to time. Basswood produces a light soft wood used for cabinets, paneling and interior finishing. The bloom is the source of excellent honey. It is an outstanding humus builder. Basswood is of minor importance to wildlife. Squirrels and other rodents eat the nutlets, rabbits and white-tail deer the twigs and foliage. The seeds apparently do not attract songbirds.

Two trees share the honor of being the largest living specimens. One is 17 feet 1 inch in circumference, 103 feet tall with a crown spread of 103 feet. It is growing at Queenstown, Maryland. The other is 16 feet 11 inches in circumference, 113 feet tall with a crown spread of 67 feet. It is growing in Grand Traverse County, Michigan.

133b. Leaves comparatively small (1 1/2 to 2 1/2 inches long). Cultivated. Fig. 217.

SMALL-LEAVED EUROPEAN LINDEN .... *Tilia cordata* Mill.

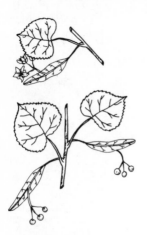

A medium-sized tree to 100 feet with spreading branches and rounded crown. Is an import from Europe where it has been planted as a shade tree since ancient times. LEAVES: often broader than long, unequally cordate at base, dark green above, 1 1/2 to 2 1/2 inches long. FLOWERS: yellowish-white, about 1/3 inch across, in nearly upright cymes. FRUIT: globose, about 1/4 inch in diameter, tomentose; faintly ribbed with thin fragile shell. Planted as an ornamental and a valuable source of bloom for honey.

134a. Leaves covered with firmly attached matted hair beneath, white or sometimes brown higher in crown. Fig. 218.

Fig. 217. Tilia cordata.

WHITE BASSWOOD .... *Tilia heterophylla* Vent.

White basswood is typically a southern species, medium size, 60 to 80 feet in height and well formed. Its growth rate is intermediate,

faster than most of the oaks but slower than yellow-poplar and northern red oak. It is moderately long lived. BARK: gray and furrowed. LEAVES: dark green and glabrous above, underside covered with brownish or white pubescence, firmly attached, 3 to 5 inches long. FLOWERS: 10 to 20 in corymb, about 1/4 inch long. FRUIT: about 1/3 inch long, brownish. TWIGS AND BUDS: similar to American basswood.

White basswood occurs on moist well drained sites along mountain streams and coves where the soils are either alluvial or colluvial. These soils contain a good amount of humus. Basswoods are listed in 16 forest types without mention of a

Fig. 218. Tilia heterophylla.

particular species. In the northern portion of its range, white basswood is associated with northern red oak, white ash, black cherry, white oak and eastern hemlock; further south, yellow buckeye, yellow birch, sweet birch, sugar maple, and yellow-poplar. Understory species representative of the types are azalea *Rhododendron* **spp.**, mountain-laurel, hydrangea *Hydrangea arborescens,* flowering dogwood, blackberry and dewberry *Rubus* **spp.**, sumac, grape *Vitis* **spp.**, and greenbrier *Smilax* **spp**.

White basswood is tolerant and a component of a more stable mesophytic forest community. The species is relatively free of serious diseases, but does experience attacks from cankers, rots, stains, leaf spots and wilts. As far as insects are concerned, many defoliators, spanworms, loopers and borers attack the species from time to time with little, if any, significant damage. It is very susceptible to damage by fire. The wood is used for cabinet work and other uses for which the light soft texture of basswood is desired. Seeds are not attractive to songbirds or game birds. Deer will, on occasion, browse the tender twigs and branches of sprouts. Like the other basswoods, it is rated as an outstanding humus builder.

The largest white basswood living and of record is 13 feet 1 inch in circumference, 80 feet in height with a crown spread of 70 feet. It is growing at Morris Arboretum, Philadelphia, Pennsylvania.

The CAROLINA BASSWOOD *Tilia caroliniana* Mill. differs from white basswood in that the pubescence on the underside of the leaf may be easily removed and the range is restricted to the Coastal Plains. Note range map 218.

135a. **Leaves entire or 2 or 3-lobed; bark and leaves aromatic. SASSAFRAS. Fig. 88.**

135b. **Leaves more or less star-shaped with 3 to 7 narrow radiating lobes. Pith 5-angled. Fig. 219.**

SWEETGUM .... *Liquidambar styraciflua* **L.**

Sweetgum is a tall symmetrical tree to 120 feet in height and has a long straight bole. Is fast growing with a medium life span. BARK: gray, deeply furrowed; corky wings on the smaller twigs and yellow or yellowish on the first year growth. LEAVES: star-shaped, 5 to 7 pointed; glossy dark green turning brilliant red in the fall. FLOWERS: monoecious, male flowers in grape-like clusters, green; female in greenish balls. FRUIT: numerous pods in a ball-like mass.

Sweetgum is adaptable to a number of different soils and sites. It makes its best growth on the moist alluvial clay and loam of river bottoms. It can

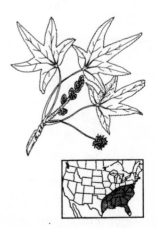

Fig. 219. Liquidambar styraciflua.

do remarkably well on dry gravelly clay uplands. It is an integral member of four major forest types where it is associated with northern red oak, mockernut hickory, pin oak, yellow-poplar and willow oak. It is a lesser component in 24 other types where it occurs along with southern yellow pines, scarlet and chestnut oaks, water hickory, beech, southern magnolia, and cottonwood. Understory is variable. Some of the more common species are dogwood, hazel *Corylus* **spp.**, azalea *Rhododendron* **spp.**, fringetree, hawthorn, strawberry bush *Euonymus americanus,* sumac, elder *Sambucus canadensis,* greenbrier *Smilax* **spp.**, and grape *Vitis* **spp.**

Fig. 219a. Around the turn of the century, this sweetgum log was brought to the saw-mill in a "float" buoyed by floating species such as cypress, cottonwood and ash. It became detached from the float and sank. It was recovered in 1938, sound as the day it was cut. Water seasoning had accentuated the depth and colour of the red heartwood and it was cut into beautiful veneer panels. The log measured 40 inches at the small end, 16 feet long and it was not the butt log from the tree. It contained 1220 boardfeet. It is hard to believe the sweetgum we see today could ever reach such size. (Miller Photo)

Sweetgum is classed as intolerant. It does well in even-aged, pure stands but toward maturity suppression takes its toll. It is a pioneer along with red cedar, persimmon and sassafras in the invasion of abandoned cultivated lands. (Fig. 10) Sweetgum can maintain itself under southern pines, then to dominance when the pine is removed. In this instance, it is subclimax. It is very susceptible to fire damage. Fire is used to control it in pine types if it is considered an undesirable species. It is highly resistant to disease and insect attacks. It is widely used for lumber, furniture, paneling and pulpwood. The heartwood is an attractive deep red color. Even though sweetgum has a wide range, it is not greatly used by wildlife. Bobwhite quail eat the seeds to some extent. Finches eat the seeds taking them from the balls. Twigs and foliage are considered a starvation diet for white-tail deer. The species is rated medium in humus building capacity.

The largest sweetgum living and of record is 17 feet 10 inches in circumference, 118 feet high with a crown spread of 81 feet. It is growing at New Madrid, Missouri.

135c. Not as in 135a or 135b 136

136a. Pith 5-angled in cross section, see Fig. 173a; leaves usually broad at base. **THE POPLARS** 96

136b. Pith nearly round in cross section; usually with long thorns. **THE HAWTHORNS** 103

137a. Pith with brownish cross partitions and short hollow spaces between. (See Fig. 159b) 138

137b. Pith without diaphragms. (See Fig. 159a) 140

THE WALNUTS: Genus JUGLANS

138a. Leaflets serrate, young twigs pubescent. Nuts rough and thick shelled 139

138b. Leaflets almost entire; twigs glabrous. Nuts thin shelled and fairly smooth. Cultivated. Fig. 220.

ENGLISH WALNUT ....
....*Juglans regia* L.

A broad round crowned tree to 80 feet in height. An import from Asia. BARK: gray with shallow furrows. LEAVES: almost wholly without pubescence; leaflets with smooth margins or nearly so. FLOWERS: male in catkins; female small green in groups of 1 to 3. FRUIT: nut with thin shell. In many cultivated forms. Is used for the commercial production of English walnuts.

139a. Fruit in long racemes covered with viscid hairs. Leaflets 11 to 17 densely serrate. Cultivated. Fig. 221.

Fig. 220. Juglans regia.

JAPANESE WALNUT .... *Juglans ailantifolia* Carr.

A small tree to 60 feet high with a broad, round crown. Introduced into this country about 1860 from Japan. BARK: brownish-gray moderately furrowed. LEAVES: with 11 to 17 leaflets, smooth above, usually glandular pubescent beneath, 8 to 15 inches long. FLOWERS: male in hanging catkins; female, small green in racemes. FRUIT: in long racemes of 8 to 20. Thick shelled. The species and many varieties are cultivated as shade trees and for the nuts. They do not appear to be as tasty as the English or American species.

Fig. 221. Juglans ailantifolia.

139b. Fruit solitary or in pairs (occasionally 3), almost spherical. Leaflets 15 to 23. Bark on limbs dark and rough. Fig. 222.

BLACK WALNUT ....*Juglans nigra* L.

Black walnut is a medium-sized tree 70 to 90 feet in height with straight bole and symmetrical crown. It has a deep tap root and wide spreading root system. It makes

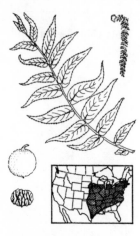

rapid growth and is long lived. BARK: dark brown and prominently ridged, upper branches dark. LEAVES: 12 to 28 inches long, 13 to 23 leaflets, glabrous above, pubescent beneath. FLOWERS: catkins, 2 to 4 inches long, May or June. FRUIT: solitary or in clusters of 2 to 3, light yellow-green; nut, oval, edible. TWIGS AND BUDS: twigs, stout, light brown; buds, terminal, short, blunt, covered by a few pubescent scales. Lateral much smaller, often superposed. Leaf scars elevated with hairy fringe on upper margin.

Fig. 222. Juglans nigra.

Black walnut is found throughout the eastern United States. It is sensitive to soil conditions and develops best on deep well-drained soils. These are frequently found in coves and stream bottoms. It grows along with many other hardwoods, but is rarely abundant. It occurs as a minor species in four major forest types where it is associated with eastern redcedar, white oak, red oak, hickories, sweetgum, beech, and sugar maple. Other occasional associates are yellow-poplar, white ash, black cherry, hackberry, and basswood. There is an antagonism between black walnut and many other plants within its root zone. Understory species found in the types along with black walnut are azalea *Rhododendron* **spp.**, mapleleaf viburnum *Viburnum acerifolium*, hydrangea *Hydrangea arborescens*, mountain-laurel, pepperbush *Clethra acuminata*, grape *Vitis* **spp.**, and sumac *Rhus* **spp.**

Fig. 222a. A black walnut plantation 2 years old. (Miller Photo)

Black walnut is intolerant and a member of several climax types but it cannot be considered more than a subclimax species. There are few insect enemies. The walnut caterpillar may cause some damage by defoliation. There are some cankers which occasionally give trouble. It is quite windfirm and the thick bark gives it good protection against fire. It is one of the most valuable, money wise, of all eastern hardwoods and walnut plantations on abandoned but fertile farmlands are not uncommon. (Fig. 222a) The lumber is used for high quality furniture, paneling and gun stocks; the nuts for flavoring and generally eaten for food. Due to the size of the nut, very few wildlife species are able to use it for food. Four species of squirrels eat the nuts. Their messy gnawing habits give the ground feeding birds an opportunity to pick up the crumbs. The red-bellied woodpecker is reported to open and eat the nut meats. Twigs and foliage are not palatable for browsing animals. It is not considered to be a soils enhancing species.

The largest black walnut living and of record is 20 feet 3 inches in circumference, 108 feet tall with a crown spread of 128 feet. It is growing in Anne Arundel County, Maryland.

139a. Fruit elongate, in compact clusters of 3 to 5, coated with rusty sticky hairs. Leaflets 11 to 17. Bark of larger limbs with smooth light areas. Fig. 223.

BUTTERNUT ....*Juglans cinerea* **L.**

Butternut is a medium-sized tree 40 to 60 feet high with spreading branches and a round crown. The bole is often divided into several ascending limbs. It is fast growing and short lived. BARK: light gray, divided into prominent fissures and flat ridges with a diamond shaped pattern. LEAVES: 15 to 30 inches long with 11 to 17 nearly sessile leaflets, hairy. FLOWERS: male flower in long yellow-green drooping catkins; the female with red fringed stigmas. FRUIT: an elongated nut 1 1/2 to 2 1/2 inches long, pit deeply corrugated with sharp ridges. TWIGS AND BUDS: twigs, stout, greenish-gray to reddish-brown, pith chambered; buds, terminal, somewhat elongated, covered by a few pubescent scales. Lateral, smaller, often superposed, covered by rusty-brown tomentum.

Fig. 223. Juglans cinerea.

Leaf scars elevated with dense hairy cushion on upper margin.

Butternut grows best on streambank sites and well drained gravelly soil. It is seldom found on dry, compact soil. It occurs most frequently on stream benches, coves, terraces, and slopes, all with good drainage. It does not occur in pure stands and is only an occasional component with other species. More commonly it occurs in three important forest types, where it grows along with black cherry, white oak, northern red oak, basswood and white ash. Over its wide range it is found along with beech, black walnut, elm, hemlock, hickory, red maple, sugar maple, and yellow-poplar. Understory varies as much as the trees with which it is associated. Some of the more common species are hazel *Corylus americana,* azalea *Rhododendron* **spp.,** mountain-laurel, strawberry bush *Euonymus americanus,* striped maple, and mountain maple, greenbrier *Smilax* **spp.,** grape *Vitis* **spp.,** and hawthorn. Butternut is an intolerant minor species in the mesophytic climax forests in eastern United States. The insects which attack butternut are those associated with neighboring trees, wood borers, defoliators, nut weevils, lacebugs, and bark beetles. A canker dieback seems to be damaging throughout its range. It is susceptible to fire damage. It is cultivated for nuts. The lumber is used in cabinet work, paneling and furniture. The nut, like that of the black walnut, is too large and rugged for general wildlife usage. Squirrels are the principal users. Its roots have the same toxic effect on the soil as black walnut.

The largest butternut living and of record is 20 feet 8 inches in circumference, 100 feet tall with a crown spread of 94 feet. It is growing outside its natural range in Portland, Oregon.

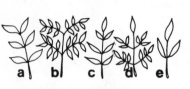

Fig. 224.

140a. Leaves evenly pinnate (a), or doubly pinnate (b), axillary buds superposed. Fig. 224a & b ..141

140b. Leaves odd pinnate (c), odd-bipinnate (d) or with only three leaflets (e). Fig. 224c, d, e 143

141a. Usually with large sharp pointed thorns, pith small 142

141b. No thorns, pith large. Fig. 225.

KENTUCKY COFFEETREE *Gymnocladus dioicus* **(L.)** K. Koch

A medium-sized tree 75 to 100 feet high with a rounded crown, coarse branches and short bole. It grows at a moderate rate and is short lived. BARK: dark gray, deeply fissured. LEAVES: twice pinnately compound, some very large. FLOWERS: staminate in clusters 2 3/4 to 4 inches long; pistillate in racemes 4 to 12 inches long. FRUIT: pod 4 to 10 inches long, 1 1/2 to 2 inches broad, remain until late winter. Seeds large and heavy. TWIGS AND BUDS: young growth hairy, stout. Leaf scars broad and shield shaped; buds, small and partly sunken in a hairy crater.

The Kentucky coffeetree occurs in rich bottomlands, moist ravines, and lower slopes. It is a minor species of the Central Hardwood region west of the Appalachians. It is associated with many species of moist forest types, among which are white oak, red oak, hickory, southern red and scarlet oaks; in the southern portion, sweetgum and black tupelo. Understory species are just as variable; some of the more common are dogwood, chinkapin, hydrangea *Hydrangea arborescens,* leatherwood *Dirca palustris,* witchhazel, redbud, pawpaw, and serviceberry *Amelanchier* **spp**. The Kentucky coffeetree is considered a tolerant species and a member of subclimax

Fig. 225. Gymnocladus dioicus.

types. It does not appear to have any serious insect enemies. It is resistant to many of the common rots. Fire is damaging to the bole and will kill the tree. The wood is used for cabinet work as it has an interesting figure and color. It is not cut in any quantity as its numbers are small. It is occasionally planted as an ornamental. It belongs to the legumes and as such the roots have nitrogen fixing characteristics. The seeds do not seem to be palatable to wildlife, in fact they may even be poisonous. Foliage and twigs do not appeal to the browsing species.

The largest Kentucky coffeetree living and of record is 14 feet 6 inches in circumference, 101 feet in height with a crown spread of 74 feet. It is growing in Bryn Mawr, Pennsylvania.

142a.   Fruit a many seeded pod 12 to 18 inches long. Fig. 226.

HONEYLOCUST ....*Gleditsia triacanthos* L.

Honeylocust is a medium-sized tree 70 to 80 feet in height with a rather short bole and open spreading crown. Clusters of branching thorns are usually present on the bole and larger limbs. Some trees may lack these. The root system is wide and deep. Honeylocust makes rapid growth and has a moderate longevity. BARK: dark gray with thin scales. LEAVES: pinnate, fern-like, or twice pinnate consisting of 18 to 28 alternate leaflets or 4 to 7 pairs of secondary leaflets; dark green, yellow in autumn. FLOWERS: polygamous; greenish, not conspicuous, May and June. FRUIT: pod 10 to 18 inches long; flat and often twisted, dark brown when ripe, flattened bean-like seeds, sweet. TWIGS AND BUDS: twigs, stout to slender zigzag, lustrous, with 3-branched thorns, 2 to 3 inches long; terminal buds wanting. Lateral, minute, superposed.

Honeylocust is typically a bottomland tree and is most commonly found only near streams or lakes. It will tolerate dry sites but makes very poor growth. It is rarely a major component of a forest stand. It is a minor associate in three forest types where it grows along with northern red oak, mockernut hickory, sweetgum, Nuttall oak, willow oak, sugarberry, American elm and green ash. Understory species with which it is associated are buttonbush, hawthorn, redbud, possumhaw, sumac, American holly, greenbrier *Smilax* **spp.**, and grape *Vitis* **spp.** Honeylocust is an intolerant subclimax species. It is relatively disease free but does suffer occasionally from a canker and root rot. It is relatively windfirm but susceptible to fire damage. It makes good fence posts and hedges well when clipped. The fruit is eaten by squirrels and other rodents; waterfowl when the site is in overflow. Rabbits seem to relish the young trees. As a member of the legumes it has the capability of nitrogen fixation in the roots. A thornless form, *Gleditsia triacanthos f. inermis* (L.) Zabel, is widely cultivated and occasionally found growing wild.

Fig. 226. Gleditsia triacanthos.

The largest honeylocust living and of record is 18 feet 9 inches in circumference, 92 feet high with a crown spread of 112 feet. It is growing in Queenstown, Maryland.

142b. Fruit a short 1 to 3-seeded pod 4 to 5 inches long. Fig. 227.

WATERLOCUST ....*Gleditsia aquatica* Marsh.

A medium-sized tree 50 to 60 feet in height with a short bole and heavy spreading branches. Branches are usually armed with thorns. It is a fast growing short-lived species. BARK: thin, dull gray to brown, with small scales. LEAVES: with 12 to 22 leaflets or bipinnate with 3 to 4 pairs of pinnae. FLOWERS: greenish in slender racemes. FRUIT: pods, usually single seeded, 1 to 2 inches long and 1 inch wide, arranged in racemes. TWIGS AND BUDS:

twigs, stout and zigzag, armed with thorns; buds, terminal wanting, lateral partly submerged.

Waterlocust is a minor species of bottomland hardwoods which occurs in extensive backwater areas subject to spring overflow. These sites are on tight clay with poor drainage. It is a minor component in three forest types where it is associated with overcup oak, water hickory, green ash, black willow, box-elder and water tupelo . Understory species commonly found in these types are swamp privet *Forestiera acuminata*, planertree, buttonbush, honeysuckle *Lonicera japonica*, greenbrier *Smilax* **spp.**, grape *Vitis* **spp.**, and poison ivy *Rhus radicans*. It is intermediate in tolerance and a subclimax species. Waterlocust is subject to attack from but very few insects or diseases. It is susceptible to damage by fire due to its thin bark. It is rarely if ever cut for lumber. There is some use made of it as fence posts. They do not, however, have the lasting qualities associated with locust. Seeds are taken by waterfowl during overflow, squirrels and other rodents.

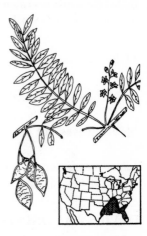

Fig. 227. Gleditsia aquatica.

The largest waterlocust living and of record is 4 feet 8 inches in circumference, 91 feet high with a crown spread of 34 feet. It is growing in Big Oak Tree State Park in Missouri.

143a. Prominent glands at tip of teeth on base of leaflets. Leaves have a disagreeable odor. Fig. 228.

AILANTHUS ....
Ailanthus altissima (Mill.) Swingle

A medium-sized tree up to 100 feet in height with an oval crown. It is rapid growing and short lived. Is an import from northern China and used for ornamentation. BARK: gray, thin, rough, young twigs green. LEAVES: pinnately compound, 12 to 40 inches long; one or more glands on each leaflet, sometimes evenly pinnate. FLOWERS: yellowish-green in large panicles. Staminate flowers emit foul odor, June. FRUIT: broad winged, spirally twisted, 1 1/2 inches long; seed in center.

Fig. 228. Ailanthus altissima

Ailanthus is escaping from cultivation and makes very fast growth even on poor hard packed soils. It puts out numerous vigorous stump sprouts when cut or burned. It does not appear to be particularly attractive to any species of wildlife The largest ailanthus living and of record is 18 feet 8 inches in circumference, 80 feet in height with a crown spread of 75 feet. It is growing at Head of the Harbor, Long Island, New York.

143b. Not as in 143a 144

144a. Leaves twice pinnately compounded 145

144b. Leaves but once compounded 146

145a. Leaves up to 4 feet long. Thorns on twigs and leaves. Fig. 229.

DEVILS-WALKINGSTICK ....*Aralia spinosa* L.

A small sparsely branched shrub-like tree to 30 feet in height. Fast growing and short lived. BARK: gray-straw colored, interspersed with stout spines or prickles; young twigs round, very stout.

LEAVES: twice pinnate, 3 to 4 feet long, 2 1/2 feet wide, clustered at the ends of branches. Five or six pairs of lateral leaflets, dark green above, pale beneath. FLOWERS: white, 1/16 inch long, appearing at midsummer in large panicles. FRUIT: black, 1/8 inch in diameter, 3 to 5 angled, purple, very juicy flesh. Seeds oblong, 1/10 inch in diameter. Ripens in autumn. TWIGS: leaf scars exceptionally large and reaching more than half way or more around the twig; bundle scars 5 or more.

Occurs infrequently in the deep, moist soils along streams, probably reaching its best growth in the foothills of the Smoky Mountains on western slopes. It is associated with Nuttall, cherrybark, live and willow oaks, sweetgum, American elm and many others. Understory varies but some of the more common species are elder *Sambucus canadensis,* sumac, haw-

Fig. 229. Aralia spinosa.

thorn, redbud, dogwood, honeysuckle *Lonicera japonica,* and grape *Vitis* **spp**. The species does not appear to have any serious insect or fungus enemies. It is susceptible to damage by fire. Fire has been used to reduce numbers of the species where it is undesirable. It has no commercial use except possibly as an ornamental. The white-throated sparrow, olive-backed and wood thrushes eat the fruits. Fox and skunk as well as squirrels and other rodents take the fruit on occasion.

The largest devils-walkingstick living and of record is 2 feet 3 inches in circumference, 26 feet in height with a crown spread of 20 feet. It is growing in the Great Smoky Mountains National Park, North Carolina.

149b. Leaves 2 1/2 feet or less in length, without thorns. Fig. 230.

CHINABERRY ....*Melia azedarach* **L.**

A small wide branching tree with a round crown, often reaching 50 feet in height. It is rapid growing and short lived. Is a native of the Himalaya and elsewhere in Asia. BARK: rather deeply furrowed. LEAVES: with ovate leaflets 1 to 2 inches long; glabrous, light green. FLOWERS: in open panicles, lilac, about 1/2 inch across. FRUIT: very abundant, yellow, 1/2 to 3/4 inch in diameter.

Chinaberry is widely planted in the South as a shade tree and an ornamental. It makes rapid height growth and sprouts rapidly from the stump. It is intolerant and does not do well where shaded. Insects and fungus seem to leave the species alone. It can be killed by fire, but will sprout. The berries are eaten by catbirds, mockingbirds, and robins and it is not uncommon to find them partially paralyzed after eating too many berries—they appear intoxicated

Fig. 230. Melia azedarach.

but after a time revive. The largest Chinaberry living and of record is 10 feet 2 inches in circumference, 82 feet tall with a crown spread of 73 feet. It is growing near Brantley, Alabama.

A very common variety, UMBRELLA CHINABERRY *Melia azedarach f. umbraculifera* (Knox) Rehd. is found throughout the South and southeast. It has a flattened crown and drooping leaves.

146a. Leaves with 3 leaflets. Fig. 231.

COMMON HOPTREE ....*Ptelea trifoliata* L.

A small tree 25 to 30 feet in height with a round crown. It is slow growing and short lived. BARK: smooth, thin, bitter, branchlets covered with fine pubescence. LEAVES: 3 leaflets, rarely 5, finely serrate, 2 to 3 inches long, green, turn clear yellow in the fall. FLOWERS: small, greenish white, June. FRUIT: thin obovate wings, 1 inch or less in diameter, dark brown, in clusters. TWIGS AND BUDS: buds depressed conical, silvery silky; leaf scars horseshoe-shaped.

The common hoptree occurs on rocky slopes following the borders of the forest. It is tolerant enough to withstand the high shade of other trees. It does not appear to be associated with any particular forest type. It does occur in the proximity of dogwood, hawthorn, wild plum, eastern redcedar, persimmon and sassafras. It frequently occurs in even-aged thickets. The species is susceptible to damage by fire. It does not appear to be subject to serious damage from insects or diseases. It is planted as an ornamental and the fruit occasionally used in the making of beer. It does not appeal to wildlife, except where the thickets provide nesting and escape cover for birds, both song and game. It has some value in erosion control as it will grow on poor soil.

Fig. 231. Ptelea trifoliata.

The largest hoptree of record is 2 feet in circumference, 37 feet tall with a crown spread of 22 feet. It is growing at Bransford, Connecticut.

Fig. 232.

149b. Branches without thorns. Bark of tree smooth. Leaflets 7 to 11. Fig. 233.

YELLOWWOOD ....*Cladrastis lutea* (Michx. f.) K. Koch

A medium-sized tree 50 to 60 feet in height with a trunk dividing into several stems forming a round and graceful crown. It is slow growing and moderately long lived. BARK: thin, smooth, beech-like, shows inner bark in delicate light streaks as the outer bark becomes fissured. LEAVES: Pinnately compound, dark green leaflets, 8 to 12 inches long, turning bright yellow in autumn. FLOWERS: pea-shaped, hanging in long stems, pure white delicately marked with yellow. FRUIT: a small pod, bean-like, hanging in clusters. TWIGS AND BUDS: buds ovoid, brownish, composed of several closely packed units; leaf scars nearly encircling the bud.

Yellowwood occurs along rich wooded limestone slopes and bluffs. Often overhanging the banks of mountain streams. It is not a major component of any particular forest type but occurs as a minor species in types with yellow birch, beech, basswood, yellow-poplar, black cherry and hemlock. In the understory it is associated with willow, mountain-laurel, azalea *Rhododendron* **spp.**, rosebay rhododendron, viburnum *Viburnum* **spp.**, greenbrier *Smilax* **spp.**, and grape *Vitis* **spp.** It is normally an understory species, or at best, in the intermediate crown class. It is tolerant and subclimax. It is susceptible to damage by fire. Insects and disease

Fig. 233. Cladrastis lutea.

do not appear to make any inroads on the species. Before commercial dyes, a yellow coloring was extracted from the wood. Now it is used occasionally for gun stocks. It is valuable in protecting stream banks from erosion. As a legume, it imparts nitrogen to the soil. Yellowwood does not appear to have any particular value to wildlife. The foliage over trout water attracts resting terrestrial insects which frequently fall into the stream for fish food.

The largest yellowwood of record is 15 feet 7 inches in circumference at 3 feet, 58 feet high with a crown spread of 70 feet. It is growing at Morrisville, Pennsylvania.

150a. Pods, twigs, and leaf stems smooth; flowers white. Fig. 234.

BLACK LOCUST ....*Robinia pseudoacacia* L.

A medium-sized tree 70 to 80 feet in height with a narrow crown. Open grown trees tend to be forked and limby. It is considered to be fast growing with a moderate life span. BARK: dark brown, very rough, dividing into strips as tree grows older. LEAVES: 7 to 19 leaflets, dark green, smooth and entire, 8 to 14 inches long. FLOWERS: white or yellowish, fragrant, in drooping racemes, 4 to 7 inches long, calyx short, 5-toothed, slightly 2-lipped, May and June. FRUIT: glabrous pod from 3 to 5 inches long containing 4 to 8 small hard seeds. TWIGS AND BUDS: twigs, moderately stout, zigzag, reddish-brown usually with stipular spines. Buds, terminal wanting; lateral, submerged beneath the leaf scar.

Black locust will grow in a variety of sites and soils but limestone soils are particularly favorable. It occurs in pure stands but more frequently in mixed stands. It is a minor component of five other forest types in which it is associated with scarlet, bear, white and red oaks, eastern redcedar, yellow-poplar, and several of the southern pines. Understory species are variable but some of the more common are flowering dogwood, redbud, azalea *Rhododendron* **spp.**, hydrangea *Hydrangea arborescens,* hawthorn, greenbrier *Smilax* **spp.**, blueberry *Vaccinium* **spp.** Black locust is an intolerant pioneer species. It is widely planted for erosion control on soil banks and other denuded sites. Several insects attack the tree, the most damaging of which is the locust borer. A leaf miner and twig borer are also locally damaging. It is subject to heart rot which often follows a borer attack. It is very susceptible to fire damage. Black locust is a legume and as such improves the soil through fixation of nitrogen. The lumber is used for construction where durability is important. It is widely planted for fence post production. Plantations are attractive cover for wildlife. Seeds are eaten by quail, pheasant and squirrel. Deer will browse the foliage. It is however rated low as an overall wildlife food species.

Fig. 234. Robinia pseudo-acacia.

The largest living black locust is 15 feet 11 inches in circumference, 85 feet in height with a crown spread of 60 feet. It is growing near Jefferson, Indiana.

150b. Twigs and leaf stems with glands; pods sticky; flowers reddish. Fig. 235.

CLAMMY LOCUST ....*Robinia viscosa* Vent. var. *viscosa*

Clammy locust is a small tree 30 to 40 feet in height with slender spreading branches. It is fast growing and short lived. BARK: dark brown, smooth. LEAVES: 11 to 21 leaflets; dark green above, white pubescent below; petiole with glandular hairs; 7 to 12 inches long. FLOWERS: reddish or flesh colored 2/3 inch long in racemes.

FRUIT: a pod 2 to 3 1/2 inches long; covered with sticky hairs; seeds reddish-brown, mottled. TWIGS AND BUDS: twigs, covered with glandular hairs.

Clammy locust occurs on drier sites and ridge tops. It is planted as an ornamental in parks and gardens. It rarely grows tall enough to even get into the intermediate crown class with other tree species. It is a minor member of the understory. It grows along with chestnut oak, scarlet oak, black tupelo, sourwood and white pine. With it in the understory are mountain-laurel, azalea *Rhododendron* **spp.**, hydrangea *Hydrangea arborescens*, blueberries *Vaccinium* **spp.**, blackberries *Rubus* **spp.**, and grape *Vitis* **spp.** It is susceptible to fire damage. It does not appear to have the number of insect enemies which infest black locust. Its only commercial use is for planting in parks and gardens. Wildlife value is very low. It is a legume with nitrogen fixing capacity.

Fig. 235. Robinia viscosa.

The HARTWIG LOCUST, *Robinia viscosa* **var.** *hartwigii* (Koehne) Ashe, is a variety which grows as a small shrub in the mountains and Piedmont plateau in North Carolina, Georgia and Alabama. It attains heights of 10 to 15 feet.

151a. Leaflets glabrous above. Fig. 236.

AMERICAN MOUNTAIN-ASH ....*Sorbus americana* Marsh.

A small tree 20 to 30 feet high with a well formed crown. It has a moderate growth rate and is short lived. BARK: light gray broken into small scales. LEAVES: 5 to 8 inches long. Leaflets 9 to 17, dark green above, pale beneath. Petioles green or reddish. FLOWERS: in large clusters, white, 1/8 inch across. FRUIT: globular, 1/4 to 1 inch in diameter, bright orange-red. TWIGS AND BUDS: twigs, brown tinged with red, large leaf scars and oblong lenticels; buds, terminal, large and conspicuous, glabrous.

Occurs on rocky sites, moist slopes and seeps. It is a minor component in four forest types where it grows under yellow birch, red spruce, Fraser fir, northern red oak, balsam fir, red maple,

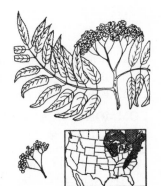

Fig. 236. Sorbus americana.

yellow buckeye and paper birch. In the variable understory it is
associated with Catawba rhododendron, hobblebush *Viburnum
alnifolium*, witherod *Viburnum cassinoides*, pepperbush *Clethra
acuminata*, fetterbush *Andromeda* **spp.**, blueberries *Vaccinium* **spp.**,
and elder *Sambucus canadensis*. Mountain-ash is an intolerant pioneer. It does not appear to have any significant insect enemies or
diseases. Fire will kill the stem. Its principal use is as an ornamental shrub which attracts songbirds in the winter. The fruit and
buds are eaten by ruffed and sharp-tailed grouse, 7 species of songbirds and squirrels. Moose browse the foliage and twigs in the
northern portion of its range.

The largest American mountain-ash living and of record is 5 feet
6 inches in circumference. It is growing in the Great Smoky Mountains National Park, Tennessee.

151b.   Leaflets pubescent on both sides. Fig. 237.

EUROPEAN MOUNTAIN-ASH .... *Sorbus aucuparia* L.

A small tree up to 50 feet with a
rounded crown. Is a native of Europe,
western Asia and Siberia and was introduced into the United States as an
ornamental and subsequently widely
cultivated. BARK: smooth and gray.
LEAVES: 9 to 15 leaflets, usually pubescent beneath, 5 to 10 inches long.
FLOWERS: 1/3 inch across; in cymes
4 to 6 inches across, white. FRUIT:
bright red remaining through the winter. It is planted as a showy winter
shrub. Numbers of songbirds are attracted to the red berries. The largest
European mountain-ash living and of
record is 3 feet 8 inches in circumference, 40 feet tall with a crown
spread of 32 feet. It is growing at Beu-
lah, Michigan.

Fig. 237. Sorbus aucuparia.

152a. Branches with short thorns 153
152b. Branches without thorns or prickles 154
153a. Flowers and fruit in axils. Leaflets 5 to 11. Fig. 238.

COMMON PRICKLY-ASH ....*Zanthoxylum americanum* Mill.

A small tree to 25 feet, more frequently a shrub. BARK: light
greenish-gray, smooth twigs with stipular, stout thorns. LEAVES:
leaflets 3 to 11, opposite, dark green above, lighter beneath.
FLOWERS: greenish-yellow, small, appear before leaves, April-
May. FRUIT: small fleshy pods with shining black seeds, red
when ripe.

Occurs in open, rocky woods along bluffs and thickets in low moist ground. It is an intolerant early subclimax species. It occurs as an understory species under beech, northern red oak, hemlock, silver maple, black willow and American elm. In the understory it is associated with dogwood, hazel *Corylus* **spp.**, sumac *Rhus* **spp.**, and elder *Sambucus* **spp.** It is susceptible to fire but has a vigorous sprouting habit which keeps the thickets going even following a hot fire. Insects and disease do not appear to damage the species. It does not have any commercial value except possibly its resin which is used in medicines. Wildlife does not utilize it as food or cover. The largest prickly-ash living and of record is 2 feet 4 inches in circumference at the base and 45 feet high with a crown spread of 22 feet. It is growing at Crystal River, Florida.

Fig. 238. Zanthoxylum americanum.

153b. Flowers and fruit in large terminal panicles. Leaflets 5 to 17. Fig. 239.

HERCULES-CLUB ....
..................*Zanthoxylum clava-herculis* **L. var.** *clava-herculis*

A small tree 25 to 30 feet in height with a round crown and short bole. BARK: thin, light gray, rough. LEAVES: with 7 to 15 leaflets shining green above, paler below, 5 to 8 inches long. FLOWERS: dioecious 1/8 to 1/4 inch across in cymes 4 to 5 inches long, greenish. FRUIT: ripening in spring or early summer, small brown capsule.

Occurs scattered throughout the Coastal Plains on light sandy soils, low bluffs, and river banks. Reaches its best growth in rich stream-side soils with good moisture and drainage. It is an understory species in several types where it occurs under longleaf, slash and loblolly pines, sweetgum, southern red oak, blackjack oak and bluejack oak. In the understory it is associated with yaupon, American holly, gallberry, hawthorn, and green-

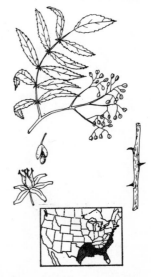

Fig. 239. Zanthoxylum clava-herculis.

brier *Smilax* **spp**. It is considered to be a moderately tolerant sub-climax species. Hercules-club does not appear to have any serious insect enemies or diseases. Fire will prune back the above-ground portion of the stem, but rarely kills the roots. It does not appear to have any commercial value except perhaps in the medicinal field. Wildlife does not find the species attractive. The largest Hercules-club living and of record is 7 feet 6 inches in circumference, 38 feet in height with a crown spread of 59 feet. It is grow-ing in Little Rock, Arkansas.

A variety of Hercules-club, *Zanthoxylum clava-herculis* **var.** *fruticosum* (A. Gray) S. Wats., is found in a restricted range in western Texas. It is called the TEXAS HERCULES-CLUB PRICKLY-ASH.

WESTERN SOAPBERRY ..... *Sapindus drummondii* Hook. & Arn.

A small tree 40 to 50 feet in height often shrub-like with erect branches. BARK: thin reddish-brown, broken into plates. LEAVES:

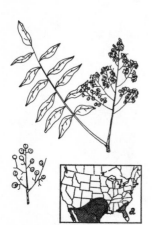

with 9 to 17 leaflets, smooth above, pu-bescent below. FLOWERS: white in panicles 6 to 9 inches long. FRUIT: ripening late, yellow, hanging on tree through winter. TWIGS AND BUDS: twigs yellow-green with lenticels show-ing plainly; buds, superposed, bundle scars 3, usually curved, not always dis-tinct.

Occurs on moist sites on clay or lime-stone uplands. The plant contains sa-ponin which is the reason for the soapy nature of the fruits. It is a showy tree for ornamental planting. The fruit has been used as a fish poison. Some people are subject to dermatitis if they handle the fruit. It has no recorded value to wildlife. The largest western soapberry of record is 7 feet 4 inches in circumference, 54 feet high with a crown spread of 52 feet. It is growing at Corsicana, Texas.

Fig. 240. Sapindus drummondii.

The FLORIDA SOAPBERRY, *Sapindus marginatus* Willd., is evergreen and grows in a restricted range in the southeastern coastal plain as shown at "a" on map.

156a. Flowers and fruit in slender axillary panicles; leaflets 7 to 13. Fig. 241.

POISON-SUMAC ....*Toxicodendron vernix* (**L.**) Kuntze

A small tree occasionally 25 feet in height with an open crown. The poisonous juice turns black upon exposure. Is fast growing and short lived. BARK: thin, light gray. LEAVES: with 7 to 13 leaflets, dark green above, paler below, very brilliant in fall, 7 to 14 inches long. FLOWERS: 1/8 inch across in open panicles, yellowish-green. FRUIT: shining white or yellow tinted. TWIGS AND BUDS: twigs, moderately stout, yellowish-brown, and rather conspicuously mottled. The terminal bud is broadly conical with somewhat hairy scales. Leaf scars shield-shaped with a number of scattered bundle scars. Knowledge of the winter characteristics are important as the twigs are poisonous if broken.

Poison-sumac occurs in wet swamps in association with a large number of species. It is a component of the understory in swamp types along with tamarack,

Fig. 241. Toxicodendron vernix.

black ash, American elm, red maple, sweetbay, swamp tupelo, water tupelo and loblolly bay. In the understory it is associated with bog rosemary *Andromeda glauciphylla,* leatherleaf *Chamaedaphne* **spp.**, yaupon, swamp cyrilla, and buckwheat-tree. It is considered to be moderately tolerant and is subclimax. Poison-sumac does not appear to have any serious insect enemies or diseases. In spite of the troubles to man from the poison of the plant, wildlife makes good use of the fruit. Perhaps this may be some small compensation for the skin irritation. Grouse, pheasant, quail and turkey eat the seeds, as well as about 20 species of songbirds. Sumac is susceptible to fire and if the swamp is dry enough to burn, the species may be killed back to the roots. It will sprout following fire.

The largest poison-sumac living and of record is 1 foot 2 inches in circumference, 31 feet in height with a crown spread of 30 feet. It is growing at Lakeville, Oakland County, Michigan.

156b. Flowers and fruit in terminal panicles. Fig. 242 ....**157**

157a. Branches and leaf stalks thickly covered with velvety hair; leaflets 11 to 31, pale on the underside. Fig. 242.

STAGHORN SUMAC ....*Rhus typhina* **L.**

A small tree 35 to 40 feet in height, frequently a shrub. The contorted branches form a flat topped crown. It has a moderate growth rate and is short lived. BARK: thin, smooth, dark brown. LEAVES: with 11 to 35 leaflets, dark green above, nearly white beneath, turning to brilliant shades in fall. FLOWERS: greenish-yellow in dense panicles. FRUIT: in panicles 6 to 9 inches long, brownish-red. TWIGS: hairy, pith yellowish and very large.

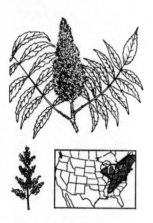

Occurs on uplands on good soil, is less common along streams and swamps. When in forest environment, it seeks the roadsides, openings, and low density stands. It is an intolerant pioneer. As an understory species it grows in forest types having such species as white, northern red, black, post, and bur oaks, loblolly, shortleaf, and pitch pines. Understory species with which it is associated are hazel *Corylus* spp., wild plum, hawthorn, blackberry *Rubus* spp., wild rose *Rosa* spp., and greenbrier *Smilax* spp. It has little if any commercial value. At one time it was used in connection with tanning leather. There are no insect enemies or diseases which significantly attack sumacs. Although sumac berries are not high quality food for wildlife, they are a staple food that is used at periods of the year when other more palatable foods are scarce. Fruits are taken by grouse, pheasant, prairie chicken, quail and turkey, about 20 species of songbirds and rodents. Twigs and foliage are browsed by deer and moose.

Fig. 242. Rhus typhina.

The largest staghorn sumac living and of record is 3 feet 4 inches in circumference, 26 feet in height with a crown spread of 26 feet. It is growing at Clawson, Michigan.

157b. Branches and leaf stalks pubescent; leaflets 9 to 21, green below. Fig. 243.

SHINING SUMAC .... *Rhus copallina* **L. var.** *copallina*

A small tree 25 to 30 feet in height with spreading branches. It grows moderately fast and is short lived. BARK: light brown and separating into papery scales. LEAVES: 9 to 21 leaflets shining dark green above; petiole wing margined between the leaves, pale, pubescent beneath, 6 to 8 inches long. FLOWERS: dioecious, in rather open panicles, greenish-yellow. FRUIT: about 1/8 inch across, red when ripe. TWIGS: covered with a fine wool; pith greenish white.

Shining sumac occurs on dry hillsides, ridges, along roads, openings in the forest and in low density stands. It is an intolerant pioneer species. It occurs in a forest environment in openings as an understory component. The forest types in which it occurs are composed of white, black, northern red and post oaks and sugar maple. Understory species with which it is associated are hazel *Corylus* **spp.**, hawthorn, wild plum, bittersweet *Celastrus* **spp.** and

Fig. 243. Rhus copallina.

greenbrier *Smilax* **spp.** Shining sumac does not appear to suffer serious damage from insects or disease. It is susceptible to fire. Very little commercial use is made of shining sumac at this time. In past years it was used in connection with dyeing and tanning. Fruits are eaten by grouse, prairie chicken, quail, turkey and about 20 species of songbirds. Foliage and twigs are browsed by white-tail deer and moose. The largest shining sumac living and of record is 1 foot 5 inches in circumference, 44 feet high with a crown spread of 19 feet. It is growing near Chattahoochee, Florida.

A southern variety of SHINING SUMAC *Rhus copallina* var. *leucantha* (Jacq.) DC. is found on the Coastal Plains and in Florida. (Below line "a", Fig. 243) The flowers differ in color from *R. copallina* var. *copallina* in that they are white instead of greenish-yellow.

157c. **Branches and leaf stalks glabrous; leaflets 11 to 31, whitish below. Fig. 244.**

SMOOTH SUMAC ....*Rhus glabra* **L.**

Commonly a shrub but occasionally becomes a tree 15 to 25 feet tall. It is widely distributed and is subject to minor variations. Is relatively fast growing and short lived. BARK: slightly ridged, thin with shreddy scales. LEAVES: 11 to 31 leaflets, yellow-green above, distinctly whitish below, 18 to 24 inches long. FLOWERS: monoecious, white to greenish-white. FRUIT: small globular drupe covered with crimson hairs, borne in loose panicles 6 to 8 inches long and 2 to 3 inches wide. TWIGS: glabrous.

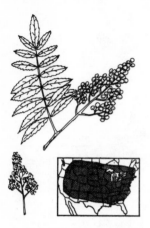

Occurs in variable sites, but makes its best growth in bottomlands along sizeable rivers. It is an intolerant pioneer. As a component of the understory, it occurs along with forest types having such species as cherrybark oak, southern red oak, willow oak, and sweetgum, American elm, red maple and sycamore. Understory species with which it is associated are dogwood, possumhaw, hawthorn, wild plum, elder *Sambucus canadensis* and wild grape *Vitis* **spp.** Smooth sumac does not appear to suffer serious damage from insects or disease. It is susceptible to damage from fire. It has no commercial value. The thickets in which it occurs are attractive to many forms of wildlife as nesting and escape cover. The fruits are eaten by grouse, prairie chicken, pheasant, turkey and 20 or more species of songbirds. Foliage is browsed by mule deer, whitetail deer and moose. The largest smooth sumac is 2 feet in circumference, 27 feet in height with a crown spread of 21 feet. It is growing at Fairfield, Texas.

Fig. 244. Rhus glabra.

THE HICKORIES: Genus CARYA

Hickories are widely distributed throughout the eastern United States. They grow on a variety of sites ranging from dry, rocky ridges to moist alluvial bottomlands. They are considered to be slow growing and relatively long lived, but not as long as the oaks. The fruits-nuts of many of the species are eaten by man. Fox, red and gray squirrel eat all species and are the principal wildlife using the nuts. Hickories are rated high in humus building capacity. Where a strong, shock resistant wood is required, hickory is available. Development of the high quality pecan through plant breeding has resulted in a major industry in the South.

158a. Bud scales few (6 or less), not overlapping; leaflets 7 to 17; fruit usually winged at the sutures. PECAN HICKORIES ....
....159

158b. Bud scales more than 6, overlapping; leaflets 3 to 9; fruit usually not winged. TRUE HICKORIES 162

159a. Nut flattened, ovoid; shell of nut thin, brittle; seed bitter 162

159b. Shell of nut smooth, thick, hard; seed sweet. Fig. 245.

NUTMEG HICKORY ..*Carya myristicaeformis* (Michx. f.) Nutt.

A large tree 80 to 100 feet in height. It is one of the minor hickories only because of its limited distribution. One of the slower growing and long lived species. BARK: smooth to shaggy, reddish-brown. LEAVES: 6 to 12 inches long, covered with silvery scales below. FLOWERS: male catkins 3 to 4 inches long, anthers yellow. FRUIT: about 1 inch long, husk very thin, shell of nut thick.

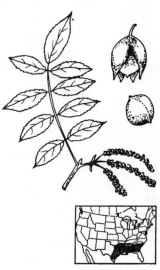

Nutmeg hickory occurs on moist rich soils within its limited range. It is not an important species in any forest type. It is a minor associate along with swamp chestnut, cherry-bark, Shumard, and willow oaks, several other hickories, white ash, and black tupelo. Common under-story species are red buckeye, eastern redbud, witch-hazel, hawthorn, and possumhaw. It is tolerant and will survive in the understory until released. It is a climax species. Fire damages trees of all ages. Several insects attack the species but only

Fig. 245. Carya myristicaeformis.

rarely become epidemic—borers, lace bugs, and girdlers. No important diseases occur in nutmeg hickory. Where it reaches merchantable sizes, it is cut for lumber and other uses for which hickory is adapted. Gray and fox squirrel as well as other rodents eat the fruit. Quail, turkey, and songbirds eat the droppings from rodent use. White-tail deer browse the foliage and twigs.

159c. Nut sub-cylindric, elongate 161

160a.   Fruit 4-winged entire length, nut with 4 sharp angles, com-
pressed. Leaflets 7 to 15, buds reddish-brown. Fig. 246.

WATER HICKORY ....*Carya aquatica* (Michx. f.) Nutt.

A slender medium-sized tree to 100 feet in height. Slow growing
and has a moderate life span. BARK: light brown separating into
loose scales. LEAVES: 9 to 15 inches long, dark green above.

FLOWERS: male in yellowish catkins;
female small, several in a spike. FRUIT:
very much flattened, seed very bitter.
TWIGS AND BUDS: buds reddish-
brown.

Water hickory grows on a variety of
moist to wet sites and is often found on
the heavy clay soils of the Mississippi
River valley. It is a major component
in two forest types where it is associated
with sugarberry, American elm, green
ash, overcup oak and Nuttall oak,
winged elm and cedar elm. In the understory, the more common species are
swamp privet *Forestiera acuminata*, buttonbush, planertree, hawthorn, greenbrier *Smilax* spp., and grape *Vitis* spp.
It is a tolerant subclimax species and
responds to release. Insects and diseases
are not serious threats to water hickory. It is subject to damage
by fire. Where it grows in good form it is cut along with the other
bottomland hardwoods. Its lumber is of lower quality than other
hickories as it is subject to "shake"—a ring separation peculiar to
trees growing on wetter sites. Waterfowl will use the fruit during
overflow. Squirrels and other rodents eat the nuts. Turkey and
some of the songbirds will eat droppings from rodent nibbling.
White-tail deer will, on occasion, browse sprout growth. The largest
water hickory living and of record is 22 feet 2 inches in circumference, 150 feet in height with a crown spread of 87 feet. It is growing near Blountstown, Florida.

Fig. 246. Carya aquatica.

160b.   Fruit 4 angled above the middle; nut smooth; leaflets 7 to
11; buds yellow. Fig. 247.

BITTERNUT HICKORY ....
.................................*Carya cordiformis* (Wangenh.) K. Koch

A well formed tree 90 to 100 feet in height with a broad crown.
It is probably the most abundant and uniformly distributed of the
hickories. It is one of the faster growing species and has a long
life span. BARK: light brown tinged with red, plate-like scaled
surface, not peeling. LEAVES: 6 to 10 inches long, dark yellowish-

green. FLOWERS: male in catkins 3 to 4 inches long, yellow, coated with hairs; female small, green. FRUIT: thin husk, narrowly 4 to 6 ridged; nut globular, thin walled, bitter. BUDS: bright yellow.

Bitternut hickory occurs on a wide variety of sites. It is found on rich, loamy or gravelly soils, wet woods and along the borders of streams as well as on dry uplands. It does not grow at the higher elevations in the eastern mountains. It is a component of three forest types where it is associated with white and red oaks in the central forest region. In the south with swamp chestnut and cherrybark oaks, shagbark hickory and yellow-poplar. Understory species are quite variable, but some of the more common are hawthorn, french mulberry *Callicarpa americana*, sweetshrub *Calycanthus* spp., American holly, strawberry bush *Euonymus americanus*, blackberry *Rubus* spp., and greenbrier *Smilax* spp. Bitternut is called an intolerant species but can survive moderate suppression as well or better than many of its associates. It is considered a member of more stable forest communities. Bitternut is easily damaged by fire. It does not seem to be particularly susceptible to rot. It is attacked by bark beetles, especially in dry years. Twig girdlers attack the young seedling. It is cut for lumber, flooring and other uses. The fruit is not palatable to humans. Squirrels and other rodents eat the nuts. Ground feeding birds pick up the pieces dropped by rodents. White-tail deer occasionally browse the foliage and twigs of sprout growth. In most game ranges the forage is looked upon as a starvation diet for deer.

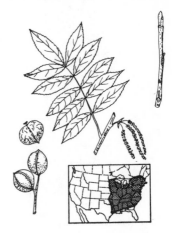

Fig. 247. Carya cordiformis.

The largest bitternut living is 11 feet in diameter, 105 feet tall with a crown spread of 80 feet. It is growing in Marcellus, Michigan.

161a. Nut elongate, cylindric, edible. Leaflets 9 to 17. Fig. 248.

PECAN ....*Carya illinoensis* (Wangenh.) K. Koch

Pecan is the largest of the hickories frequently attaining heights of 150 feet or more and has a well developed crown and long clear bole. Pecan grows at a moderate rate about the same as its associates in the bottomlands. It is long lived. BARK: light reddish-brown, roughened with forked ridges. LEAVES: 12 to 20 inches long with 9 to 17 leaflets, dark yellow-green. FLOWERS: male catkins, yellowish-green, 3 to 5 inches long; female in few to many flowered spikes. FRUIT: in clusters of 2 to 11. BUDS: yellowish-brown.

Fig. 248. Carya illinoensis.

Pecan is most common on well drained alluvial soils not subject to prolonged overflow. Its best development is on river front ridges and well drained flats, rarely on clay flats. It is a major component of but one forest type where it is associated with sycamore and American elm. It is a minor component in four other forest types, where it is associated with cottonwood, sweetgum, Nuttall and willow oaks, sugarberry, green ash and black willow. Typical understory species are roughleaf dogwood, possumhaw, swamp privet *Forestiera acuminata*, greenbrier *Smilax* spp., grape *Vitis* spp., elder *Sambucus canadensis*, and sumac. Pecan is an intolerant subclimax species. It is susceptible to fire damage at all ages. Bark beetles, girdlers, caterpillars and other insects cause slight damage. The wood of pecan is used for paneling, furniture, and other commercial uses. The species is often planted on homesteads for fruit. There are many cultivated varieties of the species which were developed for fruit production. In the fall of the year, if there are any squirrels in the forest, they will be found in pecan trees. Deer eat the fruit. Ground feeding birds follow rodents and pick up pieces dropped by them.

The largest living pecan of record is 19 feet 7 inches in circumference, 160 feet in height with a crown spread of 95 feet. It is growing near Mer Rouge, Louisiana. Pecan is the State Tree of Texas.

BITTER PECAN *Carya Xlecontei* Little, is a hybrid of pecan *Carya illinoensis* and water hickory *Carya aquatica*. It has an elongate nut somewhat flattened and 7 to 13 leaflets. In the lower Mississippi River bottoms it grows in the same environment as does water hickory, wetter than pecan will tolerate. It has the same associates in tree species and understory as water hickory.

162a. Husk of fruit thick completely splitting into sections; terminal bud 1/2 to 1 inch long; branchlets stout 163

162b. Husk thinner, usually incompletely splitting; terminal bud 1/4 to 1/2 inch long; branchlets slender 165

163a. Bark not shaggy, rough; nuts thick shelled reddish-brown, often long pointed. Fig. 249.

MOCKERNUT HICKORY ....*Carya tomentosa* Nutt.

A medium-sized tree 40 to 60 feet in height with a wide topped crown. Its growth rate is variable but on better sites it is considered to be moderate. It is long lived. BARK: gray, scaly, with shallow ridges. LEAVES: with 5 to 7 leaflets shining dark yellow-green, 8 to 12 inches long. FLOW-

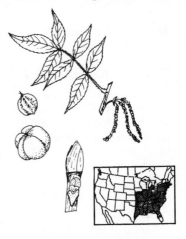

ERS: monoecious, male catkins, pale yellow, 4 to 5 inches long; female flowers, 2 to 5 inches, spikes. FRUIT: thick hull and brownish nut, sweet. BUDS: inner scales colored.

Mockernut occupies a variety of sites—in the north, it grows on better ridges, hillsides and less frequently in alluvial bottoms; in the eastern mountains, on dry sites, such as south and west slopes; in the Coastal Plains, it occurs on sandy pine sites. In the South Carolina sandhills, it occurs as a dwarf, along with yaupon. It is a major component of but one forest

Fig. 249. Carya tomentosa.

type where it is associated with northern red oak and sweetgum. It is a component in four other variable types and associated with: New England and the Coastal Plains, oaks, eastern redcedar, sweetgum, yellow-poplar; Cumberland Plateau, white oak, black and post oaks, shagbark hickory, shortleaf pine and pitch pine; Piedmont Lowland, white oak, black oak, shagbark hickory; Piedmont Upland, loblolly, longleaf and shortleaf pines, southern red oak, pignut hickory; southern bottomland hardwoods, swamp chestnut oak, Nuttall oak, cherrybark oak, water oak, green ash, white ash, American elm, black tupelo. Understory species vary as widely as those of its forest associates. Some of the more common are hazel *Corylus* **spp.**, hawthorn, wild plum, french mulberry *Callicarpa americana*, greenbrier *Smilax* **spp.**, honeysuckle *Lonicera japonica*, yellow jessamine *Gelsemium sempervirens*, and grape *Vitis* **spp.** Mockernut is considered intolerant but it does recover from suppression rapidly. It may be a climax species on moist sites but subclimax elsewhere. It is extremely susceptible to fire damage. Mockernut is host to a number of leaf and twig fungi which cause little damage. Several insects, bark beetles, borers and carpenter worms, cause some loss. The wood is used for tool handles and other forms

where strength is required. Nuts are eaten to some extent. Squirrels
and other rodents make use of the fruit. Ground feeding birds will
pick up pieces dropped by feeding rodents. White-tail deer make
casual use of sprout growth.

The largest mockernut hickory living and of record is 9 feet 2
inches in circumference, 112 feet high with a crown spread of 58
feet. It is growing at Sandy Spring, Montgomery County, Maryland.

**163b.   Bark shaggy, in long loose plates; nuts whitish; terminal
buds with inner scales bright red or yellowish** **164**

**164a.   Leaflets usually 7 to 9; nut pointed at base, shell thick.
Fig. 250.**

SHELLBARK HICKORY .... *Carya laciniosa* (Michx. f.) Loud.

A medium-sized tree 80 to 110 feet in height with a narrow open
crown. It is slow growing and probably has a life span greater than
any of the hickories. BARK: light gray, scaling from tree in long
thick plates. LEAVES: with 5 to 9 leaflets, shining dark green, 15
to 20 inches long. FLOWERS: male catkins, yellow 5 to 8 inches

long; female, in spikes of 2 to 5
flowers. FRUIT: husk thick, nut
brownish 1 1/4 to 2 1/2 inches
long, sweet. There is much variation in the shape of the nuts.
TWIGS: orange-brown or buff
colored, lenticels orange colored.

Shellbark is essentially a bottomland species doing best on
deep, fertile moist soils. It does
not do well on heavy clay soils of
first bottoms. In the northern part
of its range it occurs on dry sites
but limited to small areas. It may
occur in pure stands consisting of
several trees, but is more commonly mixed with other hardwoods. It is a minor component

Fig. 250. Carya laciniosa.

of two forest types. When grow-
ing with bur oak, it is associated with American elm, white ash,
basswood, swamp white oak, pin oak and cottonwood. In the
Swamp Chestnut Oak-Cherrybark Oak Type, it is associated with
white ash, white oak, several other hickories, water oak and sweetgum in addition to swamp chestnut and cherrybark oaks. Shellbark is one of the more tolerant of the hickories. It holds a high
position in the Swamp Chestnut Oak-Cherrybark Oak Type, a
climax type. It also occurs in the Bur Oak Type which is pioneer.

Understory species vary to quite an extent. In the Bur Oak Type, it is associated with hazel *Corylus americana,* corral berries *Symphoricarpos orbiculatus,* hawthorn, and prairie crab. In the Swamp Chestnut Oak-Cherrybark Oak Type, the understory is more likely to be roughleaf dogwood, hawthorn, elder *Sambucus canadensis,* shining and smooth sumacs, redbud and grape *Vitis* **spp.** Shellbark has no important enemies but is occasionally injured by borers, bark beetles, twig girdlers and weevils. Following fire, rot enters the bole. More than 100 fungi attack hickories and pecans. Wood is used as tools and for smoking meat. Nuts are the commercial hickory nuts. Nuts are eaten by ducks, quail and turkey. Flowers and nuts are taken by crows, jays, nuthatches, and several woodpeckers. Squirrels and other rodents eat the nuts and buds. Whitetail deer browse on twigs and foliage. The largest shellbark hickory living and of record is 12 feet 3 inches in circumference, 115 feet high with a crown spread of 90 feet. It is growing at French Lick, Indiana.

164b.   Leaflets usually 3 to 5; nut rounded at base, shell thinner. Fig. 251.

SHAGBARK HICKORY ....*Carya ovata* (Mill.) K. Koch

A medium-sized tree 70 to 100 feet in height. It is generally well formed with long bole and spreading crown. It is one of the fastest growing of the hickories and is long lived.
BARK: light gray, shaggy, separating and hanging in long thick plates. LEAVES: 5 to 7 leaflets, lower pair smaller, 8 to 14 inches long. FLOWERS: male catkins, in 3's; 4 to 5 inches long, open after leaves have attained full size; female in spikes, reddish-brown. FRUIT: globular, thick husk, deeply grooved at seams; nut white, thin shelled, sweet. TWIGS AND BUDS: twigs, dark reddish-brown, stout; buds, with loosely fitting pubescent scales.

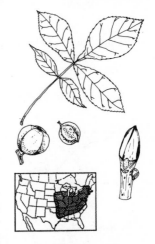

Fig. 251. Carya ovata.

Over its wide range, shagbark hickory occupies a great variety of sites. In the north, it grows on upland slopes to elevations as high as 2000 feet. Further south, it is more inclined to deep, moist alluvial soils; in the central areas on fertile uplands. In the midsouth, it occurs primarily in river bottoms. It is a minor component in three forest types. Some of the common species with which it is associated throughout its range are: Cumberland Plateau, white oak, black oak, yellow-poplar, shortleaf and pitch pine; Piedmont Lowland, white oak, northern red and black oaks, mockernut hickory; Central Region, sugar maple, black walnut, bur oak, yellow-poplar, black cherry and black tupelo; Coastal Plains, Shumard oak, southern red oak, several other hickories, white oak and chestnut oak. Understory species vary greatly; some of the more common are hazel *Corylus* **spp.**, flowering dogwood, hawthorn, greenbrier *Smilax* **spp.**, grape *Vitis* **spp.**, mapleleaf viburnum *Viburnum acerifolium*, and elder *Sambucus canadensis*. Shagbark is classed as moderately tolerant and recovers quickly from suppression. It is a climax species. At all ages it is susceptible to damage by fire. Heart rots cause considerable cull and degrade. It is attacked frequently by insects; bark beetles probably do the most damage. The wood is used for tool handles and the nuts for trade. Improved varieties produce many of the nuts of commerce. Nuts are eaten by squirrels and other rodents; ground feeding birds pick up the pieces dropped by rodents. Twigs and foliage are considered a starvation diet for white-tail deer. On occasion deer will eat the nuts.

The largest shagbark hickory living and of record is 11 feet 5 inches in circumference, 100 feet high with a crown spread of 113 feet. It is growing at Chevy Chase, Maryland.

CAROLINA HICKORY *Carya ovata* **var.** *australis* (Ashe) Little, is the southern variation. It differs in having smaller fruits and slimmer leaflets. It is common in the Piedmont Plateau, northern Georgia, Alabama, northeastern Mississippi and Tennessee. It was formerly known as *Carya carolinae-septentrionalis*.

165a. Young branches, leaves and winter buds glabrous, leaflets 5 to 7. Fig. 252.

PIGNUT HICKORY ....*Carya glabra* (Mill.) Sweet

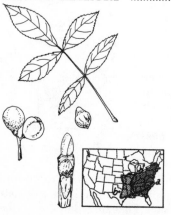

Fig. 252. Carya glabra.

A medium-sized tree with spreading or drooping branches reaching heights of 90 feet. Pignut develops a good tap root with few laterals. It is slow growing and has a moderate life span. BARK: ridged, light gray. LEAVES: with 5 to 7 leaflets, finely serrate, yellow-green, 8 to 12 inches long, Smooth above. FLOWERS: monoecious; male catkins yellow, about 2 inches long; female in small spikes. FRUIT: thick husk, nut small, smooth, not ribbed. TWIGS AND

BUDS: terminal buds short and stout, somewhat globose and glabrous.

Pignut hickory generally occurs on dry ridges and hillsides on well drained upland soils. In the southern Appalachian portion of its range, it is common on moist sites. It is a minor component of two forest types where it is associated with post oak, southern red oak, white oak, scarlet and live oaks, shortleaf and Virginia pines, red maple, hackberry, black tupelo and mockernut hickory. It is intolerant in the northeast portion of its range and tolerant in the southeast. It is a member of the more stable oak-hickory forests throughout most of its range. Understory species associated with pignut are flowering dogwood, sweetshrub *Calycanthus* **spp.**, redbud, sumac, elder *Sambucus canadensis,* several greenbriers *Smilax* **spp.**, maple leaf viburnum *Viburnum acerifolium,* and grape *Vitis* **spp.** It is susceptible to fire damage. It is attacked by several fungi, bark beetles and galls. It is cut commercially for lumber to be used in tool handles. Occasionally it is used for smoking meats. Nuts are used by squirrels and other rodents. Sap suckers frequently girdle the bole. Several songbirds eat the flowers and ground feeding game birds will pick up pieces of the nuts dropped by feeding rodents.

The largest pignut hickory living and of record is 11 feet 5 inches in circumference, 165 feet tall with a crown spread of 60 feet. It is growing in Baton Rouge, Louisiana.

Two varieties of pignut are recognized: COAST PIGNUT HICKORY *Carya glabra* **var.** *megacarpa* (Sarg.) Sarg., has a larger nut and occurs as indicated south of black line "a" on Fig. 252. RED HICKORY *Carya glabra* **var.** *oderata* (Marsh.) Little, has glabrous or slightly pubescent leaves with usually 7 leaflets. It occurs over much the same range as pignut but extends westward as indicated at "b" Fig. 252.

SAND HICKORY *Carya pallida* (Ashe) Engl. & Graebn., is distinguished by a thin hulled nut and silvery scales on the spring leaflets. It occurs in the Coastal Plains and Piedmont from New Jersey south to western Florida and Louisiana.

165b. Branchlets and leaves when young and winter buds; rusty pubescent. Fig. 253.

BLACK HICKORY ....*Carya texana* Buckl.

A small tree 30 to 50 feet in height with open widely spreading crown. It is slow growing and short lived. BARK: deeply furrowed, frequently almost black. LEAVES: 8 to 12 inches long, 5 to 7 leaflets, shining dark green. FLOWERS: male catkins rust colored. FRUIT: 1 1/4 to 1 3/4 inches in diameter; nut 4-angled above the middle. BUDS: covered with rusty pubescence mixed with silvery scales.

Occurs in dry or rocky uplands where it is associated with black and blackjack oaks and shortleaf pine. The understory is sparse

but commonly occurring are yaupon, wild plum, sumac, and chinkapin oaks. It is intolerant and subclimax. It is subject to the usual borers and insects which attack the genus Carya. Fire is damaging. It does not generally grow to sufficient size for commercial use. Squirrels and other rodents eat the nuts. Sprout growth is a starvation diet for white-tail deer.

The largest black hickory living and of record is 9 feet 4 inches in circumference, 90 feet tall with a crown spread of 86 feet. It is growing at Spears League, Harden County, Texas.

Fig. 253. Carya texana.

166a. Leaves simple 167

166b. Leaves compound 188

167a. Leaves with palmate lobes. Fruit a 2-winged "key." Fig. 254 168

Fig. 254.

167b. Leaves without lobes 176

THE MAPLES: Genus ACER

A large number of maples occur in North America. For the most part they are confined to the eastern United States. Maples are deciduous trees or sometimes shrubs. They have opposite long petioled leaves, mostly simple, palmately lobed with toothy margins. In boxelder, the leaves are pinnate with 3 to 7 leaflets. Maples are rated high in humus building capacity. Maples are widely used for shade trees, lumber and other wood products, such as flooring and furniture stock. Maple syrup comes from the sap of several species. Wildlife, birds and mammals eat the seeds, buds and flowers. Hoofed browsers use the twigs and foliage. Some of the most brilliant fall color is from maples, both native and introduced. The genus Acer is the State Tree of Rhode Island and Wisconsin.

168a. Lobes of leaves not serrate 173

168b. Lobes of leaves with serrations 169

169a. Not as in 169b 170

169b. Leaves as pictured; when young with brown pubescence beneath; twigs green with dark stripes. Fig. 255.

STRIPED MAPLE ....*Acer pensylvanicum* L.

A small tree 30 to 40 feet in height. It is rarely dominant, but grows well in the shade of other trees. It is fast growing and has a short to moderate life span. BARK: bright green turning to reddish-brown, marked by vertical white lines. LEAVES: thin, pale green 5 to 8 inches long. FLOWERS: brilliant yellow in drooping racemes. FRUIT: winged, in pairs about 2 inches from tip to tip. TWIGS AND BUDS: twigs, glabrous; buds, large and blunt.

Occurs in moist cool sites under the canopy of other trees. It is a tolerant climax species. It occurs under sugar maple, beech, yellow birch, balsam fir, paper birch, yellow-poplar, hemlock and northern red oak. In the understory its associates are pawpaw, beaked hazel *Corylus cornuta,* leatherwood *Dirca palustris,* scarlet elder *Sambucus pubens,* alternate-leaf dogwood, Canada yew *Taxus canadensis,* red raspberry *Rubus idaeus,* and blackberries *Rubus* spp. Striped maple does not appear to host any serious insects or diseases. It is susceptible to damage from fire. It does not have any commercial use except as an ornamental in urban planting. Songbirds eat the seeds in the spring as do rodents and other small mammals. Grouse will, on occasion, bud striped maple in the spring. Where it occurs in northeastern winter deer yards, it is browsed heavily.

Fig. 255. Acer pensylvanicum.

The largest striped maple living and of record is 3 feet 10 inches in circumference, 38 feet tall with a crown spread of 25 feet. It is growing in Pine Hill near Princeton, Massachusetts. The tallest striped maple is 2 feet 1 inch in circumference, 58 feet in height with a crown spread of 29 feet. It is growing in Marquette County, Michigan.

170a. Flowers appearing earlier than the leaves 171

170b. Leaves appearing earlier than the flowers 172

171a. Lobes of leaves wider above their base; flowers without petals; young fruit hairy. Fig. 256.

SILVER MAPLE ....*Acer saccharinum* **L.**

A large tree with a heavy spreading crown 100 to 120 feet in height. It is fast growing and short lived, rarely over 125 years. BARK: smooth and gray on young trees, rougher and darker on older parts, breaking up into scales. LEAVES: five-lobed, lobes plainly toothed, underside whitish, 6 to 8 inches long. FLOWERS: sessile, numerous, small, reddish, appearing before the leaves. FRUIT: winged, largest of our maples, ripens early. TWIGS: red or orange; when crushed, with a rank odor.

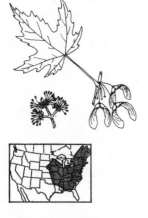

Silver maple grows in about all sites where there is good moisture throughout the growing season. It can tolerate heavy muck soils with imperfect drainage, but develops best on well drained moist sites along major rivers in the middle west. Silver maple is a component of several forest types where it is associated with American elm, red maple, basswood, swamp white oak, cottonwood, black walnut, hackberry, sweetgum, and several hickories. Understory species which are more common are roughleaf dogwood, possumhaw, elder *Sambucus canadensis,* su-

Fig. 256. *Acer saccharinum.*

macs, hawthorn, greenbrier *Smilax* **spp.**, and grape *Vitis* **spp**. On good sites, silver maple is tolerant, on poor sites very intolerant. Occasionally it appears as a pioneer on bottomland soils but is more generally regarded as subclimax. It does not stand prolonged suppression. It is particularly susceptible to heart rots and canker. Insect damage is relatively unimportant. The species is susceptible to fire damage. It cannot withstand prolonged flooding. It is cut for lumber, planted as a shade tree and the sap can be converted into syrup. It is one of the preferred trees for squirrel dens, particularly in bottomlands. The wide spreading crown apparently attracts them. The food value of the tree is relatively mediocre, but buds and seeds are taken. The largest silver maple is 23 feet 2 inches in circumference, 115 feet in height with a crown spread of 108 feet. It is growing near Stratford, Iowa.

171b. Lobes of leaves widest at their base; flowers with reddish petals; young fruit glabrous. Fig. 257.

RED MAPLE ....*Acer rubrum* **L.**

A large tree with a heavy oval or rounded crown and several main branches, 100 to 120 feet in height. It is fast growing, especially in early life. It is a short lived tree rarely living beyond 150 years. BARK: dark gray, flaky or smoothish. LEAVES: 2 to 6 inches long, 3 to 5 lobed, green above, whitish beneath, turning scarlet in early fall. FLOWERS: red or yellowish, appearing before leaves, individual flowers on long pedicels. FRUIT: winged on stems 3 to 4 inches long, ripens early. TWIGS: red or orange, no rank odor when crushed.

Red maple occupies a wide variety of sites ranging from very wet to quite dry. It reaches its best development on moderately well drained moist soils at low to intermediate elevations. In the south, it is a bottomland species; in the north, it is limited to river valleys and alluvial flats. Red maple is associated with more than 70 commercial tree species in 50 forest types. It is a major component in 3 forest types where it is associated with gray birch, black ash, and American elm in the northern forests; in the southern

Fig. 257. Acer rubrum.

types, with sweetbay, swamp tupelo, overcup oak and sugarberry. In cross section, it occurs from the dry red pine type of the northern forest to the wet baldcypress type of the southern forest—a very adaptable species. Understory species are as variable as the forest types. Some of the more common are nannyberry *Viburnum lentago,* elder *Sambucus canadensis,* willow, chokecherry, hawthorns, sumacs, buttonbush, and swamp privet *Forestiera acuminata,* greenbrier and grape. It is shade tolerant and longer lived than many of its associates. It can function as an intermediate in many forest stands. It is considered a pioneer or early subclimax species. Red maple is particularly susceptible to wounding and subsequent rots. It is host to a multitude of insects which reduce its vigor. It is susceptible to damage by fire and fire-killed trees sprout vigorously from the roots. Commercially it is used for lumber, syrup and as a shade tree. Wildlife does not make great use of the buds or seeds, but white-tail deer and snowshoe rabbit browse and eat the shoots and foliage. Young maples 3 to 6 feet high are favorite nesting sites of the prairie warbler. Where deer are abundant in the northern woods, they can do much damage to red maple by heavy browsing. Red maple is a poor soil builder. Its litter is low in nitrogen as compared to other trees.

The largest red maple is 16 feet 3 inches in circumference, 125 feet in height with a crown spread of 108 feet. It is growing in Armada, Michigan.

172a. Shrub or small tree with greenish twigs. Fig. 258.

MOUNTAIN MAPLE .... *Acer spicatum* Lam.

A small bushy tree more frequently a shrub, occasionally 25 to 30 feet tall. It is fast growing and short lived. BARK: usually

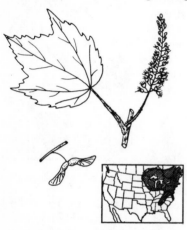

smooth, thin reddish-brown. LEAVES: 4 to 5 inches long, turning to brilliant reds and yellows in autumn. FLOWERS: monoecious, male at tip and female nearer base of slender raceme, yellow, pubescent. FRUIT: red or yellow when mature, turning brown when ripe. TWIGS AND BUDS: twigs, downy, especially near the tip; buds acute.

Occurs in sites and under similar conditions as striped maple. It is essentially a species of the understory. It occurs in a number of forest cover types where the major

Fig. 258. Acer spicatum.

components are sugar maple, beech, yellow birch, balsam fir, red fir, paper birch, yellow-poplar, hemlock and northern red oak. In the understory its variable associates are striped maple, pawpaw, beaked hazel *Corylus cornuta,* leatherwood *Dirca palustris,* scarlet elder *Sambucus pubens,* alternate-leaf dogwood, Canada yew *Taxus canadensis,* blackberries *Rubus* **spp**. Mountain maple is moderately tolerant, less than striped maple, and is a subclimax species. Except for ornamental planting in urban areas, it has no commercial value. It is susceptible to damage by fire. Insects and disease do not appear to cause significant damage. Grouse will eat the buds and flowers. Its greatest value is to deer during the winter months. Mountain maple twigs are rated high as winter deer browse.

The largest mountain maple living and of record is 1 foot 4 inches in circumference, 48 feet tall with a crown spread of 34 feet. It is growing on South Manitou Island, Leelanau County, Michigan.

172b. Large tree, leaves pubescent beneath, their petioles red; wings of fruit pubescent. Fig. 259.

SYCAMORE MAPLE ....*Acer pseudoplatanus* L.

Sycamore maple is a large spreading crowned tree with vigorous growth. It thrives in exposed situations and near salt water. It was introduced from Europe and Western Asia where it has been culti-vated for centuries. BARK: dark gray. LEAVES: 4 to 8 inches long, green above, pale and glaucous beneath. Many culti-vated varieties with leaves of different colorings and markings. FLOWERS: in hanging racemes, long stamens. FRUIT: keys with wings about at right angles, glabrous. The tall spreading crown is at-tractive to nesting orioles and other tree nesting songbirds. The principal use made of sycamore maple is for shade tree plant-ing. Its spreading crown and brilliant fall foliage make it a good choice for this purpose.

Fig. 259. Acer pseudoplatanus.

173a. Leaves often with large stipules; green and usually pu-bescent beneath. Fig. 260.

BLACK MAPLE ....*Acer nigrum* Michx.

A medium-sized tree up to 80 feet in height with a well devel-oped rounded crown. It has an average growth rate and is long lived. It occurs with sugar maple and some botanists classify it as sugar maple. Where it occurs with sugar maple, there is much variation in the characteristics of both species. BARK: deeply furrowed, scaly and dark colored. LEAVES: 5 to 7 inches long, dull green above, yellow-green and pubescent be-neath especially along the yellow veins. FLOWERS: on slender pubescent pedi-cels 2 to 3 inches long, yellow. FRUIT: usually with converging wings, glabrous. TWIGS AND BUDS: twigs smooth and shiny with prominent lenticels which are large and warty.

Black maple occurs along with sugar maple on well drained soils. The sites may be either alluvial or upland. The range of the species lies primarily in

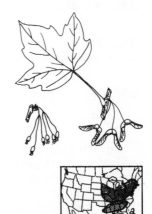

Fig. 260. Acer nigrum.

areas which have been glaciated and with relatively low relief. Best development of black maple is found in Iowa and northern Missouri. Black maple is not shown as a separate species in forest types but occurs along with sugar maple. It is associated with gray birch, red maple, white pine, beech, yellow birch, basswood, black cherry, white and northern red oaks, in addition to sugar maple. Understory species common to the types are hawthorn, prickly-ash, sumacs, elder *Sambucus canadensis*, greenbrier *Smilax* spp., bittersweet *Celastrus scandens*, grape *Vitis* spp., and Virginia creeper *Parthenocissus quinquefolia*. Black Maple is a tolerant sub-climax species. It is susceptible to a number of heart rots which may enter through logging injuries and broken limbs. It is not highly susceptible to insect damage, but defoliators, borers, aphids and other forest insects occasionally cause some local damage. There is some damage sustained by squirrels gnawing off tips of branches. It is susceptible to damage from fire. It is cut along with sugar maple for flooring, furniture and veneer. The sap is converted to syrup and maple sugar. Rodents and squirrels strip the new growth. Grouse eat the buds. White-tail deer browse the foliage on new sprout growth.

The largest black maple living and of record is 13 feet 11 inches in circumference, 116 feet tall with a crown spread of 107 feet. It is growing in Oakland County, Michigan.

The CHALK MAPLE *Acer leucoderme* Small, with range "a" as shown on the map, differs from *A. nigrum* in having pale smooth bark, glabrous petioles, and basal lobes of the leaf more deeply cut. Some authorities suggest that it and *A. barbatum* Michx. may be gradations of *A. nigrum* because of geographical range.

173b. No stipules **174**

174a. Petioles with milky sap; leaves firm and smooth usually wider than long; fruit and flowers as pictured. Fig. 261.

NORWAY MAPLE .... *Acer platanoides* L.

A medium-sized tree with a broad rounded crown to 100 feet in height. It is relatively fast growing and has a moderate life span. Introduced from Europe and the Caucasus where it has long been cultivated as a shade tree and ornamental. It is valued for its shade and ornamental potential with the large nearly horizontal spreading branches, dense crown and brilliant yellow leaves in autumn. BARK: dark gray often almost black, close and rather finely divided. Less flaky than sugar maple. LEAVES: 4 to 8 inches long, very dark green above, blade usually wider than long. (There are

a number of variable colored leaf varieties.)
FLOWERS: when leaves are half grown,
showy, yellow, in stalked corymbs, less
drooping and larger than the sugar maple.
FRUIT: with wings diverging in a straight
line; mature in fall. BUDS: smooth, the terminal conspicuous, purplish brown. Norway
maple is widely planted for shade throughout the United States. It is adaptable to
southern climate as well as the northern
cold.

174b. Petioles with watery sap. Leaves
      usually not wider than long 175

Fig. 261. Acer platanoides.

175a. Leaves usually longer than wide,
      somewhat wrinkled and with pointed
      lobes. Fig. 262.

SUGAR MAPLE ....*Acer saccharum* Marsh.

Sugar maple is a medium-sized tree 60 to 80 feet in height and
under forest conditions develops a clear straight bole. It has a
shallow spreading root system. It is considered to have moderately
fast growth and is long lived. BARK: light gray-brown, with deep
long furrows, scaly. LEAVES: 5 to 8 inches
long, dark green above, paler beneath, yellow or sometimes red in autumn. FLOW-
ERS: drooping on very slender hairy pedicels, calyx hairy at the apex, petals none,
greenish-yellow. FRUIT: wings but slightly
diverging. Matures in late summer and germination takes place the following spring.
TWIGS AND BUDS: twigs smooth and
shiny and with less prominent lenticels than
black maple, which it resembles.

Sugar maple occurs on fertile, moist and
well drained soils of all types. Although it
may be found on dry, shallow soils, it is
never thrifty; the same is true if found on
swampy sites. It is an integral member of
6 major forest types and is a component in
17 other types. In the major types it is asso-   Fig. 262. Acer saccharum.
ciated with beech, basswood, black cherry,
red spruce and yellow birch. In the other types with balsam fir,
white pine, hemlock, white spruce, northern red and white oaks,
mockernut hickory, yellow-poplar. Understory vegetation is variable,

for some of the species see *Acer nigrum*, others are beaked hazel *Corylus cornuta*, leatherwood *Dirca palustris*, scarlet elder *Sambucus pubens*, alternate-leaf dogwood, Canada yew *Taxus canadensis*, red raspberry *Rubus idaeus*, strawberry bush *Euonymus americanus*, and buffalo nut *Pyrularia pubera*. Sugar maple is very tolerant of shade and able to recover from suppression, even in pole size stands. It is considered a climax species. Of the six major forest cover types where it is an integral member, four are climax types. It is susceptible to fire damage, but will sprout. Greatest damage comes from exposing wood to entry of heart rot and other diseases. Fire and logging injuries are the principal sources of entry for fungi. The species is not highly susceptible to insect injury, but borers, loopers, aphids, and scales all work on trees in local infestations. Sugar maple is the principal source of sap for maple sugar. The quality of sap varies from tree to tree but it takes about 32 gallons of spring sap on the average to make one gallon of syrup or 8 pounds of sugar. There are tree breeding programs in action for production of high yielding orchards. Lumber is used for furniture, veneer and panels. Buds are taken by grouse; twigs and foliage, especially on sprout growth, by white-tail deer. Woodland rodents gnaw the twigs, often causing damage to the tree. Forest types in which sugar maple is a major species are excellent wildlife habitat. This is particularly true for deer and grouse.

The largest sugar maple of record and still living is 19 feet 9 inches in circumference, 116 feet tall with a crown spread of 75 feet. It is growing in Garrett County, Maryland. Sugar maple is the State Tree of New York and Vermont.

FLORIDA MAPLE *Acer barbatum* Michx., is similar to *Acer saccharum*, except for its smaller, more undulate-margined leaves, blue-green and often tomentose on the lower surface. It is also smaller and more spreading. Its southern range is shown on the map. The largest living Florida maple of record is 6 feet 6 inches in circumference, 77 feet tall with a crown spread of 46 feet. It is growing between Havana and Quincy, Florida.

176a. Leaves with serrate margins 185

176b. Leaves entire 177

177a. Pith with cross partitions or large cavities; petioles usually hollow. Fig. 263.

ROYAL PAULOWNIA ....
.......................*Paulownia tomentosa* (Thunb.) Sieb. & Zucc.

A medium-sized tree with short thick trunk and wide rounded crown, to 40 feet in height. It is fast growing and short lived. Is a native of China and was introduced in the United States in 1834.

Has escaped cultivation in the eastern states and now occurs from southern New York to Georgia. The large leaves are a prominent feature of the tree. BARK: dark gray, furrowed. LEAVES: 5 to 15 inches long, heart-shaped, occasionally 3-lobed, velvet-like. FLOWERS: blue or pale violet, 2 inches or more long in panicles, very showy. FRUIT: in cone-shaped dry capsules 1 to 1 1/2 inches long. Seeds small and numerous. Its principal use is as an ornamental in urban plantings. The largest Paulownia living and of record is 18 feet in circumference, 40 feet tall with a crown spread of 40 feet. It is growing in Portsmouth, Scioto County, Ohio.

Fig. 263. Paulownia tomentosa.

177b. Not as in 187 ....**178**

178a. **With large cordate leaves (5 to 12 inches long) usually 3 at a node; long pencil-shaped fruit. Figs. 264, 265** **179**

178b. Leaves 4 inches or less in length **180**

179a. **Flowers many in crowded panicles, lower lobe entire. Fruit pods slender, 1/4 to 1/3 inch thick and rather numerous in panicle. Fig. 264.**

SOUTHERN CATALPA ....*Catalpa bignonioides* Walt.

A small tree to 60 feet with wide rounded crown and few crooked branches. It is fast growing and short lived. BARK: light brown and fairly smooth. LEAVES: heart-shaped, 6 to 12 inches long, light green and glabrous above. FLOWERS: white, spotted with yellow and purple, appearing late in spring, in large panicles long and broad, showy. FRUIT: long pods with many winged seeds hanging on till spring, 10 to 20 inches long.

Catalpa naturally occurred along the banks of streams in the Coastal Plains of the southeast (see "a" on map). It has, however, been planted for park and ornamental plantings northward which resulted in extending its natural-

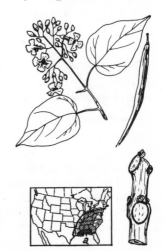

Fig. 264. Catalpa bignonioides.

ized range as indicated. As a component of the forest, it occurred along with live oak, southern magnolia, slash pine and longleaf pine, never more than in minor numbers. Understory species commonly associated with the species are swamp cyrilla, buckwheat-tree, yaupon, dahoon, hawthorn, and greenbrier *Smilax* **spp.** It is intolerant and a subclimax species. It is susceptible to damage by fire but is not attacked by any serious insects or diseases. Web-worm occasionally seeks out the catalpa. Its principal use is for shade planting in urban centers. It is the source of the catalpa worm *Ceratomia catalpae,* a prize live bait for bream fishing. Growing the catalpa worm is a commercial enterprise. The largest southern catalpa living and of record is 17 feet in circumference, 75 feet in height with a crown spread of 80 feet. It is growing on the campus of the University of Mississippi, Oxford.

179b.   Flowers fewer in open panicles, lower lobe notched. Fruit pods 1/2 inch in diameter and few in cluster. Fig. 265.

NORTHERN CATALPA ....*Catalpa speciosa* Warder

A large tree occasionally 120 feet in height with a straight trunk and slender branches forming a round crown. It is fast growing and

short lived. BARK: thick, light brown, scaly. LEAVES: entire, heart-shaped, long-acuminate, 8 to 15 inches long. FLOWERS: large, showy, in few flow-ered panicles; white, sparingly spotted with yellow and purple. FRUIT: cap-sule, 8 to 20 inches long, thick-walled. Seeds 1/3 inch wide with brownish wings terminating in fringe of hairs. The few large capsules distinguish this spe-cies from the southern catalpa which matures many capsules of small di-ameter.

Northern catalpa occurs in rich bot-tomlands as a minor species. (Compare native range to extended area over which it has been naturalized "a".) It occurs in several forest types where it

Fig. 265. Catalpa speciosa.

is associated with American elm, slippery elm, white oak, basswood, white ash, and mockernut hickory. Understory species commonly found with catalpa are elder *Sambucus canadensis,* sumacs, haw-thorns, greenbrier *Smilax'* **spp.**, and blackberries *Rubus* **spp.** It is intolerant and a member of subclimax associations. It is susceptible to fire damage. Is not significantly damaged by fungi. The catalapa worm *Ceratomia catalpae* causes serious defoliation if uncontrolled.

These larvae, however, are used for fish bait and are thus controlled and utilized. It is planted as an ornamental but is also found in plantations where it is being grown for fence posts, as its wood is durable. Growth in these situations is usually rapid—1/2 inch in diameter each year. The largest northern catalpa living and of record is 17 feet 4 inches in circumference, 93 feet in height with a crown spread of 74 feet. It is growing in Lansing, Michigan.

180a. Semitropical tree bearing a profusion of large pink flowers in open terminal panicles. Fig. 266.

COMMON CRAPEMYRTLE ....*Lagerstroemia indica* L.

A small tree to 25 feet more often a shrub due to pruning. Branches 4-angled. Was introduced in the United States from China in 1747. It has long been cultivated in the tropics and subtropics. It becomes a handsome shrub. BARK: smooth and brown. LEAVES: deciduous almost sessile 1/3 inch long. FLOWERS: bright pink, sometimes purplish or white, 1 to 1 3/4 inches across in panicles up to 10 inches long. FRUIT: a capsule. The crapemyrtle is widely planted as an ornamental shrub throughout the South. It appears to be hardy as far north as central Maryland. There are many forms ranging from pale pink to cherry red and violet; one variety has all white flowers.

Fig. 266. Lagerstroemia indica.

180b. Not as in 180a 181

181a. Leaves pinnately veined to tip 182

181b. Outer veins of leaf becoming nearly parallel with the midrib 183

182a. Leaves without stipules; flowers white, fringe-like in drooping panicles. Fig. 267.

FRINGETREE ....*Chionanthus virginicus* L.

A small tree more often a shrub to 30 feet in height. It is fast growing and short lived. It is a showy species of the spring understory. BARK: thin with brown and reddish scales. LEAVES: dark green above, paler beneath, 4 to 8 inches long. FLOWERS: white fringe-like, about 1 inch long in drooping panicles 5 to 7 inches long when leaves are about 1/3 grown. FRUIT: fleshy, dark blue drupe with glaucous bloom when ripe in autumn, 1/2 to 3/4 inches long.

Fringetree occurs as a minor understory species in many Coastal Plains, Upper Coastal Plains and mountain forest types. It prefers

moist stream banks and deeper soils, but is frequently found on dry longleaf sites in the Coastal Plains. Tree species in the types with which it is associated are longleaf, loblolly and shortleaf pines, northern and southern red oaks, yellow-poplar, white pine, several hickories, basswood and black tupelo. Understory species with which it occurs are hawthorn, dogwood, redbud, pepperbush *Clethra acuminata*, several viburnums, blueberries *Vaccinium* **spp**., and greenbrier *Smilax* **spp**. It is moderately shade tolerant and a member of subclimax associations. There do not appear to be any significant enemies of the species, insect or disease. Hot fires will kill the roots but light fire induces sprout-

Fig. 267. Chionanthus virginicus.

ing. This is the reason it still persists in the fire climax pine forests of the Coastal Plains where fire is used in management. Its only

commercial use is for ornamental plantings for which it is well suited as it produces a showy floral display in the spring. In some parts of the Coastal Plains, it is considered to be a preferred browse species for white-tail deer. Elsewhere it appears to be only moderately used. Many songbirds and animals eat the date-like fruit. Seeds are eaten by deer, quail and turkey. The largest fringetree living and of record is 4 feet 8 inches in circumference, 60 feet in height with a crown spread of 62 feet. It is growing in the National Zoological Park, Washington, D. C.

Fig. 267a. White panicles of the fringetree. (Miller Photo)

182b. Leaves with small triangular stipules, flowers cream colored in spherical heads. Fig. 268.

COMMON BUTTONBUSH ....*Cephalanthus occidentalis* L.

A small tree to 50 feet in height more often a shrub with spreading crown. It is fast growing and short lived. BARK: dark gray-brown to blackish, with broad flat ridges and deep fissures. LEAVES: dark green above, paler beneath; midrib light yellow, 2 to 7 inches long. FLOWERS: creamy white, tubular, in a head 1 to 1 1/2 inches in diameter, showy. FRUIT: red-brown when fully ripe. TWIGS: leaf scars nearly circular; stipules persistent, their scars nearly connecting the leaf scars; bundle scars crescent or U-shaped.

Fig. 268. Cephalanthus occidentalis.

Buttonbush occurs along ponds, lakes, streams and major river bottoms. It is well represented in bottomland forest types where it is associated with overcup, willow, water, Nuttall, live and cherrybark oaks, American elm, water tupelo, swamp tupelo, willow and cottonwood. Understory species with which it occurs are swamp privet *Forestiera acuminata*, planertree, roughleaf dogwood, possumhaw, sumac, and hawthorn. It is tolerant of both shade and prolonged flooding. It is a subclimax species. It does not appear to be damaged by insects or disease. Fire will kill it if the site in which it grows ever gets dry enough to burn. The only commercial use is in the field of ornamental planting in wet areas. Wildlife use is light considering the abundance and frequency with which it occurs. Perhaps this is due to the presence of more palatable species in the same game range. Waterfowl are the greatest users of the seed. Beaver eat the wood. Twigs and foliage are taken by white-tail deer in some localities in the southwest and east. Where it grows in pure stands along the shore

Fig. 268a. Flower group of buttonbush. (Miller Photo)

and out into the water in ponds and lakes, it forms good escape cover for waterfowl. Songbirds that prefer to nest over water, such as some of the flycatchers, find the spreading crown of button-bush attractive.

The largest buttonbush living and of record is 2 feet 2 inches in circumference, 29 feet in height with a crown spread of 17 feet. It is growing near Clinton, Michigan.

THE DOGWOODS: Genus CORNUS

183a. Leaves opposite. Fig. 270 184

183b. Leaves alternate, smooth above, fruit blue. Fig. 269.

ALTERNATE-LEAF DOGWOOD ....*Cornus alternifolia* L. f.

A small tree to 30 feet tall with short trunk and flat crown. It makes rapid growth but is short lived. BARK: thin, smooth, dark reddish-brown. LEAVES: rarely oppo-site, bright yellow-green above with white appressed hairs beneath, 3 to 5 inches long. FLOWERS: in terminal flat-topped cymes, cream colored. FRUIT: on red stems, dark blue when ripe, 1/3 inch in diameter. TWIGS AND BUDS: twigs, green to purple, visible bud scales usually 2 or 3.

Fig. 269. Cornus alternifolia.

Alternate-leaf dogwood occurs as an understory component in forest types throughout its range. It prefers the rich soils and borders of streams and ponds where moisture is ample. It is associated with a large number of forest types, but only in a minor way. Types under which it occurs are composed of northern red oak, Shumard oak, southern red oak, yellow-poplar, white pine, basswood, American elm, white ash and red maple. Understory species with which it is associated are flowering dogwood, elder *Sambucus* spp., and sumacs, redbud, sassafras, greenbrier *Smilax* spp., and haw-thorn. Although dogwoods as a rule are tolerant, alternate-leaf dogwood is probably the most intolerant. It is a member of sub-climax associations. Because of its thin bark, it is easily damaged by fire. The dogwood borer and several scales are damaging but it does not appear to be host to any serious diseases. The wood is occasionally used for speciality purposes such as turning. The fruit is eaten by grouse, pheasant, prairie chicken, turkey and more than 16 species of songbirds. Squirrels and small mammals eat the fruit, wood, and foliage. White-tail deer browse the twigs and foliage.

Like other dogwoods, it is considered outstanding as a humus builder.

The largest alternate-leaf dogwood living and of record is 1 foot 9 inches in circumference, 30 feet in height with a crown spread of 22 feet. It is growing in Leelanau County, Michigan.

184a. Flowers greenish surrounded by 4 large white or pinkish bracts, fruit red. Fig. 270.

FLOWERING DOGWOOD ....*Cornus florida* L.

A small tree to 40 feet in height with rounded crown. Is generally found in the understory of the forest types within its range. It is fast growing and short lived. BARK: very rough, reddish-brown, divided into blocks. LEAVES: entire, pale underneath, dark green and glabrous, scarlet in autumn, 2 to 5 1/2 inches long. FLOWERS: 4 large bracts, pinkish-white, very attractive, 1 1/4 to 2 1/2 inches wide, surrounding small greenish-yellow flowers, May-June. There are cultivated forms with pink flowers. FRUIT: ripens in fall, scarlet red, oblong drupe 3/8 inch long with thin, acrid pulp, said to be poisonous to humans. TWIGS: purplish or bluish, often with a whitish bloom, angled or diamond-shaped.

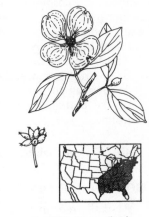

Fig. 270. Cornus florida.

Occurs in deep moist soils along streams and lower slopes which are on the alkaline side. It is a component of a number of forest types where it is a subordinate species. Some of the overstory species under which it grows are scarlet, white, northern and southern red and black oaks, hickories, yellow-poplar, chestnut oak, loblolly, shortleaf, longleaf and Virginia pines, white pine, red maple, beech and black tupelo. Understory species with which it grows are redbud, hawthorn, hydrangea *Hydrangea arborescens*, Virginia sweetspire *Itea virginica*, mountain-laurel, greenbrier *Smilax* **spp.**, grape *Vitis* **spp.**, and blackberries *Rubus* **spp.** It is the most tolerant of the dogwoods and usually found in the understory. It is considered a climax species. Dogwood is

Fig. 270a. The showy white bracts of flowering dogwood are often mistaken for petals. (Miller Photo)

susceptible to fire damage, but will sprout vigorously following a
light ground fire. Due to differences in moisture content between
hardwood and pine litter, fire can be run under dogwood without
harming it. Hardwood leaves are too wet to burn when needles
burn at the proper rate. This accounts for the abundance of dogwood in pine woods where fire is used in management. Several
borers and scale insects damage the species. It is subject to damage
from rot, canker and dieback. The wood is used for turned articles.
The tree is widely planted as a showy spring ornamental. About
all forms of birds and animals eat the fruit. Foliage and twigs are
eaten by deer, particularly sprout growth. It is highly valuable for
soil improvement as the foliage contains significant amounts of
potassium, phosphorus, calcium, magnesium and sulfur. Minor elements such as boron, copper, iron, and zinc are present in significant amounts. These of course are all incorporated into the soil as
the leaf litter decays.

The largest flowering dogwood living and of record is 5 feet 1
inch in circumference, 50 feet tall with a crown spread of 44 feet.
It is growing in Maclay Gardens State Park, Tallahassee, Florida.
It is the State Tree of Virginia and the State Flower of North
Carolina.

184b. Flowers white, leaves rough above, fruit white. Fig. 271.

ROUGHLEAF DOGWOOD ....*Cornus drummondii* C. A. Meyer

A small tree up to 50 feet with an irregular open crown. It is
fast growing and short lived. BARK: brown, with narrow ridges

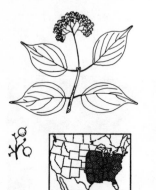

and appressed scales. LEAVES: rough
3 to 4 inches long and 1 1/2 to 2 inches
wide, dark green, the tip is prolonged.
FLOWERS: cream colored in broad
panicles. FRUIT: white on red stems
about 1/4 inch in diameter, containing
2 seeds, rarely 1.

Roughleaf dogwood occurs on low
ridges and better drained flats of alluvial bottomlands. It is an understory
tree where it occurs. Overstory species
under which it grows are overcup, willow, water, Nuttall, cherrybark oaks,
American elm, sycamore, water hickory,

Fig. 271. Cornus drummondii.   and willow. Understory species with
which it grows are buttonbush, elder
Sambucus canadensis, planertree, hawthorn, greenbrier *Smilax* **spp.**,
possumhaw, grape *Vitis* **spp.** It is moderately tolerant and a member
of subclimax associations. It does not appear to have any serious

insects or diseases. Fire is dangerous when the site is dry enough to burn. The wood is used infrequently in lathe work. Berries are eaten by many songbirds, turkey, quail and small mammals. Twigs and foliage are browsed by white-tail deer. The largest living roughleaf dogwood is 1 foot 4 inches in circumference, 10 feet tall with a crown spread of 4 feet. It is growing in the Mt. Washington Cemetery at Independence, Missouri.

185a. Mature twigs brownish. Winter buds with 2 outer scales ......
....186

185b. Mature twigs green. Winter buds with more than 2 outer scales. Flowers purple. Fig. 272.

EASTERN WAHOO .... *Euonymus atropurpureus* Jacq.

A small coarse shrub-like tree rarely reaching 20 to 25 feet in height. It is relatively fast growing and short lived. BARK: thin, ashy-gray, covered with minute scales. Young twigs green, usually with 4 yellowish ridges. LEAVES: 2 to 5 inches long, with stout midrib and primary veins, pale yellow in autumn. FLOWERS: dark, purple, usually in fours, nearly 1/2 inch across, appear May to June. FRUIT: pods smooth, deeply lobed, salmon colored, ripens in fall, seeds 1/4 inch long, scarlet, exposed from fruit.

Is widely distributed throughout the range, but not in great numbers in any one site or forest type. It occurs in rich soils along the borders of woods and on lower slopes, ravines, stream banks and alluvial bottoms. It does not do well on dry sites. It is a component of the understory and occurs in a number of forest types. Overstory species most commonly growing with wahoo are northern red

Fig. 272. Euonymus atropurpureus.

oak, white oak, sycamore, American elm, basswood, yellow-poplar and several hickories. Understory species with which it is associated are pawpaw, hazel *Corylus americana,* hawthorn, sumac, elder *Sambucus canadensis,* dogwoods, redbud, and greenbrier *Smilax* **spp.** and grape *Vitis* **spp.** It is a tolerant member of subclimax associations. Wahoo does not appear to have any significant enemies either insects or disease. Fire will damage the thin barked bole and sprouting is not vigorous. It is widely planted as an ornamental and the fruit is particularly attractive. Wildlife do not find the seed too palatable. Twigs are browsed by white-tail deer. The largest eastern wahoo living and of record is 1 foot in circumference, 13 feet tall with a crown spread of 18 feet. It is growing at Manhattan, Kansas.

186a. Petioles with marginal wings. Long pointed winter buds. Fig. 273.

NANNYBERRY ....*Viburnum lentago* **L.**

A bushy tree 20 to 30 feet in height with a rounded crown and tough tortuous branches. It is fast growing and short lived. BARK: dark reddish-brown, prominently ridged. LEAVES: lustrous dark

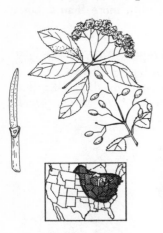

green, 2 1/4 to 5 inches long. FLOW-ERS: large flat clusters of small white flowers blooming in May or June. FRUIT: ripe in September; blue-black, borne in drooping clusters, stems red, good to eat. Stone flat, oval. BUDS: leaf buds narrowly lance-shaped, lead colored.

Nannyberry occurs as a component of the understory, rarely if ever in the high canopy except in sapling stands. It grows on rocky hillsides and moist sites along streams. Is moderately tolerant and a member of subclimax associations. Forest types under which it grows are composed of white, black, scarlet and northern red oaks, yellow-poplar, basswood,

Fig. 273. Viburnum lentago.

white pine, hemlock, sweetgum, and river birch. Understory species with which it is associated are dogwood, redbud, hazel *Corylus americana,* hawthorn, alder and wild plum. Nannyberry does not appear to have any serious enemies among the insects or fungi. It can be killed by fire. Its principal commercial use is as an ornamental shrub in urban areas. Where it grows, its fruit is eaten by such game birds as turkey, grouse, both ruffed and sharp-tailed, and pheasant, a dozen or so songbirds, squirrels and small mammals. Twigs and foliage are browsed by white-tail deer. The foliage rates high in humus building capacity.

The largest living nannyberry of record is 5 feet in circumference, 22 feet in height with a crown spread of 35 feet. It is growing at Centre Hills Country Club, State College, Pennsylvania.

186b. Without margins on petioles. Winter buds short, pointed
....**187**

187a. Petioles and underside of leaves with tangled hairs, reddish-brown. Fig. 274.

RUSTY BLACKHAW ....*Viburnum rufidulum* Raf.

A small tree with irregular open crown often 30 to 40 feet tall. It is used as an ornamental in urban areas. Is fast growing and short lived. BARK: brown, thin, irregularly roughened. LEAVES: shining dark green above, lighter and dull beneath, 2 1/2 to 4 inches long. FLOWERS: about 1/4 inch across, white, in large flattened corymbs. FRUIT: a flattened drupe 1/2 to 2/3 inch long, bright blue with whitish bloom on red stems. BUDS: dark red and tomentose.

Occurs in dry forest types and margins of streams where it is a component of the understory. Overstory species are post, blackjack, black, white and southern red oaks, sweetgum, cedar elm, loblolly, shortleaf and Virginia pines. Companion species in the understory are dogwood, hydrangea *Hydrangea arborescens,* fringetree, blackberry *Rubus* **spp.**, sumac, grape *Vitis* **spp.**, hawthorn, and greenbrier *Smilax* **spp.** It is tolerant and a member of subclimax associations.

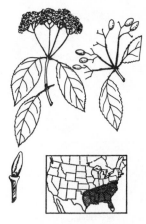

Fig. 274. Viburnum rufidulum.

Rusty blackhaw does not appear to be damaged by insects and fungi, except possibly infrequent tent caterpillar infestations. The thin bark makes it susceptible to fire damage. Its principal commercial use is for ornamental plantings. Fruits are eaten by grouse, turkey and quail, over a dozen species of songbirds, squirrels and small woodland mammals. White-tail deer eat the fruits and browse the twigs and foliage, during the summer months. The foliage is considered high in humus building capacity. The largest living rusty blackhaw of record is 3 feet 11 inches in circumference, 25 feet in height with a crown spread of 30 feet. It is growing near Washington, Arkansas.

187b. Leaves and petioles usually glabrous, winter buds with brown pubescence. Fig. 275.

BLACKHAW ....*Viburnum prunifolium* L.

A small bushy tree occasionally to 30 feet in height. Is fast growing and short lived. BARK: gray, broken by fine ridges. LEAVES: shining dark green above, paler beneath, rather thick, 2 to 3 inches long. FLOWERS: white, about 1/4 inch across in flat clusters; 2 to 4 inches across. FRUIT: a flattened drupe on red stems, dark blue with whitish bloom when ripe. BUDS: dark red and scurfy.

Occurs on dry rocky hillsides, along roads and in forest openings. It is the most intolerant of the viburnums. It rarely, if ever, occurs in the overstory canopy but is a component of the understory. It usually occurs with such overstory species as black, northern red, white, chestnut, and post oaks, American elm, white pine, pitch pine, and sweetgum. In the understory it is associated with dogwood, redbud, hazel *Corylus americana*, hawthorn, blackberry *Rubus* **spp.**, elder *Sambucus* **spp.**, and grape *Vitis* **spp.** It is one of the more intolerant members of dry site subclimax understories. Blackhaw does not appear to be plagued by insects or fungi. It is susceptible to fire damage. Roots are gathered for brewing a tea which is used as a tonic. Fruit is eaten by grouse, turkey, and quail, many songbirds and small woodland mammals. Deer browse the twigs and foliage during the summer months. The foliage is considered high in humus building capacity.

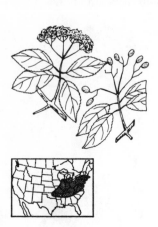

Fig. 275. Viburnum prunifolium.

The largest living blackhaw of record is 1 foot 9 inches in circumference, 20 feet tall with a crown spread of 19 feet. It is growing at Glen Mills, Pennsylvania.

188a. **Leaves palmately compound. Fig. 276** 189

188b. **Leaves trifoliate or pinnately compound. Fig. 224** 191

THE BUCKEYES: Genus: AESCULUS

189a. **Terminal buds not sticky, most often 5 leaflets** 190

189b. **Terminal buds sticky; flowers white marked with lavender and yellow. Leaflets usually 7 with sharp curve at tip. Fig. 276.**

HORSECHESTNUT ....*Aesculus hippocastanum* **L.**

A showy tree 75 to 80 feet in height with a pyramidal top. One of the most showy flowering trees and often planted as a shade tree. Introduced from southern Asia. It makes rapid growth and has a moderately long life span. BARK: dark brown, large flakes. LEAVES: palmately compound with usually 7 pointed leaflets, 10 to 15 inches long. FLOWERS: white spotted with yellow and purple in large showy panicles, May and June. FRUIT: rounded, 2 to 3 inches in diameter, covered with spines, seed 1 to 1 1/2 inches long, dark mahogany with large hilum. BUDS: sticky and nearly black.

The principal use made of the species is for shade and ornamental plantings. The bark is rich in tannin and used in medicines. Traditionally, folks have carried a nut to prevent rheumatism. An alcohol extract of the nut is considered a vasa-constrictor.

Fig. 276. Aesculus hippocastanum.

190a. Flowers red, calyx tubular; fruit without prickles. Fig. 277.

RED BUCKEYE ....*Aesculus pavia* **L.**

A small tree more often a shrub with open head, occasionally reaching heights of 40 feet. Its red flowered panicles are attractive in the spring woodlands. Is fast growing and short lived. BARK: smooth, dark gray. LEAVES: 7 to 13 inches long, shining dark green, pale yellowgreen below. FLOWERS: red, in panicles, to 8 inches long. FRUIT: spherical smooth with one or two chestnut brown seeds, their hilum small. BUDS: not sticky.

Occurs on moist, but not wet, sites on lower slopes and stream bottoms. Is an infrequent component of the understory where it is associated with dogwood, redbud, hawthorn, sumac, elder *Sambucus* **spp.**, greenbrier *Smilax* **spp.**, and grape *Vitis* **spp**. It occurs under black, southern red, northern red, scarlet and white oaks, sycamore,

Fig. 277. Aesculus pavia.

willow, cottonwood, river birch, loblolly pine and yellow buckeye. It is a tolerant member of subclimax associations. Red buckeye does not appear to have any serious insects or diseases. It is susceptible to damage by fire. It rarely grows large enough for commercial products. The fact that it blooms early in life at heights of 3 feet makes it a showy spring ornamental for urban planting.

Normally the seed is considered unpalatable or poisonous to animals. Squirrels occasionally eat the fruit in the "soft" stage apparently without fatal consequences. Deer make very little use of the foliage as browse.

A hybrid of red buckeye and the horsechestnut has leaves like the horsechestnut and red flowers. It is known as the RED HORSE-CHESTNUT.

The largest living red buckeye of record is 1 foot 1 inch in circumference, 22 feet in height with a crown spread of 14 feet. It is growing in Crawfordville, Florida.

Fig. 277a. Panicle of red buckeye, a showy flower of the spring woodlands. (Miller Photo)

190b. Flowers yellow or red, calyx bell-shaped. Fruit without prickles. Fig. 278.

YELLOW BUCKEYE ....*Aesculus octandra* Marsh.

Yellow buckeye is a medium-sized tree reaching heights of 60 to 90 feet with a well rounded crown. Is fast growing but with only a medium life span. Occasional specimens may reach older ages. BARK: dark brown, broken into irregular roundish areas.

LEAVES: 8 to 13 inches long, dark yellow-green. FLOWERS: in panicles 5 to 8 inches long, yellow or occasionally red. FRUIT: smooth, usually 2-seeded. TWIGS: stout, with nonresinous terminal buds.

Yellow buckeye occurs on sites with moisture and good drainage. It reaches its best growth in river bottoms and along banks of streams in the deep soils of the Appalachians. Throughout most of its range, it is considered a bottomland species. In the southern part however, it ascends to high elevations on mountain slopes. It is tolerant and climax. Yellow buckeye does not occur in pure

Fig. 278. Aesculus octandra.

stands but as a minor component of six forest types where it is associated with sugar maple, beech, yellow birch, black cherry, red spruce, Fraser fir, northern red oak and basswood. Many more hardwood species occur within these cover types. Understory species commonly associated with the yellow buckeye are mountain ash, dogwood, rosebay rhododendron, mountain-laurel, red buckeye, hawthorn, sweetshrub *Caly-canthus* **spp.**, and buffalo nut *Pyrularia pubera.* Yellow buckeye does not have any major insect enemies and is relatively free of disease. It is susceptible to damage from fire. It is used for furniture, paneling, caskets, artificial limbs and planted as an ornamental. Due to the poisonous gluco-cide known as aesculin in the nut, they are not used for food. In the fall, squirrels frequently eat the nut in the "soft" stage. This use is often associated with heavy squirrel populations, not food shortage. Foliage and twigs do not appear to be palatable to browsers and are reported to be poisonous to livestock.

Fig. 278a. Typical bark of yellow buckeye. (Miller Photo)

The largest yellow buckeye of record now living is 15 feet 11 inches in circumference, 85 feet high with a crown spread of 54 feet. It is growing in the Great Smoky Mountains National Park, Tenneessee.

The PAINTED BUCKEYE *Aesculus sylvatica* Bartr., differs in lacking the glandular hairs found on the pedicels and calyx of yellow buckeye. Its range is confined to the Coastal Plain and outer Piedmont from southeastern Virginia to Georgia, Alabama, and northwestern Florida. Note "a" on map. The largest painted buckeye living and of record is 13 feet 3 inches in circumference, 75 feet tall with a crown spread of 50 feet. It is growing at Sosebee Cove, Union County, Georgia.

190c. Flowers yellow, calyx bell-shaped, fruit with prickles. Fig. 279.

OHIO BUCKEYE ....*Aesculus glabra* Willd.

A medium-sized tree 60 to 90 feet tall with a spreading crown. It develops a strong tap root the first year and grows faster than oaks, but slower than yellow-poplar. It is not a long lived species.

BARK: fetid, rough, young twigs smooth gray with prominent orange lenticels. LEAVES: palmately compound with usually 5 leaflets, narrower than in horsechestnut. FLOWERS: pale yellow-green appearing in April and May in panicles 5 to 6 inches long. FRUIT: on a stout stem, pale brown, 1 to 2 inches long, with prickly valves. Seed, bright, shiny, reddish-brown. BUDS: bud scales prominently keeled.

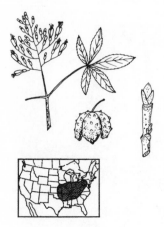

It is a moist site species most frequently occurring along river bottoms and on stream banks. It appears as a shrub on dry sites in the western portion of its range. It occurs in mixed stands in minor numbers. It is listed as a minor component in at least two forest types where it is associated with northern red oak, basswood, white ash, sugar maple, beech, black walnut, red mulberry, several hickories, and other oaks. Understory species are variable, some of the more common are dogwood, hazel *Corylus* **spp.**, hawthorn, blackhaw, maple leaf viburnum *Viburnum acerifolium*, greenbrier *Smilax* **spp.**, grape *Vitis* **spp.**, and sumacs. It is intermediate in tolerance and a tree of subclimax communities. Ohio buckeye is relatively free of disease and is not subject to serious insect damage. Rot will enter where fires have scarred the bole. The lumber is used for furniture, paneling, wooden ware and artificial limbs. Squirrels will on occasion eat the nut but other animals seem to shun it. Young shoots are poisonous to livestock. An alkaloid narcotic is found in both the nuts and foliage.

Fig. 279. Aesculus glabra.

The largest living Ohio buckeye of record is 9 feet 9 inches in circumference, 85 feet in height with a crown spread of 40 feet. It is growing in Champaign County, Ohio. Ohio buckeye is the State Tree of Ohio.

191a. Leaflets 3 to 7 with veins extending into the sharp pointed serrations, stipules present. Fig. 280.

BOXELDER ....*Acer negundo* **L.**

Boxelder is a medium-sized tree 50 to 75 feet in height with an irregular bole, shallow root system and an open spreading crown. It is fast growing and short lived. BARK: rough, greenish-gray. LEAVES: pinnately compound with 3 to 5 leaflets. FLOWERS:

very small, yellowish-green appearing before leaves. Trees distinctly male and female. FRUIT: winged 1 to 2 inches long, ripens in early summer and hangs on tree for months. TWIGS: stout, green to purplish-green, lustrous or covered with a glaucous bloom.

It occurs on a variety of sites but does best on moist soils. It is perhaps the most aggressive of the maples. Boxelder does not occur in pure stands, but is a minor component of six major forest types where it is associated with aspen, bur oak, green ash, balsam poplar, American elm, cottonwood, sugarberry, sycamore, pecan and black willow. Occurring as it does over a wide range, understory species found in the types vary greatly. Some of the more common are pawpaw, elder *Sambucus* **spp.**, hawthorn, possumhaw, sumacs, and grape *Vitis* **spp.** It is an intolerant pioneer species. Boxelder does not appear to have any serious insect enemies or diseases. It is susceptible to damage from fire. Occasionally it is cut for furniture, boxes, crates, pulpwood and fuel. The buds, twigs and seeds are eaten

Fig. 280. Acer negundo.

by grouse, turkey and several songbirds. Small mammals eat the seeds, flowers, bark and twigs. Deer occasionally browse the twigs and foliage. Generally, it is not considered a highly valuable wildlife species. In the semi-arid prairie states, it may be an important food species due to lack of other similar foods. It has been widely planted on poor sites as a shade tree. The largest living boxelder of record is 13 feet 6 inches in circumference, 81 feet in height with a crown spread of 108 feet. It is growing in Detroit, Michigan.

191b. **Leaflets entire or with rounded serrations; veins not extending into serrations** **192**

191c. **All leaves with 3 leaflets; bark with strong odor; fruit an inflated pod as pictured. Fig. 281.**

AMERICAN BLADDERNUT .... *Staphylea trifolia* **L.**
A small tree 10 to 15 feet tall but more frequently a shrub with an open crown. The foliage remains on the twigs until late fall. It is fast growing and short lived. BARK: smooth and with greenish stripes. LEAVES: trifoliate, 4 to 6 inches long, margins finely serrate, leaflets rather sharp pointed. FLOWERS: perfect, bell-shaped in drooping raceme-like clusters, yellowish-white, May. BUDS: terminal bud lacking.

Occurs in rich, moist sites often on north or eastern aspects. Frequently associated with limestone soils, alluvial sites along streams and rivers. It is a minor understory component in a number of forest types. Tree species common to the sites on which bladdernut occurs are northern red oak, hemlock, white pine, basswood, yellow birch and yellow-poplar. In the understory it is associated with hawthorn, dogwood, redbud, sumac and greenbrier *Smilax* **spp**. It is a moderately tolerant subclimax species. It does not appear to have any serious insect enemies or diseases. It is susceptible to fire, as the bark is very thin. Bladdernut is planted as an ornamental. It has some watershed value as it forms a dense underground root system, thus stopping soil movement. It does not appear to have any value for wildlife except possibly as nesting sites for low-nesting species of songbirds.

Fig. 281. Staphylea trifolia.

The largest American bladdernut living and of record is 1 foot 3 inches in circumference, 29 feet tall with a crown spread of 21 feet. It is growing near Utica, Michigan.

THE ASHES: Genus FRAXINUS

Ashes contain several important timber trees, others are used in erosion control and some are used as ornamentals in urban planting. Sixteen species of ashes are native to the United States. The group is identified by opposite pinnate leaves, with 3 to 11 leaflets, paired except at the end. They are usually sawtoothed. The winter buds are blunt. Fruit is a one-seeded samara with a long wing which matures in summer and is cast in the fall.

192a. Twigs 4-sided; leaflets 7 to 11, green on both sides. Fig. 282.

BLUE ASH ....*Fraxinus quadrangulata* Michx.

A medium-sized tree 60 to 100 feet in height with a slender crown. It grows rather fast and is moderately long lived. BARK: light gray furrowed into large plates. LEAVES: yellow-green above, paler beneath, glabrous throughout. FLOWERS: before the leaves, perfect, very simple, in open panicles. FRUIT: samara 1 to 2 inches long. TWIGS: have corky wings between the nodes.

Blue ash occurs on dry uplands, usually on limestone base soils. It is a minor component of only one forest type where it is associated with northern red oak, mockernut hickory, eastern hophornbeam, sweetgum, black tupelo, and American elm. Understory species commonly occuring in the type are redbud, dogwood, hazel *Corylus* **spp.**, hawthorn, wild plum, grape *Vitis* **spp.**, and greenbrier *Smilax* **spp.** It is a moderately intolerant species and subclimax. Blue ash does not appear to have any serious enemies, either insect or fungi. It is susceptible to damage from fire as the scars on the bole are openings for heart rot. Wood is used for lumber, handles, sporting goods, and veneer. The inner bark contains a mucilaginous substance which turns blue with exposure to air. It has been used as a dye. It is only of moderate importance to wildlife. Several songbirds eat the seed. Turkey and quail often shuck out the seed from the single wing. Small woodland rodents often eat the seed. White-tail deer frequently browse the twigs and foliage.

Fig. 282. Fraxinus quadrangulata.

The largest living blue ash is 10 feet 8 inches in circumference, 114 feet tall with a crown spread of 54 feet. It is growing in Funk's Grove, Illinois.

CAROLINA ASH *Fraxinus caroliniana* Mill., has elliptical often 3-winged samara and 5 to 7 oval blunt apexed leaflets. It occurs along the southeastern and gulf coasts. (See "a" on map)

192b. Twigs not 4-sided 193

193a. Twigs and petioles pubescent or velvety 194

193b. Twigs almost if not entirely smooth 195

194a. Fruit mostly 2 inches or more long, leaflets pubescent beneath. Fig. 283.

PUMPKIN ASH ....*Fraxinus profunda* (Bush) Bush

A medium-sized tree to 110 feet in height with a narrow open crown. Is fast growing and short lived. **BARK:** light gray, rather

272 HOW TO KNOW THE TREES

deeply ridged. LEAVES: 6 to 15 inches long, dark yellow-green. FLOWERS: dioecious, in panicles. FRUIT: samara 2 to 3 inches long.

Pumpkin ash occurs in deep swamps and overflow bottoms which are inundated several months of the year. It is a minor associate in one forest type where it is associated with baldcypress, water tupelo, black willow, swamp cottonwood and water locust. Understory species commonly found in the type are buttonbush, swamp privet *Forestiera acuminata,* hawthorn, planertree, greenbrier *Smilax* **spp.**, and peppervine *Ampelopsis arborea.* It is intolerant and subclimax. Pumpkin ash is relatively free of insects and disease. When the site upon which it grows is dry enough to burn, it is highly susceptible to fire damage. Lumber is used for boxes, veneer and some furniture. Several songbirds eat the seed. Woodduck also take the seed. Deer frequently browse the twigs and foliage. The largest pumpkin ash living and of record is 11 feet 5 inches in circumference, 96 feet tall with a crown spread of 36 feet. It is growing in Big Oak Tree State Park, Missouri.

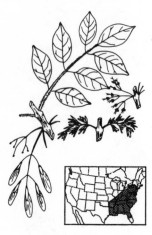
Fig. 283. Fraxinus profunda.

194b. Fruit mostly less than 2 inches long. Fig. 284.

GREEN ASH ....*Fraxinus pennsylvanica* Marsh.

Green ash is the most widely distributed of the ashes native to the United States. It is a medium-sized tree 30 to 60 feet in height. A moderately fast growing species and has a medium length life span. BARK: somewhat smooth, brown tinged with red. LEAVES: light yellow green above, pale and pubescent beneath, 8 to 12 inches long. FLOWERS: dioecious in panicles. FRUIT: samara with single wing 1 to 2 inches long. TWIGS: first season's twigs more or less velvety.

Green ash occurs on a variety of soils ranging from alluvial bottomland sites to moist uplands. It does not tolerate water-laden soils such as swamps, but

Fig. 284. Fraxinus pennsylvanica.

does well on well drained, moist soils. It can stand limited flooding. It grows pure or predominant in one forest type and is an associate in 13 other types. The species most commonly associated with green ash are boxelder, red maple, pecan, sugarberry, sweetgum, American elm, cottonwood, black willow, willow oak and sycamore. Understory species commonly found in these associations are hawthorn, roughleaf dogwood, hornbeam, Eastern hophornbeam, flowering dogwood, greenbrier *Smilax* **spp.**, and grape *Vitis* **spp.** Green ash varies from intolerant to moderately tolerant. On bare alluvial soils it acts as an invading pioneer. It is however less able to maintain itself in competition with its more tolerant associates, decreases in frequency and gives way to elm and maple. Reacting thus, it is considered a subclimax speices. The lumber of green ash is used for sporting goods, handles, veneer and boxes. It is planted as a shade tree and in the Great Plains as a shelterbelt. Several insects feed on green ash; scales, borers, sawflys, and carpenter worms. Several diseases are of minor importance; leaf spot —a defoliator, rust and heart rot. Wildlife use the seeds and browse the twigs and foliage. Greatest users are songbirds and game birds, along with white-tail deer.

The largest green ash living and of record is 14 feet 8 inches in circumference, 105 feet tall with a crown spread of 79 feet. It is growing in Big Oak Tree State Park, Missouri. Green ash is the State Tree of North Dakota.

195a. Fruit flattened, wing present its full length. Leaflets 7 to 11, sessile. Fig. 285.

BLACK ASH ....*Fraxinus nigra* Marsh.

A medium-sized tree from 50 to 60 feet in height. Is a typically northern tree. The bole is inclined to be poorly shaped. It has a very shallow root system. Black ash has an average rate of growth and medium life span. BARK: gray, slightly tinged with red, divided into large irregular plates separating into thin scales. LEAVES: pinnately compound, 12 to 16 inches long; leaflets 7 to 11, sessile, dark green above, paler below. FLOWERS: inconspicuous, without calyx or corolla, dioecious. FRUIT: winged all around, flattened, faintly-veined body. Ripens in late summer. TWIGS AND BUDS: stout grayish, terminal buds dark brown to nearly black.

Fig. 285. Fraxinus nigra.

Black ash grows commonly on peat soils. It also occurs on sands and loams where the water table is high. Typically it occurs in bogs, along streams and in poorly drained woods where there is a high water table and standing water frequently occurs. It occurs pure or predominant in one forest type where it may be associated with American elm and red maple. It is a common associate in six other forest types where it is associated with northern white-cedar, balsam fir, black spruce, hemlock, yellow birch, white spruce, paper birch and tamarack. Understory species common to the types are alder, red-osier dogwood *Cornus stolonifera,* bog laurel *Kalmia polifolia,* Labrador-tea *Ledum groenlandicum,* poison sumac, willow, blueberry *Vaccinium angustifolium*, highbush blueberry *Vaccinium corymbosum,* small cranberry *Vaccinium oxycoccus* and winterberry *Ilex verticillata.* Black ash is an intolerant subclimax species. It is relatively free from damage by insects and disease. When the site is dry enough to burn, it is highly susceptible to fire damage. The shallow roots in the peat are easily damaged by hot fires. Black ash sprouts readily from stumps. The lumber is used for furniture, veneer, cooperage and baskets. Woodducks, grouse, turkey and several songbirds eat the seeds. Small mammals eat seeds and wood. Deer heavily browse the twigs of young trees as well as sprout growth. Where it occurs in winter deer yards, the growth can be damaged by heavy browsing. It is an important winter food under these conditions. Moose browse the twigs and foliage during the summer months.

The largest living black ash of record is 9 feet 7 inches in circumference, 108 feet tall with a crown spread of 48 feet. It is growing in Wayne County, Ohio.

195b. Base of fruit cylindrical; samara wing almost wholly terminal. Leaflets pale beneath. Fig. 286.

WHITE ASH ....*Fraxinus americana* **L.**

Is the most common of the native ashes. It is medium-sized 70 to 80 feet in height with a long, straight, clear bole and somewhat open crown. The root system is deep in porus soils and shallow on rocky sites. White ash is fast growing with a moderate life span. BARK: dark brown or gray tinged with red, deeply divided by narrow fissures into broad ridges. LEAVES: pinnately compound, 5 to 11 leaflets, dark green above, pale or light green below. Purple and yellow in fall. FLOWERS: dioecious, simple, dark purple in large clusters, April-May. FRUIT: a samara, 1 to 2 inches long. TWIGS: stout, glabrous, dark green to gray-green.

White ash occurs on deep, moist fertile upland soils or well drained alluvial sites. It does not do well in swamps, but can stand short temporary flooding. It is more common on sites along streams and lower slopes as well as a variety of upland situations. It is a major species in two forest types where it is associated with northern red oak and basswood. It is a common component in 22 other forest types. Its associates vary greatly but some of the more common are yellow-poplar, black cherry, beech, several moist site oaks, hickories, red maple and willow, loblolly pine and sweetgum. Over such a wide range of sites and species, understory species are variable but some of the more common are downy serviceberry, pawpaw, American hornbeam, flowering dogwood, witch-hazel, eastern hophornbeam, and maple leaf viburnum *Viburnum acerifolium*. When young, white ash is tolerant with age, it becomes more intolerant and so is rated as intermediate-intolerant. It is an intermediate subclimax species, but reacts as a pioneer when invading abandoned fertile fields. There are about a dozen insect pests causing local severe damage; scales, sawflys, tent caterpillar and fruitworm. Several fungi such as leaf spot, canker, rusts and heartwood rot are damaging. Like many hardwoods, it is susceptible to damage by fire, mainly through fire

Fig. 286. Fraxinus americana.

scars at the base of the trunk where rot can enter. Lumber of white ash is used for furniture, veneer, sporting goods, paneling. Seeds of the tree are eaten by a number of songbirds; finches, grossbeaks, and cardinals; woodducks, quail, turkey and grouse. Small mammals eat the bark and seeds. White-tail deer browse the twigs and foliage. Heavy browsing can eliminate white ash. The largest living white ash of record is 24 feet in circumference, 80 feet tall with a crown spread of 82 feet. It is growing in Glenn Mills, Pennsylvania.

The TEXAS ASH *Fraxinus texensis* (A. Gray) Sarg., often considered a variety of white ash is a rather small tree growing on dry ground and differs from white ash by having more rounded leaflets and usually but five of them. Its range is restricted to Oklahoma and central Texas (see "a" on map).

PICTURED KEY FOR IDENTIFYING THE GENERA OF TREES IN WINTER

1a. Trees retaining green leaves throughout the winter 2

1b. Leaves falling from the tree during winter, or at least losing their green color ..11

2a. Leaves needle-like, awl-like, or scale-like, fruit a dry cone or a berry. THE CONIFERS. Turn to Fig. 19. Fig. 287.

Fig. 287.

Since almost all of the cone bearing trees which are included here have the same characteristics in winter that they possess at other seasons, the reader is referred to the regular key for further identification of this group.

2b. Leaf blades expanded. (Retained on trees, green throughout the winter.) 3

3a. Leaves with spine tipped teeth, fruit a red berry. Fig. 288. AMERICAN HOLLY Genus *Ilex*. Turn to Fig. 153.

3b. Not as in 3a 4

4a. Leaves crenate or serrate 5

4b. Leaves entire (margin not cut in any way) 6

Fig. 288.

5a. Leaves 1 to 2 inches long, oval; fruit a red berry. YAUPON Genus *Ilex*. Turn to Fig. 155.

5b. Leaves 4 to 5 inches long, wedge-shaped at base, gradually turning scarlet before falling. Buds as pictured. Fig. 289. LOBLOLLY-BAY Genus *Gordonia* Turn to Fig. 185.

6a. Leaves yellow-green, fruit an acorn. LIVE OAK Genus *Quercus*. Turn to Fig. 141.

Fig. 289

6b. Not as in 6a 7

7a. Leaves aromatic if broken. REDBAY Genus *Persea*. Turn to Fig. 78.

7b. Leaves not aromatic 8

8a. Leaves 4 to 12 inches long. ROSEBAY RHODODENDRON Genus *Rhododendron*. Turn to Fig. 80.

8b. Leaves 3 to 4 inches long. MOUNTAIN-LAUREL Genus *Kalmia*. Turn to Fig. 79.

8c. Leaves usually less than 3 inches long 9

9a. Fruit black, fleshy, 1/4 inch, leaves 1/2 to 2 1/2 inches long. TREE SPARKLEBERRY Genus *Vaccinium*. Turn to Fig. 83.

9b. Fruit, small dry capsules in long racemes 10

10a. Leaves not falling until autumn of second year, 1 1/2 to 2 inches long, thick, not veiny. BUCKWHEAT-TREE Genus *Cliftonia*. Turn to Fig. 81.

10b. Leaves 2 to 3 inches long, remaining green until spring in the South, farther north turning red and falling through the winter. SWAMP CYRILLA Genus *Cyrilla*. Turn to Fig. 82.

11a. Twigs with thick dwarf branches (from which leaves grow year after year). Fig. 290 12

Fig. 290.

11b. Twigs without dwarf branches 13

12a. Twigs scaly; fruit a cone, often present. Fig. 290a. THE LARCHES Genus *Larix*. Turn to Figs. 23 and 24.

12b. Twigs smooth yellowish-gray, no cones. Fig. 290b. THE MAIDENHAIR TREE Genus *Ginkgo*. Turn to Fig. 20.

13a. Leaf scars usually whorled (3 at each node). Long pencil-shaped brown pods usually in evidence. CATALPA Genus *Catalpa*. Turn to Figs. 264 and 265.

13b. Leaf scars opposite (2 at each node). Fig. 291 14

Fig. 292.

13c. Leaf scars alternate (only 1 at each node). Fig. 292 23

Fig. 292.

14a. Pith large usually with diaphragms (cross partitions), conical, brown fruit about 1 1/2 inches long usually in evidence. Bundle scars in an ellipse. ROYAL PAULOWNIA Genus *Paulownia*. Turn to Fig. 263.

14b. Pith solid. Bundle scars not in an ellipse or ring 15

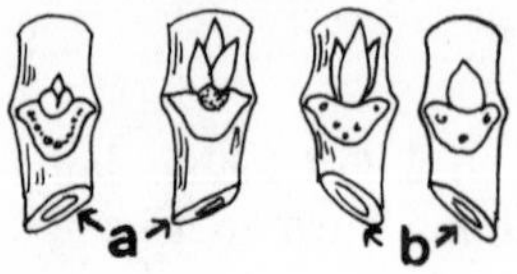

15a. Bundle scars 1 or several so closely united as to appear as 1. Fig. 293a 16

15b. Bundle scars more than 1. Fig. 293b 18

Fig. 293.

16a. Twigs green, usually bearing 4 ridges, making the twig feel square. Pith square or diamond-shaped in cross section. WAHOO Genus *Euonymus*. Turn to Fig. 272.

16b. Twigs not green; pith round or nearly so 17

17a. Leaf scars close to the bark; fruit winged; lenticels not large; buds rough or pubescent. THE ASHES Genus *Fraxinus*. Figs. 282-286.

17b. Leaf scars on short stalks, concave; lenticels large; fruit a drupe. FRINGETREE Genus *Chionanthus*. Turn to Fig. 267.

18a. With stipular scars 19

18b. Without stipular scars 20

19a. Twigs green, strongly scented; stipular scars, curved. Bladder-like fruit sometimes in evidence. BLADERNUT Genus *Staphylea*. Turn to Fig. 281.

19b. Bundle scars in broken ring; stipular scars connecting leaf scars (leaf scars sometimes in whorls of 3). Fig. 294. BUTTONBUSH Genus *Cephalanthus*. Turn to Fig. 268.

Fig. 294.

20a. At leat some of the buds 1/2 inch or more in length, with numerous scales; leaf scars (a) heart-shaped; fruit scars (b) round or oval, both large. Fig. 295. THE BUCKEYES Genus *Aesculus*. Turn to Figs. 276-279.

Fig. 295.

20b. None of the buds 1/2 inch in length 21

21a. Twigs 4-winged, glabrous. Upper buds sometimes alternating; buds 4-ranked; bundle scars in broken circle. CRAPEMYRTLE Genus *Lagerstroemia*. Turn to Fig. 266.

21b. Not as in 21a 22

22a. Terminal buds with 1 main pair of scales visible and a small pair at base. Fig. 296a. THE VIBURNUMS Genus *Viburnum*. Turn to Figs. 273-275.

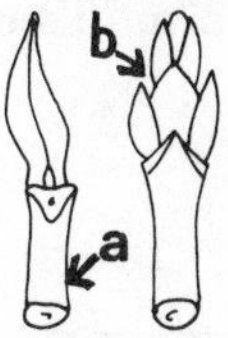

Fig. 296.

22b. Terminal buds with several pairs of visible scales. Leaf scars v-shaped with 3 to 5 bundle scars. Double-winged fruit sometimes in evidence. Fig. 296b. THE MAPLES Genus *Acer*. Turn to Figs. 255-262 and 280.

22c. Leaf scars narrow, conical; flowering buds (flowering dogwood) spherical, often flattened. THE DOGWOODS Genus *Cornus*. Turn to Figs. 269-271.

23a. Twigs with stipular scars or ridges entirely circling the twig. Fig. 297 24

23b. Twigs without complete stipular rings 27

Fig. 297.

24a. Leaf scars wholly surrounding the bud, due to leaf base having covered the bud; bark of upper limbs greenish-white. Fruit, hanging brown balls about 1 inch in diameter, often on tree through the winter. SYCAMORE Genus *Platanus*. Turn to Fig. 207.

24b. Leaf scars below the buds; terminal buds large and active 25

25a. Sap milky, pith large, very white somewhat angular and interrupted at nodes. Fig. 298. FIG Genus *Ficus*. Turn to Fig. 208.

25b. Not as in 25a 26

Fig. 298.

26a. Buds smooth, pith diaphragmed (Fig. 299a); fruit dry and brownish, as pictured, often retained during the winter. YELLOW-POPLAR Genus *Liriodendron*. Turn to Fig. 71.

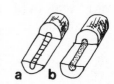

26b. Buds usually downy or with whitish bloom; pith solid. (Fig. 299b) Fruit red. THE MAGNOLIAS Genus *Magnolia*. Turn to Figs. 72-77.

Fig. 299.

27a. Trees with thorns, spines or prickles 28

27b. Trees without thorns, spines or prickles 36

Fig. 300.

28a. Stems thickly covered with prickles. Leaf scars large, nearly encircling the stem. Fig. 300. DEVILS-WALKING-STICK Genus *Aralia*. Turn to Fig. 229.

28b. With, usually, only a pair of rather heavy prickles near the nodes. Leaf scars broad but not encircling the stem. Buds pubescent. PRICKLY-ASHES Genus *Zanthoxylum*. Turn to Figs. 238 and 239.

28c. Stems without numerous prickles between the nodes 29

29a. Young twigs covered with wooly white scales; buds silvery. RUSSIAN-OLIVE Genus *Elaeagnus*. Turn to Fig. 87.

29b. Twigs not as in 29a 30

Fig. 301.

30a. One spine on each side of the leaf scar (modified stipules). Fig. 301 31

30b. Thorns not at side of buds; connected with the wood 32

31a. Leaf scar on membranes; covering two or more axillary buds. Fig. 301. LOCUST Genus *Robinia*. Turn to Figs. 234 and 235.

31b. Leaf scar below the bud; buds pubescent. PRICKLY-ASHES Genus *Zanthoxylum*. Turn to Figs. 238 and 239.

32a. With sturdy thorns on sides of twigs but not terminal thorns 33

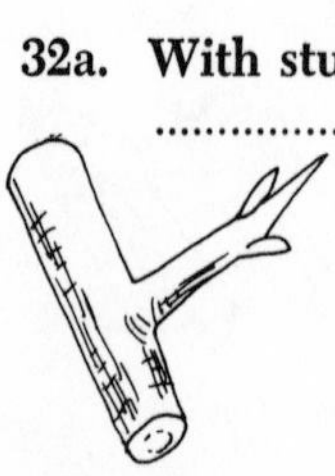

Fig. 302.

32b. Trees with terminal or spur-like branches ending in thorns; with or without thorns on sides of branches. Fig. 302 34

33a. With one sharp thorn at the side of each axillary bud. Large, orange-like fruit balls often present on tree or ground. Fig. 303. OSAGE-ORANGE Genus *Maclura*. Turn to Fig. 70.

Fig. 303.

33b. Thorns usually branched, above the leaf axils and on the trunk. Fig. 304. Fruit a flat bean-like pod. HONEYLOCUST Genus *Gleditsia*. Turn to Figs. 226 and 227.

Fig. 304.

33c. Thorns axillary, usually unbranched. Fruit a small pome with bony center. Fig. 305. THE HAWTHORNS Genus *Crataegus*. Turn to Fig. 183a-i.

Fig. 305.

34a. Terminal bud present 35

34b. Terminal bud falling off, leaving a scar. Twigs glabrous, often with prominently marked lenticels. PLUMS AND CHERRIES Genus *Prunus*. Turn to Figs. 194-206.

35a. Buds conical, pubescent; twigs yellowish-olive, smooth. Trees usually tall wtih rather slender top. PEAR Genus *Pyrus*. Turn to Fig. 188.

35b. Buds rounded, downy, or pubescent; twigs usually pubescent. Trees with rounded crown and spreading branches. THE APPLES Genus *Malus*. Turn to Figs. 189-191.

36a. Leaf scars and axillary buds in two distinct rows on the twig (first, third and fifth directly above the second and fourth). Fig. 306a 37

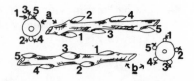

Fig. 306.

36b. Leaf scars in more than two rows on the twig. Fig. 306b 44

a   b

Fig. 307.

37a. With 3 bundle scars. Fig. 307a 38

37b. Bundle scars scattered, more than 3. Fig. 307b
....77

37c. With but one bundle scar; 2 exterior bud scales; pith often with cavities. PERSIMMON Genus *Diospyros*. Turn to Fig. 91.

38a. Pith with diaphragms, with or without cavities. Fig. 299a. THE HACKBERRIES Genus *Celtis*. Turn to Figs. 210-211.

38b. Pith solid. Fig. 299b 39

Fig. 308.

39a. Terminal bud without a covering of bud scales, hairy. Twigs zigzag; lateral buds on short stalks. Fig. 308. WITCH-HAZEL Genus *Hamamelis*. Turn to Fig. 96.

39b. Terminal bud covered with scales, slender long pointed; leaf scars narrow. SERVICEBERRY Genus *Amelanchier*. Turn to Figs. 151 and 152.

39c. Terminal bud absent, or if present, the leaf scar is oval or semi-circular 40

40a. Twigs dark brown, without speckles, leaf scars oblique. Buds not superposed 41

40b. Twigs speckled, reddish-brown; buds reddish-violet, often in clusters. Dry, brown bean-like pods, 1 1/2 to 2 1/2 inches long, often on tree during winter. REDBUD Genus *Cercis*. Turn to Fig. 209.

41a. Small tree with unbroken bluish-gray bark; trunk with prominent ridges. AMERICAN HORNBEAM Genus *Carpinus*. Turn to Fig. 108.

41b. Not as in 41a 42

42a. No catkins in evidence in winter. Twigs of some species with cork wings. Buds usually rounded. THE ELMS Genus *Ulmus*. Turn to Figs. 98-104.

42b. With young male catkins present in winter. Fig. 309 43

Fig. 309.

43a. Bark of tree usually in papery layers; terminal buds present. THE BIRCHES Genus *Betula*. Turn to Figs. 110-115.

43b. Bark divided into fine scales frequently running spirally on trunk and larger branches. No terminal bud. HOPHORN-BEAM Genus *Ostrya*. Turn to Fig. 109.

44a. With 2 or more buds at each leaf scar placed one above the other (superposed); all but one is often very small. Fig. 310a 45

(Fig. 310 illustration)

Fig. 310.

44b. Only one bud at each leaf scar or 2 or more placed side by side. Fig. 310b 52

45a. Pith with cross partitions (diaphragms) separated by open air spaces. Fig. 299a 46

45b. Pith with cross partitions but with intervening spaces filled with pith; no stipular scars; bundle scars 3. Fig. 299a. THE TUPELOS Genus *Nyssa*. Turn to Figs. 160-161.

45c. Pith solid without cross partitions. Fig. 299b 47

46a. Twigs slender, pith small, white or greenish; leaf scars a half circle. SILVERBELL Genus *Halesia*. Turn to Fig. 158.

46b. Twigs stout, pith brown; leaf scars with 3 bundle scars. THE WALNUTS Genus *Juglans*. Figs. 220-223.

47a. Buds scarcely projecting beyond the surface; tip of branch or at least the terminal bud dying 48

47b. Buds standing out prominently, though not necessarily large 50

48a. Buds surrounded by leaf scar. Fig. 311 49

48b. Buds not surrounded by leaf scar; pith large, brown. Broad thick bean-like pods often in evidence. KENTUCKY COFFEETREE Genus *Gymnocladus*. Turn to Fig. 225.

49a. Twigs often zigzag; pith small; large bean-like pods often in evidence. HONEYLOCUST Genus *Gleditsia*. Turn to Figs. 226 and 227.

Fig. 311.

49b. Twigs straight, pith larger, white. Shrub or small tree. Seeds winged. HOPTREE Genus *Ptelea*. Turn to Fig. 231.

50a. Buds surrounded by leaf scar, hairy; 5 to 9 bundle scars; small thin bean-like pods often in evidence. YELLOWWOOD Genus *Cladrastis*. Turn to Fig. 233.

50b. Buds not surrounded by leaf scar 51

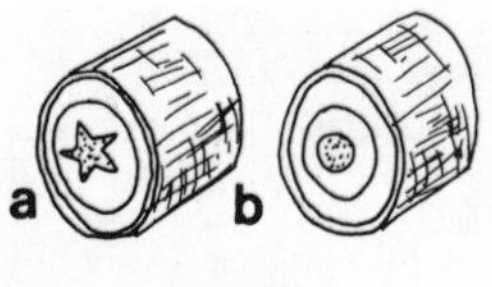

51a. Pith somewhat star-shaped in cross section, brown or yellowish (Fig. 312a); terminal buds large; fruit a nut. THE HICKORIES Genus *Carya*. Turn to Figs. 245-253.

Fig. 312.

51b. Pith round in cross section. Fig. 312b. Bundle scars 3. Shrub or small tree. SOAPBERRY Genus *Sapindus*. Turn to Fig. 240.

52a. Pith triangular in cross section, buds on short stalks (Fig. 313); catkins present throughout winter. ALDER Genus *Alnus*. Turn to Figs. 117-121.

Fig. 313.

52b. Pith not triangular, buds without stalks 53

53a. Buds surrounded by leaf scar; pith large (Fig. 314); fruit dry berries in large panicles often retained during winter. THE SUMACS Genus *Rhus*. Turn to Figs. 241-244.

53b. Not as in 53a 54

Fig. 314.

54a. Bundle scars more than one 55

54b. Only one bundle scar or several so crowded as to seem as only one. Fig. 315 75

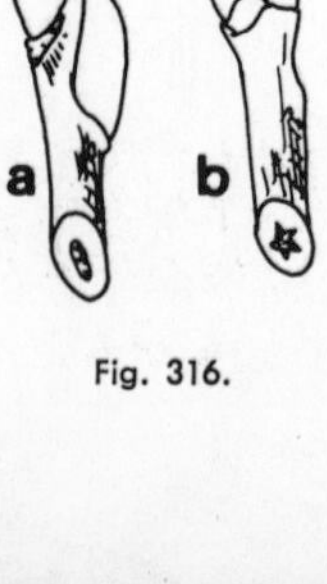

Fig. 315.

55a. Buds enclosed in single sack-like scale (Fig. 316a); bundle scars 3; stipular scars present. THE WILLOWS Genus *Salix*. Turn to Figs. 162-172.

55b. Outer covering of buds of more than one scale. Fig. 316b 56

Fig. 316.

56a. Pith somewhat star-shaped in cross section. Fig. 312a 57

56b. Pith rounded. Fig. 312b 61

57a. Several buds at tip of twigs. Fig.
317. Acorns usually in evidence on
tree or ground. THE OAKS Genus
Quercus. Turn to Figs. 123-149.

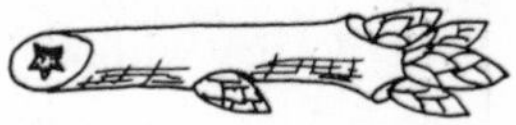

Fig. 317.

57b. Not as in 57a 58

58a. Bundle scars 3. Fig. 307a 59

58b. Bundle scars more than 3, scattered. (In groups in some of
the Hickories.) Fig. 307b 60

59a. Stipular scars present (Fig. 318);
buds often sticky. THE POPLARS
Genus *Populus*. Turn to Figs. 175-
182.

Fig. 318.

59b. Without stipular scars; buds smooth, not sticky; twigs often
with cork wings. SWEETGUM Genus *Liquidambar*. Turn to
Fig. 219.

60a. Terminal buds large with 4 or more outer scales; twigs tough,
with brown pith. THE HICKORIES Genus *Carya*. Turn to
Figs. 245-253.

60b. Buds small with few outer scales. Prickly burs of fruit usually
on tree or ground. THE CHESTNUTS Genus *Castanea*. Turn
to Figs. 106 and 107.

61a. Buds on stalks; pith solid but with
cross partitions (diaphragms). Fig.
319. THE TUPELOS Genus *Nyssa*.
Turn to Figs. 160-161.

61b. Pith with no cross partitions 62

Fig. 319.

62a. Twigs and coarse pith large, light brown;
bark ill-smelling; leaf scars large; winged
seeds often in evidence. Fig. 320. AIL-
ANTHUS Genus *Ailanthus*. Turn to Fig.
228.

62b. Not as above 63

Fig. 320.

63a. Bark with gummy, aromatic sap. Fruit in large plume-like panicles. SMOKETREE Genus *Cotinus*. Fig. 89.

63b. Bark not gummy 64

64a. Twigs without terminal bud 65

64b. Twigs with a terminal bud 68

65a. Twigs with stipular scars. Fig. 318 67

65b. Twigs with little or no evidence of stipular scars..............66

Fig. 321.

66a. Moderate sized trees of South (often umbrella-shaped). Twigs rather heavy, nearly white; buds and leaf scars as pictured. Fig. 321. CHINABERRY Genus *Melia*. Turn to Fig. 230.

66b. Twigs darker colored and smaller; buds usually smooth. THE PLUMS AND CHERRIES Genus *Prunus*. Figs. 194-206.

67a. Twigs very dark. Fruit a pome. QUINCE Genus *Cydonia*. Turn to Fig. 92.

67b. Twigs gray. Fruit small berry-like drupe. BUCKTHORN Genus *Rhamnus*. Turn to Fig. 187.

68a. Twigs green or green and red 69

68b. Twigs not as in 68a 70

69a. Twigs usually red above and green below, smooth, bark bitter. PEACH Genus *Prunus*. Turn to Fig. 192.

69b. Twigs green or greenish-yellow. Fruit, clusters of small berries, often in evidence. ALTERNATE-LEAF DOGWOOD Genus *Cornus*. Turn to Fig. 269.

70a. Bundle scars 3. Fig. 307a 71

70b. Bundle scars 5 or more in broad v-shaped leaf scars. Fruit small, red or orange pomes in clusters, sometimes in evidence. MOUNTAIN-ASHES Genus *Sorbus*. Turn to Figs. 236-237.

71a. Buds bluntly rounded 72

71b. Buds pointed; twigs sometimes with thorn-like stunted branches 73

72a. Twigs often zigzag. Fruit a small pome with bony center. Fig. 305. THE HAWTHORNS Genus *Crataegus*. Turn to Fig. 183, a-i.

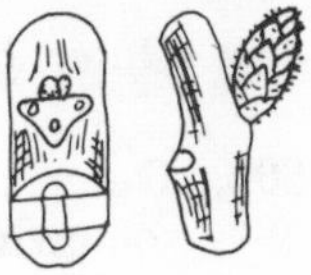

72b. Wood soft and very light; flower buds large, oval, with many scales, as pictured. Fig. 322. **CORKWOOD** Genus *Leitneria*. Turn to Fig. 90.

Fig. 322.

73a. Buds glabrous or but slightly pubescent. Lenticels often prominent; fruit with a single seed. **THE PLUMS AND CHERRIES** Genus *Prunus*. Turn to Figs. 194-206.

73b. Not as in 73a 74

74a. Twigs glabrous, usually yellowish-olive. Trees usually with slender crown. **PEAR** Genus *Pyrus*. Turn to Fig. 188.

74b. Twigs usually pubescent, if smooth then colored reddish-brown. Trees usually with rounded spreading crown. **THE APPLES** Genus *Malus*. Turn to Figs. 189 and 190.

75a. Twigs without terminal bud 76

75b. Twigs with terminal bud; twigs green, very spicy. **SASSAFRAS** Genus *Sassafras*. Turn to Fig. 88.

76a. Twigs glabrous, shining; bark sour. Fruit capsules in panicles persisting throughout the winter. **SOURWOOD** Genus *Oxydendrum*. Turn to Fig. 186.

76b. Twigs pubescent, dull, often zigzag. Fruit fleshy with flattened seeds. **PERSIMMON** Genus *Diospyros*. Turn to Fig. 91.

77a. Pith with cross partitions, solid Fig. 323; bark with ill-smelling odor; bundle scars 5 to 7. Shrub or small tree. **PAWPAW** Genus *Asimina*. Turn to Fig. 85.

77b. Pith solid; without cross partitions 78

Fig. 323.

78a. Buds 3/4 inch or longer, spike-like, with many dry scales. **BEECH** Genus *Fagus*. Turn to Fig. 105.

78b. Buds not as in 78a 79

79a. Pith star-shaped in cross section. Fig. 324. Spiny fruit burs often in evidence. **THE CHESTNNUTS** Genus *Castanea*. Turn to Figs. 106 and 107.

79b. Pith rounded in cross section 80

Fig. 324.

80a. Outer bud scales 1 to 3 81

80b. Outer bud scales more than 3; twigs brownish-yellow; sap somewhat milky. THE MULBERRIES Genus *Morus*. Turn to Figs. 213 and 214.

81a. Buds usually fleshy and often bright red; sap watery; fruit, as pictured, often in evidence. THE BASSWOODS Genus *Tilia*. Turn to Figs. 216-218.

81b. Buds conical with outer scales striated, not red; sap milky. PAPER MULBERRY Genus *Broussonetia*. Turn to Fig. 212.

PICTURED GLOSSARY

Accuminate: A leaf blade with a very sharp point or base. Fig. 325a.

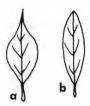

Fig. 325.

Achene: A small, dry, one-celled, unwinged but occasionally plumose, fruit. Fig. 5c.

Acute: Leaf blade with fairly sharp point or base. Fig. 325b.

Age class: One of the intervals into which the range of ages of vegetation is divided for classification.

All-aged: Applied to a stand of trees in which theoretically, trees of all ages from seedlings to maturity, are found.

Ament: A tassel-like group of flowers. Fig. 326.

Fig. 326.

Anther: The pollen-bearing part of a stamen. Fig. 3.

Aristate: With a bristle at tip of leaf. Fig. 327.

Fig. 327.

Aromatic: With spicy fragrance.

Association: Plant; A unit of vegetation essentially uniform in aspect, general appearance, ecological structure and floristic composition. Page 12.

Axil: The point on a stem immediately above the base of a leaf. Fig. 328.

Fig. 328.

Berry: A simple fleshy fruit, with seeds embedded in the pulpy mass. Fig. 5i.

Bisexual: Both sexes represented in the same tree.

Bloom: White powdery covering on fruit or leaves.

Bract: Leaf-like part at base of flower or other plant part. Fig. 329.

Fig. 329.

Bundle scar: Ends of vascular bundles showing in leaf scars. Fig. 330.

Fig. 330.

Buttress: A brace-like ridge at base of tree trunk.

Calyx: The outer floral envelope.
Cambium: A sheath of generative tissue in a woody stem between the xylem and phloem. It gives rise to secondary xylem (wood) and phloem (inner bark). Fig. 6.
Canker: A definite, relatively localized, necrotic lesion primarily of the bark and cambium.
Capsule: A dry fruit, splitting along two or more lines of suture. Fig. 331.

Fig. 333.

Fig. 331.

Carpel: One section (a) of a compound pistil (b) Fig. 332. In conifers it is the cone scale.

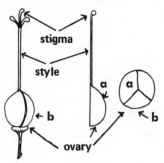

Fig. 332.

Carpellate: Having carpels; a female flower.
Catkin: A tassel-like inflorescence; an ament. Fig. 326.
Climax: Plant community or species (as used in this text); Communities or species which occur in a more stable community, are tolerant of competition and long lived. Compare with pioneer and subclimax species and communities. Page 13.
Compound: Leaves made up of several leaflets. Fig. 333.

Conical: Shaped something like a cone.
Cordate: Heart-shaped. Fig. 334.

Fig. 334.

Corolla: All of the petals of a flower taken together.
Corymb: A flat topped inflorescence in which the lower flowers bloom first. Fig. 335.

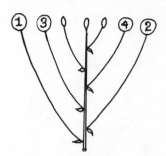

Fig. 335.

Crenate: With rounded teeth. Fig. 336.
Crown: The branches and foliage of a tree; the upper portion of a tree.

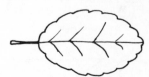

Fig. 336.

Crown class: A designation of trees in a forest with crowns of similar development and occupying similar positions in the crown cover. Fig. 9. (D) Dominant. (CD) Codominant. (I) Intermediate. (O) Overtopped.

Cylindrical: Shaped somewhat like a cylinder.

Cyme: A flat topped inflorescence in which the middle flower blooms first. Fig. 337.

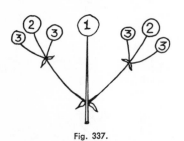

Fig. 337.

Deciduous: Falling at end of growing period, not persistent.

Dehiscent: Describes a fruit which opens by valves or slits. Compare indehiscent.

Dentate: With teeth. Fig. 338.

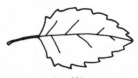

Fig. 338.

Diameter: Breast high; abbreviated as d.b.h. The diameter of a tree at 4 1/2 feet above the average ground level.

Dicotyledons: Plants with two seed leaves; usually with net-veined leaves and flower parts in 4's or 5's.

Dioecious: Unisexual, with staminate and pistillate flowers on separate plants.

Doubly serrate: With small serrations on the larger saw-like teeth. Fig. 339.

Drupe: Fleshy fruit with a single seed as plum or cherry.

Dwarf branches: Slow growing branches that bear leaves year after year.

Fig. 339.

Ecosystem: forest; an assemblage of plants and animals living in an environment of air, soil and water, each interrelated directly or indirectly with one another. This is also referred to as a forest community. Page 11.

Emarginate: Leaf notched at the tip. Fig. 340.

Fig. 340.

Entire: Leaves or other parts that are neither cut nor lobed. Fig. 341.

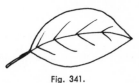

Fig. 341.

Epidermis: Leaves; a transparent layer of cells covering the upper and lower leaf surfaces and through which light readily passes.

Even-aged: Applied to a stand in which relatively small age differences exist between individual trees.

Excurrent: Descriptive of a tree with a main trunk extending to the top of the crown; as in a pine, spruce or fir.

Fasicle: A bundle or cluster.

Filament: That part of the stamen supporting the anther.

Fissures: Cracks in the bark.

Follicle: A single carpellate dry fruit splitting along one line of suture.

Forb: An herbaceous flowering plant, not a member of the grass (*Gramineae*) family.

Fruit: The seed bearing part of a plant.

Fruit scar: Mark on a stem where the fruit was attached.

Galls: Abnormal growth caused by insects.

Germinate: Starting to grow.

Glabrous: Without hairs, smooth.

Gland: A secreting cell or organ.

Glaucous: Covered with a fine white or bluish powder, bloom.

Globose: Shaped like a ball.

Hastate: Like an arrow-head, but with the basal lobes pointing outward.

Head: An inflorescence in which sessile flowers seem to arise from a common center. May be either spherical or flat-topped. Fig. 342.

Fig. 342.

Herbs: Plants with no woody tissue.

Hilum: Scar on a seed where it was attached to its stem. Fig. 343.

Fig. 343.

Humus: The plant and animal residues of the soil, litter excluded, which are undergoing decomposition.

Husk: Outer covering of nut or fruit.

Hybrid: A cross between two species.

Indehiscent: Describing a fruit which does not open by valves or slits. Compare dehiscent.

Inflorescence: Arrangement of the flowering parts of a plant.

Internode: That portion of a stem between two nodes.

Kernel: Interior part of nut or seed.

Knees: relating to trees; root structures rising out of water or wet soil; believed to aid the tree in respiration. Fig. 25b.

Lanceolate: Lance shaped. Fig. 344.

Fig. 344.

Lateral: Along the side.

Layering: Rooting of side branches.

Leaflets: Expanded parts of a compound leaf. Fig. 345.

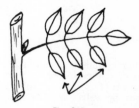

Fig. 345.

Leaf scar: Mark on stem where leaf was attached. Fig. 346.

Fig. 346.

Legume: A dry fruit, the product of a simple pistil, usually dehiscing along two lines of suture.

Lenticle: Opening in bark for respiration; often quite prominent.

Lesser vegetation: As used in this text; that part of the understory vegetation found on the ground and composed of herbaceous species.

Lignin: The second most abundant constituent of wood.

Litter: As related to the soil; the uppermost layer of organic debris, freshly fallen or only slightly decomposed. As it decomposes it becomes one of the components of humus.

Linear: Long and narrow with sides nearly parallel. Fig. 347.

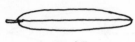

Fig. 347.

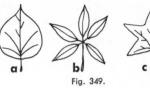

Fig. 349.

Maturity: For a given species or stand; the approximate age beyond which growth falls off or decay begins at a rate likely to increase.

Monoecious: Bearing both male and female parts on the same tree.

Mucronate: With an abruptly short sharp tip. Fig. 348.

Fig. 348.

Fig. 350.

Mutant: Plant or animal with a changed inheritance; sports.

Mycorrhiza: Rootlet of a higher plant modified through integral association with a fungus to form a constant structure which differs from either component but is attached to the root system and functions somewhat as a rootlet.

Node: Region on stem where lateral leaves and buds are attached.

Nut: Usually a one-celled, one-seeded fruit with a bony woody, leathery or papery wall and usually partially or wholly encased in an involucre or husk.

Obtuse: Blunt.

Ovary: That part of the pistil which contains the ovules.

Overstory: That portion of the trees in a forest stand forming the upper crown cover.

Ovoid: Egg shaped.

Ovule: The structure developing into a seed, after fertilization.

Palisade cells: In leaf; where chlorophyll is found and photosynthesis takes place.

Palmate: Several veins (a) or leaflets (b) diverging from one point. Fig. 349. Palmately lobed (c).

Panicle: An inflorescence in which the lateral branches rebranch. Fig. 350.

Parenchyma: Relatively unspecialized, thin walled cells, loosely packed, located between the palisade cells and lower epidermis. Contain chlorophyll and are available for storage of nutrients. Sometimes called "spongy" parenchyma.

Petal: A division, often showy, of the corolla.

Petiole: The stem of a leaf.

Phloem: Inner bark; the principal tissue concerned with the translocation of elaborated foodstuffs.

Pinnate: Parts arranged as in a feather. Pinnately lobed (a). Pinnately veined (b). Fig. 351.

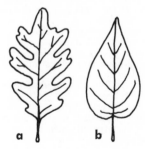

Fig. 351.

Pioneer: Plant community or species; trees or groups of trees capable of invading bare or denuded sites. They are usually aggressive, intolerant, light seeded and short lived. Page 13.

Pistil: The seed bearing organ of a flower, consisting of the ovary, stigma and style.

Pistillate: Having only pistils, a female flower.

Pith: Soft tissue at the center of a stem.

Pole: A young tree 4 inches or more d.b.h.

Polygamous: Bearing both perfect and imperfect flowers.

Pome: A fleshy fruit of the apple type in which the seeds are encased in a cartilaginous material.

Pruning: Trimming trees or other plants.

Pubescent: Covered with hairs. Pubescence refers to the covering.

Raceme: An inflorescence in which short stalked flowers arise at different places from the stem. Fig. 352.

Fig. 352.

Receptacle: The, often expanded, portion of the stem bearing the organs of the flower.

Resinous: Having a sticky sap.

Root system: That portion of the tree which occurs below the surface of the ground and where much of the food is stored.

Rounded: Referring or descriptive of a leaf base.

Rufous: Reddish brown.

Rugose: Wrinkled, used in describing leaf surfaces in which the veins are sunken.

Sagittate: Leaf shaped as an arrow, but without outward pointing lobes at the base. Fig. 353.

Samara: An indehiscent winged fruit.

Sapling: A young tree less than 4 inches d.b.h. and usually more than 2 inches d.b.h.

Fig. 353.

Scion: The plant part added in grafting.

Seedling: A tree grown from seed, generally used in connection with a very young tree. Smaller than a sapling.

Self-pruning: Twigs breaking off naturally. A desirable characteristic in valuable lumber trees, but not necessarily so in ornamentals.

Sepals: A unit of the calyx.

Serotinous: Usually meaning fruits that ripen late, but when used in connection with cones; those which remain closed not allowing dissemination of seeds. Cones may remain closed unless subjected to high temperatures.

Serrate: Having a saw-toothed margin. Fig. 354.

Fig. 354.

Sessile: Without a stem, as leaf, flower or fruit. Fig. 355.

Fig. 355.

Shrub: A perennial woody plant of low stature and usually multiple stemmed.

Simple: Leaves with but one blade.

Solitary: But one at a place.

Spatulate: Somewhat spoon shaped. Fig. 356.

Fig. 356.

Spike: An inflorescence with sessile flowers scattered along the stem. Fig. 357.

Fig. 357.

Stamens: Male parts of a flower, producing pollen and consisting of an anther and filament.

Staminate: Having stamens, a male flower.

Stand: An aggregation of trees or other growth occupying a specific area and sufficiently uniform in composition (species), age arrangement and condition as to be distinguishable from the forest or other growth on adjoining areas.

Stem: The principal axis of a plant from which buds and shoots are developed. In a tree; the trunk or bole.

Stigma: The part of the pistil that receives the pollen.

Stipular scars: Marks left on a stem where stipules were attached.

Stipules: Appendages at the base of petiole of a leaf. Fig. 358.

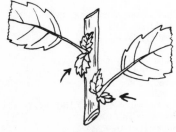

Fig. 358.

Stomata: Tiny openings in the epidermis of a leaf through which carbon dioxide and oxygen may pass.

Striate: Marked with stripes.

Strobile: Same as cone, usually refers to immature structure.

Style: The slender portion of the pistil connecting the stigma and ovary.

Subclimax: Plant community or species; trees or groups of trees which replace pioneer species and are more tolerant of competition and longer lived. Page 13.

Subglobose: Somewhat ball-shaped.

Terminal bud: The bud located at the end of the twig.

Tolerance: (Used in the most simple context) The capacity of a tree to develop and grow in the shade of and in competition with other trees.

Tomentose: Covered with dense wool-like hairs.

Trifoliate: With three leaflets. Fig. 359.

Fig. 359.

Truncate: Cut rather squarely. Fig. 360.

Fig. 360.

Twigs: Small branches.

Type, Forest: A descriptive term used to group stands of similar character as regards composition and development, due to certain ecological factors, by which they may be differentiated from other groups of stands.

Umbel: An inflorescence in which the stalked flowers all arise from one place. Fig. 361.

Fig. 361.

Understory: That portion of the trees, shrubs and vines in a forest stand, below the overstory. Lesser vegetation is the herbaceous component of the understory.

Uneven: Leaves with one side larger than the other. Fig. 362.

Fig. 362.

Uneven-aged: Applied to a stand in which there are considerable differences in ages of trees. Usually 3 or more age classes are represented.

Veins: Vascular bundles showing as lines on leaves.

Whorled: Three or more leaves or stems arising at one node. Fig. 363.

Fig. 363.

Witches brooms: A fungus growth on trees.

Xylem: The lignified water-conducting, strengthening and storage tissues of branches, stems and roots.

Index of Common Names

Index of Scientific Names